Solving the Romans Debate

Solving the Romans Debate

A. Andrew Das

Fortress Press
Minneapolis

SOLVING THE ROMANS DEBATE

Cover image: P.Mich. inv. 6238: folio: folio 20 verso, containing Romans 16:14-23. Digitally reproduced with the Permission of the Papyrology Collection, Graduate Library, The University of Michigan.
Cover design: Kevin van der Leek Design Inc.
Book design: Phoenix Type, Inc.

Library of Congress Cataloging-in-Publication Data

Das, A. Andrew.
  Solving the Romans debate / A. Andrew Das.
    p. cm.
Includes bibliographical references.
ISBN-13: 978-0-8006-3860-3 (alk. paper)
ISBN-10: 0-8006-3860-3 (alk. paper)
1. Bible. N.T. Romans—Criticism, interpretation, etc. 2. Christianity and other religions—Judaism. 3 Judaism—Relations—Christianity. I. Title.
BS2665.6.J4D37 2007
227'.106—dc22   2006024552

Manufactured in the U.S.A.
11   10   09   08   07   1   2   3   4   5   6   7   8   9   10

To Peter, Paul, and Sara,
τέκνα μου ἀγαπητά

Contents

Acknowledgments

Although this project formally began in the summer of 2004, the seeds were sown ten years earlier. In the fall of 1994, when we were graduate students at Union Theological Seminary in Virginia, Johann Kim and I initiated a year-long seminar on Romans led by Paul J. Achtemeier. At the time, Professor Achtemeier made what struck us as a surprising claim. He argued that Romans was written to a gentile audience. I had always thought that the audience of Romans included a significant Jewish contingent. I found myself skeptical of Achtemeier's thesis. Achtemeier delivered that fall a paper at the Pauline Theology Group of the Society of Biblical Literature in which he made similar claims. Scholarly reaction was also generally skeptical, but Achtemeier fielded the questions with relative ease. I tabled the matter, since I was working on another difficult project at the time, Paul's view of the Law.[1] When I returned to the situation of Romans while preparing a chapter of *Paul and the Jews* in 2000 and 2001, I ultimately concluded that Achtemeier was right about the audience of Romans.[2] I was surprised, however, when reviewers frequently passed over that chapter or incomprehensibly concluded that I was articulating the standard view of the Romans situation. (I suspect that reviewers read the introduction to the book but not the chapter on the Romans situation itself.) I also realized that I had not articulated my approach as fully as would be required to satisfy other readers of Romans. Thus the genesis of this project in the summer of 2004.

As with any such endeavor, I am indebted to many. Elmhurst College provided me a Faculty Development Research Grant for the summer of 2004 to begin work on the manuscript. Ms. Kathy Willis, our college's circulation librarian, assisted me with gaining access to innumerable books and articles not

---

1. This was published as *Paul, the Law, and the Covenant* (Peabody, Mass.: Hendrickson, 2001).

2. *Paul and the Jews* (Library of Pauline Studies; Peabody, Mass.: Hendrickson, 2003).

otherwise available. A number of scholars have generously read through the manuscript at various points. Paul Achtemeier of Union Theological Seminary in Virginia and Thomas R. Schreiner at Southern Baptist Seminary in Louisville both read through the entirety of the manuscript and offered helpful comments along the way. Robert A. J. Gagnon of Pittsburgh Theological Seminary interacted with me on Romans 16 even as he was preparing his own new monograph on Romans 3. I am indebted to conversation with Douglas J. Moo as well as several of the Ph.D. candidates in the Wheaton College Graduate School who dialogued with me on Rom 7:7–25 and 11:26. Professor Moo also offered helpful suggestions on chap. 2. Stanley K. Stowers of Brown University, whose pioneering work on Romans has proved influential in many quarters over the last decade, kindly offered help and feedback as well. John Brug and, to a lesser extent, Paul Wendland offered critical feedback on chap. 5 from a traditional standpoint. I am grateful to my mother, Mrs. Rebecca Das, who read through the entire manuscript for style. The book would not have been possible without the incredible support of my wife, Susan. This book is dedicated to the three wonderful little children who have so enriched our lives, Peter, Paul, and Sara.

As I began seeking a publisher in the summer of 2005, Fortress Press had just brought onto their team Dr. Neil Elliott, who discovered a book proposal on his desk that happened to correspond with his own research agenda. I am grateful for his interest in and encouragement of this project in its concluding phases. The Romans situation has proved to be a controversial and debated topic for several generations now. Whether or not all agree with my conclusions, I hope that this work will provide a significant stepping-stone to solving the Romans debate.

Introduction

A furious debate has raged in Pauline scholarship for the last forty years over the occasion behind the Letter to the Romans. Paul's letters generally address specific issues facing local congregations. The apostle confronted Jewish Christian teachers at Galatia. He comforted the Thessalonians when members of their congregation died shortly after his departure. He combated division at Corinth.[1] He presented a slave to his master as a new man in Christ in the Letter to Philemon. Even the Letter to the Philippians appears to be confronting the unnecessary and divisive conflict between two prominent women in the congregation.[2] When scholars turned their attention to Romans, the situation presupposed in this letter proved more elusive.

When anyone mentions in scholarly circles that Paul is writing to Roman congregations composed exclusively of gentiles, the response is usually a polite silence.[3] What is likely going through the minds of most specialists is skepticism.

---

1. John M. G. Barclay, "Thessalonica and Corinth: Social Contrasts in Pauline Christianity," *JSNT* 47 (1992): 49–74.

2. David E. Garland, "Composition and Unity of Philippians," *NovT* 27 (1985): 141–73; Nils A. Dahl, "Euodia and Syntyche and Paul's Letter to the Philippians," in *The Social World of the First Christians: Essays in Honor of Wayne A. Meeks* (ed. L. Michael White and O. Larry Yarbrough; Minneapolis: Fortress Press, 1995), 3–15. In *Paul's Letter to the Philippians in the Light of Disunity in the Church* (NovTSup 79; Leiden: Brill, 1995), Davorin Peterlin placed the dispute between the two women into a larger context of factiousness.

3. Throughout this work, I have placed "gentile" in lowercase since, unlike "Jew," the word "gentile" is not a proper name referring to a particular ethnic group but is rather a Jewish designation for the non-Jewish world (so also Neil Elliott in his 2005 presentation at the national meeting of the Society of Biblical Literature). As Christopher Stanley put it: "The use of the term 'Gentiles' (ἀλλόφυλοι or ἔθνη) to designate all non-Jews represents a 'social construction of reality' developed by a particular people-group (the Jews) in a concrete historical situation" ("'Neither Jew Nor Greek': Ethnic Conflict in

1

Paul writes in Romans about God's faithfulness to Israel, the extent that Moses' Law is relevant for believers in Christ, Abraham as the forefather of both the circumcised and the uncircumcised, the advantages and blessings that remain for the Jewish people, and the interrelationship of Jews and gentiles in the divine plan. Although the apostle identifies his audience in places as gentiles, he also turns at times to "the Jew." The letter has a "double character." Most biblical scholars have great difficulty imagining how a letter overflowing with such motifs could have been addressed to any other than a mixed audience of both gentiles and Jews.

While Pauline specialists have at various points over the years suggested an entirely gentile audience for Paul's letter, a detailed challenge to the consensus of a Jewish constituency in the Roman congregations did not present itself until the 1990s.[4] The thesis of an entirely gentile audience is usually associated with Stanley Stowers's 1994 *A Rereading of Romans*.[5] Stowers strove to situate Romans in its neglected first-century setting apart from the anachronistic imposition of doctrinal categories. Stowers maintained that Romans must be read primarily in light of Greco-Roman literature, especially the moral philosophy of the day. In this context, Paul offered gentiles, obsessed with gaining control over their passions and desires, the ultimate solution: the gospel of God's righteous action in Jesus Christ, an action that empowers a "disciplined and restored self."[6] Many have dismissed Stowers's book as idiosyncratic. While exhaustively examining Greco-Roman literature and philosophy, Stowers largely ignored the scholarly emphasis on the Jewish and biblical traditions embedded in Paul's letter.[7] Stowers claimed that "Greek texts often control the scripture" while conceding in the next breath that these very Greek texts are ostensibly "in the background."[8] Stowers also spent an inordinate number of pages on Rom 1–4 (two hundred and fifty) while neglecting the remaining twelve chapters (eighty pages)! Several reviewers also noted that he followed Krister Stendahl, Lloyd Gaston, and John Gager in claiming that the Christ event in Paul's gospel was relevant primarily, or perhaps

---

Graeco-Roman Society," *JSNT* 64 [1996]: 101–24) When I have placed "gentile" in lowercase in a quotation from the NRSV, that is identified as "NRSV, mod."

4. For instance, see the brief case for an entirely gentile audience in Johannes Munck, *Paul and the Salvation of Mankind* (Atlanta: John Knox, 1959), 200–209.

5. Stanley K. Stowers, *A Rereading of Romans: Justice, Jews, and Gentiles* (New Haven: Yale Univ. Press, 1994). Wayne Meeks wrote in his endorsement for the book, "I'll never read the letter the same way again."

6. Ibid., 42.

7. Jouette M. Bassler, review of Stowers, *A Rereading of Romans, JBL* 115 (1996): 366. So also Richard B. Hays, "'The Gospel Is the Power of God for Salvation to Gentiles Only'? A Critique of Stanley Stowers's *A Rereading of Romans*," *CRBR* 9 (1996): 37.

8. Stowers, *Rereading Romans*, 316.

even exclusively, for the gentiles and not Jews.[9] The gentiles needed to be made right with God; the Jews were *already* God's covenant people.[10] Both Richard Hays and John M. G. Barclay devoted significant portions of their reviews to disputing this element of Stowers's thesis.[11] Such perceived idiosyncrasies have prompted investigators to dismiss his basic thesis of a gentile audience. Ironically, Hays and Barclay misread Stowers's *Rereading*.[12] In Stowers's own words: "Paul clearly says that both Jews and gentiles are subject to sin (3:9–20) and fall short of the glory of God (3:23), that God is now angry with the Jews as a whole . . . , and that the gospel has the power to save Jews from God's anger."[13] "At the present historical moment both Israel as a whole and the other nations stand equally before God as disobedient peoples (not every individual member)."[14] Stowers insisted against Gaston that, for Paul, Jesus was *Israel's* Messiah.[15] That interpreters of the caliber of Hays and Barclay misread Stowers demonstrates the need for greater care and attention to what he actually wrote.[16] The case for a gentile readership has been dismissed too quickly.

Stowers was not the first to present a detailed case for a gentile audience to the letter. Neil Elliott had actually championed the thesis a few years before Stowers's book appeared.[17] Elliott's published dissertation did not emphasize the non-Jewish, Greco-Roman background to the letter to the extent that Stowers's

---

9. Krister Stendahl, "Paul among Jews and Gentiles," in *Paul among Jews and Gentiles* (Philadelphia: Fortress Press, 1976), 1–77; Lloyd Gaston, *Paul and the Torah* (Vancouver: Univ. of British Columbia Press, 1987); John Gager, *The Origins of Anti-Semitism* (Oxford: Oxford Univ. Press, 1983).

10. For a detailed critique of the two-covenant approach of Stendahl, Gaston, and Gager, see A. Andrew Das, *Paul and the Jews* (Library of Pauline Studies; Peabody, Mass.: Hendrickson, 2003), 96–106.

11. Hays, "'The Gospel Is the Power of God,'" 29–30, 38–40; John M. G. Barclay, review of Stanley K. Stowers, *A Rereading of Romans, JTS* 46 (1995): 648–51. So also Jeffrey Peterson's review of Stowers, *A Rereading of Romans, ResQ* 39 (1997): 52–53.

12. Note the very title of Hays's review: "'The Gospel Is the Power of God for the Gentiles Only'?"

13. Stowers, *Rereading Romans*, 129.

14. Ibid., 197.

15. Ibid., 364 n. 5; note also Stowers's seconding Räisänen's critique of Gaston on p. 297 for denying the very real problem for Paul of Israel's *apistia* in 3:3; 9:1–5; 10:1; 11:20, 23.

16. Stowers titled his unpublished response to Richard Hays's review "Misreadings of a Rereading." I am indebted to Stowers for sharing his response.

17. Neil Elliott, *The Rhetoric of Romans: Argumentative Constraint and Strategy and Paul's Dialogue with Judaism* (JSNTSup 45; Sheffield: Sheffield Academic, 1990; Fortress Press edition, 2006).

book did. Elliott argued rather that Paul was hoping to strengthen the Romans in their lives of obedience, since their obedience as gentiles would guarantee the sanctity of the offering Paul was taking to the Jerusalem believers.[18] The Roman gentiles were urged to put aside their potential differences over Jewish observances and cooperate with Paul by their prayers in this offering.[19] The dialogue with the fictive "Jew" in Rom 2 functioned rhetorically to motivate the gentile audience. If the Jew, a member of God's privileged people, was not exempt from God's punishment for sin, how much less the gentile.[20] Elliott's work did not receive the attention that Stowers's work provoked. Robert Morgan, in a rare review, while complimentary, felt that Elliott's book needed to be expanded into a larger work "before many will be persuaded."[21] Wendy Dabourne's review noted the inordinate attention to Rom 1–4 also in Elliott's work and his concession that Rom 14:1 — 15:13 identified Jewish Christians in the Roman church.[22] She concluded:

> This means that as a matter of historical fact, Paul's letter was addressed to and read to a Christian community comprising a Gentile majority and a Jewish minority, in a situation in which the relationship between Jewish and Gentile believers was a key pastoral and theological issue for the Church. How were the Jewish believers supposed to respond while the diatribe passages were being read to their Gentile-Christian brothers and sisters in Christ?[23]

In other words, the concession of a Jewish Christian minority in Rom 14–15 undermined Elliott's entire thesis.[24]

Stowers's and Elliott's books share certain weaknesses that have prevented scholars from accepting their basic thesis of a gentile audience for the letter. They both spend little time with Rom 16. Stowers dismissed the Jewish people identified in the chapter with criticism of specialists who have conflated the empirical and encoded readers of the text.[25] Most commentators have drawn upon the

---

18. Ibid., 93.

19. Ibid., 94.

20. Ibid., 270.

21. Robert Morgan, "Romans Re-visioned," review of Neil Elliott, *The Rhetoric of Romans, ExpTim* 102 (1991): 279–80.

22. Wendy Dabourne, review of Elliott, *The Rhetoric of Romans, JTS* 43 ns (1992): 608–9.

23. Dabourne, Review of Elliott, *The Rhetoric of Romans*, 609.

24. Stowers, for his part, distinguished the encoded readers of Romans from actual readers.

25. Stowers, *Rereading of Romans*, 22–23, 30. The actual presence of Jews in the audience is irrelevant. Paul wrote his letter for *gentiles*. On the distinction between

list of names in chap. 16 as decisive evidence that Jews in fact numbered in the Roman congregations. Hays remarked on Stowers's brief treatment of chap. 16: "This is surely not coincidental, for some of the strongest evidence for the mixed Jewish-gentile composition of the Christian community at Rome comes from that chapter."[26] Elliott likewise concluded from chap. 16 that there was probably a Jewish Christian minority in Rome.[27] Further, both Stowers and Elliott did not satisfactorily account for the evidence from Rom 14:1 — 15:13 that Paul is also writing to the *Jewish* "weak." Many have noted that the customs described in these two chapters stemmed from Moses' Law. Hays found remarkable that Stowers passed over 15:7–13 "with virtually no supporting exegetical argument" when Paul urged his readers to welcome one another. The Romans were to follow the example of Christ in welcoming Jews and gentiles in order that these two groups might join together in praise of God.[28] Several scholars, such as C. E. B. Cranfield, Richard Hays, and Steve Mason, even wondered whether the explicit identifications of the audience as gentile were as decisive as Stowers and Elliott thought. For instance, Stowers and Elliott pointed to Rom 1:5–6 as proof.[29] Paul speaks of the gentiles "among whom (ἐν οἷς) you also are called." The prepositional phrase, however, is ambiguous and may be translated *geographically* as "*among whom* you are." The Romans — whether Jew or gentile — found themselves in the midst of a gentile world.[30] Stowers and Elliott, these critics have contended, wrongly pressed the evidence too far when they argued for an *entirely* gentile audience, whether actual or encoded.[31]

Again, many cannot conceive a letter written to gentiles that discusses at such length Judaism, its heritage, customs, and fate. Elliott and Stowers both struggled mightily to show how the "double character" of the letter can be resolved as a sort of "trap" ensnaring the proud gentile. Romans 11:26 asserts that "all Israel will be

---

encoded and empirical readers, see the critique of Alain Gignac, "Déconstruire notre lecture de *Romains* pour reconstruire notre théologie? Á propos de l'ouvrage de S. K. Stowers: *A Rereading of Romans,*" *LTP* 54 (1995): 181–93.

26. Hays, "'The Gospel Is the Power of God,'" 37. Similarly, Barclay noted that Rom 16 is "strangely left out of account, although the chapter is otherwise mined for information about the social status of the addressees" (review of Stowers, 647).

27. Elliott, *Rhetoric of Romans,* 94 n. 1.

28. Hays, "'The Gospel Is the Power of God,'" 37.

29. As Elliott explained, although the Romans were a mixed audience of both gentiles and Jews, Paul *addresses* them as exclusively gentile: "I've always imagined that a predominantly gentile audience *that included Jews* was nonetheless addressed *as gentiles*" (private communication).

30. Hays, "'The Gospel Is the Power of God,'" 35.

31. Ibid., 35–36.

saved." This climactic declaration completes a rhetorical movement that began with the critique in the early chapters of the letter of the Jew who boasts in his or her ethnic identity and heritage and who relies on works done in accordance with Moses' Law. No sooner does Paul chastise the "Jew" in Rom 2:17–29 than he lays the bait for the trap sprung in Rom 11:11–26 in which he criticizes gentile boasting of having supplanted Israel in the divine plan. The gentiles are in danger of the same sort of ethnic pride as the Jew and, ironically, at the expense of the Jew. On the other hand, the sheer extent of Paul's discussion of the Jews and Israel causes one to wonder whether such a discussion would have been necessary had Jews not actually been present in the audience or its immediate context. Thomas Schreiner in his commentary on Romans was categorical that Stowers and others who held to an entirely gentile audience were simply "wrong."[32]

The "mystery of Romans" need remain a mystery no longer. The pieces of the puzzle may be arranged in a manner that satisfies the full range of the evidence. What follows is a proposed solution to "the Romans debate" that not only builds on prior work in favor of a gentile audience for Romans but also advances the position further. To set the stage for this unfolding argument, chap. 1 briefly reviews some of the key positions that have been taken through the years in the debate over the situation and purpose behind Paul's letter. Even to speak of a letter begs the question of the literary integrity and limits of Romans. Did the letter originally include all sixteen chapters? Fifteen? Or even fourteen? The ancient manuscript evidence is hardly uniform. If Rom 14, 15, and 16 are integral to the letter, then a solution to the Romans debate must duly account for these chapters. Some have wondered whether Paul was writing primarily to the Romans or if he had a different audience in mind. Perhaps he was writing a general treatise summarizing his struggles and his thinking as it developed in the East. Perhaps he was anticipating his upcoming trip to Jerusalem or possibly to Spain. If Paul intended this letter primarily for his Roman audience, what did he intend? Perhaps Paul was aware of a situation in the Romans church. Many scholars have pointed to Rom 14:1 — 15:13 for that situation, but others have wondered whether Rom 14:1 — 15:13 concretely identifies Jewish and non-Jewish characteristics for the "weak" and the "strong," respectively. In narrowing the options, chap. 1 provides a foundation for the ensuing discussions.

The notion that Paul was writing to both Jewish and gentile Christians must ignore how he actually addresses his audience. Chapter 2 builds on recent work to demonstrate that the critics are not able to account for the letter's explicit

---

32. Thomas R. Schreiner, *Romans* (BECNT 6; Grand Rapids: Baker, 1998), 13 n. 25.

identifications of the audience.[33] Paul's turn to "the Jew" in places such as Rom 2:17 and the double character of the letter also beg treatment. A thorough analysis of Rom 14–15 and Rom 16 will demonstrate that that these chapters actually *support* a gentile audience. While it is true that Paul's letter is saturated with references to the Jews, their Scriptures, and their heritage, the content of the letter bespeaks members in the audience who had interacted with the synagogues as God-fearers. The discussion in chaps. 14–15 regarding the Law's customs points to other members of the gentile Christian assemblies without the same appreciation for Judaism. This chapter will therefore account for the full range of evidence within the letter itself.

A letter to Christ-believing gentiles that discusses at length the Jewish people, their Scriptures and heritage would also be plausible in the context of a gentile subgroup of the Roman synagogues. Mark Nanos has heeded Stowers's and Elliott's call for a recognition of the encoded gentile audience, but he has also recognized the inability of all-gentile proponents to resolve the "double character" of a letter that addresses the place of Israel in God's plan.[34] He neatly resolved the tension by positing gentiles who have learned about the Jewish Messiah in the synagogues and who have continued to meet in that context. As ingenious as his approach is, Nanos has his critics, particularly Robert A. J. Gagnon.[35] Nanos, for his part, has responded at length. Resolving this hearty and instructive debate is the task of chap. 3. Ultimately, this chapter demonstrates that a break had indeed taken place between the gentile audience of Romans and the Jewish synagogues.

Chapter 4 reviews the situation behind the infamous Edict of Claudius recorded by Suetonius. Many commentators still think that the Jews were forced by Claudius to leave Rome en masse and that, when they returned, the Christ-believing Jews began to meet for worship alongside the gentiles. The belief that a widespread expulsion of the Jews took place under Claudius is problematic. More likely, a limited action took place that affected the troublemakers, particularly the followers of "Chrestus." Even a more limited action would have impacted the relationship between the followers of Christ and the synagogues. Gentile Christians who had attended synagogue gatherings would have been forced to

---

33. See especially the recent work of Runar M. Thorsteinsson, *Paul's Interlocutor in Romans 2: Function and Identity in the Context of Ancient Epistolography* (ConBNT 40; Stockholm: Almqvist & Wiksell, 2003).

34. Mark D. Nanos, *The Mystery of Romans: The Jewish Context of Paul's Letter* (Minneapolis: Fortress Press, 1996).

35. Robert A. J. Gagnon, "Why the 'Weak' at Rome Cannot Be Non-Christian Jews," *CBQ* 62 (2000): 64–82.

form their own house churches. A reconstruction of the historical events in Rome offers suggestive, confirming parallels to Paul's letter itself.

Chapter 5 examines some of the implications of a gentile audience for reading the letter. The role of the Jewish people in a letter addressed to Roman gentiles requires investigation. Paul's gospel remains "to the Jew first." A revised understanding of the audience enhances the climactic sense of the declaration in Rom 11:26 that all Israel will be saved. The identity of the "I" of Rom 7:7–25 has also been a difficult issue in Pauline scholarship, but the "I" as a gentile God-fearer neatly resolves the riddles of this chapter and demonstrates the exegetical value of recognizing a gentile audience. In short, this solution to "the Romans debate" incorporates the pieces of the puzzle into a coherent whole.

Chapter 1

The Romans Debate:
Narrowing the Options

In his 1988 book *The Reasons for Romans*, A. J. M. Wedderburn wrote: "Why Paul wrote Romans is still something of an enigma. There is as yet no consensus as to why Paul should write precisely this letter with these contents to this church at this moment in his, and its, history."[1] He added: "That there should be so much disagreement over the purpose of Romans is disconcerting in a letter that has perhaps received more learned attention and research than almost any other piece of literature in human history."[2] Karl Donfried's *The Romans Debate*, published first in 1977 and then revised and expanded in 1991, featured a collection of essays representing the major approaches to the letter. The sheer array of interpretive possibilities in this volume exposes the difficulty specialists have had reaching any sort of consensus. Not a year passes without the appearance of at least a handful of essays and a monograph or two. With few exceptions, the major options were already articulated in *The Romans Debate*. In 1996 Mark Nanos titled his first major work *The Mystery of Romans*. Mysteries are hard to resist, particularly for scholars. Like any mystery, the Romans debate requires a bit of sleuthing — the collection of clues, the formation of hypotheses, and the elimination of alternatives until the pieces fit together in a satisfactory framework.

To speak of a "Romans debate," of course, assumes a stable object of inquiry. The early to mid-twentieth century witnessed a flurry of activity with respect to

---

1. A. J. M. Wedderburn, *The Reasons for Romans* (SNTIW; Edinburgh: T&T Clark, 1988), 1.
2. Wedderburn, *Reasons for Romans*, 2.

the integrity and unity of Romans. Several scholars followed ancient manuscript traditions in positing fourteen- and fifteen-chapter forms of Romans. Others defended the full sixteen-chapter version of the letter. Still others wondered if the Christians in subsequent generations had combined separate letter strands or included their own ruminations in Paul's original product. Because of the variants in the manuscript tradition, a sixteen-chapter form of the letter requires some defense.

Once researchers settled on an original form of the letter, they delved into the situation behind the letter and the letter's purpose. Was Paul offering the Romans a compendium of Christian doctrine or a summary of his thinking as it developed from his conflicts in the East? Perhaps he was seeking the Romans' prayers as he prepared to go to Jerusalem. Or perhaps he was enlisting their support for his missionary journey to Spain. Did the Roman church lack a proper apostolic foundation? Was he anticipating opposition to his gospel in Rome? Many have contended that Paul was hoping by his letter to address a concrete situation in Rome. F. F. Bruce and A. J. M. Wedderburn both rightly emphasized multiple reasons for Paul's authoring this letter.[3] The crucial question is whether any of these proposals may serve as the *primary* rationale for Paul's writing Romans. The last decades of the twentieth century witnessed one approach becoming increasingly popular in the commentaries: Paul was hoping to alleviate tensions that had arisen between Rome's gentile Christian majority and a Jewish Christian minority regarding Mosaic observances. This chapter will weigh the major proposals in the Romans debate and seek new horizons for interpretation.

The Integrity of the Letter

Radical Partition Theories

Over the years several scholars have concluded that the current form of Romans, with all its complexities and difficulties, is actually a composite of two, three, or even several separate letters. If Romans were indeed such a composite, the situation behind one strand could be entirely different from the situation behind another. To search for a single occasion behind the entire document would be an error. Partition theories must therefore be considered first in order to resolve

---

3. F. F. Bruce, "The Romans Debate — Continued," *BJRL* 64 (1981–82): 334–59; repr. in *The Romans Debate* (rev. and enl. ed.; ed. Karl P. Donfried; Peabody, Mass.: Hendrickson, 1991), 175–94. Note the very *title* of Wedderburn's work: *Reasons for Romans*. He did, however, gravitate toward a particular situation in the Roman congregation as receiving special attention in this letter.

the situation(s) and occasion(s) behind Romans. Scholarly questioning of the unity of Romans was more frequent a generation ago. Walter Schmithals in a 1975 monograph and again in his 1988 commentary argued that Romans is a composite of two originally separate letters: Letter A, penned in Ephesus earlier in Paul's ministry prior to the problems at Corinth (Rom 1:1 — 4:25; 5:12 — 11:36; 15:8–13), and a later Letter B (Rom 12:1–21; 13:8–10; 14:1 — 15:4a, 7, 5–6, 14–32; 16:21–23; 15:33).[4] In a 1964 article Junji Kinoshita hypothesized three letters behind Romans: a sermon on the gentile mission, the original letter (1:1–32; 2:6–16; 3:21–26; 5:1–11; 8:1–39; 12:1 — 13:14; 15:14–33); "The Manual of Instruction on Jewish Problems" (2:1–5; 2:17 — 3:20; 3:27 — 4:5; 5:12 — 7:25; 9:1 — 11:36; 14:1 — 15:3; 15:4–13); and Rom 16, a later appendix.[5] J. C. O'Neill's 1975 commentary identified *several* fragments and interpolations.[6]

Schmithals's approach may be considered representative of the various partition theories. Schmithals noted conflicting purposes and occasions throughout Romans. In Rom 1:10, 13 Paul claims that he was being hindered from traveling to Rome, but in Rom 15:22–25 the hindrance appears to be in the past and Paul has a firm confidence in his future travel plans, which include a possible visit.[7] In 15:20 Paul expresses reluctance to build on someone else's foundation with respect to the Romans, and yet in chap. 1 he envisions producing some fruit in Rome. In 15:24 he plans to visit Rome in order to gain support for a missionary venture in Spain, but in chap. 1 he desires to visit the Roman Christians for their own sake with Spain nowhere in view.[8] To resolve such conflicting statements, Schmithals concluded that Rom 1 and 15 must not be from the same original letter. Positing originally separate letter fragments would resolve the contradictions. On the other hand, in his search for consistency Schmithals was at a loss to explain why someone would have edited and combined the letter strands so poorly into such a contradictory final product.

---

4. Walter Schmithals, *Der Römerbrief als historisches Problem* (SNT 9; Gütersloh: Gerd Mohn, 1975); idem, *Der Römerbrief: Ein Kommentar* (Gütersloh: Gerd Mohn, 1988), esp. pp. 25–29, 33–45, 417–24, 543–53. In Schmithals's theory, Rom 5:1–11 and 13:11–14 belong to the Thessalonian correspondence.

5. Junji Kinoshita, "Romans: Two Writings Combined," *NovT* 7 (1964): 258–77. A by-product of Kinoshita's reasoning: Paul's editor and not the apostle himself was the great mind who addressed the relationship between Jews and gentiles.

6. J. C. O'Neill, *Paul's Letter to the Romans* (Baltimore: Penguin, 1975), 13–18, 264–74; see also the supporting comments in the commentary itself.

7. Schmithals, *Römerbrief als historisches Problem*, 167.

8. Ibid., 168–69.

In a comprehensive critique of Schmithals's position, A. J. M. Wedderburn appealed to the text-critical principle of giving preference to the more difficult reading as original, in this case the text of Romans in its current form. The complexities of Romans are better accounted as a result of Paul's own authorship rather than of subsequent editing.[9] Further, Wedderburn questioned whether the tensions Schmithals identified were sufficiently serious enough to require different letters. Whereas Schmithals contrasted Paul's sense of being hindered from travel in 1:13 with the greater confidence of 15:23–25, Wedderburn responded that even in 1:13 the hindrance had already been removed ("up until now"; note also the aorist verb). The path had already been cleared for the travel plans of chap. 15. As for Paul's general policy of not wanting to build on another's foundation and yet hoping for fruit in Rome, Schmithals himself recognized that positing separate letters would not remove the contradiction.[10] Wedderburn was not convinced of a contradiction. Although Paul does speak of "evangelizing" in both 1:15 and 15:20, the contexts are very different. In 1:15 Paul is speaking to those already converted, whereas in 15:20 he is speaking of initial missionary work. In chap. 1 he is maneuvering delicately and sensitively with respect to a group he has not yet visited. The general principle of 15:20 does not necessarily rule out Paul's preaching where Christianity has already been planted. As for the omission of any mention of the trip to Spain in chap. 1, to highlight plans for Spain at the beginning of the letter would be to "call into question the extent of his interest in the Romans."[11] The apostle's desire to be mutually encouraged by the Romans' faith in 1:12 parallels his desire to be refreshed by their company in 15:32.[12] The extant textual evidence provides no evidence for separate strands behind Romans. As Leander Keck, a leading specialist on Romans, caustically commented: "Schmithals is probably the only student of Romans who believes all this."[13] Richard Hays, in his response to Keck's essay, chastised him for even bothering to review "the wildly speculative hypotheses" and "idiosyncratic musings" of Schmithals, Kinoshita, and others: "Such theories belong in a museum

---

9. A. J. M. Wedderburn, "The Purpose and Occasion of Romans Again," *ExpTim* 90 (1979): 137–41; repr. in *The Romans Debate* (rev. and enl. ed.; ed. Karl P. Donfried; Peabody, Mass.: Hendrickson, 1991), 195–202, esp. p. 198. See also the parallel discussion in Wedderburn, *Reasons for Romans*, 25–29.

10. Schmithals, *Römerbrief als historisches Problem*, 172.

11. Wedderburn, "Purpose and Occasion," 199.

12. See also the detailed critique of Schmithals by Ulrich Wilckens, *Der Brief an die Römer* (3 vols.; 3d ed.; EKKNT 6; Neukirchen-Vluyn: Neukirchener, 1997), 1:28–29.

13. Leander E. Keck, "What Makes Romans Tick?" in *Pauline Theology 3: Romans* (ed. David M. Hay and E. Elizabeth Johnson; Minneapolis: Fortress Press, 1995), 9.

of exegetical curiosities rather than a serious discussion of the theological coherence of Romans. These hypotheses demonstrate nothing more than the inability of their authors to tolerate dialectical complexity."[14] Such theories suffer from a complete absence of evidence in the ancient manuscript tradition and are unable to offer a satisfactory explanation for how and why later redactors of Romans would weave the fragments together into its current form.

A Fourteen-Chapter Version of Romans

The witness of the ancient manuscript tradition, an Achilles' heel for radical partition theories, raises yet a new set of issues. Several textual difficulties beset Romans. First, are Rom 1:7 and 1:15, with their identification of the Roman addressees, original to the letter or the product of later scribal editors? The manuscript tradition is by no means unanimous. Second, were Rom 15 and 16 part of the original letter? One or both of these chapters may be questioned on the basis of the extant textual evidence. Third, is the doxology (16:25–27) original, and does it belong at the end of the letter? The doxology is positioned at the end of chap. 14 in some manuscripts, at the end of chap. 15 in others, and at its current location in still others. To summarize the textual data:[15]

1:1 — 14:23	15:1 — 16:23; 16:25–27	p^{61}, $\aleph$, B, C, bo, sa, D, e, f, vg, sy^p
1:1 — 14:23; 16:25–27	15:1 — 16:23; 16:25–27	A, P, min
1:1 — 14:23; 16:25–27	15:1 — 16:24	sy^h
1:1 — 14:23	15:1 — 16:24	F, G, g, Archetype of D
1:1 — 14:23; 16:24–27		vg^{2089}, Old Latin, according to Cyprian's chapter lists
1:1 — 15:33; 16:25–27	16:1–23	p^{46}

---

14. Richard B. Hays, "Adam, Israel, Christ: The Question of Covenant in the Theology of Romans: A Response to Leander E. Keck and N. T. Wright," in *Pauline Theology 3: Romans*, 76. Hays's comments also target as perceptive an interpreter of the letter as Keck, who was all too ready to consider such theories and had himself been tempted to perform arguably unnecessary radical surgery on the text of Romans (e.g., 13:1–7; 16:17–20). Such radical surgery should be an interpretive device of last resort.

15. Werner Georg Kümmel, *Introduction to the New Testament* (rev. and enl. ed.; trans. Howard Clark Kee; Nashville: Abingdon, 1975), 315. For a more thorough listing of the manuscript evidence for the various configurations, see Harry Gamble, Jr., *The Textual History of the Letter to the Romans* (SD 42; Grand Rapids: Eerdmans, 1977), 23–24.

A number of manuscripts support a fourteen-chapter version of the letter by the positioning of the doxology (16:25–27) after 14:23. In other manuscripts, the doxology follows *both* 14:23 and 16:24. In addition, an early Vulgate manuscript (Codex Amiatinus) contains short summaries (*breves*) of the various sections of the letter. The fiftieth summary recaps 14:13–23 and is followed by the fifty-first on 16:25–27. Romans 15:1 — 16:23 does not appear to have been available to the author. Codex Fuldensis as well as other Vulgate manuscripts maintain the fifty-one-section Amiatine pattern.[16] The Marcionite prologue claims that Romans was written from Athens, even though Rom 15–16 points to a Corinthian origin. The Marcionite prologue must therefore have been based on a version of the letter without chaps. 15–16.[17] Tertullian never cited Rom 15–16 and referred to Rom 14 as "the conclusion of the letter" (*clausula epistolae*). Irenaeus and Cyprian did not cite chaps. 15–16 either.[18] So Kirsopp Lake concluded that Paul wrote the fourteen chapters of Romans as an "anti-Judaistic letter" and added Rom 1:7, 15 and chap. 15 when he sent the letter to Rome. Somehow the letter to Ephesus (Rom 16) was appended.[19] If this hypothesis were correct, the Romans may not have been the original recipients of the letter. To speak of a "Romans debate" would be a misnomer.

While the Roman letter circulated in some quarters in a fourteen-chapter form, the shortened version is likely not the original. An originally fourteen-chapter version of Romans cannot account for how the Old Latin manuscripts that end after chap. 15 developed. Scholars have generally agreed that Rom 15:1 to at least Rom 16:16, if not to 16:24, are Pauline in style and content. Further, Paul's discussion of the strong and the weak does not conclude until 15:6 or 15:13.[20] No one has been able to provide a viable hypothesis why 15:1–6 or 15:1–13 would have been subsequently and rather artificially added to a fourteen-chapter Romans. No one has been able to explain why a later addition to Romans would have continued a discussion that belonged with the original situation of the letter.[21]

An original longer letter was more likely abbreviated into a fourteen-chapter version. Discerning the rationale for this alteration, on the other hand, has proven

---

16. Gamble, *Textual History*, 16–18.

17. Ibid., 19–20.

18. Ibid., 20–21.

19. Kirsopp Lake, *The Earlier Epistles of St. Paul: Their Motive and Origin* (2d ed. London: Rivingtons, 1919), 335–50, 361–65, and esp. pp. 365–69.

20. J. B. Lightfoot, *Biblical Essays* (New York: Macmillan, 1893; repr., Grand Rapids: Baker, 1979), 363–64; Lake, *Earlier Epistles*, 361–65.

21. Gamble, *Textual History*, 99.

more difficult. Paul himself would not have been the source of the abbreviation since the discussion of the weak and the strong from 14:1 properly continues until 15:6 or 15:13, and textual evidence is entirely lacking for a form of the letter ending at either 15:6 or 15:13. Origen claimed that the fourteen-chapter version of Romans was Marcion's handiwork: he removed the doxology and then "cut away" (*dissecuit*) all that followed 14:23. Although the Latin verb *dissecuit* could be taken to suggest that Marcion altered the contents of chaps. 15–16, most scholars think Origen claimed that Marcion *deleted* chaps. 15–16.[22] A Marcionite alteration is possible but by no means certain. Origen never hinted at why Marcion would delete the last two chapters. Elements in those chapters would surely be at odds with Marcion's animosity toward Judaism and its Scriptures — especially the Scriptural citations in 15:3, 9–12, 21, the commendation of the Scriptures' value (15:4), and the description of Jesus as the servant of the circumcised (15:8). A complete removal of the two chapters, however, would be largely unprecedented even for Marcion. He typically removed only the material he found offensive and left what remained.[23] Further, Origen is the only source tracing the fourteen-chapter version to Marcion. The array of Western witnesses to the shortened form, especially in the Old Latin tradition, is difficult to reconcile with a Marcionite origin, since at the time of the Latin texts "catholic opposition to Marcion was at its zenith."[24] In view of Marcion's radical practices, Origen's charge is understandable, but Marcion's influence remains uncorroborated. Another hypothesis has traced the fourteen-chapter version to liturgical use, but liturgical function does not explain why the break came after 14:23 and not after 15:6 or 15:13, because the early verses of Rom 15 would be suitable for liturgy. The notion of fixed lectionary texts by the early second century is without evidence. Even if such a lectionary system existed, it is questionable whether at this early date such a system would influence the textual transmission so strongly.[25] Perhaps the fourteen-chapter version was the result of an accident in which the last pages of a manuscript were lost. The problem with this hypothesis is that not only are the last two chapters missing, but also missing is the twofold identification in chap. 1 of the audience as located in

---

22. Thus William Sanday and Arthur C. Headlam, *A Critical and Exegetical Commentary on the Epistle to the Romans* (5th ed.; ICC; Edinburgh: T&T Clark, 1902), xcvi–xcvii; G. Zuntz, *The Text of the Epistles: A Disquisition upon the* Corpus Paulinum (London: British Academy, 1953), 227; Franz J. Leenhardt, *The Epistle to the Romans: A Commentary* (London: Lutterworth, 1961), 26.

23. Gamble, *Textual History*, 106.

24. Ibid., 106. See Gamble's full discussion, 100–14.

25. Ibid., 114–15.

Rome.[26] The omission of the last two chapters, in combination with the deletion of specific verses from Rom 1, appears to be deliberate.

Harry Gamble considered the possibility that Romans was shortened into a more general form to appeal to a wider audience the most likely explanation.[27] A few manuscripts omit ἐν Ῥώμῃ in 1:7 and τοῖς ἐν Ῥώμῃ in 1:15. Gamble noted that these omissions coincide with the fourteen-chapter form of Romans attested in the Western bilinguals. Romans 1:7, 15, and chaps. 15–16 together specify the addressees.[28] Romans appears to have been deliberately shortened.[29] Although Gamble cited the unnaturally abrupt break after 14:23 as a weakness in other theories, surprisingly, he did not recognize the problem the break in Paul's discussion would pose for his own position.[30] One would expect such a "catholicized" version of Romans to end after 15:6 or 15:13 with the completion of the discussion of the weak and the strong and prior to the specifics of Paul's travel plans in the latter part of the chapter and the greetings of chap. 16. A satisfactory account of the origin of a fourteen-chapter variant has yet to be proposed. The only relative certainty is that the fourteen-chapter form itself is not original.

A Fifteen-Chapter Version of Romans

In 1829 David Schulz proposed that Paul wrote Rom 1–15 to the church at Rome and then added chap. 16 with its extensive list of greetings for the church at Ephesus. T. W. Manson's 1962 essay advanced Schulz's original proposal.[31] The strongest textual evidence for Manson's thesis is p[46], which uniquely places the doxology (16:25–27) after chap. 15. Also, Manson considered it unlikely

---

26. Ibid., 115. One must also explain the fifteen-chapter version attested by p[46].

27. Ibid., 115–24. This has remained the most popular position.

28. Ibid., 29–33.

29. So also Lightfoot, *Biblical Essays*, 311–20, 352–74 (Lightfoot's original essay along with his response to Hort).

30. For instance, Gamble, *Textual History*, 36, cited the unnatural break at 14:23 as decisive against the fourteen-chapter theory. It is inexplicable why someone would create such an unnatural break in Paul's discussion in order to shorten the letter for a wider audience.

31. T. W. Manson, "St. Paul's Letter to the Romans — and Others," in *Studies in the Gospels and Epistles* (ed. M. Black; Manchester: Manchester Univ. Press, 1962), 225–41; repr. in Donfried, *The Romans Debate*, 3–15, esp. pp. 10–12. Manson also favored a subsequent Marcionite removal of Rom 15 along with the 1:7 and 15. On Schulz's original proposal, see Kümmel, *Introduction*, 318 n. 45.

that Paul would have had twenty-six personal friends, some apparently intimate, in the churches of a city he had never visited (1:10–15; 15:19–23).[32] Ephesus would have been a different matter because of Paul's extensive ministry there according to the Book of Acts. In fact, the people otherwise known on the Rom 16 list are associated with Asia, especially Ephesus. Prisca and Aquila (Rom 16:3–5) traveled with Paul to Ephesus in Acts 18:18, established a church there (1 Cor 16:19), and resided there at the time of 2 Tim 4:19. If Prisca and Aquila were in Rome at the time of the authoring of Rom 16, then the couple would have left Rome, resided in Ephesus, proceeded back to Rome, established a church there, and ended up back at Ephesus according to 2 Tim 4:19–22 (cf. 1:15–18). Is it not more likely that they had simply left Rome and remained in Ephesus?[33] An audience including Epaenetus, "the first convert in *Asia*" (Rom 16:5; emphasis added), would also match an Asian Ephesian destination.[34] The warning in Rom 16:17–20 seems harsh and abrupt when no false teachers in Rome are singled out in an otherwise irenic letter.[35] Even the discussion of the strong and the weak in Rom 14:1 — 15:13 provides no hint of opposition. On the other hand, scholars have often inferred from 1 and 2 Timothy the presence of false teachers at Ephesus. Manson noted points of contact between Rom 16:17–20 and the warnings of Acts 20:29–32 in an Ephesian context.[36] Manson concluded from the evidence that as Paul reflected on the conflicts he had endured at Corinth and Galatia over the relationship between the new faith and its Jewish roots, he decided to send a summary of his thinking (chaps. 1–15) to Rome. He then sent a copy of the letter to Ephesus along with a cover letter, chap. 16.[37] Romans 16 also served as a letter of recommendation for Phoebe (Rom 16:1–2).[38] If Manson were right, Rom 16 would be of no value for reconstructing the situation behind chaps. 1–15.

Most specialists have not found Manson's case compelling. The textual evidence overwhelmingly favors the inclusion of chap. 16 in the letter. Even in p[46],

---

32. See also Lake, *Earlier Epistles*, 326.

33. Ibid., 327–9; Schmithals, *Römerbrief: Ein Kommentar*, 547.

34. Lake, *Earlier Epistles*, 327; Kümmel, *Introduction*, 318.

35. Lake, *Earlier Epistles*, 326–27.

36. Manson, "St. Paul's Letter," 13 n. 23; Gamble, *Textual Issues*, 39–40.

37. For most of these arguments, see also Schmithals, *Römerbrief: Ein Kommentar*, 546–49.

38. J. I. H. McDonald, "Was Romans XVI a Separate Letter?" *NTS* 16 (1969–1970): 369–72, cited several shorter ancient letters with extensive greetings (and sometimes recommendations) that would parallel Rom 16:1–23 as its own letter — for instance, Dius's letter to his father Horion (Oxyrhynchus Papyrus 1962).

Manson's prime exhibit, 16:1–23 follows immediately after the doxology.[39] According to the principles of textual criticism, the earliest reading is the one that can explain the origin of all the variants. In that regard, p[46] fails as the original reading of the text.[40] Manson supposed that a scribe melded the original fifteen-chapter version of Romans with a later fourteen-chapter form that included the doxology (1:1 — 14:23; 16:25–27) to create the version attested by p[46] (1:1 — 15:33; 16:25–27; 16:1–23). Manson's reconstruction requires positing three unattested forms in the manuscript tradition, including an unlikely hypothetical intermediate (1:1 — 15:33; 16:25–27).[41] Peter Lampe demonstrated several peculiarities of vocabulary and grammatical style that are common between Rom 1–15 and 16.[42] The δέ in Rom 16:1 presupposes preceding text and proves that chap. 16 did not stand on its own.[43]

The greetings of Rom 16 function much better in a Roman context than in an Ephesian context. Paul could very well have known twenty-six people in Rome.[44] Travel throughout the empire was common for many, especially

---

39. Peter Lampe, "The Roman Christians of Romans 16," in Donfried, ed., *The Romans Debate*, 217. Miniscule 1506 is the only manuscript with chap. 15 but without 16:1–23, although there is a blank half page between chap. 15 and 16:25–27. The copyist of 1506 apparently knew of Rom 16. The manuscript is not viable evidence for the original text of Romans, because it is a descendant of Marcion's fourteen-chapter Romans as well as texts with chaps. 15 and 16 together.

40. Peter Lampe, "Zur Textgeschichte des Römerbriefes," *NovT* 27 (1985): 273–77; Mark A. Seifrid, *Justification by Faith: The Origin and Development of a Central Pauline Theme* (NovTSup 68; Leiden: Brill, 1992), 252–53.

41. Rom 15:33 already forms an adequate conclusion; Kurt Aland, "Der Schluss und die Ursprüngliche Gestalt des Römerbriefes" in *Neutestamentliche Entwürfe* (TB 63; Munich: Chr. Kaiser, 1979), 295–97. p[46] is more easily explained as a universalized form of the sixteen-chapter version of Romans (Gamble, *Textual History*, 96–126).

42. Peter Lampe, *From Paul to Valentinus: Christians at Rome in the First Two Centuries* (trans. Michael Steinhauser; Minneapolis: Fortress Press, 2003), 160–64.

43. Wolf-Henning Ollrog, "Die Abfassungsverhältnisse von Röm 16," in *Kirche: Festschrift für Günther Bornkamm zum 75. Geburtstag* (ed. Dieter Lührmann and Georg Strecker; Tübingen: J. C. B. Mohr [Paul Siebeck], 1980), 226–27; Lampe, "Roman Christians," 217. As Ollrog pointed out, the Ephesian hypothesis requires several unnecessary additional steps. Romans 16 must be broken off from its preceding text and then abnormally appended to Rom 15. Far simpler is the recognition that Rom 16 naturally follows on the heels of Rom 15.

44. As Ollrog noted, it is impossible to prove whether or not Paul might have known twenty-six people in Rome. Assumptions regarding whom Paul may or may not have

travel to and from Rome.[45] Although Paul, by his descriptive characterizations, betrays personal knowledge of only nine of the people on his list, the rest could have been well-known individuals in the Roman communities.[46] By greeting so many people he is forging links to a place he had yet to visit and is proving his credentials by means of his contacts with the congregations.[47] Ollrog wondered why it seems so amazing to some that Paul would have known of twenty-six people in Rome when his close companions Prisca and Aquila were in Rome and could have informed him of the congregation's members, especially in view of Paul's plans to visit Rome.[48] Prisca and Aquila likely left Rome because of the Edict of Claudius (Acts 18:2) and could have returned subsequently with the accession of Nero in 54, or even sooner. They may have returned then to Ephesus for business.[49] Travel and migration from the Aegean region to Rome was not unusual in this period.[50] Ancient inscriptions bear witness that the names of Rom 16 were otherwise attested in Rome.[51] Further, Paul refers to those who reside in the households of Aristobulus and Narcissus (Rom 16:10–11). This Narcissus was perhaps the powerful Roman freedman who exerted influence in Claudius's circles. Aristobulus may well have been the grandson of Herod the

---

known offer a shaky foundation for conclusions regarding the authenticity of Rom 16 ("Die Abfassungsverhältnisse," 226).

45. Kümmel, *Introduction*, 319; Wedderburn, *Reasons for Romans*, 15; Donfried, "Short Note," 44–52, esp. pp. 49–50. Lampe, "Roman Christians," 219, cited CIG 3920, in which the craftsman Flavius Zeuxis brags of seventy-two trips from the East to Italy. While he is exceptional, he demonstrates the possibilities. See also Wayne A. Meeks, *The First Urban Christians: The Social World of the Apostle Paul* (New Haven: Yale Univ. Press, 1983), 16–23; Abraham J. Malherbe, *Social Aspects of Early Christianity* (2d ed.; Philadelphia: Fortress Press, 1983), 62–68.

46. Gamble, *Textual History*, 47–48; Lampe, "Roman Christians," 219–20.

47. Wedderburn, *Reasons for Romans*, 14.

48. "Die Abfassungsverhältnisse," 226.

49. Lampe, "Roman Christians," 221, surprisingly concluded that 2 Tim 4:19 must be historically in error to claim that Prisca and Aquila were back in Ephesus. Lampe himself pointed out (p. 220) that Aquila had already moved at least three times in 1 Cor 16:19: Acts 18:1–2; cf. 18:18, 26 (Pontus — Rome — Corinth — Ephesus). So, Lampe asked, why not a fourth trip back to Rome? Indeed, why not a business trip or extended visit to Ephesus? Lampe (p. 219) cited inscription CIG 3920 where the craftsman Flavius Zeuxis brags on his epitaph that he had sailed seventy-two times from the East to Italy. While an exceptional instance, the epitaph demonstrates the possibilities for travel. See also Ollrog, "Die Abfassungsverhältnisse," 238.

50. Ollrog, "Die Abfassungsverhältnisse," 239.

51. Gamble, *Textual History*, 51 (relying on Lightfoot).

Great and brother of Agrippa I. The Herodian Aristobulus lived in Rome.[52] Ephesian inscriptions do not bear witness to the names Urbanus, Phlegon, Persis, and Asyncritus; Roman epigraphs do.[53] Identifying Epaenetus as the first convert *in Asia* (16:5) makes little sense if addressed to Asian Ephesians who would already know Epaenetus.[54] The Romans, on the other hand, may not have realized Epaenetus's significance.[55] Along similar lines, would the Ephesians not *already have known* that Prisca and Aquila were Paul's co-workers?[56] They would have known that Timothy was his co-worker (16:21). In contrast: "Other persons are named without any personal reference or intimate detail whatsoever, which seems absurd if Paul had worked with them for almost three years, as was the case in Ephesus."[57] Considering their importance for the community, the descriptions of Andronicus and Junia (16:7) seem rather impersonal (cf. Apollos in 1 Cor 3:5–9).[58] The lack of personal detail in some of the greetings would have been tactless had Paul been in close contact with those individuals. The lack of detail suggests, contrary to the Ephesian hypothesis, that Paul only knew these leaders by reputation but not personally.[59] Why append greetings directed to a particular audience—Ephesians—to a letter being sent to an entirely different audience in a distant land?[60] The number of people greeted in Romans actually militates *against* an Ephesian destination. Paul did not in any other letter send such an extensive set of greetings to a church with which he was familiar. Surely in Ephesus Paul would have known more than the twenty-six he mentioned: "It

---

52. Ibid., 50. Certainty is not possible in either case. "Narcissus" is attested as the name of a Roman slave in at least fifty instances; Lampe, *From Paul to Valentinus*, 165. As for Aristobulus, however, note the reference to "Herodion" in v. 11.

53. Lampe, "Roman Christians," 216.

54. Leon Morris, *The Epistle to the Romans* (Grand Rapids: Eerdmans, 1988), 27. Ollrog ("Die Abfassungsverhältnisse," 239) noted that Paul met Prisca and Aquila in Acts 18:1–3, and they went on together to Ephesus. It would not be surprising, then, that the first convert of Asia should remain associated with Prisca and Aquila when they went on to Rome in 16:5.

55. Kümmel, *Introduction*, 319.

56. Gamble, *Textual History*, 49; Ollrog, "Die Abfassungsverhältnisse," 237–38.

57. Robert Jewett, "Paul, Phoebe, and the Spanish Mission," in *The Social World of Formative Christianity and Judaism: Essays in Tribute to Howard Clark Kee* (ed. Jacob Neusner, Peder Borgen, Ernest S. Frerichs, and Richard Horsley; Philadelphia: Fortress Press, 1988), 148; Ollrog," Die Abfassungsverhältnisse," 240 (the point was originally made by Ollrog).

58. Ollrog, "Die Abfassungsverhältnisse," 237. Nothing is said regarding their relationship to the community or their coworkers.

59. Ibid., 236–41.

60. John Knox, "The Epistle to the Romans: Introduction," *IB* 9:367.

would have been invidious to make a selection."[61] Paul would have risked offending Ephesians who were not singled out. Had Ephesus been the destination for this chapter, Paul strangely does not refer to his experiences or future plans with the Ephesians, quite unlike the others letters to churches he had founded.[62] A Roman destination makes better sense of the list as Paul greeted everyone he knew or had heard of in a city that he had yet to visit.[63] He was thereby establishing his authority and commending his ministry by means of his associations with respected persons in the Romans' midst who could serve as character references.[64] They could attest to the validity of his gospel.[65] The ecumenical greeting "all the churches of Christ greet you" (16:16) is fitting in Romans, since Paul would have been sending greetings from the eastern churches while he was considering a new ministry in the West in Spain.[66] In greeting and highlighting his contacts in Rome, he was laying the foundation for that future work.[67]

Many commentators have found in the abrupt, harsh warning of Rom 16:17–20 further evidence that Rom 16 was not part of the original letter. Paul adopts such a friendly tone elsewhere in the letter. Such abrupt disruptions, however, are not unusual for Paul.[68] As for the irenic tone elsewhere in Romans, Paul never claims in Rom 16:17–20 that such teachers are already present in Rome. These verses may well signal a *potential* threat.[69] The vocabulary and motifs of this passage parallel language earlier in the letter. For instance, in 16:17

---

61. Morris, *Romans*, 24–25.

62. Ollrog, "Die Abfassungsverhältnisse," 237.

63. Gamble, *Textual History*, 48; Lampe, "Roman Christians," 217.

64. Jeffrey A. D. Weima, "Preaching the Gospel in Rome: A Study of the Epistolary Framework of Romans," in *Gospel in Paul: Studies on Corinthians, Galatians and Romans for Richard N. Longenecker* (ed. L. Ann Jervis and Peter Richardson; JSNTSup 108; Sheffield: Sheffield Academic, 1994), 362.

65. Lampe, "Roman Christians," 218. These individuals need not be members of the Roman congregations themselves.

66. Ibid., 218.

67. Ollrog, "Die Abfassungsverhältnisse," 241–42.

68. See, for instance, 1 Cor 16:20b compared with 1 Cor 16:22a. Karl Paul Donfried, "A Short Note on Romans 16," in idem, *The Romans Debate*, 51–52; repr. from *JBL* 89 (1970): 441–49. David E. Garland has provided an excellent defense of the unity of Philippians with its rather abrupt change of tone in 3:2 ("Composition and Unity of Philippians," *NovT* 27 [1985]: 141–73). For additional instances of abrupt changes of tone, see Phil 3:18–19; and 1 Thess 2:15–16 and the discussion of Markku Kettunen, *Der Abfassungszweck des Römerbriefes* (AASF 18; Helsinki: Suomalainen Tiedeakatemia, 1979), 71–72.

69. Gamble, *Textual History*, 43. The hypothesis of Rom 1–15 as a circular letter reflecting on Paul's past dialogues with Jewish Christian opposition assumes a uniformity

παρακαλῶ δὲ ὑμᾶς, ἀδελφοί ("I urge you, brothers and sisters") is similar to the expressions Paul employs in 12:1 and 15:30. As for "dissensions" (διχοστασία), note the divisions in 11:17, 20; 14:1–5, 10, 13 and the peaceful opposites in 12:16 and 14:19. For "stumbling blocks" (σκάνδαλα), see 14:13; cf. 9:33; 11:9. The "teaching" (διδαχή) of v. 17 finds precedent in 6:17. Compare Rom 16:18 and its reference to the "belly" (κοιλία) with the concerns of Rom 14:1 — 15:7.[70] Paul also praises the Roman believers in v. 19 as he had in 1:8, 12; 15:14. Romans 16:19b is similar in thinking to 1 Cor 14:20. Romans 16:20 is comparable to 1 Cor 15:24–28. J. Paul Sampley even noted how God's crushing Satan under the Romans' feet in 16:20 parallels the Roman government's crushing its opponents to maintain peace (cf. Rom 13:1–7).[71] Finally, Sampley outlined verbal and thematic connections that vouch for the authenticity of this paragraph. The harsh reproach of deviation in Rom 16:17–20 parallels Paul's harshness elsewhere (esp. Gal 1:9; 1 Cor 16:22). The emphasis on "my gospel" parallels Rom 2:16, "my God" parallels Rom 1:8, and "my ways in Christ" parallels 1 Cor 4:17.[72]

Harry Gamble demonstrated throughout both Hellenistic and Pauline letters the elements that typify epistolary conclusions: hortatory remarks, wish of peace, greetings, and grace benedictions. The concluding elements may vary somewhat from letter to letter and are not rigid in form. The elements of Rom 16 are typical of a Pauline letter closing: greetings (16:3–15), kiss of peace (16:16), admonition (16:17–20), and grace benediction (16:20).[73] If Rom 16 were intended for Ephesus, 15:33 would be the conclusion of the letter with its wish of peace, but Paul does not conclude any other letter with a wish of peace.[74] Such wishes of peace elsewhere in Paul and elsewhere in the New Testament precede the greetings, as is the case in Rom 16.[75] The grace benediction of Rom 16:20b, 24, on the other hand, is exactly what would be expected of

---

in the history of opposition to Paul's ministry and likely distorts the identity of such opponents.

70. Philip F. Esler, *Conflict and Identity in Romans: The Social Setting of Paul's Letter* (Minneapolis: Fortress Press, 2003), 127; see, however, the discussion of Karl Olav Sandnes's study below.

71. J. Paul Sampley, "Romans in a Different Light: A Response to Robert Jewett," in Hay and Johnson, *Pauline Theology 3: Romans*, 127.

72. Sampley, "Romans in a Different Light," 128.

73. Gamble, *Textual History*, 84–95.

74. Ibid., 54.

75. Phil 4:9; 2 Cor 13:11; 1 Thess 5:23; 2 Thess 3:16; Heb 13:20; 3 John 15. Galatians 6:16 and Eph 6:23 do not conclude letters (note the grace benedictions that follow). First Peter 5:14 is the only exception and is non-Pauline; Ollrog, "Die Abfassungsverhältnisse," 226; Lampe, "Roman Christians," 217.

a Pauline ending.[76] Indeed, after the lengthy introduction (1:1–7), the longest in the Pauline corpus, it is not likely that the letter's conclusion would be the shortest. Further, the hypothesis that Rom 16 had been its own letter of commendation and greetings is implausible since such a letter would be unparalleled in the Pauline corpus.[77] A letter of recommendation for Phoebe is unnecessary when Paul's letters typically include subforms of various genres. Paul appends a commendation of Timothy to the Corinthians at the conclusion of his letter (1 Cor 16:10–11).[78] Gamble noted the parallel with the recommendations at the end of some of Cicero's letters. A letter consisting almost exclusively of greetings, however, is unattested in antiquity.[79] Evidence is also entirely lacking for the speculative thesis that chap. 16 had been part of a different but now lost letter.[80] Jeffrey Weima demonstrated several concerns of Romans exemplified in the letter's closing (15:33 — 16:27).[81] Donfried could therefore write of a shift in scholarship in which Rom 16 is now understood as an integral part of the letter.[82] Any reconstruction of the situation within the Roman churches must employ the full sixteen chapters.[83]

---

76. Ollrog, "Die Abfassungsverhältnisse," 226–27.

77. Lampe, "Roman Christians," 216.

78. Gamble, *Textual History*, 85–87.

79. Ibid., 85; Kümmel, *Introduction*, 319.

80. Gamble, *Textual History*, 45–46.

81. "For a careful study of the letter closings reveals that Paul commonly shapes and adapts this epistolary unit in such a way that it relates directly to — sometimes, in fact, even summarizes — the major concerns and themes taken up in the bodies of their respective letters" (Weima, "Preaching the Gospel," 359).

82. Donfried, *The Romans Debate*, lxx.

83. As for Rom 16:25–27, Kümmel, *Introduction*, 316, and Hans Lietzmann, *Einführung in die Textgeschichte der Paulusbriefe an die Römer* (5th ed.; HNT 8; Tübingen: J. C. B. Mohr [Paul Siebeck], 1933; repr., 1971), 130–31, thought that the most likely textual explanation for the ending of Romans is that an original text consisting of 1:1 — 16:23 was shortened into the version Marcion had (1:1 — 14:23). A doxology was added to Marcion's text (1:1 — 14:23; 16:26–27). When the revised form of Marcion's text was later compared with the original reading, the doxology in some instances remained after 14:23 with 15:1 — 16:24 added, or in other instances the doxology was deleted (1:1 — 14:23; 15:1 — 16:24), or the doxology was moved, either to after 15:33 or after 16:23, or the doxology was repeated after 16:23. See also the case against the authenticity of 16:25–27 in Raymond F. Collins, "The Case of a Wandering Doxology: Rom 16,25–27," in *New Testament Textual Criticism and Exegesis: Festschrift J. Delobel* (ed. A. Denaux; BETL 161; Leuven: Leuven Univ. Press, 2002), 293–303. For a defense of the authenticity of 16:25–27, see Schreiner, *Romans*, 810–17; I. Howard Marshall, "Romans 16:25–27: An Apt Conclusion," in *Romans and the People of God: Essays in Honor*

The Origin of the Roman Church

The surviving clues are too scant to form a clear picture of the origins of the Roman Christian community. History has left only the barest hints. In the early fourth century the church historian Eusebius traced Roman Christianity's origin to the preaching of Peter, who had followed Simon Magus there in 41 CE, during the second year of the emperor Claudius.[84] The *Catalogus Liberianus* from 354 CE recognized Peter as the founder of the Roman church. He then served as its first bishop for twenty-five years.[85] Eusebius and the *Catalogus Liberianus* appear to be basing their accounts on legends, which speculated on Peter's destination after he left Jerusalem "for another place" in Acts 12:17.[86] These traditions are doubtful, because both Acts 15:6–7 and Gal 2:7–9 place Peter in Jerusalem for either one or two separate meetings, depending on how one reconciles these texts. In other words, both Luke and Paul associate Peter with the eastern Mediterranean region. Several sources from the late first and second centuries labeled Peter and Paul "founders" of the Roman community, likely because of their martyrdom there and the Roman church's possession of their remains.[87] At the time of his writing, Paul recognizes that the Roman Christian assemblies had already been in existence "for many years" (Rom 15:23). So Paul could not have been the community's "founder" in the sense of being the first to bring the Christian message. Peter was not likely the first to bring the Christian message

---

of Gordon D. Fee on the Occasion of His 65th Birthday (ed. Sven K. Soderlund and N. T. Wright; Grand Rapids: Eerdmans, 1999), 170–84; Larry W. Hurtado, "The Doxology at the End of Romans," in *New Testament Textual Criticism: Its Significance for Exegesis: Essays in Honor of Bruce M. Metzger* (ed. Eldon Jay Epp and Gordon D. Fee; Oxford: Oxford Univ. Press, 1981), 185–99; Weima, "Preaching the Gospel," 364–65. Udo Borse, "Schlußwort des Römerbriefes: Segensgruß (16,24) statt Doxologie (VV.25–27)," SNTU 19 (1994), 173–78, who noted several connections between 16:25–27 and 14:1 — 15:6 (as well as the rest of the Pauline corpus).

84. *Hist. eccl.* 2.14.6; 2.17.1; *De viris illustribus* 1 (PL 23.638); Orosius, *Historiae adversus paganas* 7.6 (CSEL 5.447).

85. For a full discussion of this text, see Richard Adelbert Lipsius, *Chronologie der römischen Bischöfe bis zur Mitte der vierten Jahrhunderts* (Kiel: Schwers'sche, 1869), 40–76.

86. Joseph A. Fitzmyer, *Romans* (AB 33; New York: Doubleday, 1993), 29. The much later tradition in the *Catalogus Liberianus* is also at odds with Ignatius's and Irenaeus's much earlier reports of both Peter's and Paul's involvement with the Roman church.

87. Ignatius, *Rom.* 4:3; Irenaeus, *Haer.* 3.1.1, 3.3.2; *1 Clem.* 5–6. For a full discussion of these texts, see Oscar Cullmann, *Peter: Disciple, Apostle, Martyr* (trans. Floyd V. Filson; Philadelphia: Westminster, 1958), 91–115.

to Rome either. Paul frequently refers to the founding apostles of other locations (1 Thess 3:2–5; 1 Cor 3:5–9; Col 1:7; 4:12–13) but never mentions Peter or anyone else as having planted the message of the gospel in Rome — and Paul is certainly not shy about mentioning Peter (for example, Gal 1:18; 2:6–14; 1 Cor 1:12; 9:5). Luke demonstrates keen interest both in Rome and in Peter's missionary activity. He would not likely have omitted a visit by Peter to Rome, the climactic destination of the Acts narrative, had he known such a visit had taken place.[88] It is questionable whether Paul would have written to the Romans as under his sphere of influence if Peter had founded the churches there.[89]

If neither Peter nor Paul were the founders of the Roman churches, their origins may perhaps be traced to the Roman visitors to Jerusalem at Pentecost in Acts 2:10. Raymond Brown rejected this possibility since the Jews described in Acts 2 were *resident* (κατοικοῦντες) at Jerusalem.[90] On the other hand, the Roman Jews on the list are singled out from the rest as "sojourners" (ἐπιδημοῦντες).[91] The possibility of Roman sojourners taking the message about Christ back to Rome remains as viable an option as any. Quite apart from the Jews present at Pentecost in Acts 2:10, Christ-believing slaves, merchants, and artisans could have brought the message to Rome. Perhaps a missionary movement had reached Rome from Jerusalem or Antioch.[92] Brown thought "that Christianity was brought to Rome by Jewish Christians from Palestine."[93] The ancient Christian author Ambrosiaster concluded that the Roman church was not based on an apostle but rather was formed in the Jewish communities that then passed the message on to the gentiles.[94] Brown went so far as to claim that

---

88. Raymond E. Brown and John P. Meier, *Antioch and Rome: New Testament Cradles of Catholic Christianity* (New York: Paulist, 1983), 97–98, 102–3.

89. John Wenham's extensive formulation that Peter founded the Roman church is therefore unlikely (*Redating Matthew, Mark and Luke: A Fresh Assault on the Synoptic Problem* [Downers Grove, Ill.: InterVarsity, 1992], 146–72).

90. Brown and Meier, *Antioch and Rome*, 104 n. 215; E. A. Judge and G. S. R. Thomas, "The Origin of the Church at Rome: A New Solution?" *RTR* 25 (1966): 83.

91. Elliott, *Rhetoric of Romans*, 47 n.3; note the qualification in Judge and Thomas, "Origin," 83.

92. Peter Stuhlmacher, "The Purpose of Romans" in *The Romans Debate*, 231–42, esp. p. 238; trans. of "Der Abfassungszweck des Römerbriefes," *ZNW* 77 (1986): 180–93.

93. Brown and Meier, *Antioch and Rome*, 104, 110.

94. CSEL 81.1.5–6. Translation available in Wedderburn, *Reasons for Romans*, 51. So also Mark Reasoner, "Rome and Roman Christianity," in *Dictionary of Paul and His Letters* (ed. Gerald F. Hawthorne, Ralph P. Martin, and Daniel G. Reid; Downers Grove, Ill.: InterVarsity, 1993), 853.

the Roman Christians were predominantly Jewish. Although not many have followed Brown in concluding a predominantly Jewish audience for Romans, the Jewish influence on Roman Christianity seems clear from what evidence remains. Such Jewish influence must be accounted for if Romans is conceived as written to a predominantly gentile audience.[95]

The Occasion and Purpose of Romans

As scholars continue to struggle with Paul's purpose in authoring this letter, Karl Donfried's *The Romans Debate* helpfully surveys the options. Many of the options are not mutually exclusive. Scholars continue to struggle with this question. Any system of classification will inevitably be imperfect and incomplete. Nevertheless, in surveying the major options, the central question is Paul's *primary* purpose in writing to the Romans.

Summary of Paul's Theology[96]

For centuries Romans was understood as a summary of Paul's theology.[97] Philipp Melanchthon, Luther's colleague, called Romans "a compendium of Christian doctrine."[98] Anders Nygren concluded in his classic commentary from the mid-twentieth century that Romans "impresses one as a doctrinal writing, a theological treatise, which is only externally clad with the form of a letter."[99] For Nygren, the letter had little to do with the concrete circumstances of a particular congregation.[100] The specific occasion behind this letter is certainly not as clear as

---

95. For a summary of the history of Jews in Rome, see Wolfgang Wiefel, "The Jewish Community in Ancient Rome and the Origins of Roman Christianity," in Donfried, *The Romans Debate*, 86–92; trans. of "Die jüdische Gemeinschaft im antiken Rom und die Angfänge des römischen Christentums," *Judaica* 26 (1970).

96. The classifications of the various approaches in this section are by no means hard and fast. Even in theories classified separately, overlaps are frequent, and in theories categorized together, significant differences are common.

97. For instance, Lightfoot, *Biblical Essays*, 315.

98. *Loci Communes*, as cited in Peter Stuhlmacher, *Paul's Letter to the Romans: A Commentary* (trans. Scott J. Hafemann; Louisville: Westminster John Knox, 1994), 2. Romans sets forth the doctrines of God's being, human weakness, law, sin and punishment, promise, the Redeemer, the Son of God and his suffering, resurrection, grace, righteousness, the church, eternal blessedness and punishment.

99. Anders Nygren, *Commentary on Romans* (Philadelphia: Fortress Press, 1949), 7.

100. Nygren, *Commentary on Romans*, 4, 7–9.

in other Pauline epistles (for example, 1 Corinthians or Galatians), and Romans does appear to be more extensive in the scope of its teachings. On the other hand, Paul says little in this letter about his understanding of the church (Rom 12:3–8 is rather meager), the Lord's Supper (cf. 1 Cor 11:17–34), the resurrection (cf. 1 Cor 15; 1 Thess 4:13 — 5:11), or Christology (cf. Phil 2:6–11). If a theological treatise, the letter is hardly comprehensive!

In defending Romans as a doctrinal treatise, Nygren neglected the introduction to the letter (1:1–15), offered only a few, less-than-compelling paragraphs on the exhortation (12:1 — 15:13), and ignored the entirety of the concluding material (15:14 — 16:27).[101] In other words, he did not incorporate into his thesis those aspects of the letter that offer the greatest clues to the situation behind the letter. Nygren claimed that the Romans "greatly needed" Paul's answer to their problems, and yet he was never able to identify the concrete problems that necessitated the response.[102] Consequently, Nygren was never able to account for the selection of issues in this particular letter for this particular audience.

T. W. Manson did not accept the traditional perspective that Romans is a systematic handbook of the apostle's doctrine. Manson nevertheless theorized that Paul is summarizing his thinking as it had developed during his struggles in the East at Galatia, Corinth, and Philippi. Günther Bornkamm agreed with Manson that Paul is generalizing his views as they had developed in the East. He noted the extensive points of contact with the Galatian and Corinthian correspondence.[103] Bornkamm called Romans Paul's unintended "last will and testament."[104] He did not mean this literally but rather, as he concluded his essay:

> This great document, which summarizes and develops the most important themes and thoughts of the Pauline message and theology and which elevates his theology above the moment of definite situations and conflicts into the sphere of the eternally and universally valid, this letter to the Romans is the last will and testament of the Apostle Paul.[105]

---

101. Ibid., 3–37.

102. Ibid., 8. See also the critique of James C. Miller, *The Obedience of Faith, the Eschatological People of God, and the Purpose of Romans* (SBLDS 177; Atlanta: Society of Biblical Literature, 2000), 6–8.

103. For a helpful chart outlining Bornkamm's parallels, see Fitzmyer, *Romans*, 71–72.

104. Günther Bornkamm, "The Letter to the Romans as Paul's Last Will and Testament," in Donfried, *The Romans Debate*, 27–28; repr. from *ABR* 11 (1963).

105. Bornkamm, "Letter to the Romans," 27–28.

Unlike Manson, however, Bornkamm felt that the Roman destination is firmly etched in the letter, the ninth-century codex G's omission of "Rome" notwithstanding. Bornkamm recognized that Paul's reflections in this letter are prompted by "definite situations and conflicts," even if the letter ultimately transcended those situations. Bornkamm proposed that the letter represents Paul's reflections as he anticipates his trip to Jerusalem with the collection and the potential reception there. In Rom 15:30–31 Paul seems worried about the possibility of persecution at the hands of Jews who no doubt consider him an apostate, with the result that the Jerusalem church might not accept the collection. Bornkamm believed that questions still lingered in Jerusalem from the apostolic council (cf. Acts 15): Is Paul's Law-free gospel legitimate, and can gentiles really be equal members of the church? Bornkamm theorized that these concerns prompted the extended reflections that Paul sent to Rome. If Paul seriously anticipated disagreement and opposition at Jerusalem to the extent that the collection might be jeopardized, it is surprising that he never identified the Jerusalem groups and their positions.[106] Bornkamm never explained why the Romans would even be interested in "a last will and testament" more concerned with issues that would arise at Jerusalem rather than in Rome. Why send a letter *to Rome* in this particular manner and style?[107] Why write a "testament" for a church he had neither founded nor visited?[108] Bornkamm further hypothesized that Paul wanted to introduce himself to the Romans in preparation for his planned trip to Spain. "But it is not at all clear that this is the 'natural' form for a letter of introduction to take — especially if these convictions have been shaped by Eastern controversies and an imminent trip to Jerusalem in which Rome was not involved."[109] Paul's plans to visit Rome strike some interpreters as vague — too vague to require a "letter of introduction" in preparation for that visit.[110] Finally, any specific knowledge of the Roman congregation Paul betrays within the letter would undermine Bornkamm's thesis. Bornkamm therefore minimizes the value of Rom 14–15 for reconstructing the situation at Rome. In short, Romans is no mere summary of Paul's theology, nor can the letter be characterized as his "last will and testament."

---

106. M. Jack Suggs, "'The Word Is Near You': Romans 10:6–10 within the Purpose of the Letter," in *Christian History and Interpretation* (ed. W. R. Farmer, C. F. D. Moule, and R. R. Niebuhr; Cambridge: Cambridge Univ. Press, 1967), 291.

107. Suggs, "'The Word Is Near You,'" 291–92; Donfried, "Short Note," 46.

108. Wedderburn, *Reasons for Romans*, 8.

109. Suggs, "'The Word Is Near You,'" 292.

110. William S. Campbell, "Why Did Paul Write Romans?" *ExpTim* 85 (1973–74): 265.

The Jerusalem Trip as the Purpose for Paul's Writing

M. Jack Suggs's 1967 essay on Rom 10:6–10 devoted a significant opening section to the purpose of Romans. Suggs agreed with Manson and Bornkamm that Paul was not "intimately acquainted with the Roman church." In the absence of evidence for any communication from Rome to Paul, Suggs proposed that the apostle must be writing Romans in anticipation of the trip to Jerusalem. Like Bornkamm, Suggs's Paul is concerned that non-Christian Jews at Jerusalem might be hostile toward him (15:31) and that the Jerusalem Jewish Christians, should they receive Paul positively, could face further difficulties if their fellow Jews perceived them to be aligned with Paul and the gentile Christians. Thus in Romans Paul is anticipating the questions that the Jerusalem Jews would have regarding his missionary activity to the gentiles and regarding his reputed views on Israel and the Law. A letter to the strategic and powerful Roman church as well as to the churches in the East (including Ephesus), which outlines a "partially moderated position . . . *in advance* of the delivery," could prove useful during the visit to Jerusalem.[111] Suggs's Paul wants to explicate his gospel with respect to the Mosaic Law and Israel in such a way that his presence at Jerusalem would not harm the Jerusalem church. Suggs did not consider that Paul may have received information about the Roman congregation through his contacts apart from a formal letter. Should Paul have had any concrete knowledge of the Roman congregations, Suggs's thesis would be undermined. Suggs also overemphasized the mention in Rom 15 of the Jerusalem collection. Jeffrey Weima, in his essay on the opening and closing chapters of Romans, contended that the references to Jerusalem and Spain explain Paul's failure to come to Rome in person. The discussion of the Jerusalem collection serves the rhetorical purpose of substantiating the success of Paul's gospel ministry. If the churches in Macedonia and Achaia have recognized Paul's authority to the point of contributing to his collection for Jerusalem (of all places!), how much more should the Roman Christians recognize him and his ministry![112]

Jacob Jervell also concluded that Paul is writing Romans with Jerusalem primarily in mind. Jervell proposed that as the apostle writes about the relationship between Jews and gentiles, he is imagining what he will say to the Jerusalem church when he arrives with the collection. Paul, as the apostle of the gentiles, anticipates conflict with the Jerusalem Christians. Nevertheless, Paul never asks that the Romans pray that the truth of the gospel be upheld against opponents at Jerusalem. Paul never gives any indication in his letter that there was even an

---

111. Suggs, "'The Word Is Near You,'" 296–97.
112. Weima, "Preaching the Gospel," 357.

issue over the circumcision of gentiles. If gentile circumcision were still an issue, why would he not refer to the earlier Jerusalem agreement (cf. Gal 2)? If Paul were experiencing or anticipating conflict with Jerusalem, such anticipated conflict would figure more prominently in Romans.[113] Is preparation for a potential Jerusalem conflict really the overarching concern of an apostle who is so highly critical of the "Jew" in 2:17–29?[114] Romans 2:17–29 would only exacerbate the tensions. Paul never mentions the Jerusalem trip as a major reason, let alone *the* reason, that he is writing to the Romans.[115] Ernst Fuchs briefly argued Jervell's basic thesis a decade earlier, and Karl Donfried's problem for Fuchs would apply equally to Jervell's thesis: "Why send such a 'secret letter,' one which actually has Jerusalem in mind, to Rome?"[116] Mark Seifrid noted that Paul does not seek representatives from Rome for his journey to Jerusalem, merely their prayers (Rom 15:30–32): "It is hard to believe [as per Jervell] that Paul sent a lengthy letter simply to request prayer from a congregation which as a whole was still unknown to him."[117] As Neil Elliott pointed out in his review of Jervell: "As to Paul's reference to 'strengthening' and 'evangelizing' the Romans in chap. 1, it would seem preferable to *balance* these indications of purpose relating to the letter's explicit audience with Paul's concern regarding Jerusalem, rather than to simply cancel them out or collapse them into the Jerusalem 'target.'"[118]

Jervell struggled over the course of several pages with the question of why Paul should be writing this particular letter to the Roman church. He ultimately argued that the Roman church occupied a preeminent position, since the church was located in the heart of the gentile world. Paul's claim to be the apostle to the gentiles would ring hollow to the Jews at Jerusalem if he had yet to visit Rome. Paul needed the entire gentile Christian world in the West united behind him before going to Jerusalem.[119] Joseph Fitzmyer commented on this reasoning: "Yet that is to allow the tail to wag the dog. This may be a minor preoccupation

---

113. Seifrid, *Justification by Faith*, 195.

114. Ibid., 196. Seifrid also questions how Jerusalem could be the object of a letter so clearly addressed to gentile readers at other points (e.g., 6:19).

115. Angelika Reichert, *Der Römerbrief als Gratwanderung: Eine Untersuchung zur Abfassungsproblematik* (FRLANT 194; Göttingen: Vandenhoeck & Ruprecht, 2001), 23.

116. Donfried, "Short Note," 46; Ernst Fuchs, *Hermeneutik* (2d ed.; Bad Cannstatt: R. Müllerschön, 1958), 191.

117. Seifrid, *Justification by Faith*, 196.

118. Elliott, *Rhetoric of Romans*, 27.

119. Jacob Jervell, "The Letter to Jerusalem," *ST* 25 (1971): 61–73; repr. in Donfried, *The Romans Debate*, 53–64, esp. pp. 62–64.

as Paul composes the letter, but the collection to be taken to Jerusalem cannot explain the major thrust of his letter or be the chief 'clue' to its interpretation."[120] Bent Noack, who took a similar approach to Jervell's, went so far as to understand 1:18–3:8 and chaps. 5–8 — significantly large portions of the letter — as "backwater" in a document intended to justify a Jerusalem trip.[121] Elliott commented on Noack's and Jervell's approach: "It is evident from these statements that this solution to the letter's double character is purchased at the cost of the rhetorical integration of the letter frame and body at the crucial hingepoint of 1:15–18."[122] Too much of the letter appears to be targeting issues in Rome and not Jerusalem, especially Paul's counsel against gentile Christian smugness over against Judaism in Rom 11.[123] The lengthy admonitions in Rom 12–15 do not appear to have the Jews at Jerusalem in mind. Keck asserted that "the claim that [concerns for Jerusalem] shaped the letter to the Romans is a remarkably apt instance of the proverbial red herring."[124] In a move that would hardly play well in Jerusalem, Paul sides with the "strong" against the Law-observant "weak" in recognizing that the distinction between "clean" and "unclean" has been superseded in Christ (14:14; 15:1). Wedderburn likewise demurred: "Such a line of argument makes no sense addressed to the Jerusalem church, but makes excellent sense addressed to the Roman church and to what is . . . a predominantly gentile church."[125] Jervell was simply unable to explain the situation that led to Paul's writing of Romans. He could only account for a portion of chap. 15 in his theory. When the letter is considered as a whole, mention of the Jerusalem trip

---

120. Fitzmyer, *Romans*, 725.

121. Bent Noack, "Current and Backwater in the Epistle to the Romans," *ST* 19 (1965): 164.

122. Elliott, *Rhetoric of Romans*, 28.

123. The more one finds Romans to be addressing a particular situation in the churches there, the less likely is Jervell's thesis. As a variation on Jervell's basic approach, Martin Luther Stirewalt identified Romans as a "letter-essay" ("The Form and Function of the Greek Letter-Essay," in Donfried, *The Romans Debate*, 147–71). Although letters were intended for a specific audience regarding specific issues, they were also intended to be read by others besides the addressees. Such letters supplement or are a substitute for a past or future work of the author and are intended as a tool of instruction (Stirewalt, "Form and Function," 169–71). Certainly Paul is explaining his gospel message to the Romans, but nothing in this letter would suggest that the letter is meant to be a substitute or supplement for another work or that Paul ever had a wider audience than the Romans in view (Wedderburn, *Reasons for Romans*, 8–9).

124. Keck, "What Makes Romans Tick?" 17; so also Reichert, *Der Römerbrief*, 23.

125. Wedderburn, *Reasons for Romans*, 20.

appears to be tangential.[126] The Jerusalem audience is obviously not the target audience of this letter. Paul's purpose in mentioning the trip to Jerusalem, the home of the apostles, is simply to buttress his own authority in Rome.[127]

In yet another variation of the "Jerusalem collection thesis," Wedderburn thought that the collection might have been controversial in Rome. Perhaps Paul wanted to resolve issues in the *Romans'* minds.[128] Yet Paul assumes the Romans already know about the collection when he refers to it obliquely in 15:31 as "my service in Jerusalem." He is not defending the project but openly soliciting the Romans' prayers on its behalf as he fears "unbelievers" (and not fellow believers) at Jerusalem.[129] The notion that the Jerusalem collection is the central factor motivating the letter overextends the evidence.

Romans as Preparation for the Spanish Mission

If Paul were not writing primarily to prepare for an anticipated trip to Jerusalem, some have suggested that he wanted to introduce himself to the Romans in the hope of drawing upon their support for a mission to Spain. Dieter Zeller argued this thesis in 1973.[130] Robert Jewett agreed that the entire Letter to the Romans was Paul's means of enlisting their support for the Spanish project (15:28).[131] When Paul requests that the Romans offer Phoebe whatever help she might need in 16:2, he has that mission in mind. The greetings in chap. 16 enlist support from key individuals for the mission.

Since Erasmus in the sixteenth century, many scholars have also recognized an apologetic function in Romans as a crucial component of the preparations

---

126. Fitzmyer, *Romans*, 75.

127. Weima, "Preaching the Gospel," 357.

128. Wedderburn, *Reasons for Romans*, 70–75.

129. Miller, *Obedience of Faith*, 16.

130. Dieter Zeller, *Juden und Heiden in der Mission des Paulus: Studien zum Römerbief* (FB 1; Stuttgart: Katholisches Bibelwerk, 1973), 38–77.

131. Jewett, "Paul, Phoebe, and the Spanish Mission," 142–61, esp. p. 143; Robert Jewett, "Romans as an Ambassadorial Letter," *Int* 36 (1982): 5–20; idem, "Ecumenical Theology for the Sake of Mission: Romans 1:1–17 + 15:14 — 16:24," in Hay and Johnson, *Pauline Theology 3: Romans*, 89–108; Arthur J. Dewey ("ΕΙΣ ΤΗΝ ΣΠΑΝΙΑΝ: The Future and Paul," in *Religious Propaganda and Missionary Competition in the New Testament World: Essays Honoring Dieter Georgi* (ed. Lukas Bormann, Kelly Del Tredici, and Angela Standhartinger E NovTSup 74; Leiden: Brill, 1994], 321–49). Dewey thought that Paul's universal gospel message to both Jews *and* Greeks required a trip to Spain to fulfill the grand vision. In the passages Dewey cited, however, Paul himself does not make any connection to Spain.

for Spain.[132] Philipp Vielhauer thought that Paul was concerned with opponents at Rome who would undermine his credibility there and ruin the potential for a mission to Spain.[133] For Marku Kettunen, these opponents were Judaizers jeopardizing the Roman launching point.[134] In soliciting the Romans' agreement with his gospel, Paul would be garnering the necessary support for further missionary work.[135] Angelika Reichert likewise saw Romans serving an apologetic function clearing the way for the Spanish mission. Although many scholars who have concluded that Paul is preparing for a Spanish mission have also thought that the letter serves an apologetic function, these two notions will be tackled separately (see also "An Apologetic Purpose," below).

Paul refers to his trip to Spain only very briefly in this letter and does not in any way link the content of the letter with his future missionary endeavors.[136] The concrete issues that he tackles rather directly in Rom 14:1 — 15:13 far exceed what one would expect for a letter of self-recommendation or a letter of recommendation for Phoebe. If, according to Jewett, Paul were trying to unify the Roman church in preparation for the Spanish mission, J. Paul Sampley wondered: "Is Roman divisiveness wasting resources? How would greater unity yield more support? Are contacts for hospitality in Spain less likely with contention among the churches? Could not Paul secure those contacts from the different Roman churches? How many translators might a Spanish mission need?"[137] Jewett's suggestion that Paul wants a unified base of operations in Rome for his

---

132. F. Godet, *Commentary on St. Paul's Epistle to the Romans* (trans. A. Cusin; New York: Funk & Wagnalls, 1883), 53.

133. Philipp Vielhauer, *Geschichte der urchristlichen Literatur: Einleitung in das Neue Testament, die Apokryphen und die Apostolichen Väter* (Berlin: Walter de Gruyter, 1975), 181–84.

134. Kettunen, *Abfassungszweck*, contended that Paul wanted to elicit the Romans' agreement with his gospel (and against his opponents), an agreement that would then serve him in the Spanish mission. James C. Miller, *Obedience of Faith*, 17, also highlighted Paul's need of Roman support for his anticipated trip to Spain and his concern about opponents in the East arriving in Rome and stirring up controversy, which would neutralize the possibility of using Rome as a launching point.

135. So also Michael Theobald, *Römerbrief: Kapitel 1–11* (3d ed.; SKK 6; Stuttgart: Katholisches Bibelwerk, 2002), 21–23: As he clarified his gospel message as the apostle to the gentiles, he was hoping to pave the way for their support when he mentioned Spain with its gentile populace at the end of the letter.

136. Cf. Reichert, *Der Römerbrief*, 26.

137. Sampley, "Romans in a Different Light," 112. He added (p. 112): "Jewett's conception of Paul's mission focuses too much beyond Rome; it does not do justice to Paul's mission *in Rome*" (emphasis his). Sampley argued that, if anything, Jerusalem is in mind far more than Spain.

mission to Spain remains unstated in the text and raises more questions than answers. Paul recognizes that he was writing "rather boldly" in 15:15. As Robert A. J. Gagnon observed with respect to this boldness:

> One does not take chances when one's primary aim is to curry favor. At least in 14:1 — 15:13, and probably also in some other risky sections (particularly in 6:1 — 8:17 and 11:11–36), Paul recognizes that some of the Roman believers may get the impression that he, the outsider, has overstepped his bounds.[138]

Weima responded that the mention of Spain, like the mention of the upcoming Jerusalem collection trip, would enhance Paul's authority with the Romans. The support Paul received for the collection throughout the East, his impending visit to the very birthplace of Christianity in Jerusalem, as well as his planned trip to the furthest reaches of the West in Spain — Greece, Asia Minor, Jerusalem, Spain — provide a breathtaking vista of his apostolic labors and ministry.[139] Surely the Romans would want to heed his gospel and advice and share in those labors. Mark Seifrid explained that the mention of Spain alongside Rome responds to a potential objection to his failure to visit: "It should be remembered too, that Paul's depiction of his visit to Rome as a 'passing through on the way to Spain,' was necessary to his appearing consistent to his audience. If for years he had failed to come to Rome because of unevangelized areas in the East, how could he ignore pioneering work in the West?"[140] The reference to Spain in 15:27–29 is then followed by Paul's request for welcome in Rome in 15:30–33: "The two sections of the 'apostolic parousia' are independent, self-contained units, which by their very parallelism suggest that they stand in a coordinate, not subordinate relation."[141] Seifrid also observed that the discussion of Spain is absent in the concluding appeal of 15:30–33 with its focus on Rome. As Seifrid put it so well: "The [Spanish] mission is not mentioned directly until the conclusion of the letter, and then in a minor key."[142]

Providing an Apostolic Foundation for a "Church"

In Rom 15:20 Paul claims that he would not build on another's foundation, and yet, as Günter Klein observed, the apostle is doing just that as he wrote. Klein's

---

138. Gagnon, "The 'Weak' at Rome," 64–82.
139. Weima, "Preaching the Gospel," 357.
140. Seifrid, *Justification by Faith*, 194.
141. Ibid.
142. Ibid.

1969 essay concluded that Paul must have thought that the Roman churches lacked a proper apostolic foundation (see 1 Cor 3:1, 10–17). They were not *authentic* churches of God. This would explain, for Klein, why Paul never called the Roman churches ἐκκλησίαι in the first fifteen chapters. By preaching the gospel to them through his letter and by a future visit (1:13–15; 15:20), Klein's Paul would rectify the lack of an apostolic foundation at Rome.[143] On the other hand, if the Roman churches lacked a proper apostolic foundation, as Klein supposed, why would Paul speak so highly of them? He hopes to benefit from their faith (1:12), a faith known throughout the world (1:8). He writes "by way of reminder" (15:15) and is "confident" that they are "filled with all knowledge, and able to instruct one another" (15:14). Paul's statement that he does not build on another's foundation in preaching the good news simply articulates a general practice and not an inflexible rule.[144] Romans 15:20 should not be interpreted so narrowly as to rule out any sort of activity in mission areas started by others, even if Paul's primary intention is virgin territory, such as Spain. Paul does not object to other missionaries who are active in the church he started at Corinth. His activities at Corinth demonstrate that he worked cooperatively in the mission field with fellow laborers on behalf of Christ (for example, 1 Cor 3:5–11; 16:12; 2 Cor 1:2–4; 10:12–18).[145] As Fitzmyer suggested, Paul may simply be "watering" what others "planted" in Rome (1 Cor 3:6).[146] Donfried: "The phrase 'thus making it my ambition to preach the gospel, not where Christ has already been named' must be understood as an apology as to why Paul has *not yet* been

---

143. Günter Klein, "Paul's Purpose in Writing the Epistle to the Romans," in Donfried, *The Romans Debate*, 29–43; trans. of "Der Abfassungszweck des Römerbriefes," in *Rekonstruktion und Interpretation: Gesammelte Aufsätze zum Neuen Testament* (BevT 50; Munich: Chr. Kaiser, 1969), 129–44. So also Schmithals, *Römerbrief*, who supported the thesis with a rather questionable reconstruction of the various literary strands that were subsequently woven together into the final version of the letter (see above).

144. Rightly Fitzmyer, *Romans*, 715–16; C. E. B. Cranfield, *A Critical and Exegetical Commentary on the Epistle to the Romans* (2 vols.; Edinburgh: T&T Clark, 1975, 1979), 2:765.

145. Sigfred Pedersen, "Theologische Überlegungen zur Isagogik des Römerbriefes," *ZNW* 76 (1985): 51–57, esp. pp. 51–53.

146. Fitzmyer, *Romans*, 76. George Smiga contended that chaps. 1–11 fulfilled Paul's intention to "preach the gospel" in 1:15 and the exhortations and encouragement of chaps. 12–16 fulfilled his desire for "mutual encouragement" in 1:12 ("Romans 12:1–2 and 15:30–32 and the Occasion of the Letter to the Romans," *CBQ* 53 [1991]: 257–73). Both request sections (12:1–2 and 15:30–32) are linked to the opening thanksgiving section and communicate Paul's desire that mutual benefit accrue to his Roman hearers and himself.

in Rome — viz., his first responsibility was to preach Christ where He had not yet been preached, in the area 'from Jerusalem as far round as Illyricum' (15:19)." Paul had been delayed from reaching Rome for good reason, but nevertheless he expresses his hope to use Rome as a launching point to further unreached territory in Spain (15:22–25, 28).[147] Peter Stuhlmacher translated Rom 1:15: "Therefore for my part I was prepared to preach the gospel to you in Rome as well." Paul wanted — past tense (thus vv. 13–15) — to evangelize in Rome, but others had reached the city before him. In writing to the Romans, Paul now wants their unity and their participation in the gospel proclamation as he proceeds farther west.[148] Paul never identifies the need of an apostolic foundation for Rome as a rationale for his visit in Rom 15:24, 32 and writes instead about Jerusalem and Spain.[149]

Klein considered the absence of the word ἐκκλησία in Rom 1–15 proof that the Romans lacked a proper apostolic foundation as a church. The word *does*, however, appear in chap. 16. By way of comparison, Paul is rather casual in delaying reference to the Philippians as an ἐκκλησία until Phil 4:15 where the word appears to be used only incidentally. Generally, Paul identifies his recipients as an ἐκκλησία in his epistolary openings, but in Romans he prefers the appellations "called" and "beloved" as he anticipates his line of reasoning later in Rom 9:25–26, where he employs these same terms in connection with Hos 1:10 and 2:23.[150] Paul also recognizes the Romans as "one body in Christ" (12:5). The absence of ἐκκλησία is therefore explicable. Even if Klein were right, could Paul remedy the lack of an apostolic foundation by merely passing through town on the way to Spain (15:24)?[151] Further, very little of the content of Romans can be marshaled in support of Klein's proposed purpose for Paul's writing the letter. Why, for instance, does Paul write about the fate of ethnic Israel in chaps. 9–11 in a letter primarily to Roman gentiles?[152] Finally, William Campbell wondered if Paul did not label the Romans an ἐκκλησία because of tensions within the congregations.[153] Klein's approach to Paul's primary purpose for writing has not garnered much support in scholarly circles.

---

147. Donfried, "Short Note," 45.

148. Stuhlmacher, "Purpose of Romans," 237.

149. Thus Reichert, *Der Römerbrief*, 27–28.

150. Kettunen, *Abfassungszweck*, 36–67. Wedderburn, *Reasons for Romans*, 49, agreed: "Perhaps rather the use of such a term [ἐκκλησία] seemed superfluous and redundant after such eloquent expressions of God's favour and electing grace."

151. Donfried, "Short Note," 45.

152. Reichert, *Der Römerbrief*, 27.

153. W. Campbell, "Why Did Paul Write Romans?" 266, 269.

Exercising Authority as Apostle to the Gentiles

L. Ann Jervis compared Romans' epistolary frame to the opening, thanksgiving, apostolic parousia, paraenesis, and conclusion of each of Paul's other letters as well as Greek letters in general.[154] On the basis of the letter's frame, Jervis agreed with Klein that Paul was indeed exercising authority over the Romans as the apostle to the gentiles. Jeffrey Weima likewise limited himself to the epistolary frame and, not surprisingly, came to a similar conclusion: Paul was asserting his apostolic authority so that the Romans would heed his gospel message in the body of the letter. Historical and social issues, such as the relationship between Jews and gentiles, remain subordinate to Paul's preaching of the gospel.[155] Although Jervis's and Weima's analyses of the opening and closing of the letter are unsurpassed, neither has demonstrated how an understanding of the letter's frame illumines the body of the letter or explains Paul's primary purpose for writing. With so little (or no) attention to the body of the letter, neither Jervis nor Weima was able to discount the possibility that Paul is grounding his authority as an apostle in the frame of the letter in order that the Roman audience, which he has yet to meet, would be open to the content of the letter, including his advice for concrete contingencies at Rome. Jervis and Weima have not explained the choice of topics in this letter. For instance, neither scholar has accounted for the emphasis on Judaism in a letter to gentiles or the relationship between the "strong" and the "weak." Paul is grounding his apostolic authority not as an end in itself but in order that his advice for the situation at Rome would not fall on deaf ears.

The Lack of a Concrete Situation at Rome

Some scholars, such as Wayne A. Meeks and J. Paul Sampley, have questioned whether Paul's letter offers clear and sufficient evidence for a specific reconstruction of the identity of the "weak" and "strong" in Rom 14:1 — 15:13 and the Roman situation in general.[156] Paul takes a rather "oblique approach" and

---

154. L. Ann Jervis, *The Purpose of Romans: A Comparative Letter Structure Investigation* (JSNTSup 55; Sheffield: Sheffield Academic Press, 1991).

155. Weima, "Preaching the Gospel," 337–66.

156. Wayne A. Meeks, "Judgment and the Brother: Romans 14:1 — 15:13," in *Tradition and Interpretation in the New Testament* (ed. Gerald F. Hawthorne and Otto Betz; Grand Rapids: Eerdmans, 1987), 290–300; J. Paul Sampley, "The Weak and the Strong: Paul's Careful and Crafty Rhetorical Strategy in Romans 14:1 — 15:13" in *The Social World of the First Christians: Essays in Honor of Wayne A. Meeks* (ed. L. Michael White and O. Larry Yarbrough; Minneapolis: Fortress Press, 1995), 40–52.

employs "rather vague formulation[s]."[157] According to these scholars, when Paul addresses specific situations in the various churches he founded, he generally identifies the situation more directly than he does in Romans.[158] He had never visited the Roman congregation. Perhaps the content of the letter reflects circumstances in Paul's own life and ministry at this turning point in his apostolic career with the completion of his work in the East (Rom 15:18–24) rather than any particular circumstance in Rome. He had completed and is preparing to deliver the collection for the Jerusalem saints (15:25–28). The apostle to the gentiles is anxious about the reception of a collection that embodies his hopes for the unity of Jewish and gentile Christians (15:30–33). Jerusalem's acceptance of the gentiles' gift would legitimize the status of the churches founded by Paul and ensure the unity of the entire Christian church.

In a related thesis, Robert J. Karris concluded from his review of Rom 14:1 — 15:13 that Paul was reprising in a more generalized manner to the "weak" and "strong" of Rome his exhortation to the "weak" and "strong" in Corinth regarding meat sacrificed to idols.[159] On the other hand, the peculiar details of Rom 14–15 and the differences between Rom 14–15 and 1 Cor 8–10 defy the conclusion that Paul was only generalizing to the Romans comments originally intended for a concrete situation elsewhere.[160] The differences suggest diverging situations for these two letters. Several critical details in the discussion in 1 Corinthians are absent in Romans. Paul never mentions food offered to idols in Romans, as he does in 1 Cor 8:1, 4, 7, 10, 12 and 10:19–22. The possibility of eating in an idol temple is not a concern for the Romans (cf. 1 Cor 10:19–22).[161] Paul does not emphasize "knowledge" in Romans, as he does in 1 Cor 8:1–11. In Romans he never refers to the "conscience," as he does in 1 Cor 8:7, 10, 12; 10:25, 27–29. Conversely, several details in Paul's exhortation to the Romans are absent in 1 Cor 8–10. Unlike the weak in Corinth, the weak in Rome eat vegetables (Rom 14:2) and observe days (Rom 14:5). Abstention from wine (Rom 14:21)

---

157. Sampley, "Romans in a Different Light," 124; idem, "The Weak and the Strong," 42. Or with Meeks: "Paul takes up the topic [of clean and unclean food] out of his experience, not theirs, because it is well suited to show in behavioral terms the outworking of the main theses of the letter" ("Judgment and the Brother," 292).

158. Meeks, "Judgment and the Brother," 292, warns of excessive "mirror-reading" in Rom 14:1 — 15:13. Such caution is certainly warranted.

159. Robert J. Karris, "Romans 14:1 — 15:13 and the Occasion of Romans," CBQ 25 (1973): 155–78; repr. in Donfried, The Romans Debate, 65–84.

160. The same may be said of the differences between Romans and Galatians. For instance, consider the variations in how Abraham is employed in both letters; Beker, Paul the Apostle, 94–104.

161. Schreiner, Romans, 706.

does not characterize the Corinthian weak. Paul's admonitions to "welcome" or "accept" one another in Rom 14:1, 3; 15:7 (twice) and not to judge (14:1, 10, 13) are absent in 1 Corinthians. In 1 Corinthians Paul does not admonish the "weak" as he does in Romans. The difference between the strong and the weak in Romans centers on faith (Rom 14:1, 22, 23 [twice]), but faith is never an issue in 1 Cor 8–10. Unlike the Roman weak, the Corinthian weak do not consider meat to be "common" or "unclean" (κοινός).[162] Romans 14:1—15:6 occupies a prominent position as the climax of Paul's exhortations to this community. Surely such a positioning in the letter reflects the community's needs. The fact that Paul aligns himself with "the strong" in 15:1 demonstrates that he is aware of the issues and the parties involved at Rome.[163]

The unique aspects in the discussions of the weak and the strong in Romans and 1 Corinthians correspond to emphases elsewhere in the respective letters. The Corinthians were puffed up with knowledge and their consciences untroubled by horrendous sin in 1 Cor 8–10 (for example, 8:1–3, 10–12) as elsewhere in the letter (for example, 1 Cor 1:18—2:16; 5:3–13; 6:9–20). After Paul's discussion of Moses' Law and the place of Israel in God's plan in Rom 9–11, in Rom 14–15 the apostle exhorts the Roman "weak" who are practicing certain aspects of the Law in the presence of the "strong" who are not. "Common" or "unclean" foods pose a stumbling block preventing some members of the church from welcoming or accepting others. The "summary" in Romans is far longer than the "original" in 1 Corinthians, even without the added Scriptural citations. Clearly Paul is not summarizing in Rom 14:1—15:13 a discussion originally targeting a different audience.[164] What Paul writes in Romans appears directly relevant to the needs of the Roman Christians.[165] As John M. G. Barclay put it:

---

162. Mark Reasoner, "The Theology of Romans 12:1—15:14," in Hay and Johnson, *Pauline Theology 3: Romans,* 288–89 n. 5; James D. G. Dunn, *Romans 9—16* (WBC 38B; Dallas: Word, 1988), 795; John M. G. Barclay, "'Do We Undermine the Law?' A Study of Romans 14.1—15.6," in *Paul and the Mosaic Law* (ed. James D. G. Dunn; Tübingen: J. C. B. Mohr [Paul Siebeck], 1996), 287–308; Wayne A. Meeks, "Judgment and the Brother," 293.

163. Barclay, "'Do We Undermine the Law?'" 288–89.

164. For further critique of Karris's thesis, see Karl Paul Donfried, "False Presuppositions in the Study of Romans," *CBQ* 36 (1974): 332–58; repr. in idem, *The Romans Debate,* 102–25 esp. pp. 107–12.

165. Nelio Schneider devoted an entire monograph to this question and concluded that the discussion in Romans reflects the peculiarities of the situation there (*Die 'Schwachen' in der christlichen Gemeinde Roms* [Theologie 5; Münster: Lit, 1996]). Schneider also provided a thorough critique of Hellenistic and Gnostic asceticism and concluded that Jewish purity concerns offer the most likely background for the "weak," especially the

Moreover, the space which Paul devotes to this theme, his careful description of opposing positions and the prominence of this passage at the end of the paraenesis all suggest its immediate applicability in Rome. The fact that Paul can confidently number himself among "the strong" (15.1) also indicates that he knows the issues involved. If he can predict his allegiance with one of the two groups in the debate, he must know where they stand: he would hardly donate his authority as a blank cheque cashable by any Pauline group claiming to be "the strong."[166]

The specifics in Rom 14:1 — 15:13 offer the possibility of reconstructing elements of the situation behind this letter.

Some interpreters have objected that the apostle's language in Rom 14:1 — 15:13 admits a more general application than a specific dispute over Jewish customs.[167] Paul does not identify the weak as Jews. He avoids mention of the Sabbath and speaks instead of observing the days. Rather than conclude, as have some, that Paul has no knowledge of the Romans' situation, the apostle may merely be phrasing his discussion in such a way as to be paradigmatic for other divisions between Christians over matters of indifference.[168] Or perhaps Paul is attempting to proceed with tact by speaking more generally and obliquely since he had neither founded nor visited this church.[169] The obliqueness may be a rhetorical device. By applying more general language and by not identifying the strong and weak more directly, Paul could address the issue without exacerbating the problem. As Walters explained: "By utilizing an oblique approach Paul was able to speak to the issue at hand in terms of appropriate behavior in Christ without respect to the ethnic origin of the convictions."[170]

---

uniquely Jewish usage of κοινόω. Her conclusion that the "weak" were Jewish Christians, however, represents the conventional view.

166. John M. G. Barclay, "'Do We Undermine the Law?'" 288–89.

167. Meeks, "Judgment and the Brother," 290–300.

168. "Paul's oblique approach puts no Roman group in the spotlight" (J. Paul Sampley, "The Weak and the Strong," 42). The chapters permit broader application even if pertaining primarily to Jewish customs. So also Reichert, Römerbrief, 271–333), who envisioned the advice with respect to the "weak" and "strong" of value for the Romans' potential mission work in Spain, should Paul himself be unable to initiate that endeavor.

169. Thus Barclay, "'Do We Undermine the Law?'" 289.

170. James C. Walters, Ethnic Issues in Paul's Letter to the Romans: Changing Self-Definitions in Earliest Roman Christianity (Valley Forge, Pa.: Trinity Press International, 1993), 87. On the other hand, Paul was specific that vegetarianism was at issue; contra Walters, Ethnic Issues, 86.

The view of some specialists that Romans reflects only personal concerns at a turning point in Paul's career is problematic. In the first place, he indicates in Rom 16 that he knows of at least twenty-six people in Rome and would likely possess some knowledge of the Roman church through his contacts.[171] Wedderburn wrote:

> [I]f Romans 16 with its extensive list of greetings sent to persons known to Paul, or known of by him, is part of the original letter to Rome, then the supposition that Paul knew little of what was going on in the church there becomes far more difficult to sustain. *Such extensive knowledge of who was in the church there is in itself impressively detailed knowledge of this aspect of the life of the church in Rome and indicates that Paul's lines of communication with it were functioning quite well.*[172]

Specific knowledge of the situation at Rome may be evident at several points in the letter: Paul praises the Romans' faith (1:8), maturity (15:14), and obedience as "known to all" (16:19). "The congratulatory language of 1:8 and 15:14 is no doubt exaggerated, but must at least have some basis in fact, otherwise it would be read as sarcasm — which is hardly what Paul would want."[173] In Rom 6:17 he refers to the "teaching" the Romans had received and is confident in 15:14–15 that his instructions are serving only as "a reminder." Likewise in 16:17 he speaks of the teaching they had learned. Some commentators have even thought that Paul's instructions in 13:6–7 regarding taxes are a response to a developing situation in Rome at the time of the letter.[174] Paul assumes that his audience is already aware of his desire to visit (1:9–11, 13; 15:18–23). The brief comments on the collection in 15:26 assume the audience's prior knowledge of his efforts on behalf of Jerusalem. The Romans, for their part, may even have been aware of criticisms of Paul in the East (3:8). Such passages cumulatively indicate that he had at least some knowledge of the situation within the Roman church.[175] The general indirectness with respect to the Roman situation that many have noted is understandable since he had not been to Rome. His policy had been one of

---

171. Paul's knowledge of the Roman situation is rendered more likely by the general recognition of chap. 16 as an integral part of the letter; see especially Gamble, *Textual History*.

172. Wedderburn, *Reasons for Romans*, 13.

173. Dunn, *Romans 1–8*, xviii.

174. Ibid.; idem, *Romans 9–16*, 759. Paul is drawing in these verses on conventional Jewish wisdom and early Christian tradition (see, for instance, 1 Pet 2:13–17; Wis 6:3–4). These traditions do not, however, offer advice regarding taxation. Paul's comments in this regard therefore appear to have been motivated by his knowledge of an issue specific to Roman Christianity.

175. See Miller, *Obedience of Faith*, 116–21.

non-interference in the churches founded by others. That policy would certainly have included a Roman congregation he had never visited (Rom 15:20–22; 2 Cor 10:13–16). The Letter to the Romans therefore represents a departure from his usual pattern of writing to churches he knew. That departure alone may account for his tactful reserve. Karl Donfried even concluded from the circumstantial nature of Paul's other correspondence that the burden of proof is on those who think Romans was *not* written to a specific situation.[176]

An Apologetic Purpose

Paul's other letters target very specific situations in the congregations being addressed. The letter to the Galatians, far from being an abstract expression of the apostle's thinking, addresses the concrete situation of Jewish Christian evangelists who had entered into the Galatian gentile churches. First Thessalonians consoles and advises a young congregation shortly after the apostle had departed when death had intervened and prevented several members from witnessing Christ's imminent return (1 Thess 4:13–18).[177] First Corinthians combats divisions within the congregation (1 Cor 1:10).[178] Likewise, Philippians appears to have been written in large part to settle a dispute between two women in the congregation (Phil 4:2–3).[179] Paul's message in each letter appears tailored to the situation within a particular church. The question presents itself whether a situation had arisen at Rome that had come to the apostle's attention.[180]

---

176. Donfried, "False Presuppositions," 103–4.

177. See John M. G. Barclay, "Thessalonica and Corinth: Social Contrasts in Pauline Christianity," *JSNT* 47 (1992): 49–74.

178. Barclay, "Thessalonica and Corinth"; Margaret M. Mitchell, *Paul and the Rhetoric of Reconciliation: An Exegetical Investigation of the Language and Composition of 1 Corinthians* (Louisville: Westminster John Knox, 1991).

179. Thus Garland, "Composition and Unity of Philippians," 141–73. Nils A. Dahl independently came to the same conclusion in his essay "Euodia and Syntyche," 3–15. Peterlin, *Paul's Letter to the Philippians,* highlighted a larger context of disunity in the congregation in which the women's dispute played a central role.

180. Already in 1836 Ferdinand Christian Baur was seeking the specific situation addressed by Romans; "Über Zweck und Veranlassung des Römerbriefs und die damit zusammenhängenden Verhältnisse der römischen Gemeinde," in *Tübinger Zeitschrift für Theologie* 3 (1836): 59–178; repr. in *Historishe Untersuchungen zum Neuen Testament* (*Ausgewählte Werke in Einzelausgaben* 1; Stuttgart/Bad Cannstatt: Friedrich Frommann, 1963), 147–266.

Peter Stuhlmacher concluded from Rom 3:8 and 16:17–20 that opponents of Paul's ministry were already present in Rome.[181] Douglas Campbell doubted whether Paul's opponents had already reached Rome. Campbell contended that in passages such as Rom 3:8 and 16:17–20 Paul expected that Jewish Christians who would counter his message in Rome would soon arrive from the East.[182] A fuller exposition of his thinking on the Mosaic Law, circumcision, the Old Testament Scriptures, and the place of Israel in God's plan would be necessary to answer their objections.[183] James C. Miller in his survey of the Romans debate agreed with Campbell that Paul is anticipating critics of his message arriving in Rome shortly. They would find fertile soil in the conflict between the weak and the strong to promote their Law-observant approach to Christianity. Miller relied primarily upon Rom 16:17–20.[184] Such an approach does not adequately account for the climactic place of Rom 9–11 in the body of the letter prior to the paraenesis. These chapters staunchly maintain the place of Israel against potential *gentile* arrogance. For Campbell and Miller, Paul is less concerned with gentile arrogance against Judaism than he is with the pressure of Jewish false teachers from the East with their objections to Paul's message. Nowhere do Paul's admonitions in 12:1 — 15:13, which build on the foundation laid in chaps. 1–11, ever instruct the Romans with respect to potential Jewish teachers like those Paul encountered in the East. Paul never provides any indication that the Romans had objections to his message or harbored suspicions about him because of a supposed reputation for controversy in the East.

Although Angelika Reichert prioritized Paul's hopes to travel from Jerusalem on to Rome and Spain — plans he had had for years (15:23; 1 Cor 16:3–4; 2 Cor 8:19; 10:15–16), she thought that the apostle is reckoning seriously with

---

181. Stuhlmacher, "Purpose of Romans," 239.

182. Douglas A. Campbell, "Determining the Gospel through Rhetorical Analysis in Paul's Letter to the Roman Christians," in *Gospel in Paul: Studies on Corinthians, Galatians and Romans for Richard N. Longenecker* (ed. L. Ann Jervis and Peter Richardson; JSNTSup 108; Sheffield: Sheffield Academic Press, 1994), 320–31.

183. This explains, for many, the extensive discussion of the Jews and their Scriptures throughout the letter; Stuhlmacher, "Purpose of Romans," 239–40. Paul is essentially entering into an extended dialogue with the Jews, contends J. Christiaan Beker, *Paul the Apostle: The Triumph of God in Life and Thought* (Philadelphia: Fortress Press, 1990), 74–91.

184. Miller, *Obedience of Faith*, 11, 131–32, 138–50, linked this paragraph of Romans to other passages in Galatians and Philippians in which he was combating Jewish Christian opponents. Romans 3:8 also proved, for Miller, that objections to Paul's gospel were already known in Rome.

the possibility that trouble in Jerusalem could prevent him from realizing these plans (15:25–32).[185] Paul therefore has a double purpose in writing: both to prepare for the possibility of his arrival in Rome on the way west to Spain and to steel the Romans for the arrival of different voices in case he is prevented from realizing his plans. The Letter to the Romans could turn out to be his first *and last* communication to the congregations. He is equipping the Romans as a sort of Pauline community in order that they could potentially function independently.[186] If unable to realize his plans for the Spanish mission personally, Paul hopes that the Romans will be able to spread the gospel westward in his stead.[187] On the other hand, he never actually articulates the possibility that the Romans would take on the Spanish mission in his absence, as Reichert recognized. Paul never makes such a request of the Romans. Reichert assumed that Paul is anticipating the Romans' independent evangelizing activity in the very places in the letter where he mentions only *his own* apostolic activity (for example, 1:13–15; 11:13–14).[188] While Paul certainly expects the Romans' assistance with his anticipated Spanish mission, whether he plans on the Romans to assume the burden for that mission in his stead or not, is not clear from the letter and is incapable of demonstration.[189] As for preparing the Romans to deal with divergent voices that could show up in Rome, this element of her thesis paralleled Campbell's and Miller's approaches.

Romans 16:17–20 remains a crucial text for both Campbell's and Miller's positions. In this passage, they have asserted, Paul clearly identifies potential false teachers, advocates of a Law-observant form of Christianity. Mention of their devotion to the "belly" in Rom 16:18 has understandably led commentators to think of the food laws at issue in Rom 14:1 — 15:13. When the apostle warns against people who cause scandals (16:17), Campbell and Miller both interpreted the offenses in light of Rom 14 and the conflict of the strong against the weak who favored legal observances.[190] Miller also noted the parallel to the "belly" language in Phil 3:19 in the context of Jewish opponents. The flattery and deceit of the smooth talkers in Rom 16:17–20 reminded Miller of the deceitful

---

185. Reichert, *Römerbrief*, 77–82.

186. Ibid., 92–110.

187. Ibid., 83–91.

188. Ibid., 125–36.

189. The reasoning is therefore circular; so also Heike Omerzu, review of Angelika Reichert, *Der Römerbrief als Gratwanderung: Eine Untersuchung zur Abfassungsproblematik, JBL* 123 (2004): 771.

190. Miller, *Obedience of Faith*, 142.

Jewish Christian workers in 2 Cor 11:13–15.[191] If Campbell and Miller were correct, then the problem at Rome and the potential opposition to Paul would stem from those aligned with the Law-observant position of the "weak."[192]

Karl Olav Sandnes, in his recent study of "belly" language in the Pauline corpus, demonstrated that in Rom 16:17–20 the apostle is concerned not with Jewish Christian teachers or the Law-observant but rather with the possibility of a vocal and aggressive group representing a position shared by *the strong*.[193] Sandnes observed that Paul employs a cluster of images in 16:18–20: belly-worship, deceivers, and Satan. This cluster of images derives from Gen 3:15. Satan "deceived" Eve (ἀπατάω in Gen 3:13 LXX, a cognate of the word in Rom 16:18). As Paul opposes those who had transformed themselves into (Satanic) messengers of light in 2 Cor, he uses the same word in 2 Cor 11:3 for Satan's deception of Eve in the Garden of Eden (ἐξαπατάω). As for the belly imagery in Rom 16:17–20, since Satan commandeered the serpent for his purposes, God cursed the serpent to crawl on its belly. Finally, in Rom 16:20 Paul envisions the Romans' crushing Satan under their feet in language recalling the promise of Gen 3.

Paul is not the first to reflect on Gen 3:15 and this cluster of motifs. Sandnes noted the narration by Philo of Alexandria, a near contemporary of Paul, of the snake's tempting of the woman in the garden (*Opif.* 55–59 §§156–66). Philo recognizes in the serpent, as it slithered on its belly, a perfect image of pleasure's temptations of the soul (*Leg.* 3.23 §76). The "belly" was a common symbol in Greek literature for bodily pleasures. For Philo, snakes are unable to raise themselves up off their bellies and so are always oriented away from heaven toward earthly realities. As Philo read from Gen 3:14–15 that the snake was cursed to slither on its belly and eat earth all the days of its life, he compares this state to a person who loves pleasure and who cannot lift his head. Such a person grovels in dirt and feeds on the earth rather than on the heavenly nourishment of wisdom. Philo notes one other aspect about this snake that lives life slithering on its belly. It has venom in its teeth. The pleasure seeker, then, is like a poisonous snake looking for a victim (*Opif.* 56 §158). The snake speaks with a human voice to

---

191. Ibid., 144–45.

192. On Rom 16:17–20 (as well as elsewhere in the letter), Miller, *Obedience of Faith*, 19, followed Douglas Campbell, "Determining the Gospel," 328–30, and others. Miller's Paul anticipated the arrival from the East of opponents who would exacerbate tensions already simmering along the Jew/gentile divide.

193. Karl Olav Sandnes, *Belly and Body in the Pauline Epistles* (SNTSMS 120; Cambridge: Cambridge Univ. Press, 2002), esp. pp. 165–80.

deceive. It teaches a lifestyle of drunkenness (οἰνοφλυγία), gluttony (ὀψοφαγία), and greed (λαιμαργία). Philo: "These [vices], causing the cravings of the belly to burst out and fanning them into flame, make the man a glutton, which they also stimulate and stir up the stings of his sexual lusts." The snake, devoted to its belly, is a symbol for Philo of gluttony and excess, sexual and otherwise. After all, the serpent beguiles the woman to *eat*, the temptation of *pleasure* in food (*Opif.* 59 §§165–66; cf. *Sacr.* 5 §§19–22; *QG* 1 §33 [Gen 3:1]). Philo admonishes people to live lives of self-control instead. The reason why the Law of Moses treated reptiles as unclean, Philo explains, is because these animals devote themselves to their bellies and pay tribute to the stomach — to strong drink, meat, wine, fish, delicacies, all of which animate the passions. The path of self-control leads upward, but serving the belly leads downward to the earth since the belly is the reservoir of all pleasure (*Leg.* 3.47 §§138–39). The belly is the foundation of the passions and the mother of all evil (*Leg.* 3.49, 51 §§145, 149).

Paul in Rom 16 observes how belly worshipers approach speaking good or flattering words (χρηστολογία) and blessings (εὐλογία). They are cunning deceivers, even as the snake had been cunning with Eve. In *Life of Adam and Eve* and *Apocalypse of Moses*, Jewish literature from Paul's day, Satan transforms himself into an angel of light. In *Life of Adam and Eve* (9:1–5), Satan shows up and pretends to weep with Eve and thereby deceives her with his cunning. In *Apocalypse of Moses* (15), Eve recognizes, after her fall, that the enemy had deceived her. Satan informed the snake that he was going to use it as a vessel to "deceive" Eve. The author of *Apocalypse* uses the same word for deception as Paul uses in Rom 16:18 (ἐξαπατάω). In fact, Satan disguises himself as an angel praising God — in other words, as a true worshiper of God — in order to deceive and destroy Eve. So Satan uses pretense, disguise, and soft words as tools of deception to lead Adam and Eve to desire, which for the author of *Apocalypse* "is the origin of every sin" (19:1).

Paul warns the Romans against flattering speech from the false teachers or belly worshipers. Plutarch, another near contemporary of Paul, describes the flatterer as one who transforms himself into a friend and changes his appearance like a chameleon (*Mor.* 52b–c; 52c–f; 53d). Athenaeus (*Deipn.* 6.254e) speaks of flatterers as those who use sweet words to devour their victims. So Paul warns against satanic false teachers who speak smooth and sweet but deceiving words in the name of Christ. Such deception will only lead people away to the service of sinful pleasure. This is the crucial point: if belly worship is always bound up with pleasure or *excess*, these people are not pressuring the Romans to observe the Mosaic Law. Paul never says that the weak were foisting their food laws on the strong. Rather, Rom 14:1 — 15:13 targets *the strong* for their excess, for eating whatever they want right in front of their weaker brethren. From a Jewish standpoint, devotion to the Law of Moses and its food laws would deliver an individual from slavery to the passions of the belly and sin. For Jews such as Philo, those who *abandon* the Mosaic Law are belly worshipers. If Jewish authors promised that the Law would deliver from the passions of the belly and warned that abandoning the Law would lead to belly worship, then it is unlikely that Paul is describing advocates of the Law.[194] Paul is not warning against the sort of Jewish Christian opponents he encountered in the East. He has in mind, rather, the most vocal and stubborn advocates among the "strong" of Rom 14–15, who were selfishly insisting on their freedom from Jewish food laws at the expense of their weaker neighbors. The issue here is not the weak's adherence to food laws, but rather the selfishness of the strong.

In Rom 16:19 Paul juxtaposes good and evil: "I want you to be wise in what is good and guileless in what is evil." The last time he juxtaposed good and evil was in Rom 3:8 in quoting those at Rome who wrongly concluded from his theology: "Let us do evil so that good may come." Some have charged Paul's teaching, according to 3:8, as paving the way for sin and evil. His gospel and teaching would lead to an indulgent lifestyle and the service of the belly and sinful desires. Paul vigorously denies this claim and revisits it in Rom 6 when he heralds Christ as the real power that delivers from sin and death. He asks there: "Shall we go on sinning that grace may abound? May it never be." Rather, in 6:12 he warns that any who oppose his gospel of Christ would end up serving their desires. Faith and baptism *free* one from an enslavement to sin (thus Rom 6:6, 12, 14, 17, 19). When Paul returns to these matters again in Rom 16, he is claiming that false teachers in their departures threaten to rob the gospel of Christ of its power and abandon people to the desires of the flesh. Once again, connections with the earlier sections of the letter converge and suggest an overbearing expression of freedom by the strong which would lead to the very situation some had feared with Paul's message itself. His concern, then, is

---

194. Philippians 3:19 employs belly-language as well, but see Sandnes's helpful analysis of the rhetoric of 3:17–21 in *Belly and Body in the Pauline Epistles*, 136–64. Sandnes chided scholars for seeking all too quickly to find opponents behind these verses. This paragraph must be considered alongside the body language elsewhere in Philippians. Again, Paul is combating an indulgent lifestyle, not doctrinal aberration. The Philippians must renounce themselves even to the point of suffering. Sandnes (p. 164): "Paul's concern to present a holy and blameless congregation has a bearing upon bodily practices. The body is either an instrument for glorifying Christ or a means of worshipping oneself. Thus belly-devotion appears as a contrast with the true worship of Christ. This is so since worshipping Christ involves the body; Christ's bodily sufferings as well as his glorious body form two aspects with which believers identify." Sandnes's treatment of Phil 3:17–21 supplements and confirms his approach to Rom 16:17–20.

not with deliberate opposition to his message as such but with the possibility that some of the strong would take their freedom to an extreme and would express that freedom in a manner that would hurt the weak. While not setting out to oppose Paul, these potential teachers' false message and practice would nevertheless represent a serious departure from his apostolic teaching. Romans 16:17–20 does not seem to envision Jews or Jewish Christians as the potential culprits.[195]

Since Rom 16:17–20 is of no apparent value in identifying Jewish Christian objectors in Rome, then the case must rest on Rom 3:8, a verse of even less help in identifying opponents. Romans 3:8 is rather vague: "And why not say (as some people slander us by saying that we say), 'Let us do evil so that good may come'? Their condemnation is deserved." Although Stuhlmacher has not wavered in his insistence that this verse proves the presence of Jewish Christians, James D. G. Dunn's objections remain unanswered:

> The vagueness of the allusion tells against the view that Paul was directing his comment against particular individuals among the Roman congregations. The evidence of his other letters is that Paul was much more direct in his address to those who criticized his teaching. And though the challenge posed is an important one for him (6:1), and had certainly been raised against his teaching elsewhere . . . , both here and in 6:1 it appears as a corollary to his own exposition and not as a question asked by his readers.[196]

Dunn then carefully explained how the objection lodged in 3:8 furthered the logic of Paul's developing argument. Nothing, then, would suggest actual opponents at Rome.

Leander Keck wondered how to account for the *content* of Romans if the epistle were intended to respond to charges laid against the apostle. In listing several controversial topics in Paul's other letters *not* included in Romans, Keck wrote:

> [T]he more one regards Romans as Paul's means of persuading the readers that, contrary to what they heard, his gospel is sufficiently consistent with "mainstream" Christianity that they need not hesitate to welcome him and

---

195. Romans 14–15 does not combat libertinism as such, since the issue is the strong's *relation* to the weak with regard to customs that are ordinarily a matter of freedom (and not sin). The opposition in Rom 16:17–20 remains a *potential* reality should some of the strong not yield to his instructions regarding the weak. The warning will function hopefully as an effective curb.

196. Dunn, *Romans 1–8*, 137.

then support him in Spain, the more baffling is the omission of so much Pauline theology.[197]

Firm evidence is simply lacking for an apologetic function for the letter to the Romans.

Separate Jewish Christian and Gentile Christian Assemblies Urged to Worship Together

Francis Watson identified what he thought was the concrete situation behind the Letter to the Romans: Paul is writing primarily to unite divided communities. The Roman Jewish Christians are meeting for worship separately from the gentile Christians, and Paul wants both groups to come together even if the Jewish Christians are forced to leave the synagogues in the process.[198] The Jewish Christians should view their observance of the Law as a matter of personal piety and ultimately optional. Peter Lampe argued that the Roman Christians were indeed gathering in separate locations.[199] Watson pointed to Paul's admonition to "welcome one another" (προσλαμβάνομαι) in Rom 14:1 and 15:7. Paul similarly urges the Corinthians to welcome one another (ἐκδέχομαι) in 1 Cor 11:33 in the context of a meal during which some had too much to drink while others had too little even to eat.[200] Since Paul admonishes the Corinthians, who were experiencing friction and conflict, to "welcome one another," the admonition in Romans to "welcome one another" must be directed to a situation of friction and conflict as well.

According to Watson's proposal, the Roman gentile "strong" are to "welcome" the Jewish Christian "weak" who are visiting their gatherings. Watson did not countenance the possibility that the weak and the strong could both be gentile when Paul urges non-Law-observant gentiles to welcome the Law-observant "into" their house churches.[201] Whether the weak were really newcomers to the strong's gatherings is questionable. The word "welcome" (προσλαμβάνομαι) in Rom 14:1 and 15:7 does not demonstrate that the weak and

---

197. Keck, "What Makes Romans Tick?" 19.

198. Francis Watson, "The Two Roman Congregations: Romans 14:1 — 15:13," in *Paul, Judaism and the gentiles: A Sociological Approach* (SNTSMS 56; Cambridge: Cambridge Univ. Press, 1986), 94–105; repr. in Donfried, *The Romans Debate*, 203–15.

199. Lampe, "Roman Christians," 229–30.

200. That the problems arose in the context of the Corinthians' meal together, see A. Andrew Das, "1 Corinthians 11:17–34 Revisited," CTQ 62 (1998): 188–93.

201. Thus Gagnon, "The 'Weak' at Rome," 65–66.

the strong were previously meeting separately *as groups*. Mark Nanos objected that προσλαμβάνω is used in these verses in the middle form in the sense of to "accept" or "receive." Paul is not a stranger in relation to Philemon, and yet he admonishes his dear friend and coworker to "welcome" him.[202] Dunn defined προσλαμβάνω as "everyday recognition and practice of brotherhood, not an official act of reception" (see 2 Macc 10:15; Acts 28:2; Phlm 17; so also Rom 15:7).[203] The strong and the weak are not separate groups but factions *within* the same gatherings. Likewise, the admonitions for Jews and gentiles to worship together in Rom 15:7–13 would function just as well if the groups were experiencing friction within their meetings alongside each other. The various house churches in Rom 16 are not distinguished as Jewish or gentile gatherings. Romans 16 even seems to distinguish more than two gatherings. "In 16:3–26 the intermingling of Jewish and gentile names is more obviously understood to reflect mixed Jewish/gentile groups than two groups precisely distinguished as one Jewish and the other gentile."[204] Romans 14:1 and 15:7 simply cannot bear the weight of Watson's thesis. It is difficult to imagine how one group could place a stumbling block in their brothers and sisters' way if they were meeting separately (14:13, 20). The problem is that the strong and the weak were frowning upon each other's practices when they were *together*.[205]

Watson contended that Paul's "sole aim" is to "maintain and defend" the "separation of his Gentile Christian churches from the Jewish community."[206] Watson's Paul wanted the Jewish Christian congregation to "abandon their belief in the vital importance of observing the law of Moses" and adopt "an attitude of sectarian separation from non-Christian fellow-Jews." They need to make a "final break."[207] James Dunn found these assertions "astonishing."[208] The apostle pointedly reminds the gentiles in Rom 11:11–32 that they have been grafted on

---

202. Mark D. Nanos, "A Rejoinder to Robert A. J. Gagnon's 'Why the "Weak" at Rome Cannot be Non-Christian Jews,'" 4 [created 14 July 2000; updated 20 June 2003; cited 1 August 2005]. Online: http://mywebpages.comcast.net/nanosmd/Gagnon-rejoinder-6-20-03.pdf.

203. Dunn, *Romans 9–16*, 798.

204. Dunn, *Romans 1–8*, lvii.

205. See the critique of William S. Campbell (depending on Robert Jewett) in "Did Paul Advocate Separation from the Synagogue? A Reaction to Francis Watson: Paul, Judaism and the Gentiles: A Sociological Approach," *SJT* 42 (1989): 457–67, esp. p. 466.

206. Watson, *Paul, Judaism and the Gentiles*, 22.

207. Ibid., 106.

208. Dunn, *Romans 1–8*, lvii.

as wild olive shoots to Israel's tree and heritage. The gentiles do not form their own separate tree but are *dependent* upon Israel. Paul even looks forward to a day when "all Israel will be saved." Far from urging his audience to sever all ties with the Jews, the apostle holds out hope for his people and wants the gentile Romans to think similarly. He never asks the "weak" to abandon their Jewish practices in 14:1 but calls instead for mutual acceptance (15:7). The Roman gentiles represent the fulfillment of the promises to "all" Abraham's seed (4:16). Abraham is the Jews and gentiles' mutual "father" in 4:12. Such logic is incomprehensible if, with Watson, Paul is urging a break from the synagogues.

The Tension between the Strong and the Weak over Mosaic Customs in the Wake of the Edict of Claudius

The record of an Edict of Claudius expelling the Jews from Rome because of a squabble over "Chrestus" has inspired perhaps the most popular theory for the situation behind Romans. If "Chrestus" refers to Christ, then Christians were present in the Roman synagogues in the late 40s. After Claudius's harsh edict of expulsion, usually placed in the year 49 CE, the Jews and Jewish Christians were forced to leave Rome. The gentiles, who had learned of Christ from the Jewish communities, had to form their own assemblies. When Nero acceded to the throne in 54, the expelled Jews and Jewish Christians were able to return to Rome only to find Christianity thriving in gentile house churches. During the years the Jews were absent from Rome, gentile converts to Christianity had joined the house churches. These gentile converts would not have had the same appreciation for Judaism as the Christians from the synagogues would have had. Some of these converts may not have appreciated the Jewish roots of Christianity. The gentile "strong" found themselves in conflict with the returning Jewish Christian "weak." Jewish Christians, who had comprised the majority of Christians in Rome prior to the expulsion in 49 CE, found themselves in the minority upon their return five years later. The non-Law-observant majority questioned the ethnic practices of the returning Jewish Christians. Paul is therefore writing to resolve the tensions between the gentile non-Law-observant strong and the Jewish, Law-observant weak.[209] Such tensions would require Paul to summarize his gospel message insofar as it concerns the relationship between gentiles and Jews in God's historic plan for Israel. He would have to exposit his gospel more fully to be successful in persuading an audience that did not personally know

---

209. While Paul commends the Romans, that does not mean that there are not tensions. Paul commends, of all congregations, the Corinthians in 1 Cor 1:4–9.

him and his preaching. Paul hopes to unify the divided factions of Christian Jews and gentiles (thus 15:7–13).[210]

Conclusion

After having completed his work in the East (15:19), Paul is preparing to go to Jerusalem with the collection (15:25–26), and from there on to Spain (15:24, 28) by way of Rome (15:23; 1:10–13). His sixteen-chapter letter would serve, to some extent, as a means of self-introduction. The upcoming trips to Jerusalem and Spain certainly figure into his purpose in writing, but these trips should not be overemphasized as the *primary* rationale for Paul's letter. Many scholars have gravitated toward the position that Paul's primary purpose in writing Romans is to address a concrete situation of division and strife between the gentile strong and the Jewish weak. Perhaps the unity Paul urges in Rome would provide a stronger base of support for his mission to Spain (15:22–24). Most of the theories surveyed in this chapter assume that Paul is writing in Romans to a mixed audience of Jews and gentiles. A fresh, new approach would be necessary, however, if this assumption of a mixed Jewish/gentile audience should prove questionable. The next chapter raises questions regarding this very assumption.

---

210. So Willi Marxsen, *Introduction to the New Testament: An Approach to Its Problems* (trans. G. Buswell; Philadelphia: Fortress Press, 1968), 95–107. Marxsen's thesis was expanded by Wiefel, "The Jewish Community in Ancient Rome," 85–101. Among the advocates of this popular approach are: H. W. Bartsch, "Die historische Situation des Römerbriefes," in *SE* IV/1 = TUGAL 102 (Berlin: Akademie-Verlag, 1968), 281–91; Ernst Käsemann, *Commentary on Romans* (Grand Rapids: Eerdmans, 1980), 405; Dunn, *Romans 1–8*, xliv–liv; N. T. Wright, "Romans and the Theology of Paul," in Hay and Johnson, *Pauline Theology 3: Romans*, 35, 62–63; Donfried, "Short Note," 46–49; idem, "False Presuppositions," 104–6; Bruce, "The Romans Debate — Continued," 177–86; Stuhlmacher, *Paul's Letter to the Romans*, 6–8; Walters, *Ethnic Issues*, 56–64, 84–92; idem, "The Purpose of Romans"; Jeffrey A. Crafton, "Paul's Rhetorical Vision and the Purpose of Romans: Toward a New Understanding," *NovT* 32 (1990): 320–25.

Chapter 2

The Ethnic Identity of the Roman Congregations: The Internal Evidence

"We who are strong ought to put up with the failings of the weak, and not to please ourselves" (Rom 15:1). For most interpreters, Paul wrote his Letter to the Romans primarily to reconcile a gentile Christian "strong" with a Jewish Christian "weak." To the gentile majority that did not have a proper appreciation for the Jewish roots of the Christian faith, Paul's reasoning reaches its climax with the proclamation, "All Israel will be saved" (11:26). Like wild olive shoots grafted onto the cultivated tree of Israel, the gentiles may be cut off as quickly as they were engrafted (11:11–24). To gentiles who express disdain for brothers and sisters who practice various Jewish customs comes a letter that is saturated with references to the Jewish Scriptures and that outlines the proper relationship between Jew and gentile. Paul demands that the Roman Christians "welcome one another as Christ has welcomed them" (15:7).

A handful of scholars—Stanley Stowers, Neil Elliott, and Runar Thorsteinsson—have contended that Romans addressed an entirely or almost entirely gentile audience.[1] The response to their position has been largely negative. For whom would Paul's outline of Jewish-gentile relations resonate if not to mixed congregations? Why did Paul elaborately allude to and cite the Jewish Scriptures

---

1. See also Paul J. Achtemeier, "Unsearchable Judgments and Inscrutable Ways: Reflections on the Discussion of Romans," in *SBLSP 1995* (ed. Eugene H. Lovering, Jr.; Atlanta, Ga.: Scholars, 1995), 521–34; repr. (with corrections) in *Pauline Theology 4: Looking Back, Pressing On* (ed. E. Elizabeth Johnson and David M. Hay; SBLSS 4; Atlanta: Scholars, 1997), 3–21.

if he were not writing to those who read and treasured those Scriptures? How would one explain the turn to "the Jew" in Rom 2:17 or the greetings to several fellow Jews in 16:1–16? Who were the Roman congregations' "weak" members who were identified by their practice of the Jewish Sabbath and food laws (14:1—15:6)? The case for a Jewish contingent within the Roman congregations appears almost indisputable—almost. In recent years evidence has been mounting from various quarters that calls into question the entire consensus. The most compelling evidence against the consensus comes directly from the letter itself.

An Exclusively Gentile Audience

At several key points in the letter, Paul identifies or describes the members of his audience as gentiles. The apostle identifies his addressees in this letter more than in any other. A conspicuously doubled description of the audience greets the reader in the first verses of the letter in its opening (1:1–7) and thanksgiving sections (1:8–15).[2] Toward the end of the letter, as Paul narrates his travel plans, he again identifies his first readers as gentiles (15:15–16). He directly addresses the Roman "gentiles" in 11:13. In 6:17–19, he describes them in language that would hardly befit Jews. Defenders of a Jewish contingent claim that such passages do not at all suggest an exclusively gentile audience. A compelling case for a gentile audience based on these key texts will therefore have to account for and disqualify alternate interpretations that favor a mixed audience.

The Letter Opening (1:1–7)

Paul opens the Letter to the Romans as "a servant of Jesus Christ, called to be an apostle, set apart for the gospel of God," a gospel that was promised long before in the prophets (1:1–2). This good news concerns God's Son, Jesus Christ our Lord, "through whom we have received grace and apostleship to bring about the obedience of faith *among all the gentiles* for the sake of his name, *including yourselves* who are called to belong to Jesus Christ" (1:3–6, NRSV, mod.; emphasis

---

2. Arguably, the thanksgiving continues through 1:16–17, since these verses are grammatically subordinated to the preceding paragraph; Paul J. Achtemeier, *Romans* (Interpretation; Atlanta: John Knox, 1985), 35–37. Thomas R. Schreiner, *Romans* (BECNT 6; Grand Rapids: Baker, 1998), 58–59, while recognizing the validity of Achtemeier's observation, nevertheless highlighted the thematic centrality of 1:16–17.

added). Paul appears in the NRSV, as in several other modern English versions, to number his audience among the gentiles. To summarize Paul's logic:

> First premise: "I have received apostleship from Christ to preach the gospel among all the gentiles."
>
> Second premise: "You believers in Rome belong to that group of people, the gentiles."
>
> Conclusion: "I, therefore, have a divine responsibility to share my gospel with you."[3]

Paul's apostleship is for the "obedience of faith" among all the gentiles for the sake of his name" (1:5a). The Romans therefore number within the sphere of Paul's apostolic authority because they too are gentiles.[4]

C. E. B. Cranfield, in his survey of grammatical options, proposed another translation of 1:5–6: Paul is writing to those who are called *among* (and *distinguished from*) the gentiles (ἐν οἷς ἐστε καὶ ὑμεῖς κλητοὶ Ἰησοῦ Χριστοῦ). The addressees would not themselves be gentiles. The passage would refer to geographical location rather than ethnic makeup.[5] In support, Cranfield reasoned, an identification of the ethnic composition of the audience would be out of place in v. 6 since Paul did not formally identify the audience until the adscription of v. 7. Verse 6 was merely a parenthetical comment that interrupted the flow of the salutation.[6] Cranfield did not consider, however, that by interrupting the salutation, the comments about the audience in v. 6 draw attention. Thorsteinsson rightly observed that "such an 'unexpected' placement of the clause would

---

3. Jeffrey A. D. Weima, "Preaching the Gospel in Rome: A Study of the Epistolary Framework of Romans," in *Gospel in Paul: Studies on Corinthians, Galatians and Romans for Richard N. Longenecker* (ed. L. Ann Jervis and Peter Richardson; JSNTSup 108; Sheffield: Sheffield Academic, 1994), 343.

4. Ibid., 343–44; Douglas J. Moo, *The Epistle to the Romans* (NICNT; Grand Rapids: Eerdmans, 1996), 53–54.

5. C. E. B. Cranfield, *A Critical and Exegetical Commentary on the Epistle to the Romans* (ICC; Edinburgh: T&T Clark, 1975), 1:68; see also Rom 15:15–16; Markku Kettunen, *Der Abfassungszweck des Römerbriefes* (AASF: Dissertations Humanarum Litterarum 18; Helsinki: Suomalainen Tiedeakatemia, 1979), 40–43. For earlier advocates of this approach, see William Manson, *The Epistle to the Hebrews: An Historical and Theological Reconsideration* (London: Hodder and Stoughton, 1951), 173; Franz J. Leenhardt, *The Epistle to the Romans: A Commentary* (London: Lutterworth, 1961), 40.

6. Cranfield, *Romans*, 1:67.

almost certainly have had the opposite effect on Paul's audience. It would have appeared emphatic rather than parenthetic."[7]

Cranfield also contended that, had Paul wanted to identify the audience of Rom 1:6 as *a part of* the gentiles mentioned in the preceding clause in v. 5, he would have used the construction ἐξ ὧν ἐστε καὶ ὑμεῖς κλητοί.[8] Adolf Schlatter (on whom Cranfield depended) argued that with ἐξ ὧν a partitive sense would have been clearer.[9] The Romans would be undeniably included among the gentiles. Schlatter and Cranfield did not reckon with the well-attested partitive sense of the preposition ἐν in Paul's day (BDF §164 [1]). For instance, Luke describes Gamaliel in Acts 5:34 as a member of the Sanhedrin (τις ἐν τῷ συνεδρίῳ). Paul writes that he has advanced in Judaism beyond many of his people (ἐν τῷ γένει μου) of the same age (Gal 1:14). He refers to "some of you" (ἐν ὑμῖν τινες) in 1 Cor 15:12. The surprising and unexpected disruption of the Romans salutation is hardly necessary in order to remind the Romans of the obvious fact that they reside in the midst of a gentile world.[10] Paul wants to emphasize that the Romans are within the realm of his apostolic authority as

---

7. Runar M. Thorsteinsson, *Paul's Interlocutor in Romans 2: Function and Identity in the Context of Ancient Epistolography* (ConBNT 40; Stockholm: Almqvist & Wiksell, 2003), 105.

8. Cranfield, *Romans*, 1:68 n. 2.

9. Adolf Schlatter, *Romans: The Righteousness of God* (trans. Siegfried S. Schatzmann; Peabody, Mass.: Hendrickson, 1995), 11, followed by Cranfield, *Romans*, 1:68 n. 2; and Philip F. Esler, *Conflict and Identity in Romans: The Social Setting of Paul's Letter* (Minneapolis: Fortress Press, 2003), 385 n. 23. Schlatter added:

> [I]t is significant that the Roman Christians live "among the Gentiles," and for them this has particular importance. Throngs of Gentiles moved through the streets of Rome; all nations gathered there. However, in the midst of the Gentiles they live as "those who are called by Jesus Christ."

Wilhelm Julius Mangold (1884) made the same point long before; J. Christiaan Beker, *Paul the Apostle: The Triumph of God in Life and Thought* (Philadelphia: Fortress Press, 1990), 76.

10. Contra Christopher Bryan, *A Preface to Romans: Notes on the Epistle in Its Literary and Cultural Setting* (Oxford: Oxford Univ. Press, 2000), 218. In other words, if the Romans live amidst a *gentile* world and if it is gentiles to whom Paul's ministry is directed (Bryan cited 11:13; Gal 1:16; 2:7–9), how would these premises include the Romans in his apostolic commission? The Romans are not all gentiles. They are *not*, then, necessarily included in Paul's missionary sphere. The obvious fact that they live in the midst of a gentile world would therefore be meaningless for the Roman Jewish Christians whom Paul is also addressing. If the Romans are gentiles, on the other hand, mention by the apostle to the gentiles of the Romans' gentile world would make more sense.

gentiles. Paul stresses that he has been commissioned for the obedience of faith of *all* the gentiles (v. 5), and so he emphasizes that he is writing "to *all* the beloved of God who are in Rome" (v. 7's adscription). The repeated stress in vv. 5 and 7 links the audience to Paul's commission to the gentiles.[11] Without grammatical break and in the immediate context of the universalizing emphasis in v. 5 on "all the gentiles" (ἐν πᾶσιν τοῖς ἔθνεσιν), Paul adds: "including yourselves" (ἐν οἷς ἐστε καὶ ὑμεῖς, v. 6). Paul's commission to bring about the obedience of faith of the gentiles therefore serves as the warrant for his writing those in Rome.[12] Far from a mere parenthetical comment, the identification of the audience as gentile grounds Paul's rationale for writing.

Douglas Moo noted that Cranfield had not accounted for Rom 1:5's "also" (καί), which implied that "the Roman Christians are *part of*—not just 'in the midst of'—the Gentiles of v. 5."[13] The use of καί ("also") suggests the *inclusion* of the Roman audience among the gentiles, as most commentators recognize.[14] Francis Watson and Steven Mason offered a potential explanation for this difficulty in Cranfield's reading. They contended that the "also" modifies the phrase that *follows*: "called to belong to Jesus Christ" (v. 6). The Romans were (also) "called" even as Paul himself was "called" (v. 1); and even as Paul was called (as a Jew) in the midst of gentiles, so too were the Romans.[15] Watson and Mason's reasoning does not withstand scrutiny. "Called" in v. 1 modifies "apostle." The Romans are certainly called of Jesus Christ, but they are not called as apostles. Their "call" remains distinct from Paul's own.[16] Watson's reasoning would require that the clause "including yourselves who are called" (ἐν οἷς ἐστε καὶ ὑμεῖς κλητοί) be interpreted by the more distant v. 1 rather than the immediately preceding phrase (ἐν πᾶσιν τοῖς ἔθνεσιν), which the clause grammatically modifies. Cran-

---

11. Thorsteinsson, *Paul's Interlocutor*, 106.

12. Angelika Reichert, *Der Römerbrief als Gratwanderung: Eine Untersuchung zur Abfassungsproblematik* (FRLANT 194; Göttingen: Vandenhoeck & Ruprecht, 2001), 114–15.

13. Moo, *Romans*, 54 n. 79.

14. See, for instance, James D. G. Dunn, *Romans 1 — 8* (WBC 38A; Dallas: Word, 1988), 18–19, and Joseph A. Fitzmyer, *Romans* (AB 33; New York: Doubleday, 1993), 238.

15. Francis Watson, *Paul, Judaism, and the Gentiles: A Sociological Approach* (SNTSMS 56; Cambridge: Cambridge Univ. Press, 1986), 103; Steven Mason, "Paul, Classical Anti-Jewish Polemic, and the Letter to the Romans," in *Self-Definition and Self-Discovery in Early Christianity* (ed. David J. Hawkin and Tom Robinson; Lewiston, N.Y.: Edwin Mellen, 1990), 214. Mason has championed the unique thesis that Paul is writing to an audience consisting *exclusively* of Jews.

16. Thorsteinsson, *Paul's Interlocutor*, 103.

field himself posed a problem for Watson and Mason's interpreting the Romans' "call" in v. 6 alongside Paul's own. A further description of the Romans as "called" belongs more naturally in the following adscription in v. 7 (note v. 7's κλητοῖς ἁγίοις). That Paul located "called of Jesus Christ" in v. 6 indicates that the phrase explicates the gentiles of v. 5: "We should probably therefore put a comma after ὑμεῖς, and understand the words to mean: 'among whom are you also, you who are called. . . .'"[17] Paul therefore had a right to address the Romans, since they were "also" included as gentiles in the realm of his apostolic authority.[18] Mason and Watson's reading mistakenly rendered secondary the relationship between the readers and Paul as the apostle who is bringing forth the obedience of faith of the gentiles.[19]

Philip Esler recently offered support for Cranfield's brief suggestion that the terms normally translated "Jew" ('Ιουδαῖος) and "gentile" (ἔθνος) are geographical designations. Esler preferred the translation "Judeans" and "Non-Judeans." Esler did not deny that the Greek words function as ethnic designations, but he asserted that ethnicity must necessarily include a link with a geographical homeland — whether a memory of the former occupation of this land or a current occupation by some or all of the group — along with a common name, a myth of common ancestry, a shared history or shared memories of a common past, a common culture (including customs, language, and religion), and a sense of communal solidarity.[20] Although a geographical component should certainly be included as a component of ethnicity, an emphasis on the homeland may or may not be primarily in view in any particular discussion of that ethnic group. In other words, the question is whether a *primarily* geographic designation is likely in the context of Rom 1:5 (as Cranfield's argument requires — "among/in the midst of the nations [outside Judea]"). Esler disapproved of Moo's (and

---

17. Cranfield, *Romans*, 1:67.

18. Ibid., 1:67–8.

19. Reichert, *Römerbrief*, 115, incomprehensibly wrote: "Danach wären die Adressaten dem Verfasser nicht primär gegenüber, sondern *an die Seite* gestellt." Cranfield's arguments against Mason and Watson's approach apply equally against Reichert's entertaining of their approach (*Römerbrief*, 118).

20. Esler, *Conflict and Identity*, 43–44, relying on Fredrik Barth, John Hutchinson, and Anthony D. Smith. Note Esler's critique, pp. 68–74, of Shaye J. D. Cohen, *The Beginnings of Jewishness: Boundaries, Varieties, Uncertainties* (Berkeley: Univ. of California Press, 1999), 69–139. "Judean" may perhaps be a more accurate term than "Jew," but I have opted for the latter in order to emphasize the focus in Paul on the people rather than their respective lands and to signal a primarily non-geographic construal of 1:5–6, 13 (contra Cranfield).

Dunn's and Fitzymer's) contention that ἔθνη in 1:5 could not mean "nations" in a "strictly geographic sense" and that ἔθνη referred to gentiles instead of Jews.[21] Esler, on the other hand, has not provided evidence that ἔθνη is being used in v. 5 in a "strictly geographic sense." A "strictly geographic sense" would be at odds with Esler's own definition of ethnicity in which geography is only one component.[22] As Sean Freyne put it: "*Ioudaioi* were those who lived according to a set of ancestral laws and customs rather than inhabitants of the province of Judea."[23] Or with Stephen G. Wilson: "By the Roman period the term refers overwhelmingly, perhaps exclusively, to Jews wherever they hailed from."[24]

Not surprisingly, Esler cited with approval Christopher Stanley's study of the use of the term "Hellene" for ethnic Greeks residing in Asia Minor.[25] The problem with Stanley's study, as commentators have frequently noted, is that Paul in Gal 3:28 divides the entire world into "Jew" and "Greek" even as the entire world may be divided into male and female and slave and free (so also Rom 1:16; 2:9, 10; 3:9!). These oppositions characterizing "all" humanity suggest that Paul is using "Greek" synonymously with "gentile" (ἔθνος) or non-Jew rather than in terms of a particular ethnic group.[26] In other words, the Pauline text itself must be the arbiter of the fruitfulness of Stanley's (and Esler's) proposals.

---

21. Dunn, *Romans 1–8*, 18–19; Fitzmyer, *Romans*, 238.

22. Esler, *Conflict and Identity*, 112–15.

23. Sean Freyne, "Behind the Names: Samaritans, *Ioudaioi*, and Galileans," in *Text and Artifact in the Religions of Antiquity: Essays in Honour of Peter Richardson* (ed. Stephen G. Wilson and Michel Desjardins; SCJ 9; Waterloo, Ontario: Wilfrid Laurier Univ. Press, 2000), 395. He referenced John Ashton's remarks that people regularly speak of Poles in Britain and Irish in North America without ever assuming anything beyond a "special relationship with 'the folks back home.'" He concluded: "Thus, in the case of the Jews (and the Irish and the Poles also) the religio-cultural meaning builds on the geographical one but takes on the extended meaning in the process" (p. 395).

24. Stephen G. Wilson, "ΟΙ ΠΟΤΕ ΙΟΥΔΑΙΟΙ: Epigraphic Evidence for Jewish Defectors," in Wilson and Desjardins, *Text and Artifact*, 357. See the highly critical remarks against associating the term Ἰουδαῖος/*Iudaeus* with a Judean provenance in Pieter W. van der Horst, *Ancient Jewish Epitaphs: An Introductory Survey of a Millennium of Jewish Funerary Epigraphy (300 BCE–700 CE)* (CBET 2; Kampen: Kok Pharos, 1991), 69–70; Margaret H. Williams, "The Meaning and Function of *Ioudaios* in Graeco-Roman Inscriptions," *ZPE* 116 (1997): 249–62, esp. pp. 252–3 (thus the use of the term also for proselytes).

25. Esler, *Conflict and Identity*, 74–6; Christopher D. Stanley, "'Neither Jew nor Greek': Ethnic Conflict in Graeco-Roman Society," *JSNT* 64 (1996): 101–24.

26. So also Dieter Zeller, *Juden und Heiden in der Mission des Paulus: Studien zum Römerbief* (FB 1; Stuttgart: Katholisches Bibelwerk, 1973), 13–14.

Ultimately, Esler has not provided useful evidence that would identify "Judeans" in Paul's audience any more than gentiles/foreigners who had formerly associated with the Roman synagogues. This is a letter intensely concerned with the fundamental distinction between Jew/Judean and gentile/foreigner — members of differing ethnic groups. Paul uses "gentile"/foreigner (ἔθνος) elsewhere in this letter for non-Jews/Judeans (for example, 9:30–32, 11:24–25 alongside 11:30, 28, 17–18).[27] Romans 1:5–6, 13 are therefore emphasizing the non-Judean recipients of Paul's apostolic activity and commission. Finally, Esler inherited the weaknesses of Cranfield's, Watson's, and Mason's interpretation of these verses. Esler did not resolve the problems associated with the taking of v. 6 as a mere (trite) parenthetical comment about the Romans living in the midst of a foreign world. The audience consists of non-Judeans. To summarize, Paul speaks of gentiles/foreigners as the rightful recipients of his apostolic ministry in v. 5 and then emphasizes that the Romans number "also" among those foreign recipients.

The Thanksgiving Section (Romans 1:8–15)

After including the Romans among the gentiles called through his apostolic ministry to Jesus Christ, Paul expresses his incessant prayers for the Romans (Rom 1:9) and his fervent desire to visit them in order to impart a spiritual gift (vv. 10–11). In 1:13 Paul writes: "I want you to know, brothers and sisters, that I have often intended to come to you (but thus far have been prevented), in order that I may reap some harvest among you as I have among the rest of the gentiles" (NRSV, mod.; καὶ ἐν ὑμῖν καθὼς καὶ ἐν λοιποῖς ἔθνεσιν). Paul refers to "the rest" of the gentiles in relation to his Roman audience. The most natural reading is that Paul is thereby indicating (again) the gentile identity of his Roman readers. Cranfield, on the other hand, questioned the value of this verse for identifying a gentile audience.[28] He contended that Paul is expressing his hope to

---

27. For a comprehensive listing of passages throughout Romans and other Pauline literature that contrast the gentiles/nations with the Jews/Judeans, see Moo, *Romans*, 53 n. 76. Contrast is the norm. Romans 4:17 may be the only Pauline exception in which the Judeans are included among the nations.

28. Cranfield, *Romans*, 1:20, followed by Anthony J. Guerra, *Romans and the Apologetic Tradition: The Purpose, Genre and Audience of Paul's Letter* (SNTSMS 81; Cambridge: Cambridge Univ. Press, 1995), 26, and Esler, *Conflict and Identity*, 115. So also W. Manson, *Hebrews*, 174, who reasoned that the gentiles are treated in the *third* person in 1:18–22 and hence these people in 1:14–15 must be Jews. For an earlier advocate of this position, see Leenhardt, *Romans*, 44–45.

bear fruit in Rome even as he has throughout the rest of the gentile world (with geography as the primary referent of "the rest").[29] Paul is not necessarily implying that the Roman church is gentile. Contrary to Cranfield's contention that the apostle uses "gentile" to designate geographic territory, Paul employs "gentile" in Romans to designate people, non-Jews.[30] Paul goes on to write of *peoples* in vv. 14–15: "I am a debtor to Greeks and to barbarians, both to the wise and to the foolish — hence also my eagerness to proclaim the gospel to you also who are in Rome." Paul says nothing of Christian Jews in Rome.[31]

Actually, the NRSV of Rom 1:14–15 is most likely incorrect, because it is based on a mispunctuation, as Runar Thorsteinsson has shown. Thorsteinsson translated vv. 13–15:

> But I do not want you to be ignorant of, brothers, that I have frequently intended to come to you — but was hindered until now — in order that I may reap some harvest among you as I have among the rest of the gentiles, Greeks as well as barbarians, wise as well as ignorant.

---

29. Bryan, *Preface to Romans*, 218, considered 1:13 another reference to the Romans being located in the midst of a gentile world, as had been the case, for Bryan, in 1:5. The doubled emphasis on Rome being located in a gentile world seems utterly trivial. *Why* doubly emphasize the Romans' location? If the emphasis is on Rome as the capital of a gentile world, as per Bryan, is not the emphasis still on the gentile character of the Roman congregation? And why not actually *say* that Rome is the capital of the gentile world if that is the point?

30. See, for instance, Rom 2:14, 24; 3:29; 9:24, 30; 11:11–13, 25; 15:9–12, 16.

31. Steven Mason, "Paul," 214–45; idem, "'For I Am Not Ashamed of the Gospel' (Rom. 1.16): The Gospel and the First Readers of Romans," in *Gospel in Paul: Studies on Corinthians, Galatians and Romans for Richard N. Longenecker* (ed. L. Ann Jervis and Peter Richardson; JSNTSup 108; Sheffield: Sheffield Academic, 1994), 271, thought the reference to barbarians in Rome too insulting. Paul must be speaking of the "remainder" of the gentiles beyond the Greek world in Spain. Mention of Spain, however, does not come until much later in the letter. Mason also thought the οὕτως in v. 15 does not connect to v. 14 but rather to v. 16: "[For] I am obligated to both Greeks *and* barbarians, to both wise *and* foolish. [That is why I plan to head West; cf. 15.19–24]. Hence the readiness on my side . . . to bring the *euangelion* also (καί) to you who are in Rome: for I am not ashamed of the *euangelion*" ("'For I Am Not Ashamed of the Gospel,'" 273). Thorsteinsson's reconstruction of the text, however, demonstrated that the paired groups of v. 14 primarily describe "the rest of the gentiles" and not the Romans. The paired terms describe the entirety of the remaining gentile world and are not referring to any particular subgroup. Further, a prospective οὕτως, as Mason proposed, would be an unwarranted, unnatural grammatical construction; so also Reichert, *Römerbrief*, 105 n. 20.

I am bound, then, to announce the gospel with goodwill to you also who are in Rome.[32]

The advantages of his translation are numerous. Taking "Greeks as well as barbarians, wise as well as ignorant" in apposition to "gentiles" matches Paul's grammatical constructions in Rom 2:9, 10, and 1 Cor 1:24. In each case, groups linked appositionally by τε καί modify the *preceding* noun.[33] Further, Paul nearly always uses the verb ὀφείλω with an infinitive, and the choice of ὀφειλέτης εἰμί and ὀφείλω is merely a matter of emphasis. He uses ὀφειλέτης εἰμί with infinitives in Rom 8:12 and Gal 5:3. When he uses this phrasing (ὀφειλέτης εἰμί) with a noun, the noun is genitive and not dative (thus Rom 15:27).[34] The complement to ὀφειλέτης εἰμί is therefore εὐαγγελίσασθαι, and τὸ κατ᾽ ἐμὲ πρόθυμον functions as an adverbial accusative of respect.[35] With this more likely translation, Paul is further explaining and emphasizing the delay caused by his work in the East among the gentiles by specifying these gentiles as Greeks and barbarians, wise and ignorant. The sheer extent of Paul's evangelistic effort has thus far prevented him from bringing his gospel message to the Romans.[36] The Romans must be understood alongside these other specifically gentile peoples among whom Paul has labored. Again, Paul is identifying gentile *peoples* and not geographical designations — further proof that Esler has been too extreme in his formulation. As Neil Elliott summarized vv. 13–15, "In 1:13 Paul at once explains why he has not yet come to Rome, thus reinforcing an ethos of pastoral concern, *and* also indicates why he should want to come to Rome in the first place. It is important to note that both statements cohere in Paul's divine commission as apostle to the gentiles."[37] The Romans were "also" the objects of Paul's

---

32. Runar M. Thorsteinsson, "Paul's Missionary Duty towards Gentiles in Rome: A Note on the Punctuation and Syntax of Rom 1.13–15," *NTS* 48 (2002): 531–47.

33. Ibid., 540.

34. Ibid., 540–41. For explanation of other aspects of the translation, see pp. 541–44.

35. Ibid., 541–42.

36. The focus in these verses remains on *Paul's* missionary activity and delay, not on the Romans' potential cooperation in those endeavors. Nothing in this text would suggest their present or future participation in this evangelizing activity; contra Reichert, *Römerbrief*, 127–28. Reichert has forced 1:13–15 into a preconceived mold based on her interpretation of Paul's plans in chap. 15. Although Paul is describing the recipients of his message in the East, she saw in the word "barbarian" a hint of what Paul actually envisions in the back of his mind (but does not express) — Spain (p. 129).

37. Neil Elliott, *The Rhetoric of Romans: Argumentative Constraint and Strategy and Paul's Dialogue with Judaism* (JSNTSup 45; Sheffield: Sheffield Academic, 1990; Fortress Press edition, 2006), 81. Elliott added that the emphasis in this verse is on Paul's desire to be present, which is corroborated by the following verses (pp. 81–82):

evangelizing activity in v. 15 along with the gentiles of v. 14.[38] Elliott noted that Rom 1:16–17 remains part of the disclosure period that began in v. 13. He tied "gospel" (εὐαγγέλιον) in v. 16 to the "evangelization" (εὐαγγελίσασθαι) of the Romans in v. 15.[39] The same gospel ministry that called the Romans to faith continues to call forth an obedient response (cf. 15:18; 1:5).[40]

"The hindrance, elaborated in terms of his obligation to 'Greeks and barbarians, wise and uncultured' (1.14) and identified at the end of the letter as preoccupation in other mission areas (15.22), springs from the same motive that continues to drive him toward Rome, and now impels him to write, although he would much rather see the Romans face to face." Paul views the likewise gentile Romans as those to whom he has been called to minister.

38. Francis Watson's claim in *Paul, Judaism, and the Gentiles: A Sociological Approach* (SNTSMS 56; Cambridge: Cambridge Univ. Press, 1986), 103, that Paul is using καὶ ὑμῖν in v. 15 (or καὶ ἐν ὑμῖν in v. 13) "somewhat loosely" signals his inability to incorporate Paul's wording into his preferred interpretation. The apostle is *not* "simply addressing them as inhabitants of Rome" (Watson, *Paul, Judaism, and the Gentiles*, 103). Paul is "evangelizing" (εὐαγγελίσασθαι) the Romans (ὑμῖν). Watson also complained of the tension between 1:15 and the principle of 15:20 of not evangelizing where Christ has already been named, but other solutions are available for this classic conundrum (see chapter 1).

39. Elliott, *Rhetoric*, 83–84.

40. Ibid., 85–86. Elliott wrote of the connections between 1:1–17 and 15:14–32, "Whereas in the *exordium* Paul 'zoomed in' from a wide view of his apostolic responsibility to *all* gentiles (1.1–5) toward a sharp focus on his intention and desire to be *among the Romans*, in ch. 15 the view moves *outward* from his writing to the Romans in fulfillment of his 'commission'... and 'divine service'... to his boast of what Christ has done through him in other parts of the world (15.19–23) and his plans to go on to Spain (15.24, 28)." He added: "Just as there is no reference to Spain in ch. 1, so here in ch. 15 there is no talk of 'evangelizing' the Romans. That language is reserved now for locations to the west of Rome (15.20–24)." As for the contradiction between 1:15 and 15:24, Elliott writes (p. 87), "The simplest explanation of the discrepancy between Paul's much desired visit to evangelize the Romans (1.15) and the anticipated stopover for 'refreshment' in 15.24 is that they are not references to the same trip; that is, Rom. 1.15 describes the visit Paul would like to have made, *but cannot*; Rom. 15.24 refers to the visit he *will* be able to make after delivering the collection to Jerusalem (15.25–29). 'Evangelizing' the Romans is absent from Paul's future plans, not because that was never really his intention, but because that intention *has been achieved* between chs. 1 and 15, that is, *by the letter itself*." Schreiner, *Romans*, 55 n. 13, objected that if Paul is resolving his apostolic obligation by a letter, why not send the letter earlier? Paul has already answered that. He would have preferred to minister in person. Only when such a visit was no longer possible because of hindrances did he pen the letter. Perhaps a more likely resolution of the difficulty is to recognize that "to evangelize" is a broader term that refers not only to preaching to non-Christians but also to strengthening the

John W. Taylor has recently proposed that the phrase ἐκ πίστεως εἰς πίστιν in 1:17 is best interpreted as a reference to the growing faith among gentile Christians as evidence that God's righteousness is being revealed. ἐκ + A + εἰς + A, explained Taylor, is a Greek idiom that, with abstract nouns, expresses "increase, progression, or movement from a lower to a higher state."[41] Biblical antecedents for the phrase δικαιοσύνη γὰρ θεοῦ ἐν αὐτῷ ἀποκαλύπτεται (Ps 98:2; also Isa 51:4–8 [which pairs righteousness and salvation; cf. 52:10; 56:1]; 53:1) include the nations in God's actions on behalf of Israel.[42] The phrase therefore refers to the growing number especially of gentile believers. Taylor's results draw further attention to the gentile focus that dominates 1:8–17. Gentile faith proves that God's eschatological salvation has indeed arrived.[43]

The Apostolic Parousia (Romans 15:15–16)

Romans 15:15–16 offers further evidence that the audience is gentile. Paul is addressing the audience in its entirety. That much is clear from Paul's wording: "I wrote to you" (ἔγραψα ὑμῖν), that is, the Roman audience.[44] Paul justifies in these verses his boldness in writing the letter *because of* his calling as a "minister of Christ Jesus to the gentiles." Paul's ministry to the gentiles therefore offers him a warrant to write to the Romans "boldly." He also writes to the Romans "*so that* the offering of the gentiles may be acceptable." Paul is a priestly servant of the divine "gospel" (εὐαγγέλιον) as he offers the gentiles to God. "Therefore, Paul's action of boldly preaching his gospel in the body of the letter should be viewed by the Roman Christians as a fulfillment of his God-given responsibility to the Gentiles."[45] The apostle adds in v. 18: "For I shall not dare (τολμήσω) to say anything except of what Christ has accomplished through me *for the obedience of the gentiles*" (NRSV, mod.).

Cranfield thought that these verses proved only that the gospel had been planted in the gentile world with little or no implication regarding the composition

---

faith of people who are already Christian (Cranfield, *Romans*, 1:86; Elliott, *Rhetoric*, 85). Paul employs the term in writing to Christians in 1 Cor 9:12–18; Gal 4:13; cf. 2 Tim 4:5. He uses the word for his apostolic ministry in general in 1 Cor 1:17; Gerhard Friedrich, "εὐαγγελίζομαι," *TDNT* 2:719–20.

41. John W. Taylor, "From Faith to Faith: Romans 1.17 in the Light of Greek Idiom," *NTS* 50 (2004): 341–43.

42. Ibid., 344–46.

43. Ibid., 346.

44. Thorsteinsson, *Paul's Interlocutor*, 111–12.

45. Weima, "Preaching the Gospel," 356.

of the Roman church.[46] Cranfield (again) adopted a strictly geographical interpretation of these verses. In his Letter to the Galatians Paul claims that he had been called from the very beginning to preach the gospel to the nations/gentiles (ἔθνη, Gal 1:16). If Paul were called to go to the Jews too, it would be difficult to imagine why he would agree to the limitation of his work to the "gentiles" (ἔθνη), uncircumcised non-Jews, while Peter would to go to the circumcised (Gal 2:7, 9). Paul's apostleship is therefore to the "gentile" peoples and not to the "nations" as a geographical entity with no discrimination between Jew or gentile.

Romans 15:15–16 must be considered in connection with the evidence of Rom 1:5–6, 13–15. Several scholars have noted the *inclusio* formed by 1:5–15 and 15:14–32:

Verbal/Thematic Link	Opening/Thanksgiving	Apostolic Parousia
1. Praise of the Roman Christians	1:7–8	15:14
2. Paul's apostleship		
a. An act of grace	1:5 (χάριν)	15:15 (χάριν δοθεῖσάνμοι)
b. Its "service" character	1:9 ("whom I serve")	15:15 ("in priestly service")
c. Directed to the gentiles	1:5, 13 (τὰ ἔθνη)	15:16, 27 (τὰ ἔθνη)
d. To win obedience	1:5 (εἰς ὑπακοὴν)	15:18 (εἰς ὑπακοὴν)
3. Paul's gospel		
a. References to the gospel	1:1, 9, 15	15:16, 19, 20
b. His service to the gospel	1:9 (εὐαγγέλιον)	15:16 (εὐαγγέλιον)
c. His task to preach the gospel	1:15 (οὕτως … εὐαγγελίσασθαι)	15:19 (πεπληρωκέναι τὸ εὐαγγέλιον) 15:20 (οὕτως … εὐαγγελίζομαι)
4. Visit to the Christians in Rome		
a. Desire/intention to come	1:10, 11, 13, 15	15:22, 23, 24, 29, 32
b. Inability to come	1:10 (implied), 1:11	15:22

---

46. Cranfield, *Romans*, 1:20; Guerra, *Romans and the Apologetic Tradition*, 28. Note the lack of discussion in Cranfield and Guerra. For an earlier articulation of this view, see Lightfoot, *Biblical Essays*, 312–15.

Verbal/Thematic Link	Opening/Thanksgiving	Apostolic Parousia
c. Submissive to God' will	1:10 (θέλημα τοῦ θεου)	15:32 (θέλημα θεου)
d. Expectation of mutual benefit	1:12	15:23–24, 28–29, 32
5. Obligation	1:14 (ὀφειλέτης εἰμί)	15:25–27 (ὀφείλω [2x])
6. Reference to praying	1:9–10 (Paul)	15:30–32 (Romans)[47]

Romans 15:15–16 must therefore be interpreted in a parallel fashion to 1:5–6, 13–15. If Paul is grounding his relations with the Romans in his apostolic commission to the gentiles in chap. 1, he is most likely doing the same in chap. 15. The same reasoning would apply equally in reverse. Consistently and conspicuously in each of these passages, Paul mentions the Romans in the context of his apostolic mission to the gentiles. In other words, Paul is *identifying* the Romans as within the sphere of his apostolic labors. If these verses were merely saying, with Cranfield, that Paul labored among the nations of the world, then Paul would be stating the obvious and the repetitious emphasis (1:5–6, 13–15; 15:15–16) would be unnecessary.

Romans 15:15–16 follows shortly after the direct address of the audience in v. 10: "Rejoice, O gentiles, with his people." As Elliott pointed out:

> The simplest reading of the causal links in 15.14–16 (διά, εἰς τὸ εἶναι, ἵνα) implies that in Paul's view, the sanctity of the "gentiles' offering," the προσφορὰ τῶν ἐθνῶν, depends on the Romans' response to this letter. Paul has directed an admonitory letter (νουθετεῖν, 15.14) to the Romans, on the basis of "grace" or "commission" (χάρις; cf. 1.15) given to him to be a minister of Christ Jesus to (all of) the gentiles, "*in order that* the offering of the gentiles may be acceptable, sanctified by the Holy Spirit."[48]

The Romans will contribute to this offering by their obedience (thus chaps. 12–15). The paraenesis of these chapters closes in 15:9–12 with praise for God's turning the gentiles' hearts to thanksgiving.[49]

---

47. Dunn, *Romans 1–8*, 857; Andreas B. Du Toit, "Persuasion in Romans 1:1-17," *Biblische Zeitschrift* ns 33 (1989): 199–200; chart compiled by Weima, "Preaching the Gospel," 355.

48. Elliott, *Rhetoric*, 91–92. On Elliott's larger thesis that the letter functions as a *substitute* for Paul's personal preaching of the gospel, see Schreiner's critique, *Romans*, 55 n. 13.

49. Elliott, *Rhetoric*, 92–93. Note that Paul *never expresses any concern* about Jewish opposition to his views or that his trip stands in jeopardy. It is the "acceptability" or

A Direct Address of the Audience (Romans 11:13)

In Rom 11:13 Paul speaks directly to his audience and identifies them as "you gentiles." Steve Mason contended that the address of Rom 11:13 is nothing more than a rhetorical device. He found it "remarkable" that anyone should see this as evidence of a gentile audience for the letter. The turn to gentiles in 11:13 proved, for Mason, that all that had preceded in the letter was indeed addressed to Jews. Further, the gentiles addressed in 11:13 were not members of the Roman church. Paul was talking about those who have been "grafted in" — his gentile converts in the East.[50] Romans 11:13–32, for Mason, was a "rhetorical aside." Thorsteinsson faulted Mason for confusing the second person singular of diatribal rhetoric (for an aside) with the second person plural of direct address, as employed here.[51] Romans 11:25 further demonstrates that 11:13–32 is direct address to Paul's actual audience: "Brothers and sisters (ἀδελφοί), I want *you* to understand." Likewise, 12:1–8 continues the address to the entire audience as "brothers and sisters" (ἀδελφοί) who form one body. Romans 11:13–32 offers no indication of a shift in audience between vv. 13 and 25 (or between 11:13 and 12:1–8 for that matter).[52] The audience remains the gentiles of 11:13.

Does the δέ at the beginning of Rom 11:13 signal a turn to the gentile *portion* of the audience? Moo noted how Paul's phrasing supports a gentile audience: "Paul does not say 'I am speaking to those of you who are Gentiles.'"[53] The emphasis in 11:13 is on the word "you" (ὑμῖν), since this word is placed first in the sentence. The shift in v. 13 is not from one part of the audience to another but rather from the consistent use of third person pronouns for Israel and the Jews in the paragraphs that preceded to the second person pronouns for Paul's

---

"sanctity" of the offering that is at stake, i.e., the obedience of the gentiles (15:18).

50. Mason contended that every use of "gentile" in the letter refers to Paul's converts in the East; "'For I Am Not Ashamed of the Gospel,'" 273–74; "Paul," 216–17. In reckoning real gentiles in the East as those to whom Paul rhetorically turns, Mason's critique of a *fictive* dialogical partner in Rom 2:17 would not apply in the same way as Mason's reasoning in 11:13; contra Reichert, *Römerbrief*, 107. Mason left the tension between his interpretation of 2:17 and 11:13 unresolved.

51. Thorsteinsson, *Paul's Interlocutor*, 109 n. 73.

52. Theodor Zahn, *Der Brief des Paulus an die Römer* (KNT 6; 2d ed.; Leipzig: A. Deichert [Georg Böhme], 1910), 532–4, considered it the most natural reading that the addressees should remain the same. He was followed by Reichert, *Römerbrief*, 107, although neither Zahn nor Reichert considered this argument decisive. Zahn considered 12:1–8 to be directed to *all* the Romans, that is, including Jews.

53. Moo, *Romans*, 691 n. 39. Unlike Rev 2:24 with its similar grammatical construction, Paul does *not* describe "you" as "the rest" (τοῖς λοιποῖς) of the audience.

audience itself—"a change of focus from those being spoken of to those being spoken to."[54] As Stanley Stowers pointed out: "The *menoun* with *de* after *hymin* makes it almost impossible to understand Paul as turning to one group within the letter's audience (the gentile portion) rather than to the letter's audience as a whole."[55] Stowers explained: "The part of the sentence set in contrast by *menoun* corrects any mistaken impression that the discussion of Israel's future has no place in this letter so wholly addressed to gentiles and the gentile situation."[56] Paul never offers a corresponding "you Jews" (similarly 11:17–18, 24).[57] The explicit identification of the audience as "you gentiles" stands beside Paul's discussion of Israel in the third person. The "you" (gentile) / "they" (Israel) contrast, which begins in 11:13, continues through 11:32. So "you" are the wild olive shoots while "they" are the natural branches (11:17–24). Or in 11:28: "As regards the gospel *they* are enemies of God for *your* sake; but as regards election *they* are beloved, for the sake of *their ancestors*" (emphasis added). Similarly, in 10:1 Paul addresses his audience as "brothers and sisters" and then speaks of Israel in the third person in 10:1–3 (see also 9:30–32). This third-person "Israel" *includes* the remnant that believes in Christ. Paul's point throughout 9:6–23 is that "not all Israelites truly belong to Israel" (v. 6). God has always been working with a remnant *within* Israel (see also 9:27; 11:1–10). The "brothers and sisters," to whom Paul communicates concerning Israel in 10:1, whether the bulk of Israel or the believing remnant, must therefore be gentiles. Even as Paul consistently distinguishes "you" Romans from the Israelites ("they"), he speaks of "them" as "*my* own people, *my* kinsmen according to the flesh" (9:3 (emphasis added); cf. 11:1). Finally, with respect to 11:13, note that once again Paul identifies his gentile audience in connection with his ministry as "apostle of the gentiles" (εἰμι ἐγὼ ἐθνῶν ἀπόστολος). This is the same juxtaposition of gentiles and Paul's apostolic ministry that is repeatedly emphasized in 1:5–6, 13–15, and 15:15–16. Romans 11:13 therefore offers further proof that Paul is including the Romans *as gentiles* within the domain of his apostolic authority.

---

54. Thorsteinsson, *Paul's Interlocutor*, 110, who followed Hort: "Exposition has here passed into exhortation and warning, and the warning is exclusively addressed to Gentiles; to Christians who had once been Jews not a word is addressed" (cited by Thorsteinsson, 110–11 n. 76).

55. Stanley K. Stowers, *A Rereading of Romans: Justice, Jews, and Gentiles* (New Haven: Yale Univ. Press, 1994), 288–89.

56. Ibid., 288.

57. See the discussion of Rom 2:17–29 later in this chapter.

Further Evidence of the Addressees as Gentiles
(Romans 6:19; 13:11–14)

Paul occasionally describes his readers in language more appropriate for gentiles. Romans 6:19 is a striking instance: "For just as you once presented your members as slaves to impurity (τῇ ἀκαθαρσίᾳ) and to greater and greater iniquity (τῇ ἀνομίᾳ), so now present your members as slaves to righteousness." Dunn observed in his commentary on this verse: "The Jewish character of the new elements is very marked. ἀκαθαρσία, ἀνομία, and the theme of ἁγιάζειν/ ἁγιασμός are all characteristic of and prominent in Jewish thought . . . and much less typical of wider Hellenistic concerns."[58] This is the only place in Romans where Paul, of his own choice, employs "lawlessness" (ἀνομία—note the doubled use of the word).[59] Later in Rom 14 Paul speaks of those who observe the distinction between "clean" (καθαρά) and "unclean" (κοινός) foods, a distinction from Moses' Law.[60] To characterize a Roman audience that included Jews in language that was associated with gentiles would be insulting and rhetorically self-defeating. The Jewish members of the Roman congregations would hardly appreciate being described as formerly "Law-less" and "unclean." The Jewish people, who "have the law" (τὰ νόμον ἔχοντα—by contrast in 2:14) and are "[in] the law" (ἐν νόμῳ—2:14) stand opposed to those "who do not possess the law" (2:14).[61] Although Dunn thought that Paul was writing to a mixed audience of both Jews and gentiles, he conceded that the use of the terms "impurity" and "iniquity" (or better, "Law-lessness") "strengthened the implication that Paul was writing the letter with Gentiles largely or principally in view."[62]

Paul exhorts his audience in Rom 13:11–14 to "lay aside the works of darkness" that formerly characterized them and to "put on the armor of light." Living "honorably as in the day" entails avoidance of reveling (κώμοις), drunkenness (μέθαις), sexual excess (κοίταις), licentiousness (ἀσέλγεια), quarreling (ἔρις), and jealousy (ζῆλος). This list of vices is reminiscent of the vice list of Rom 1:18–32 that, for many commentators, typified Jewish polemic against gentiles. If 1:18–32 were indeed targeting gentile vices, and if Paul were now saying that such behavior characterized his audience's past, then Rom 13:11–14 would be

---

58. Dunn, *Romans 1–8*, 346.

59. The usage in Rom 4:7 is in an OT quotation; Dunn, *Romans 1–8*, 346.

60. See the discussion of these terms later in this chapter.

61. In Phil 3:5–6 Paul describes his pre-Christian existence as "blameless" with respect to the righteousness of the Law. He speaks of non-Christ-believing Jews' misguided "zeal" for Moses' Law in Rom 10:2–3.

62. Dunn, *Romans 1–8*, 347.

describing the audience's past as gentiles. On the other hand, Jews on occasion may have been guilty of the vices in 13:11–14. Even in 1:18–32 Paul hardly limits his criticism to gentiles, although gentiles would be primarily in mind.[63] The emphasis on idolatry and the worst sexual sins in 1:18–32 are more characteristic, from a Jewish standpoint, of gentile behavior. Only one of the vices in 13:11–14 (ἔρις) overlaps with 1:18–32. The overlap of vices would likely have been greater had Paul wanted the connection to be unmistakable. Both 1:18–32 and 13:11–14 are, however, vice lists, and insofar as the passages parallel each other, Rom 13:11–14 may offer some evidence that the audience is gentile.

Romans 6:19 and 13:11–14 do not exhaust the evidence for a gentile audience. For instance, in 8:15 Paul claims that his readers have received the "spirit of adoption" (πνεῦμα υἱοθεσίας). This befits a gentile audience. The Jews, on the other hand, already received that privilege centuries before (9:4 — ὧν ἡ υἱοθεσία).[64] Cumulatively, this evidence parallels the direct identification of the audience as gentile recipients of Paul's apostolic ministry. The strength of the evidence for a gentile audience demands attention!

The Category of God-Fearer

Although Romans is ostensibly addressed to gentiles, Jewish concerns dominate throughout. Interpreters have long noted the "double character" of this letter. Despite the strong evidence for a gentile audience in the opening verses, the thanksgiving, and the apostolic parousia, the intense focus on Jewish customs and Scriptures leads most commentators to conclude that a significant number of Jews were in the audience.[65] Jews, however, were not the only ones intensely interested in the unique heritage of Israel. Many gentiles found the Jewish Scriptures and customs attractive as well. They were called God-fearers.

The archetypal "God-fearer" in the Book of Acts is Cornelius, the Roman military officer.[66] Because of Cornelius's gentile identity, Peter was hesitant to enter his household.[67] Yet Luke describes him as "righteous" (δίκαιος, 10:22), "pious" (εὐσεβής; 10:2), and a respected man (10:22) who was known for his

---

63. See esp. Rom 1:23 and the discussion in A. Andrew Das, *Paul, the Law, and the Covenant* (Peabody, Mass.: Hendrickson, 2001), 171–77.

64. So Thorsteinsson, *Paul's Interlocutor*, 120.

65. For example, Mason, "Paul," 210–11; Anthony J. Guerra, "Romans: Paul's Purpose and Audience with Special Attention to Romans 9–11," *RB* 97 (1990): 224–25, 237.

66. Acts 10:1–2, 4, 7, 14, 17, 22, 28, 34–35; 11:3.

67. Acts 10:28, 34–36, 38, 45; 11:2–3, 17–18.

alms to Israel (10:2, 4, 31). Luke also calls him a "fearer of God" (φοβούμενος τὸν θεόν; 10:2, 22). Scot McKnight demonstrated that Cornelius was only the first of several instances of gentile sympathizers attending synagogues in the Book of Acts. In Acts 13:16, 26, 43 at Pisidian Antioch, Luke juxtaposes two distinct and contrasting groups. The first is labeled "Israelites," "brothers," or "Jews," and the second is labeled "God-fearers" or "devout proselytes." When the Jews opposed Paul in 13:45, he turned to the gentiles. In other words, when the first group disagreed, Paul focused his efforts on the second group — *gentile* "God-fearers" and "proselytes."[68] Paul's turn from the Jews to gentiles is confirmed by a pattern that dominates throughout the remainder of Acts: Paul and his companions responding to Jewish rejection by preaching to gentiles (for example, 18:1–7; 19:8–10; 28:25–28).[69] In Acts 17:4 Paul preaches to Jews and to "Greek God-fearers" (τῶν σεβομένων Ἑλλήνων). Acts 17:17 is ambiguous (τοῖς σεβομένοις), but the article is most likely anaphoric and refers back to the same class of gentile God-fearers participating in synagogue services in 17:2–4. In Acts 18:7 Titius Justus, a "worshiper of God" (σεβομένου τὸν θεόν), takes Paul into his home next door to the synagogue after the apostle has been rejected by the Jews.[70] As

---

68. Scot McKnight, *A Light among the Gentiles: Jewish Missionary Activity in the Second Temple Period* (Minneapolis: Fortress Press, 1991), 111. Note also the synonymous usage of "God-fearer" and "proselyte" for the second group; Luke does not appear to be concerned with making a strong distinction. Both terms would refer to gentiles. McKnight therefore challenged Max Wilcox's conclusion, in "The 'God-Fearers' in Acts: A Reconsideration," *JSNT* 13 (1981): 108–9, that the "proselytes" of 13:43 must be converts to Judaism as opposed to those born as Jews and identified in the first group of that verse. McKnight, *Light among the Gentiles*, 157–58 n. 61, suggested that, rather than read an understanding of "proselyte" from Acts 2:10 and 6:5 into 13:43, one may just as well move from 13:43 backward to the definition of proselyte in 2:10 and 6:5.

69. The prominent women of 13:50 (listed alongside the leading [gentile] men of the city) are not likely Jewish (cf. the parallel description of the gentile Lydia in 16:14 [Luke employs the phrase for gentiles]); McKnight, *Light among the Gentiles*, 111; Beverly Roberts Gaventa, *Acts* (ANTC; Nashville: Abingdon, 2003), 237; Ben Witherington III, *The Acts of the Apostles: A Socio-Rhetorical Commentary* (Grand Rapids: Eerdmans, 1998), 493; again, contra Wilcox, "God-Fearers,'" 110. Even though Wilcox admitted that Lydia is a gentile because of her name, her connection with Thyatira, and the reference to Philippi in 16:12, he preferred to read this verse in light of his doubtful assumption of Jewish women in 13:50 rather than recognize 16:12 as further proof that his reading of 13:50 was on the wrong track.

70. Note the gentile identity of Titius Justus implied by the turn to the gentiles in 18:6. His name also suggests a Roman citizen. See McKnight, *Light among the Gentiles*, 112; James D. G. Dunn, *The Acts of the Apostles* (Valley Forge, Pa.: Trinity Press

John Collins remarked: "Luke would scarcely have given such prominence to a category that was not known to exist at all."[71] Although Luke does not appear to be using phrases such as "fearers of God" (φοβούμενοι τὸν θεόν) and "reverencers of God" (σεβόμενοι τὸν θεόν) as technical terms for gentile sympathizers, the concept of gentile sympathizer or God-fearer is demonstrable both in Acts and in the wider Greco-Roman world. That is, many gentiles throughout the Roman empire frequented synagogues and were sympathetic to Judaism.[72] They remained distinct from ordinary Jews or proselytes.

The very existence of the category of God-fearer has been vigorously challenged by the work of A. T. Kraabel, who considered the category a Lukan invention.[73] Luke needed the category, Kraabel argued, to explain how Christianity

---

International, 1996), 243. McKnight, *Light among the Gentiles*, 112, also concluded that Luke conceptualizes two kinds of proselytes (a broader classification): full converts and "God-fearers." In other words, a "God-fearer" should be distinguished from ordinary gentiles even though he or she is not a full convert.

71. Collins, "Symbol of Otherness," 183. Irina Levinskaya, *The Book of Acts in Its Diaspora Setting* (*The Book of Acts in its First Century Setting* 5; ed. Bruce W. Winter; Grand Rapids: Eerdmans, 1996), 120–26, also demonstrated that the "disappearance" of the God-fearers in Acts "is justified not by the theological, but by the historical setting" (p. 125): "If the Jewish community in a particular place decided to put a stop to the Christian mission, it was by far the easiest way to do so by using their influence on the God-fearers, among whom there were socially high-ranking and influential people. Consequently God-fearers, in places where these happened, ceased to be responsive to the Christian message and the missionaries found that those Gentiles who were not connected with the synagogues were easier to approach." God-fearers, then, are rightly stressed by Luke since they could be either the core group for new gentile Christian communities or the greatest obstacle to Christianity's spread.

72. Against the technical usage of this language (even if not agreeing with every aspect of their interpretation of Acts), see Kirsopp Lake, "Proselytes and God-Fearers," in *The Acts of the Apostles* 5 (*The Beginnings of Christianity* 1; ed. F. J. Foakes Jackson and Kirsopp Lake; London: Macmillan, 1933; repr. Grand Rapids: Baker, 1979), 85–88; Wilcox, "'God-Fearers,'" 102–22; Witherington, *Acts of the Apostles*, 342–44 (who struck the right balance between the lack of technical designation and yet the existence of the category itself). Ancient authors could use this language (φοβούμενοι; σεβόμενοι) for both Jews and gentiles (e.g., *Jos. Asen.* 4:7; 23:9–13; 27:1; 28:7; 29:3; Josephus, *Ant.* 1.3.1 §96; 20.2.4 §41).

73. Acts 10:2, 22, 35; 13:16, 26, 43, 50; 16:14; 17:14, 17; 18:7 (φοβούμενοι τὸν θεόν, "fearers of God"; σεβόμενοι τὸν θεόν, "reverencers of God"). A. Thomas Kraabel, "The Disappearance of the God-Fearers," *Numen* 18 (1981): 113–26; repr. in *Diaspora Jews and Judaism: Essays in Honor of and in Dialogue with A. Thomas Kraabel* (ed. J. Andrew Overman and Robert S. MacLennan; SFSHJ 41; Atlanta: Scholars, 1992); idem, "Synagoga Caeca: Systematic Distortion in Gentile Interpretations of Evidence

became a largely gentile phenomenon. Ancient inscriptions did not bear witness to the category, and Greco-Roman literature only offered a few references of dubious value. After removing Luke's testimony from consideration, Kraabel saw the application of "God-fearer" terminology (φοβούμενοι τὸν θεόν; σεβόμενοι τὸν θεόν) limited in antiquity to Jews or their converts. For instance, the pseudepigraphic *Joseph and Asenath* describes the patriarchs Levi, Benjamin, and Joseph as θεοσεβής (4:9; 21:1; 23:9–10; cf. 8:7, 9). A Miletus inscription would seem to confirm Kraabel's conviction that Jews "are also God-fearers."[74] Several scholars have followed Kraabel in expressing skepticism about the evidence for God-fearers.[75]

Kraabel posed a serious and useful challenge to the conventional view that "God-fearers" were gentile sympathizers of Judaism. Although Kraabel thought that Luke invented the category of "God-fearer," he ignored likely antecedents for Luke's language in the Septuagint. The Septuagint employed the phrase οἱ φοβούμενοι in 2 Chr 5:6; Pss 115:9–11 (LXX: 113:17–19); 118 (LXX 117):2–4; 135 (LXX 134):19–20; and Mal 3:16. Second Chronicles 5:6 appears to distinguish οἱ φοβούμενοι from the assembly of Israel mentioned separately. The Psalms passages also appear to distinguish οἱ φοβούμενοι τὸν κύριον from the house of Israel, the house of Aaron, and the house of Levi. Luke's phrasing (φοβούμενοι τὸν θεόν) may well be borrowed from the Septuagint.[76] J. Andrew Overman considered it possible that Luke derived the notion of a group of gentiles sympathetic with Judaism from the Septuagint.[77] The Septuagintal term προσήλυτος (Heb. גר) may have referred to resident aliens who had not

---

for Judaism in the Early Christian Period," in *"To See Ourselves as Others See Us": Christians, Jews, "Others" in Late Antiquity* (ed. Jacob Neusner and Ernest S. Frerichs; SPSH; Chico, Calif.: Scholars, 1985), 224–32; repr. in Overman and MacLennan, *Diaspora Jews and Judaism*; Robert S. MacLennan and A. Thomas Kraabel, "The God-Fearers: A Literary and Theological Invention," *BAR* 12/5 (1986): 46–53, 64; repr. in Overman and MacLennan, eds., *Diaspora Jews and Judaism*.

74. Adolf Deissmann, *Light from the Ancient East* (trans. Lionel R. M. Strachan; New York: George H. Doran, 1927), 451–52: "Place of the Jews, who are also God-fearing" (Τόπος Ειουδέων τῶν καὶ θεοσεβίον).

75. For example, Judith M. Lieu, *Neither Jew nor Greek? Constructing Early Christianity* (SNTIW; London: T&T Clark, 2002). This recent volume includes her 1994 essay "Do God-Fearers Make Good Christians?"

76. Malachi 3:16, on the other hand, employs οἱ φοβούμενοι for righteous Israelites as opposed to those Israelites who "test God."

77. J. Andrew Overman, "The God-Fearers: Some Neglected Features," *JSNT* 32 (1988): 21.

converted to Judaism.[78] Although the Rabbis employed the term גֵּר for a full convert to Judaism, in the pre-Rabbinic period Philo provided evidence that the term προσήλυτοι could be used for uncircumcised gentiles who had renounced idolatry and had associated with the Jews apart from full conversion.[79] Septuagintal precedent would explain, then, why Luke considered the προσήλυτοι to be distinct from the Jews even while associated with them (Acts 2:10; 13:43).[80] As for Luke himself, John Collins observed: "Even if one regards the account of Paul's missionary activity in Acts as largely fictional, the fiction requires verisimilitude to establish plausibility."[81]

Kraabel argued from silence when he claimed that gentiles interested in Judaism must not have existed since the epigraphic remains never identified them as such. Kraabel wrongly limited himself to the term θεοσεβής to the neglect of other epigraphical and papyrological evidence for gentile sympathizers. An Aphrodisias inscription from Asia Minor appeared after Kraabel's initial study. The inscription commends two groups that contributed to a Jewish building. The "God-fearers" (θεοσεβεῖς) are listed separately (under their own heading) from the Jewish contributors (including proselytes).[82] J. M. Reynolds and J. M. Tannenbaum painstakingly demonstrated that the names of labeled "God-fearers" proved that they were gentiles. Of the fifty-four listed, only two names might be of Jewish origin. The majority of the names of those labeled as full members of the Jewish community were, in fact, Jewish.[83] The names therefore offer excellent evidence for "God-fearers" as a separate group from Jews and proselytes (!) in the synagogues.[84] The Aphrodisias inscription's use of "God-fearer" for non-Jews renders the conclusion more likely that "God-fearers" in other ancient

---

78. Ibid., 18–9.

79. Philo, *Virt.* 20 §§102–3; *QE* 2 §2; Thomas M. Finn, "The God-Fearers Reconsidered," *CBQ* 47 (1985): 82–83; Overman, "The God-Fearers," 19; Harry Austryn Wolfson, *Philo: Foundations of Religious Philosophy in Judaism, Christianity, and Islam* (Cambridge: Harvard Univ. Press, 1948), 2:369–74.

80. Overman, "The God-Fearers," 20.

81. John J. Collins, *Between Athens and Jerusalem: Jewish Identity in the Hellenistic Diaspora* (2d ed.; Grand Rapids: Eerdmans, 2000), 270.

82. Irina Levinskaya, *The Book of Acts*, 70–74.

83. J. M. Reynolds and J. M. Tannenbaum, *Jews and God-Fearers at Aphrodisias* (CPSSup 12; Cambridge: Cambridge Philological Society, 1987), 1–131.

84. See the popular summary of Reynolds and Tannenbaum's work in Robert F. Tannenbaum, "Jews and God-Fearers in the Holy City of Aphrodite," *BAR* 12/5 (1986): 54–57; also the helpful summary of the evidence in Colin J. Hemer, *The Book of Acts in the Setting of Hellenistic History* (WUNT 49; Tübingen: J. C. B. Mohr [Paul Siebeck], 1989; repr., Winona Lake, Ind.; Eisenbrauns, 1990), 444–47.

inscriptions are likewise gentiles. Certainty of whether the Aphrosisias God-fearers and contributors attended the synagogues themselves or entertained the Jewish God along with others or were merely patrons is not possible.[85] In an inscription from Acmonia (*CIJ* 766), Julia Severa, the high priestess in the imperial cult (under Nero's reign), erected a building which she then donated to the Jewish community to use as a synagogue.[86] Most of the Aphrodisias gentiles may likewise have been only benefactors, but they were at least demonstrating some degree of interest in the Jewish community by providing financial support.[87] Some of the Aphrodisias God-fearers, on the other hand, served in ways beyond

---

85. Levinskaya, *Book of Acts*, 76–78. Jerome Murphy-O'Connor, "Lots of God-Fearers? *Theosebeis* in the Aphrodisias Inscription," *RB* 99 (1992): 422, pointed out that the inscription was near a soup kitchen for the poor and vagrants. Gentiles may only have contributed out of their sense of civic duty for the less advantaged. The patrons may only have been interested in the Jewish vote. Murphy-O'Connor contrasted the level of synagogue involvement of the gentiles on face b of the inscription with the Jews, proselytes, *and God-fearers* listed on face a.

86. Thomas Kraabel granted that Julia Severa "is proof of the attractiveness of Acmonian Judaism to Gentiles in the first century" ("Judaism in Western Asia Minor under the Roman Empire [diss., Harvard University, 1968], 242, as cited by Overman, "The God-Fearers," 22, 26). That Julia Severa's beneficence should be viewed in terms of "social allegiance and status" rather than "personal religious needs and commitment," see Judith M. Lieu, "Do God-Fearers Make Good Christians?" in *Crossing the Boundaries: Essays in Biblical Interpretation in Honour of Michael D. Goulder* (ed. Stanley E. Porter, Paul Joyce, and David E. Orton; Biblical Interpretation Series 8; Leiden: Brill, 1994), 337–38. Lieu, however, was too quick to minimize gentile *religious* interest in Judaism. Certainly attraction to Jewish ritual customs may not *necessarily* be in the context of a relationship with the Jewish community (p. 341), but such a relationship is the most natural context for this interest.

87. Paul R. Trebilco, *Jewish Communities in Asia Minor* (SNTSMS 69; Cambridge: Cambridge Univ. Press, 1991), 158–59 (cf. 252 n. 60), has argued the likelihood that gentile God-fearers served as benefactors for the Sardis synagogue. Several members of the Jewish community played a prominent role in the city's life. Their involvement in public life would likely have stirred gentile interest in the Jewish community. The synagogue forecourt may have been the site of a public fountain. Finally, the grandeur of the synagogue building itself appears to be designed to advance the status of the Jewish community in their immediate gentile world.

On gentile, non-community members being granted the title of *archisynagogos* for their patronage to the community (with perhaps little or no other connection to the community), see Tessa Rajak and David Noy, "Archisynagogoi: Office, Title and Social Status in the Greco-Jewish Synagogue," *JRS* 83 (1993): 88–89. Rajak and Noy also noted Tyrronius Cladus, an *archisynagōgos* for life, has the same *nomen* as several prominent pagans in Acmonia.

mere patronage by devoting themselves to study and prayer, as did the Jews.[88] Alongside the face of the block with the list of God-fearers (side b), the first face of the block lists Jewish patrons at Aphrodisias. The words, "Below (are) listed the (members) of the decany of the students (or disciples or sages) of the law, also known as those who fervently (or continuously) praise God."[89] Included in the list of those who study the Mosaic Law and praise the Jewish God are two "*theosebeis*," Emmonios and Antonios. Murphy-O'Connor writes:

> In other words, Emmonios and Antonios belong to a Jewish group which met for prayer and study. Morever, they are formally distinguished from the three proselytes, who have adopted Jewish names. In a word they are precisely what NT scholarship has traditionally considered God-fearers to be, namely, Gentiles who, without going through the rite of conversion, participate fully in the life of the synagogue.[90]

A manumission inscription from Panticapaeum (*CIRB* 71) offered further epigraphic evidence for "God-fearers." This inscription dates significantly to the first century CE and may be translated: "I free in the *proseuchē* Elpias, my household slave, so that he will be undisturbed and unassailable by any of my heirs, on condition that he show diligence towards the *proseuchē* under the guardianship of the congregation of the Jews, and reveres God [θεὸν σέβων]."[91] H. Bellen and Baruch Lifshitz both independently suggested emending the text to read θεοσέβων (God-fearer), but their arguments were decisively overturned by Irina Levinksaya.[92] Binder pointed out in response that, irrespective of Levinskaya's objections, Elpias must have been the equivalent of a gentile God-fearer, since a Jew or proselyte would not have been required to attend synagogue services as a condition of release.[93] Binder noted four other inscriptions from Phangoria and Panticapaeum making similar stipulations for at least eight other released

---

88. Tannenbaum, "Jews and God-fearers," 57.

89. Reynolds and Tannenbaum, *Jews and God-Fearers at Aphrodisias*, 41.

90. Murphy-O'Connor, "Lots of God-Fearers?" 423; contra Kraabel.

91. Translation by Donald D. Binder, *Into the Temple Courts: The Place of Synagogues in the Second Temple Period* (SBLDS 169; Atlanta: Society of Biblical Literature, 1999), 385. For the original text, see Levinskaya, *Book of Acts*, 74.

92. Heinz Bellen, "Die Assuage einer bosporanishen Freilassungsinschrift (CIRB 71) zum Problem der 'Gottfürchtigen,'" JAC 8 (1965): 171–76; Baruch Lifshitz, "Notes d'épigraphie grecque," RB 76 (1969): 95–96; Levinskaya, *Book of Acts*, 75–76.

93. The emancipated slave remained closely connected to the *proseuche*, but the precise obligations are debated and difficult to determine.

slaves.[94] Most scholars in recent years have concluded that the inscriptional evidence does indeed support the category of "God-fearer."

Josephus spoke of Fulvia—who converted to Judaism—as a "proselyte" (προσεληλυθυῖαν τοῖς Ἰουδαϊκοῖς, *Ant.* 18.3.5 §82), but he referred to Nero's wife Poppaea—who was not exclusively interested in Judaism—as a "God-fearer" (θεοσεβής). Poppaea had intervened on behalf of the Jews when they asked Nero not to tear down a Temple wall that prevented Agrippa from viewing the sacrifices (*Ant.* 20.8.11 §§189–96).[95] At another point, Josephus managed to secure the release of some Jewish priests by appealing to Poppaea (*Life* 3 §16).[96] Josephus's use of the term "God-fearer" for Poppaea paralleled Luke's usage (Acts 16:14; 18:7, σεβόμενοι τὸν θεόν). Josephus referred to "God-fearers" again in *Ant.* 14.7.2 §110: "But no one need wonder that there was so much wealth in our temple, for all the Jews throughout the habitable world, and those who

---

94. Binder, *Into the Temple Courts*, 386; cf. Levinskaya, *Book of Acts*, 74–76. For additional inscriptional evidence that supports the semi-technical status of "God-Fearers," see Levinskaya, *Book of Acts*, 51–74.

95. The use of θεοσεβής here in Josephus contradicts Kraabel's thesis that the term refers exclusively to Jews. J. Andrew Overman faulted Kraabel for ignoring Josephus, who speaks of gentiles interested in the Jewish religion (e.g., *Ag. Ap.* 2.39 §282); "The God-Fearers: Some Neglected Features," *JSNT* 32 (1988): 22; repr. in Overman and MacLennan, *Diaspora Jews and Judaism*. As for Kraabel's distinction between θεοσεβής and Luke's σεβόμενοι τὸν θεόν, John Gager rightly noted that the first is simply an adjectival contraction of Luke's phrasing. The variety of Luke's expressions for the God-fearers does not argue against the existence of gentile sympathizers, who are otherwise well attested. Gager concluded from the large number of texts that speak of sympathetic gentiles that such texts' "weight and number cannot be ignored. Furthermore, there can be little doubt that these texts refer primarily to Gentiles who were not full converts. They were certainly not regarded as full Jews. Yet they were welcomed, as were Christians at a later date, by many synagogues. Indeed, they appear to have been designated by a recurrent, if unofficial set of terms, and to have been the intended audience for a body of Jewish literature. In short, far from it being the case that the many literary texts have been read in the light of Acts, one must say that an interpretation of Acts that ignores them must be said to lack plausibility" ("Jews, Gentiles, and Synagogues in the Book of Acts," *HTR* 79 [1986]: 92–93).

96. Some have doubted whether a Roman queen would have repudiated idolatry. Although Josephus does not explicitly call Poppaea a Jewish "sympathizer," Louis H. Feldman, *Jew and Gentile in the Ancient World: Attitudes and Interactions from Alexander to Justinian* (Princeton, N.J.: Princeton Univ. Press, 1993), 351–52, contended that these favorable actions toward the Jews only make sense if she were. At this point, the primary issue is Josephus' support or lack of support for the category of "God-fearer." I take up the question of Poppaea's status as a "God-fearer" at greater length in chap. 4—with a positive verdict.

worshiped God [God-fearers; πάντων τῶν κατὰ τὴν οἰκουμένη Ἰουδαίων καὶ σεβομένων τὸν θεόν], even those from Asia and Europe, had been contributing to it for a very long time." Years ago Kirsopp Lake noted the lack of the article before σεβομένων τὸν θεόν and concluded that the phrase further described *the Jews* and not a separate class of people.[97] Ralph Marcus, however, corrected Lake's faulty conclusion regarding the lack of the article before σεβομένων τὸν θεόν: "In good Greek when two different classes are associated in some activity or state, the article is omitted before the noun which designates the second of the two classes" (BDF §276).[98] Further, the phrase "even those from Asia and Europe" would be redundant if referring to the Jews "throughout the habitable world."[99] "God-fearers" is therefore a distinct group from the Jews. Josephus's terminology, again, parallels Luke's description of gentile "God-fearers" in Acts (13:16, 26, 50; 16:14; 17:4, 17; 18:17).[100] Similarly, Josephus spoke of Greeks attracted to Jewish religious ceremonies who were "in some measure" incorporated with the Jews (*War* 7.3.3 §45; see also *Ant.* 3.8.9 §217). On Josephus's use of the word

---

97. Lake, "Proselytes and God-Fearers," 85.

98. Ralph Marcus, "The Sebomenoi in Josephus," *JSS* 14 (1952): 249; also Daniel B. Wallace, *Greek Grammar beyond the Basics: An Exegetical Syntax of the New Testament* (Grand Rapids: Zondervan, 1996), 270–90, esp. pp. 286–87. This Josephus reference proves Kraabel wrong in his contention that the precise word combination for "God-fearer" in Acts does not occur outside the NT in any Christian or Jewish text (*Synagoga Caeca*, 27). Note also Louis H. Feldman's change of mind (*Jew and Gentile*, 350) in favor of Ralph Marcus's reading of this text as favoring "God-fearers."

99. As a reference to "God-fearers," the descriptive phrase identifies them as residing *beyond* nearby Egypt and Syria — thus Trebilco, *Jewish Communities in Asia Minor*, 147–48.

100. This is not to deny that sometimes "God-fearer" may also refer to proselytes (e.g., Acts 13:43), with John J. Collins, "A Symbol of Otherness: Circumcision and Salvation in the First Century," in "*To See Ourselves as Others See Us*," 180–81. On the other hand, as Levinskaya, *Book of Acts*, 120–26, demonstrated, often the "God-fearer" is *not* a proselyte. Cornelius in his duties would have participated in the official cult. The women of high standing in Acts 13:50 were likely not proselytes, since such instances are exceedingly rare in the first century, and even those few instances are disputed. The "Hellenes" in Acts 17:17 are typically gentiles who are not proselytes. Collins granted that Cornelius is a "God-fearer" who is *not* a proselyte.

Also, Overman, "The God-Fearers," 18–20, cautioned that Luke's use of "proselyte" most likely refers to what moderns would consider "God-fearers" rather than full converts. If so, Luke's presentation of gentile sympathizers of Judaism may be more wide-ranging than Kraabel realized. Overman demonstrated parallels to this use of "proselyte" in Jewish literature contemporary to Paul and claims the technical use for full converts, while paralleled in the first century, would not come until the Rabbis.

"incorporated" (μοῖραν), Thomas Finn commented that "Josephus elsewhere uses [this word] to denote sharing in fate, lot, or destiny. Implied, at least, is some kind of (undisclosed) status which distinguished these synagogue adherents from other Gentiles."[101] These gentiles did not become full proselytes. Josephus (*War* 2.17.10 §454) described Metilius, the commander of the Roman garrison at Jerusalem, who saved his life by promising to "turn a Jew" (ἰουδαΐσειν) even to the point of circumcision (μέχρι περιτομῆς). Feldman commented on this passage: "The fact that Josephus adds 'even to be circumcised' indicates that there is probably a distinction between 'turning Jew' (i.e., Judaizing) and becoming a full Jew."[102] Josephus described people journeying for four months to venerate God at the Jewish Temple, but Moses' Law did not permit them as gentiles to partake of the sacrificial victims (*Ant.* 3.15.3 §318).[103] With exaggeration he boasted: "The masses have long since shown a keen desire to adopt our religious observances; and there is not one city, Greek or barbarian, nor a single nation" (*Ag. Ap.* 2.39 §282 [Thackeray, LCL]).

Several other sources further substantiate that "God-fearer" is a viable first century category, especially in Rome. Louis Feldman observed: "We have more information about 'sympathizers' in Rome than we do for any other region in the ancient world."[104] Scot McKnight concluded similarly: "[T]here is evidence for a rather consistent presence of 'God-fearers,' or Jewish sympathizers, in Rome from the earliest times."[105] Martial derided "the breath of fasting Sabbatarian women" (*Epigrammata* 4.4, lines 7–12).[106] Plutarch decried the Greek adoption of barbarian superstitions, including the "keeping of the Sabbath" (*Superst.* 3.166a).[107] Quintus Caecilius was suspected by Plutarch of having Judaized (ἔνοχος ' Ἰουδαίζειν). Cicero, who took up the case that Caecilius wanted to prosecute, remarked: "What has a Jew to do with Verres?" (Plutarch, *Cic.* 7.6.5). In other words, people thought that Caecilius was practicing some but apparently not all of the Jewish customs. He certainly could not have become a full Jew because of his position and duties on behalf of Rome. Suetonius related the early first century grammarian Diogenes' refusal to lecture on any other day

101. Finn, "The God-Fearers Reconsidered," 82.

102. Feldman, *Jew and Gentile*, 350.

103. Binder, *Into the Temple Courts*, 383, faulted Kraabel for ignoring this sort of literary evidence.

104. Feldman, *Jew and Gentile*, 344.

105. McKnight, *Light among the Gentiles*, 74.

106. As translated by Menahem Stern, *Greek and Latin Authors on the Jews and Judaism* (Jerusalem: The Israel Academy of Sciences and Humanities, 1974), 1:523–24.

107. Stern, *Greek and Latin Authors*, 1:549.

than the Sabbath. The Emperor Tiberius, put off by this response, mockingly ordered him to "return seven years later," that is, in a sabbatical year (Suetonius, *Tib.* 32.2). Suetonius (*Tib.* 36) also narrated Tiberius's banishment in 19 CE of the Jews and those of the same race (*gentis*) along with those "pursuing" (*sectantes*) similar beliefs (*similia*).[108] Suetonius therefore distinguished Jews of the same race (*gentis*) from others who pursued similar beliefs as the Jews — in effect, "God-fearers."[109] Seneca, during the reign of Nero, remarked on how "The conquered [Jews] have given laws to the conquerors" and then observes that most of the people observe the Sabbath with little understanding of the origin and meaning of the rite.[110] Petronius in the mid-first century CE distinguished those who worship the "pig god" [Jewish dietary laws] from those who were circumcised and observed the Sabbath.[111] Feldman commented on this text: "Such a passage, we may add, coming from a satirist, has force only if the situation is sufficiently frequent to be recognized by the reader."[112] Epictetus noted the individual who merely played "the part (ὑποκρίνη) of a Jew when you are a Greek." Epictetus then added: "Whenever we see a man halting between two faiths (ἐπαμφοτερίζοντα), we are in the habit of saying, 'He is not a Jew, he is only acting the part (ὑποκρίνεται)'" (*Diatr.* 2.9.19–21 [Oldfather, LCL]). Epictetus contrasted, in typical Greco-Roman fashion, an individual's words or appearance (λόγῳ) with their deeds/reality (ἔργῳ). Some people were only acting the part of a Jew but had not yet become one. At the end of the first century, in his tax on the Jews Emperor Domitian distinguished those who lived as Jews without acknowledging the Jewish faith (*vel inprofessi Iudaicam viverunt vitam*) and those who concealed their Jewish origin (Suetonius, *Dom.* 12.2). The first group could not refer to Christians since by this point in time the Roman government knew the difference between Jews and Christians. The first group must therefore have referred to "sympathizers."[113] Dio Cassius (67.14.2) spoke of Flavius Clemens and his wife, Flavia Domitilla, "drifting" (ἐξοκέλλοντες) into Jewish ways at the end of the first century CE As Feldman pointed out: "[I]t is hardly likely that a consul would have practiced Judaism fully as a proselyte and have avoided participating in the state religious celebrations that

---

108. Feldman, *Jew and Gentile*, 345.

109. Ibid.

110. As quoted by Augustine, *Civ.* 6.11 (*NPNF*¹ 2:120–21).

111. Fragment 37 (Poem 24 in Heseltine, LCL); cited as fragment 50 (*AL* 696, Bu 47) in *Petronius* (ed. and trans. R. Bracht Branham and Daniel Kinney; Berkeley: Univ. of California Press, 1996), 163.

112. Feldman, *Jew and Gentile*, 346.

113. Ibid., 347.

were so integrally a part of the Roman Empire. . . . "['Drifted'] can hardly refer to conversion, which is an absolute step; it almost surely refers to step-by-step adoption of one practice of Judaism after another."[114] In the early-second century CE the satirist Juvenal referred to full, circumcised, Jewish proselytes (*metuunt*; *Sat.* 14.101, "fear") alongside "sympathizers" to Judaism just a few lines earlier (14.96, *metuentes*). He wrote: "Some happen to have been dealt a father who respects the sabbath. They worship nothing except the clouds and the spirit of the sky. They think there is no difference between pork, which their father abstained from, and human flesh. In time, they get rid of their foreskins" (*Sat.* 14.96–99 [Braund, LCL]). This was "a process which begins with the paternal generation attracted to Judaism and ends with the filial converted to it."[115] The first generation of "sympathizers" observing Sabbath (*metuentem sabbata*) and dietary laws influences a second generation to undergo circumcision (*praeputia ponunt*) and full conversion.[116]

To conclude, many gentiles throughout the ancient world found various aspects of Judaism attractive.[117] Ancient authors frequently commended the antiquity of the Jewish religion, their virtue — whether wisdom, courage, temperance, or piety — and their leader (Moses).[118] References to God-fearers frequently identify gentile individuals or groups with varying degrees of interest in Judaism — from patrons who are also worshiping other gods, to those interested in certain Jewish customs, to uncircumcised gentile sympathizers devoted to the Jewish God, to actual proselytes.[119] Greco-Roman commentary on the

---

114. Ibid.

115. Thomas M. Finn, "The God-Fearers Reconsidered," 81. Finn faulted Kraabel for not appreciating the significance of such a passage.

116. Feldman, *Jew and Gentile*, 347.

117. For a helpful survey of the evidence of widespread interest in Judaism and its customs, see especially Louis H. Feldman, "Reflections on Rutgers's 'Attitudes to Judaism in the Greco-Roman Period,'" *JQR* 86 (1995): 153–70, but Leonard Victor Rutgers's critique of widespread Jewish proselytizing activity needs to be heeded ("Attitudes to Judaism in the Greco-Roman Period: Reflections on Feldman's *Jew and Gentile in the Ancient World*," *JQR* 85 [1995]: 361–95). Martin Hengel and Anna Maria Schwemer, *Paul between Damascus and Antioch: The Unknown Years* (Louisville: Westminster John Knox, 1997), 75–76, helpfully suggested "not 'mission' but 'power of attraction.'" Gentiles simply found much about Judaism attractive (see the full discussion in Hengel and Schwemer, *Paul between Damascus and Antioch*, 61–80).

118. Feldman, *Jew and Gentile*, 177–200 (for admiration of the antiquity of Judaism), 201–32 (for the virtue of the Jews), 233–87 (on Moses).

119. See the helpful classification in Shaye J. D. Cohen, "Crossing the Boundary and Becoming a Jew," *HTR* 82 (1989): 14–15. See also John M. G. Barclay, "Paul among Diaspora Jews: Anomaly or Apostate?" *JSNT* 60 (1995): 89–120. For a useful catalog

gentile practice of Jewish customs, Jewish descriptions of gentiles attracted to the ancestral faith, and the narrative of Acts all converge to suggest that gentile God-fearers were often well integrated into the synagogue communities. The category of "God-fearer" or "sympathizer" may prove helpful for the Romans debate, especially when considering the double character of the letter.

Potential Evidence for Jewish Addressees

For most scholars, the double character of Romans — a letter addressed to gentiles but dominated by Jewish concerns — requires the presence of Jews in the audience. The extensive quotations and allusions to the Jewish Scriptures, the sustained focus on the place of the Jewish people in God's plan, and the discussions of Abraham, the Mosaic Law, and the blessings of Israel all point toward the presence of Jews in the Roman congregations. At one point, Paul even directly addresses "the Jew" (Rom 2:17). Paul does seem to be identifying Christ-believing Jews in the Roman audience when he lists several of his "kins-people" in Rom 16:21. This evidence militates — conclusively for most — against an entirely or almost entirely gentile audience. The "weak" in Rom 14:1 — 15:6 observe the typically Jewish distinction between "clean" and "unclean" food along with the Sabbath. Romans 14:1 — 15:6 should be considered lastly since this passage offers additional, critical clues into the situation at Rome beyond the ethnic identity of the audience.

Knowledge of the Scriptures

The content of Paul's letter clearly reflects the influence of the Jews and their synagogues in Rome. What would necessitate such an extended discussion of the Mosaic Law (Rom 2–3, 7, 13), justification by faith, circumcision (Rom 4), and God's faithfulness to "Israel" (Rom 9–11)? These are precisely the sort of issues that do *not* figure in Paul's first letter to the gentile Thessalonians, a congregation

---

of evidence for gentile sympathizers toward Judaism in general, quite apart from the argument over the term "God-fearers," see Louis H. Feldman, "The Omnipresence of the God-Fearers," *BAR* 12/5 (1986): 58–69. Feldman, *Jew and Gentile*, 288–341, even made a case that the Jews were indeed active in seeking converts to their religion (against the current consensus as represented by McKnight, *Light among the Gentiles*, and Martin Goodman, *Mission and Conversion: Proselytizing in the Religious History of the Roman Empire* [Oxford: Oxford Univ. Press, 1994]). Again, see Rutgers's critique of Feldman, "Attitudes to Judaism in the Greco-Roman Period," 361–95, and the remarks of Erich S. Gruen, *Diaspora: Jews amidst Greeks and Romans* (Cambridge, Mass.: Harvard Univ. Press, 2002), 46–47.

impacted very little, if at all, by a Jewish Christian constituency. Paul even claims that his Roman readers are, in whole or in part, "people who know the law" (7:1; cf. 15:4), and he offers an extended discussion of the fate of ethnic Israel in chaps. 9–11. Whereas the Scriptural passages Paul cites in Galatians appear to be largely those already in use by his opponents (or passages employed by Paul to counter his opponents' texts), he assumes that his Roman addressees will know the Scriptures and be able to follow his reasoning. He freely draws upon and discusses the Scriptural heritage of the Jews (for example, 1:17; 4:6–8, 17). He may even be assuming knowledge of Jewish-Christian creedal formulae (1:3–4; 3:24–25; 4:25). This knowledge of the Jewish Scriptures, including perhaps even the "mercy seat" (ἱλαστήριον, 3:25), could only be accounted for if at least some of the members of the Roman audience of Paul's letter had been in contact with the synagogues, in which they had been instructed in the Septuagintal translation of the Jewish Scriptures.

The Septuagint was not otherwise known in Greco-Roman circles.[120] Louis Feldman has been a lone voice in modern scholarship arguing otherwise.[121] He agreed with the early-twentieth-century position that Hellenistic Jewish literature often had a missionary purpose.[122] He was convinced that the Septuagint was read in non-Jewish circles. He pointed to gentile sources aware of Gen 1: Pseudo-Longinus's *On the Sublime* 9.9; Ocellus Lucanus (an allusion to Gen 1:28).[123] Feldman speculated that the Septuagint served as a source for the works

---

120. Collins, *Between Athens and Jerusalem*, 6; Donald Juel, *Messianic Exegesis: Christological Interpretation of the Old Testament in Early Christianity* (Philadelphia: Fortress Press, 1988), 16.) Whereas Feldman cited a long list of Jewish works that profess an interest in potential gentile readers, Goodman rightly recognized that there is no evidence of actual gentile interest in that literature (e.g., Wisdom of Solomon, Fourth Maccabees, *Joseph and Asenath*).

121. Louis Feldman, "Jewish Proselytism," in *Eusebius, Christianity, and Judaism* (ed. Harold W. Attridge and Gohei Hata; Detroit, Mich.: Wayne State Univ. Press, 1992), 381–86.

122. So also G. Klein, *Der älteste christliche Katechismus und die jüdische Propaganda-Literatur* (Berlin: Georg Reimer, 1909), esp. pp. 242–45; Peter Dalbert, *Die Theologie der hellenistisch-jüdischen Missionsliteratur unter Ausschluss von Philo und Josephus* (TF 4; Hamburg-Volksdorf: Herbert Reich, 1954), e.g., p. 20: "Es ist in verschiedenen Schriften deutlich zu spüren, wie sehr es den Verfassern ein Anliegen ist, ihre Kult- oder Zeremonialgesetze den Heiden verständlich zu machen." See, however, the rather telling critiques by Goodman, *Mission and Conversion*, 78–81, and McKnight (*Light among the Gentiles*, 57–62, 75–76). Victor Tcherikover was the first to expose the inadequacy of the evidence that non-Jews were reading Jewish literature, in "Jewish Apologetic Literature Reconsidered," *Eos* 48 (1956): 171–83.

123. Feldman, "Jewish Proselytism," 401 n. 79.

of Tacitus (*Hist.*, Book 5) and Pompeius Trogus. Feldman also noted several monographs written about the Jews and key Scriptural figures (Abraham, Joseph, Moses, Job, Solomon, and Jeremiah). On the other hand, only one non-Jewish author, Pseudo-Longinus, quoted directly from the Septuagint, and even this author did not demonstrate any knowledge of the Septuagint beyond Gen 1. Feldman tried to argue otherwise by noting that "Longinus" did not provide the name Moses. Feldman concluded from this omission that Longinus not only knew that the "lawgiver of the Jews" was Moses but also that his audience would be equally familiar with the Torah and its author. Surely, Feldman reasoned, Longinus would not cite a source unfamiliar to his audience. From this textual silence, Feldman surprisingly concluded: "[I]t seems clear that he was acquainted with much more from the Bible than this passage alone."[124] The fact that Feldman, who is rather encyclopedic in his references, was only able to cite gentile knowledge of the Septuagintal Gen 1 demonstrates that the translation was not read outside Jewish communities. As for Rome, church tradition corroborates that the first Christians there were ultimately indebted to the Jewish community for their knowledge of the Scriptures. Ambrosiaster, in an important passage from ca. 375 CE, asserts:

> It is established that there were Jews living in Rome in the times of the apostles, and that those Jews who had believed [in Christ] passed on to the Romans the tradition that they ought to profess Christ but keep the law. . . . One ought not to condemn the Romans, but to praise their faith; because without seeing any signs or miracles and without seeing any of the apostles, they nevertheless accepted faith in Christ, although according to a Jewish rite [*ritu licet Judaico*].[125]

Ambrosiaster's description confirmed that the Roman church had its origin within a Jewish context. So why not conclude from this evidence the presence of Christ-believing Jews in Rome? Indeed, through the years many interpreters have concluded that Jewish Christians were even the majority of the Roman church.[126]

---

124. Ibid., 382.

125. *PL* 17.46, cited from A. J. M. Wedderburn, *The Reasons for Romans* (SNTIW; Edinburgh: T&T Clark, 1988), 51; see also Raymond E. Brown and John P. Meier, *Antioch and Rome: New Testament Cradles of Catholic Christianity* (New York: Paulist, 1983), 110–11. See also the additional evidence cited by Mason, "'For I Am Not Ashamed of the Gospel,'" 262.

126. Thus Ferdinand Christian Baur, *Paul, the Apostle of Jesus Christ: His Life and Works, His Epistles and Teachings; A Contribution to a Critical History of Primitive Christianity* (2 vols.; London: Williams & Norgate, 1873–1875; repr. Peabody, Mass.: Hendrickson, 2003), 1:346–47; W. Manson, *Hebrews*, 172–84; T. Fahy, "St. Paul's Romans Were Jewish Converts," *ITQ* 26 (1959): 182–91; Theodor Zahn, *Der*

Paul assumes that his audience knows the Jewish Scriptures when he refers to them as "you who know the law" (Rom 7:1). Scholars often overlook the fact that gentile "God-fearers" *also* associated with synagogue Jews and had learned to treasure the Jewish Scriptures. Juvenal (*Sat.* 14.96–106, esp. 101) wrote of Roman gentiles who actively studied the Jewish Scriptures without having been circumcised.[127] Luke similarly presupposes a knowledge of the Scriptures among the "God-fearers" (Acts 13:16–41; 17:2, 4). Even while Paul identifies his readers as people "who know the law" (7:1), the immediate context suggests that they are God-fearers. In 7:4–6 Paul describes the Romans as having "died to the law" and being "discharged from the law." Just prior to 7:1, in 6:19, Paul identifies his audience as former slaves to "impurity" and greater and greater "lawlessness." Impurity and lawlessness would better describe God-fearers of the Law rather than Law-observant Jews.[128] In other words, Paul's assumption that his audience "knows the law" does not require the presence of Jewish Christians since gentile Christians, with experience in the Roman synagogues, could account for knowledge and appreciation of the Law.[129] Thorsteinsson rightly observed with respect to 7:1:

> Indeed, the fact that Paul makes this mention at all strongly suggests the opposite, viz. that the addressees here are of non-Jewish origin. There would have been no reason for him to add this observation to an address to Jews, since no Jew would not have "known the Law." What Paul's remark reveals instead is that he presupposes at least some familiarity with the Law by his readership.[130]

Brief des Paulus an die Römer (KNT 6; 2d ed.; Leipzig: A. Deichert [Georg Böhme], 1910), 18–20; idem, *Introduction to the New Testament* (Grand Rapids: Kregel, 1953), 1.421–34; and, more recently, Mason, "Paul," and idem, "For I Am Not Ashamed of the Gospel." For Zahn, Romans 11:13 represents the first turn to the gentiles in the letter. For other advocates of a strong Jewish presence or even a majority Jewish presence, see Guerra, *Romans and the Apologetic Tradition*, 22–42; and Steven Mason. Guerra (p. 40) faulted Wedderburn: "A second error, in my view is his conclusion that the audience of Romans is predominantly Gentile."

127. Peter Lampe, *From Paul to Valentinus: Christians at Rome in the First Two Centuries* (trans. Michael Steinhauser; Minneapolis: Fortress Press, 2003), 70.

128. See the discussion of 6:19 earlier in the chapter.

129. Dunn, *Romans 1–8*, 359, stressed a Roman audience inclusive of just such gentile Christians: "Certainly the phrase ['knows the Law'] does not constitute grounds for seeing the bulk of the Roman believers as Jewish Christians."

130. Thorsteinsson, *Paul's Interlocutor*, 119. Mason, "Paul," 211–13, therefore overextended the evidence to assume that Paul's cautious approach to the Scriptures proves a Jewish audience.

At the same time, Christopher Stanley emphasized in his recent study of Paul's use of Scripture that the knowledge of the Hebrew Bible on the part of the Roman audience should not be overestimated. The citations of Scripture serve a rhetorical purpose to enhance the authority of Paul's argument. The apostle frames his Scriptural reasoning "in such a way that a person with little or no specific knowledge of the Jewish Scriptures could grasp his essential point."[131] Stanley concluded that the Roman audience possessed a broad knowledge of the stories and laws of the Jewish Scriptures but would not have had to supply the original context of the quotations. Even those gentiles who had not had experience in the synagogues would have been able to follow the argument. The Scriptural quotations would rhetorically reinforce Paul's reminder of the Jewish roots of the Christian faith for any who would be disdainful. The likelihood that gentile Christians would be familiar with this particular aspect of Moses' Law is increased, however, by Jesus' interpretation of Deut 24:1–4 and Paul's appropriation of that teaching in 1 Cor 7:10–11, 39–40.[132]

Paul's supposed use of pre-Pauline Jewish-Christian traditions is of little or no use in identifying the audience. Although older scholarship was convinced of a Jewish Christian creedal tradition behind the "mercy seat" reference in Rom 3:25–26, recent scholarship has raised serious doubts whether these verses are, in fact, pre-Pauline.[133] Similarly with respect to Rom 1:2–4, nothing in these verses requires that they are pre-Pauline.[134] Even if pre-Pauline traditions in Romans were placed on a firmer footing, these traditions would say more about Paul than his readers (unless Paul expected his audience to recognize the source of the traditions — which he does not). Peter Lampe wrote tellingly with respect to 1 Clement, another document from early Roman Christianity that included Jewish traditions:

---

131. Christopher D. Stanley, *Arguing with Scripture: The Rhetoric of Quotations in the Letters of Paul* (New York: T&T Clark, 2004), 140; see the full discussion of Romans on pp. 136–70.

132. Peter J. Tomson, "What Did Paul Mean by 'Those Who Know the Law'? (Rom 7.1)," *NTS* 49 (2003): 573–81, esp. pp. 576–77.

133. For a critical but sympathetic review of the "mercy seat" identification in Rom 3:25, see Das, *Paul, the Law, and the Covenant*, 137–42. For a thorough refutation of the evidence usually cited for pre-Pauline material in 3:25–26, see ibid., 133–37.

134. James M. Scott, *Adoption as Sons: An Exegetical Investigation into the Background of ΥΙΟΘΕΣΙΑ in the Pauline Corpus* (WUNT 2/48; Tübingen: Mohr [Siebeck], 1992), 229–36; Vern S. Poythress, "Is Romans 1:3–4 a *Pauline* Confession After All?" *ExpTim* 87 (1975–76): 180–83; Christopher G. Whitsett, "Son of God, Seed of David: Paul's Messianic Exegesis in Romans 2 [sic]:3–4," *JBL* 119 (2000): 661–81.

As a Gentile Christian, Clement takes up Jewish traditions that were alive in the urban Roman Christian community. How did those traditions manage to get there? Who imported them? Were these carriers Jewish Christians? We may also think of Gentile Christians, who as *sebomenoi* had absorbed the intellectual richness of the synagogue. One must therefore be cautious in making conclusions.[135]

Clearly, some of the members of the Roman congregations had been in contact with the synagogues, but from this involvement one cannot determine whether they were Jews or gentile "God-fearers" or a combination of the two groups.

Direct Address to "the Jew" (Romans 2:17–29)

Paul does appear to address his audience as "you Jews" in Rom 2:17–29, but most interpreters, following the groundbreaking work of Stanley Stowers, have recognized these verses as a rhetorical address since the section conforms to the style of diatribe in which fictive addressees were standard fare.[136] The main features of this style include vivid dialogue with second-person singular address to an imaginary interlocutor who has introduced objections, questions, or new points. The authorial response to the interlocutor often includes (1) a vocative, which can range in tone from the negative (ταλαίπωρε) to the more neutral (ἄνθρωπε), (2) a phrase of rejection, such as μὴ γένοιτο, and (3) a characteristic particle (for example, ἀλλά, τί οὖν, γάρ, τί δέ) introducing a supporting statement.[137]

Not all have found the diatribal style of these verses convincing evidence that the "Jew" is fictive. Richard Hays considered Rom 2:17 "potentially fatal to Stowers's reading." The text explicitly identified a Jew as part of the encoded audience. Further, even if one were to grant a fictive address, Stowers conceded that 2:17–29 would censure any in the audience who fit this particular type of

---

135. Lampe, *From Paul to Valentinus*, 76. That Rom 3:24–25 with its allusion to the "mercy seat" would be comprehensible in a God-fearing context and to gentiles in the Roman congregations in general, see especially Stephen Finlan, *The Background and Content of Paul's Cultic Atonement Metaphors* (Academia Biblica 19; Atlanta: Society of Biblical Literature, 2004), 142–43.

136. Stanley K. Stowers, *The Diatribe and Paul's Letter to the Romans* (SBLDS 57; Chico, Calif.: Scholars Press, 1981), 177; Thorsteinsson, *Paul's Interlocutor*, 124–30; Paul J. Achtemeier, "Romans 3:1–8: Structure and Argument," in *Christ and His Communities: Essays in Honor of Reginald H. Fuller* (ed. Arland J. Hultgren and Barbara Hall; ATRSup 11; Cincinnati: Forward Movement, 1990), 77–87.

137. Abraham J. Malherbe, "*Me Genoito* in the Diatribe and Paul," in *Paul and the Popular Philosophers* (Minneapolis: Fortress Press, 1989), 25–33; repr. from *HTR* 73 (1980): 231–40; Thorsteinsson, *Paul's Interlocutor*, 125.

person.[138] Hays concluded that since the particular type of person identified in 2:17–29 boasted in the possession of the Mosaic Law, Jews or Jewish Christians must be included in the audience.[139] Hays does not account, however, for the harshness of Paul's language with respect to the interlocutor (for example, 2:24), a harshness which would hardly befit *Christ-believing* Jews in Paul's audience.

Douglas Campbell disputed whether Paul was addressing an imaginary opponent, as scholars such as Stowers and Thomas Schmeller contended.[140] Campbell faulted Stowers and Schmeller for relying on formal, literary publications within the Greco-Roman philosophical tradition or classroom notes reworked for publication. Paul's letters addressed practical situations in ways this literature did not.[141] Romans surely was not a school exercise or pedagogical text.[142] Campbell also doubted whether actual class discussions were as controlled as the carefully crafted texts might otherwise suggest: "If the diatribe reflects the classroom, it will probably also at times reflect the interaction in that context."[143] Paul also employed the diatribal style in passages where he appeared to be addressing specific objections from actual objectors (for example, Gal 2:17–18, the objection of Paul's rivals; Rom 11:13, gentile arrogance within his audience; Rom 3:8, an actual charge).[144] Diatribal rhetoric never addressed an entirely imaginary interlocutor with absolutely no connection to a situational context.[145]

---

138. Stowers, *Rereading of Romans*, 11–12.

139. Hays, "'The Gospel Is the Power of God,'" 36.

140. Stowers, *Diatribe and Paul's Letter*, 96–98, 112–13; idem, "Paul's Dialogue with a Fellow Jew in Rom. 3.1–9," *CBQ* 46 (1984): 707–22; idem, "Social Stature, Public Speaking and Private Teaching: The Circumstances of Paul's Preaching Activity," *NovT* 26 (1984): 59–82; Thomas Schmeller, *Paulus und die "Diatribe": Eine vergleichende Stilinterpretation* (NTAbh ns 19; Münster: Aschendorff, 1987).

141. Douglas A. Campbell, "Determining the Gospel through Rhetorical Analysis in Paul's Letter to the Roman Christians," in *Gospel in Paul: Studies on Corinthians, Galatians and Romans for Richard N. Longenecker* (ed. L. Ann Jervis and Peter Richardson; JSNTSup 108; Sheffield: Sheffield Academic, 1984), 325–26.

142. Ibid., 327.

143. Ibid.

144. Ibid., 326–27.

145. Ibid., 325–31. In "False Presuppositions in the Study of Romans," *CBQ* 36 (1974): 112–19; repr. in *The Romans Debate*, 102–25 (rev. and enl. ed.; ed. Karl P. Donfried; Peabody, Mass.: Hendrickson, 1991), Karl Donfried critically reviewed Bultmann's original thesis on the diatribe. He too questioned whether the diatribal rhetoric bore no connection to the situation at Rome: "We might well ask, how can Paul deal with the sensitive question of Jewish-gentile Christian relations in Rome without first entertaining the more general question of the relationship between Jew and Gentile in God's plan of history" (p. 116).

A diatribal style did not, then, exclude the presence of genuine opponents in Paul's letter. To conclude, as Campbell did, that Rom 2:17 *requires* Jews or Jewish Christian opponents within the audience of the letter overextends the evidence. The Romans could simply have been attracted to or interested in Jewish customs without actually *being* Jewish. Such an interest alone would warrant the rhetorical turn to "the Jew." *Gentiles* inclined toward Jewish observances could well have been feasible targets for Paul's rhetoric. Paul may even have been laying a trap for those in his audience who were *less* sympathetic toward Judaism. Paul would spring that trap later in the letter.[146]

Campbell's foremost objection to an imaginary interlocutor in Rom 2:17 was that Stowers and others wrongly extrapolated from formal literary works to such ordinary epistolary writings as Romans. Runar Thorsteinsson agreed with Campbell that Stowers's examples of the style were largely from non-epistolary works. Discerning an imaginary interlocutor, as opposed to a very real person, is difficult in actual letters. Nevertheless, ample evidence abounds from the letters of Cicero, Seneca, Diogenes, and others that the diatribal style with its employment of imaginary interlocutors could figure in ordinary letters as well. The ancients viewed letters as a substitute for an actual dialogue and therefore employed dialogical elements, which included rhetorical questions and answers. Although these dialogues engaged the addressee, some letters did indeed employ an imaginary conversational partner. As with the diatribal style attested in other genres, the interlocutor is introduced by a verb of saying, an interrogative phrase, or a conjunction. The context of the letter demonstrates that an imaginary interlocutor is envisioned. As in other genres, such letters employ the diatribal style to introduce objections that will advance the discussion. Some of the letters that employ the diatribal style are even addressed to multiple recipients as is the case in Paul's letter to the Romans. These parallels suggest that Paul is engaging a fictitious Jewish teacher for the sake of his own argument.[147]

---

146. James C. Miller, *The Obedience of Faith, the Eschatological People of God, and the Purpose of Romans* (SBLDS 177; Atlanta: Society of Biblical Literature, 2000), 135, inexplicably dismissed this possibility in spite of the evidence provided by the frame of the letter. He devoted a substantial portion of his study, pp. 23–60, to the frame (1:1–15; 15:14—16:2) and yet never reckoned with the repeated inclusion of the Romans among the rest of the gentiles. See the full discussion of Miller's thesis in chap. 1, above. In short, Miller is without strong support for Jewish objectors as the target of Paul's argumentation. Gentile sympathizers with the Jewish Law would equally suffice.

147. Thorsteinsson, *Paul's Interlocutor*, 126–44. Thorsteinsson went further to introduce the novel but ultimately questionable thesis that Paul is turning to a *gentile* interlocutor in 2:17–29: the individual *calls himself* a Jew. The textual issues that led Thorsteinsson to this thesis may be resolved without recourse to his hypothesis. Thorsteinsson

The Listing of Jews in Romans 16:1–16

Romans 16 has been cited by most interpreters as a decisive passage proving that a significant portion of the Roman congregations was Jewish.[148] Paul's Jewish co-workers Prisca and Aquila (Acts 18:2) are present. Further, Paul had referred to his fellow Jews as "compatriots" (συγγενής) in Rom 9:3 and employs the same word in Rom 16 for Andronicus, Junia (v. 7), and Herodion (v. 11). Peter Lampe, in his important study of Rom 16, cited three names from the chapter that are paralleled in the Jewish inscriptions from Rome — Maria, Rufus, and Julia — but Lampe also pointed out that these names could equally refer to gentiles. He concluded that they were probably gentiles since Paul did not call them his "compatriots."[149] Interpreters have concluded that at least five of the

---

believed that Paul was combating gentiles in his audience who were proselytes or on the verge of proselytism by undergoing circumcision. Paul wishes to dissuade his addressees of their desire for circumcision. In that case, would Paul really say to this gentile, or any gentile Christian: "What is the value of circumcision? Much in every way" (3:1). Or 2:25: "Circumcision indeed is of value if you obey the law." If Thorsteinsson were correct, the differences between Romans and Galatians would be difficult to comprehend. Paul in Galatians is vociferous against gentile reception of circumcision. The same tone is hardly evident in Romans in the discussion of circumcision. Thorsteinsson also did not reckon with the possibility that Paul may not have misread Isa 52:5 after all. The oppression of the nations in Isa 52 may not be distinguished from Israel's own sin that leads to exile in the Isaianic context (40:2; 42:24–25; 43:22–28; 50:1). "Paul rightly applies this text to the Jews of his own day. . . . [F]or Paul the deliverance [from exile] had come in the good news about Jesus Christ (Isa. 52:7–10), but many of his Jewish contemporaries had rejected this message" (Schreiner, *Romans*, 135). Stanley Stowers found the motif of the Jews as a light to the nations in 2:19–20, 24; 3:2 incomprehensible if addressed to anyone other than Jews. Jewish disobedience is precisely what provokes gentile slander (2:25 is connected by γάρ to the preceding paragraph) (review of Runar M. Thorsteinsson, *Paul's Interlocutor in Romans 2*, *JTS* 56 [2005]: 564–55).

148. On the authenticity of Rom 16 as an integral component of Paul's letter, see the discussion in chap. 1, above, and esp. Harry Gamble Jr., *The Textual History of the Letter to the Romans* (SD 42; Grand Rapids: Eerdmans, 1977); James G. D. Dunn, *Romans 9–16* (WBC 38B; Dallas: Word, 1988), 884–85; Karl Donfried "A Short Note on Romans 16," in *The Romans Debate*, 44–52 (rev. and enl. ed.; ed. Donfried; Peabody, Mass.: Hendrickson, 1991; repr. from *JBL* 89 [1970]: 441–49.

149. Peter Lampe, "The Roman Christians of Romans 16," in Donfried, *The Romans Debate*, 224–25; idem, *From Paul to Valentinus*, 75–76; contra Esler, *Conflict and Identity*, 118, who, in the absence of any firm evidence, could only speculate that a number of the individuals *may have been* Judeans/Jews. Judeans "*may have* approached 50 percent"(!) of the Roman Christians (emphasis added).

people mentioned in Rom 16:1–16 must be Jewish: Prisca, Aquila, Andronicus, Junia, and Herodion.

Metaphorical Kinship Language

Although Peter Lampe touted "compatriots" (συγγενής) as firm evidence of Jews in the Roman congregations, he never considered that the Greek word he and others translated as "compatriot" ordinarily means "relative" or "kin" throughout Greek literature rather than "fellow national."[150] The six, non-Pauline occurrences of this word in the New Testament *all* mean "family member." Romans 9:3 is the only departure from this rule, and Paul goes out of his way to signal the departure from ordinary usage by modifying συγγενής with the words κατὰ σάρκα ("according to the flesh"; note the lack of such a qualification in Rom 16).[151] While *the context* of Rom 9:3 suggests "compatriot," nothing in the context of Rom 16 requires a departure from the usual meaning of the word as "relative."[152]

Paul regularly and frequently employs familial language metaphorically for members of the Christian movement.[153] He identifies his addressees as "brothers and sisters" or "family members" (for example, ἀδελφός, 1 Thess 1:4; 2:4 [cf. 4:9]; 1 Cor 8:11, 13; 15:58; Phil 3:1; 4:1). Epaphroditus and Timothy are his "brothers" (ἀδελφός, Phil 2:25; 1 Thess 3:2). Apphia is a "sister" (ἀδελφή, Phlm 2). A Christian wife is also a "sister" (1 Cor 9:5). Paul refers to himself as "father" (πατήρ, 1 Cor 4:15, 1 Thess 2:11; Phlm 10). Timothy and Onesimus are Paul's "children" (τέκνον, 1 Cor 4:17; Phil 2:22; Phlm 10; Philemon himself is only a "brother"). The Corinthians are Paul's "children" (1 Cor 4:14–15; 2 Cor 6:13; 12:14). The patriarchs are πατέρες ἡμῶν (our ancestors/ forefathers). Some only bear the name of "brother" (ἀδελφὸς ὀνομαζόμενος; 1 Cor 5:11; 2 Cor 11:26).[154]

---

150. See LSJ and BDAG.

151. See chap. 3 on the unusual and qualified use of "brothers" (ἀδελφοί) in Rom 9:3.

152. Rightly Mason, "For I Am Not Ashamed of the Gospel," 259.

153. This is a point recognized more frequently in the last decade. See especially Reidar Aasgaard, *"My Beloved Brothers and Sisters!" Christian Siblingship in Paul* (JSNT-Sup 265; London: T&T Clark, 2004); Karl Olav Sandnes, *A New Family: Conversion and Ecclesiology in the Early Church with Cross-Cultural Comparisons* (SIHC 91; Bern: Peter Lang, 1994). On family language in 1 Thessalonians, see Trevor J. Burke, *Family Matters: A Socio-Historical Study of Kinship Metaphors in 1 Thessalonians* (JSNTSup 247; London: T&T Clark, 2003).

154. For further discussion of the relationship between household and church, see Ekkehard W. Stegemann and Wolfgang Stegemann, *The Jesus Movement: A Social*

David Rhoads even considered the metaphorical kinship of the Galatians as "children of Abraham, children of God" the central organizing concept of Paul's letter.[155] The Galatian rivals contended that God's children are the children of Abraham, and those children are marked by circumcision. Paul responds that God is already the Galatians'"Father" (1:1, 4). Those who believe are the children of Abraham (υἱοί; 3:7). So "if you belong to Christ, then you are Abraham's offspring" (σπέρμα; 3:29). As recipients of adoption (υἱοθεσία; 3:5), the Galatians have the rights and privileges of "sons" (υἱοί) and may call God "Abba, Father" (Αββα ὁ πατήρ, 4:6; cf. Mark 3:31–35 par). They are "minors" and "heirs" who have come of age and are no longer under guardians and trustees (4:1–2). Paul laments in 4:19 over "his children" (τέκνα μου) for whom he is again in the pains of labor. He speaks of children birthed by the free woman and children birthed by the slave woman. The free woman is the Jerusalem above "and she is our mother" (4:21–26). The child of the slave, however, will not share the inheritance (4:30; cf. the "false brothers" of 2:4). As "children of the promise," the Galatians should care for one another in love (5:16 — 6:10) as members of the "household of faith" (οἰκείους τῆς πίστεως). Paul closes with yet another reference to the Galatians as "brothers and sisters" (6:18; cf. 1:11; 3:15; 4:12; 5:11, 13; 6:1).

The Letter to the Romans employs metaphorical familial language frequently and similarly. Paul regularly refers to the Romans as "brothers and sisters" (ἀδελφός, Rom 1:13; 7:1, 4; 8:12, 29; 10:1; 11:25; 12:1; 15:14, 30). Abraham is the Romans' forefather on the basis of faith apart from his circumcision (4:9–12). Jesus is the firstborn of many siblings (8:29) and co-heirs (8:17). They are to treat one another as brothers and sisters (14:10, 13, 15, 21; φιλαδελφία, 12:10). Believers in Christ, according to Rom 8:15–17, 23 are "children" (τέκνα) adopted (υἱοθεσία) by God who now call him "Abba" and "Father" (ὁ πατήρ).

Paul metaphorically employs terms of familial affection throughout Rom 16. Several of those greeted are Paul's "beloved" (ἀγαπητόν μου, vv. 5, 8, 9, and 12). Phoebe is Paul's "sister" (ἀδελφή, Rom 16:1). Rufus's mother is Paul's *own* mother (v. 13). Paul speaks frequently of his "brothers and sisters" (vv. 14, 15, 17). The frequent references to "fellow workers" in vv. 3, 6, 9, and 12 and the use of words with the συν-prefix heighten the sense of familial kinship. Whenever συγγενής is employed in contexts with words such as "brother," "sister," or

---

History of Its First Century (trans. O. C. Dean, Jr.; Minneapolis: Fortress Press, 1999), 277–80.

155. David Rhoads, "Children of Abraham, Children of God: Metaphorical Kinship in Paul's Letter to the Galatians," *CurTM* 31 (2004): 282–97.

"mother" in ancient Greek literature, the meaning is always "relative."[156] Paul is using "affectionate language" "to build bridges" with the Roman congregation.[157] Bruce Malina employed the term "fictive kin group" to describe the early Christian communities. Loyalty and trust in the first century were primarily to one's blood relatives. This loyalty was extended to the Christian community.[158] By meeting in private homes, the first Christians naturally evolved into fictive kin groups.[159] David Rhoads prefers the term "metaphorical kinship" since, for Paul, these kin are hardly fictive. They are more real than blood relations.[160] Rom 16 reflects this development.

Familial Language in Associations

Philip Harland has demonstrated the use of familial language within Greco-Roman associations. Several associations considered themselves a gathering of "brothers (and sisters)," and the association's benefactors could be called a "mother," a "father," a "son" or a "daughter."[161] Debate has raged throughout the

---

156. The relationship between these words is syntagmatic; Moisés Silva, *Biblical Words and Their Meaning: An Introduction to Lexical Semantics* (rev. ed.; Grand Rapids: Zondervan, 1994), 119, 141–43, 195–97.

157. As Mason pointed out ("For I Am Not Ashamed of the Gospel," 260).

158. Bruce J. Malina and Jerome H. Neyrey, "Honor and Shame in Luke-Acts: Pivotal Values of the Mediterranean World," in *The Social World of Luke-Acts: Models for Interpretation* (ed. Jerome H. Neyrey; Peabody, Mass.: Hendrickson, 1991), 32; note also their mention of "fictive family."

159. Bruce J. Malina, "'Religion' in the World of Paul," *BTB* 16 (1986): 92–99, esp. p. 99. S. Scott Bartchy, in summarizing and drawing upon Malina's work, extended the notion of fictive kin groups to include also patron-client relationships in the Greco-Roman world as well as the sharing of community property in the book of Acts; "Community of Goods in Acts: Idealization or Social Reality?" in *The Future of Early Christianity: Essays in Honor of Helmut Koester* (ed. Birger A. Pearson; Minneapolis: Fortress Press, 1991), 312–18. See also Reta Haltmann Finger, who, in "Open Homes and Fictive Kin Groups: Jesus Invents the Family," *Daughters of Sarah* 20.1 (1994): 18–22, attempted to show how widespread this concept is in the NT. For a broad survey of household and familial language in Paul, see Robert Banks, *Paul's Idea of Community* (rev. ed.; Peabody, Mass.: Hendrickson, 1994), 47–57.

160. Rhoads, "Children of Abraham, Children of God," 284.

161. Philip A. Harland, *Associations, Synagogues, and Congregations: Claiming a Place in Ancient Mediterranean Society* (Minneapolis: Fortress Press, 2003), 31–33. Samuel Dill, *Roman Society from Nero to Marcus Aurelius* (London: Macmillan, 1911), helpfully cited several examples using these familial terms. For "brotherhood," see p. 256. For "mothers" and "daughters," he cited (p. 271) the language of the college of smiths in Tarraconensis (*Or. Henz.* 4055). For the language of "brothers" and "sisters" and the day

past century over whether the earliest Christian churches should be classified as *collegia*.[162] Regardless of the outcome of that debate, the Roman collegia offer ample precedent for familial language.[163] Inscriptions have survived from several hundred *collegia domestica*, including the imperial household, the house of Livia, and many private households.[164] *Patresfamilias* often acted as patrons of such *collegia domestica* by hosting the groups in their own homes or by providing buildings for meeting. Members frequently included people not physically

---

sacred to "dear kinship" he cited *Or. Henz.* 2417, 4055, 2392, 3774, 3815, 1485, 4134 ("brothers" and "sister"); 2417 ("kinship") (p. 280). More recently, see Philip A. Harland's review of inscriptional evidence for familial language in the associations of the Greek East, "Familial Dimensions of Group Identity: 'Brothers' (Ἀδελφοί) in Associations of the Greek East," *JBL* 124 (2005): 491–513. Against Meeks and others who minimize brotherly language in the associations, Harland noted that (Christian) epistolary materials differ significantly from (Greco-Roman) inscriptional evidence. Note that brotherly language is absent in the earliest available Christian inscriptions from the late second century, despite the literary attestation (ibid., 495–96). Harland's study is therefore remarkable in finding inscriptional evidence for "brother" and "sister" for association members, and "father," "mother," or "papas" for association leaders.

162. For a helpful survey of the debate sympathetic to the possibility of understanding the churches as *collegia*, see John S. Kloppenborg, "Edwin Hatch, Churches and *Collegia*," in *Origins and Method: Towards a New Understanding of Judaism and Christianity: Essays in Honour of John C. Hurd* (ed. Bradley H. McLean; JSNTSup 86; Sheffield: Sheffield Academic, 1993), 212–38. For a survey of differences between churches and *collegia*, see Wayne O. McCready, "*Ekklesia* and Voluntary Associations," in *Voluntary Associations in the Graeco-Roman World* (ed. John S. Kloppenborg and Stephen G. Wilson; London: Routledge, 1996), 59–73. On outsiders in subsequent centuries viewing Christian churches as voluntary associations, see Robert L. Wilken, "Collegia, Philosophical Schools, and Theology," in *Early Church History: The Roman Empire as the Setting of Primitive Christianity* (ed. Stephen Benko and John H. O'Rourke; London: Oliphants, 1971), 268–91. Harland, "Familial Dimensions," 494–95, concluded that the familial language employed in small group association settings offers a useful parallel for early Christian gatherings.

163. Greek associations did not tend to use the language of "brothers" (ἀδελφοί) except under Roman influence; Franz Bömer, *Untersuchungen über die Religion der Sklaven in Griechenland und Rom* (2d ed.; FAS 14; Weisbaden: Franz Steiner, 1981), 1:172–78; see, however, Harland, "Familial Dimensions," 491–513.

164. John S. Kloppenborg, "Collegia and *Thiasoi*: Issues in Function, taxonomy and membership," in Kloppenborg and Wilson, eds., *Voluntary Associations*, 23; Andrew D. Clarke, *Serve the Community of the Church: Christians as Leaders and Ministers* (First Century Christians in the Graeco-Roman World; Grand Rapids: Eerdmans, 2000), 64–65; Harry O. Maier, *The Social Setting of the Ministry as Reflected in the Writings of Hermas, Clement, and Ignatius* (Ontario: Wifrid Laurier Univ. Press, 1991), 22–23.

related to the family of the *paterfamilias* but associated with the household. On the basis of the Agrippinilla inscription, Bradley H. McLean demonstrated the existence of a fairly large association that employed a familial structure.[165] McLean concluded: "Religious associations created a network of fictive kinship which served to structure relationships and nurture loyalties. A religious association such as the Dionysiac association of Agrippinilla created this 'kinship network' by relating individuals — especially in extended family alliances — to a common god who acted as a patron, bestowing material and spiritual benefits."[166] Likewise Andrew Clarke: "Thus the associations provided the opportunity for many of those without a public identity, to be part of a fictional kinship group in the otherwise pluralist, multi-cultural and highly-stratified society of the Roman empire."[167] This structure would parallel the Roman churches that were also based in private homes. Such an environment would likewise lend itself to the notion of a fictive kinship network. The Pauline churches may have taken familial language to new heights, both in the extent and the range of usage. Even slaves could be considered brothers alongside their masters.[168]

Several recent studies have noted parallels between synagogues and *collegia*.[169] Others have claimed that little or no evidence is available to suggest that the synagogues were considered *collegia*. The impression that the Jewish synagogues were considered *collegia* rests primarily upon a questionable passage in Josephus (*Ant.* 14.10.9 §215).[170] Josephus cited an alleged document that employed an

---

165. Bradley H. McLean, "The Agrippinilla Inscription: Religious Associations and Early Church Formation," in idem, *Origins and Method*, 247–49, 254–57.

166. Ibid., 266. McLean's study offers a more detailed analysis that ultimately concurs with Wayne A. Meeks's initial conclusion in *First Urban Christians* (New Haven: Yale Univ. Press, 1983), 31: "The hierarchy of the cult association's officers largely reproduced that of the household, with Agrippinilla as priestess at the head." Lead figures were often called "father" (*pater*) or "mother" (*mater*); Kloppenborg, "Collegia and Thiasoi," 25–26; Clarke, *Serve the Community*, 68.

167. Clarke, *Serve the Community*, 68.

168. Bömer, *Untersuchungen über die Religion der Sklaven*, 1:178. McCready, "Ekklesia and Voluntary Associations," 63–64, noted the intimacy of the early Christians and the household as the basic unit of the church throughout the NT.

169. For instance, see Peter Richardson, "Early Synagogues as Collegia in the Diaspora and Palestine," in Kloppenborg and Wilson, *Voluntary Associations*, 90–109. Note the similar conclusions reached in several other essays in this volume.

170. Suetonius spoke on two occasions of the disbanding of all but ancient *collegia*, but the inclusion of the Jews, who are not mentioned, remains an assumption. As Margaret H. Williams in "The Structure of the Jewish Community in Rome," in *Jews in a Graeco-Roman World* (ed. Martin Goodman; Oxford: Oxford Univ. Press, 1998), 221, noted: "If the traditional date for the 'foundation' of Roman Jewish community

"extremely implausible Roman titulature" for the Roman official issuing the document. The document also mistakenly claimed that Gaius had forbidden *all* non-Jewish associations, although, in fact, several were exempted. That a Roman official would suppress all religious societies except those of the Jews is hardly plausible. Margaret H. Williams concluded from the difficulties in this passage that it was a later addition into the text.[171] Erich S. Gruen observed that Josephus's official was not purporting to quote Caesar's measure. He was simply drawing upon the measure for support in order to allow the Jews to practice their religion unhindered (as had Caesar). An exemption to Caesar's measure for Jews alone may reflect liberties taken on the part of the official, or perhaps taken by Josephus himself.[172] Gruen noted that the Jews never used the term *collegium,* never employed the terms of such an organization, and had not in all likelihood received government sanction. Membership in the Jewish people was by birth and ethnic identity, and not by trade or profession. Their bonds went beyond the local synagogue, even to the point of sending contributions well beyond the borders of the local organization to Jerusalem.[173] Christian fictive kinship language did not likely derive from the synagogues as *collegia.*

Some evidence exists for the use of familial language in the Judaism of Paul's day. The Torah spoke of the Jewish community as "kin" or "kinsfolk" (Deut 3:18; 24:7 [in apposition to the "sons of Israel"]; see also Exod 2:11; Lev 19:17). Second Maccabees, a letter from the Greek-speaking diaspora, was addressed from brothers (ἀδελφοί) to brothers. The Qumran community spoke of its members as "brothers" (for example, 1QS VI, 10, 22; CD VI, 20; VII, 1; XX, 18). Wayne Meeks cited such passages, along with the familial language employed by the Jewish syncretistic cult to the Highest God in the Bosporan kingdom, as a possible precedent for the first Christians.[174] Meeks's evidence remains rather slender, and none of his evidence is of direct value for the Roman Jews. Meeks complained that the evidence for familial language in the associations was limited, but the evidence for such language in a Jewish context was rare. A more viable explanation for the use of familial language among the first Christians is that they adapted and expanded upon the familial language of the Roman *collegia domestica* since they were meeting in private homes. The use of the term

---

is accepted (i.e. the late second to early first century BCE), none of the synagogues in Caesar's time will have been very old."

171. Williams, "Structure of the Jewish Community," 221.

172. Gruen, *Diaspora,* 26.

173. Ibid., 24–5, 121.

174. Meeks, *First Urban Christians,* 87, 225.

"relative" does not, then, justify the confident conclusion on the part of many scholars that Andronicus, Junia, and Herodion were Jewish.

A Handful of Jews in the Audience?

Eldon Jay Epp heartily affirmed "the Apostle Junia" in a recent monograph.[175] Epp's affirmation suggests the question of whether Andronicus and Junia (Rom 16:7) numbered among the original Jewish followers of Jesus. Some have thought that the second name in this pair in the original text is not a female Junia but rather a male Junias. Did the pair number *among* the apostles, or were they well-known *to* the apostles? If they numbered *among* the apostles, what sort of apostles were these? Although Epp included Junia (and Andronicus) among those who held the high apostolic office, his discussion is imbalanced. As a specialist in textual criticism, he devoted sixty-eight of the seventy-eight pages of the body of his book to demonstrating decisively that Junia is a woman in the original text. Only ten pages address the remaining interpretive issues.

Paul uses the term "apostle" with flexibility.[176] Paul sometimes employs the term for a group that has seen the Lord, which includes "the twelve," as well as himself, Jesus' brothers, and Barnabas (1 Cor 9:1–7). In 1 Cor 15:5, 7, 9 Paul *distinguishes* the apostles as a group, including himself, from "the twelve." Paul belabors his apostleship (for example, 2 Cor 12:11–12) and defines it as having encountered the risen Christ (1 Cor 9:1–2; Gal 1:1, 15–17) and having received a commission to proclaim the gospel (Rom 1:1–5; 1 Cor 1:1; Gal 1:15–17).[177] Paul also uses the term "apostle" for those serving as itinerant missionaries (for

---

175. Eldon Jay Epp, *Junia: The First Woman Apostle* (Minneapolis: Fortress Press, 2005), xvii.

176. Rudolf Schnackenburg's conclusion years ago remains valid: "Paul did not know of a uniform concept of apostleship which had clear-cut criteria" ("Apostles before and during Paul's Time," in *Apostolic History and the Gospel: Biblical and Historical Essays presented to F. F. Bruce on his 60ᵗʰ Birthday* [ed. W. Ward Gasque and Ralph P. Martin; Grand Rapids: Eerdmans, 1970], 301). See also the discussion of J. B. Lightfoot, *The Epistle of St. Paul to the Galatians* (3d ed.; Grand Rapids: Zondervan, 1962), 95–99.

177. Elisabeth Schüssler Fiorenza noted that Andronicus and Junia had been fellow prisoners with Paul; she considers this evidence of their apostleship in the narrower sense of having seen and been commissioned by the Lord ("Missionaries, Apostles, Coworkers: Romans 16 and the Reconstruction of Women's Early Christian History," *Word & World* 6 [1986]: 430–31). The problem is that Epaphroditus, a "messenger/apostle of the church" of Philippi has also suffered nearly to the point of death. Suffering is not just a mark of an apostle. It is a mark of Christian existence for Paul (e.g., 1 Thess 3:3–4). Fiorenza is therefore pressing the description of Andronicus and Junia

example, Silvanus and Timothy in 1 Thess 1:1; 2:7). The use of "apostle" for itinerant evangelists and missionaries was common in the first and early-second centuries (for example, *Did.* 11:3–6). These itinerants did not exercise the same sort of authority as Paul. Andronicus and Junia may therefore be an itinerant missionary couple much like Prisca and Aquila. Epaphroditus, who serves on behalf of the Philippian church, is labeled an "apostle" in yet a third sense as a messenger or emissary of the church (Phil 2:25: "your" apostle). Paul labels others in the same way as "messengers of the churches" (2 Cor 8:23).

The brief description of Andronicus and Junia in Rom 16:7 does not permit a firm conclusion, and commentators have remained divided. If Paul is describing the couple as "apostles" — a question in itself — they may be apostles in the sense of those who have seen the Lord, messengers of the churches, or itinerant missionaries. If Andronicus and Junia were apostles in the narrower sense of having seen and been commissioned by the Lord, they were likely Jewish.[178] E. Earle Ellis, however, concluded that the added description of the pair as "who were in Christ before me" would have been a "meaningless redundancy" had Paul included them among the apostles who had seen and been commissioned by the risen Christ (cf. 1 Cor 15:8).[179] Paul also does not identify them in the same way as he identifies himself, as apostles "of Jesus Christ" (1 Cor 1:1; 2 Cor 1:1; Col 1:1).[180] Paul does not identify Andronicus and Junia as messengers of a specific church.[181] On the other hand, Paul may have assumed the Romans' knowledge of the pair's activity on behalf of a church or churches, presumably their own. The

---

as "fellow captives" too far. Also, it is not clear whether the couple had been prisoners *with* Paul or imprisoned *as* Paul.

178. If an "apostle" in this sense includes the five hundred mentioned in 1 Cor 15:6, then gentile apostles are a distinct possibility. Schnackenburg, "Apostles before and during Paul's Time," 292, wondered why, if that were the case, such an apostolic "army" did not leave a greater trace in the early Christian writings.

179. E. Earle Ellis, "Paul and His Co-Workers," in *Dictionary of Paul and His Letters* (ed. Gerald F. Hawthorne, Ralph P. Martin, and Daniel G. Reid; Downers Grove, Ill.: InterVarsity, 1993), 186.

180. Thus Ben Witherington III, *Women in the Earliest Churches* (SNTSMS 59; Cambridge: Cambridge Univ. Press, 1988), 115–16, who considered the couple itinerant missionaries and not apostles in the sense of Paul himself. That they minister as a couple matches the description of itinerant missionaries in Luke 10:1. Similarly, the other apostles may take along spouses when they enter the mission field (1 Cor 9:5).

181. Thus Richard Bauckham, *Gospel Women: Studies in the Named Women in the Gospels* (Grand Rapids: Eerdmans, 2002), 180. Bauckham did not address the possibility that Andronicus and Junia may have been itinerant missionaries, and he offers no evidence that the pair were members of the group who had seen and been commissioned by the risen Jesus beyond the fact that this group was significantly larger than the twelve.

most likely conclusion is that Paul considers Andronicus and Junia "apostles" in the sense of itinerant missionaries.[182] As "messengers of the churches" or itinerant missionaries, these "apostles" would not necessarily even be Jewish.

Yet another issue is whether or not Andronicus and Junia are even being numbered *among* the apostles. Michael H. Burer and Daniel B. Wallace searched ancient Greek literature for instances of ἐπίσημος + ἐν + personal dative (as in Rom 16:7) and ἐπίσημος + personal genitive. They concluded that the personal genitive construction is always inclusive ("outstanding *among*") whereas the ἐν + personal dative construction is almost always exclusive ("well known *to*").[183] Burer and Wallace noted only one clear exception to the rule that ἐν + personal dative is exclusive, an instance in the second century CE author Lucian (*Merc. Cond.* 28).[184] In a follow-up study, Heath R. Curtis demonstrated that the context of the Lucian quote, when scrutinized more closely, is actually exclusive rather than an exception to Burer and Wallace's rule.[185] If the rule holds, then

---

182. Schnackenburg, "Apostles before and during Paul's Time," 302–3, asserts, "It makes no sense to play the 'charismatic' and 'institutional' concepts of an apostle one against the other. Rather, the concept of an apostle, at the beginning was not carefully defined. During this period Paul had to be active as an apostle and needed to succeed against those who contested his apostleship. He faced all the requirements, the ones which came from the 'apostles before him' in Jerusalem, as well as those who were presented by 'apostles during his time,' and in this he clarified his own understanding of apostolic authority." He also wrote, "If one considers Paul's choice of words in I Thessalonians 3:7, I Corinthians 4:9; 12:28f., and Romans 15:7, it appears that in the mission field he clearly associated himself more readily with the usage which regarded apostles as preachers and missionaries of Christ" (p. 302).

183. Michael H. Burer and Daniel B. Wallace, "Was Junia Really an Apostle? A Re-examination of Rom 16.7, *NTS* 47 (2001): 76–91.

184. The paragraph is 28 and not 2.8, a typographical error in Burer and Wallace. Burer and Wallace noted one other possible exception in Josephus (*War* 2.17.4 §418) but concluded that this passage is not useful since the adjective is functioning as a technical term with no notion of comparative force.

185. Heath R. Curtis, "A Female Apostle?: A Note Re-examining the Work of Burer and Wallace Concerning ἐπίσημος with ἐν and the Dative," *CJ* 28 (2002): 437–40. See esp. p. 439, concerning Harmon's translation in the LCL ("conspicuous among the claque"): "This would imply that Lucian's reader should worry about how some third party will interpret the praise of all the household slaves:'take pains that, among all those praising, you be conspicuous [to those listening].' But we know from the context that Lucian is warning his reader of the importance of what *the other slaves* will think because it is they who might report one's behavior to higher authority. Therefore, one must'take pains to be conspicuous *to* the folks [slaves] who are praising and to be the *chorus director* [not a member of the claque].' Lucian's point is that one should be conspicuous to the

Andronicus and Junia are not apostles themselves but rather are well known to the apostles. Several authors have strongly challenged Burer and Wallace's study for various reasons.[186] As the dust settles from this debate, a few conclusions are in order. Paul chose not to employ the genitive construction in Rom 16:7, a construction which definitely includes a comparative notion. The ἐν + personal dative construction of Rom 16:7, in view of that construction's use elsewhere in Greek literature, may be *either* inclusive or exclusive. The context of Rom 16:7 simply does not offer evidence to decide this question. Andronicus and Junia may number among the apostles, or they may be well known to the apostles.[187] If well known to the apostles, Rom 16:7 provides no hint at all whether they are Jewish.

Other evidence may suggest a Jewish identity for Andronicus, Junia, and Herodion. Paul describes Andronicus and Junia as "in Christ" prior to himself. The timing of their conversion during the early stages of the Christian mission increases the likelihood that they were Jewish. On the other hand, the possibility of a mission to the gentiles prior to Paul denies any firm conclusion.[188] The

---

slaves and be seen by them to stand apart from them so much as to become the director and not a mere member of the chorus of flatterers."

186. Epp, *Junia*, 72–78. Richard Bauckham, *Gospel Women*, 172–79, faulted them for not adequately summarizing *all* the ancient evidence available. He also thought the sample sizes are too small for sure conclusions. Linda Belleville, "'Ιουνιᾶν . . . ἐπίσημοι ἐν τοῖς ἀποστόλοις: A Re-examination of Romans 16.7 in Light of Primary Source Materials," *NTS* 51 (2005): 231–49, disputed the interpretation of several instances. In personal communication, Daniel Wallace has indicated that Michael Burer will respond to these critiques in a forthcoming work.

187. Early church fathers, e.g., Origen and Chrysostom, typically understood the construction as "outstanding among"; see Belleville, "Re-examination of Romans 16:7," 232 n. 1.

188. J. Christiaan Beker, in *Paul the Apostle*, 143–44, concluded from passages such as Acts 11:19–26 that the evangelizing of gentiles began prior to Paul's conversion with Hellenistic Jewish Christians. James D. G. Dunn, *The Partings of the Ways: Between Christianity and Judaism and their Significance for the Character of Christianity* (Philadelphia: Trinity Press International, 1991), 121–22, attributed Paul's persecution of the Jewish Christians to their reception of gentiles into their community as gentiles. The Hellenist believers were threatening Israel's covenant. Hengel and Schwemer, *Paul between Damascus and Antioch*, 83, have likewise thought that the first Christians were attracting gentiles to their movement much as had gentiles been attracted to Judaism in general. Paul persecuted the Damascus Christians, claimed Hengel and Schwemer (p. 89), for this offensive messianic sect's claim that their God-fearers had an equal status in the world to come. Hengel and Schwemer's thesis is that the attitude toward God-fear-

NRSV may well be correct in translating the description of Andronicus and Junia (συναιχμαλώτους μου) with "who were in prison with me." Paul boasts of his imprisonments in 2 Cor 11:23. They may have shared his experience of imprisonment, or they may have been imprisoned *with* Paul. If they were his fellow captives (and "apostles"), then they are, like Prisca and Aquila, associated with his gentile missionary labors. Paul's "Herodion" (v. 11) is listed in proximity to those belonging to the family of Aristobulus in v. 10. This Aristobulus may well be Herod the Great's grandson, the friend of Claudius whose household was in Rome (Josephus, *War* 2.11.6 §§221–22; *Ant.* 18.8.4 §§273–76; 20.1.1 §13). "Herodion" is a name not otherwise attested in Rome. The related "Herodianus" is attested in an inscription of Coestus, a slave of Herod who later became a slave of Augustus.[189] Peter Lampe concluded that the unique "Herodion" has the same meaning as "Herodianus" and indicates status as a slave or freedman in Herod's household. A synagogue of the Herodians in Rome (συναγωγὴ᾿ Ηροδίων; *CIJ* 1.173) supports this supposition.[190] On the other hand, the question remains whether *all* the slaves in Herod's household were Jewish? What would render this name inappropriate for a gentile slave of Herod? "Herodion" is likely Jewish, but a gentile identity is possible.

Prisca and Aquila are Paul's Jewish missionary co-laborers (Acts 18:2; 1 Cor 16:19) even to the point of risking their lives for him. Andronicus and Junia, like "Herodion," are of uncertain Jewish identity. If the two were "fellow captives" of Paul (Rom 16:7), they were associated with Paul's missionary labors as well. In other words, at least one of the pairs, if not both, labored as missionaries alongside Paul in his activities as the apostle to the gentiles (Rom 11:13). Of the five names that provide evidence for Jews in the congregations of Rome, at least two and arguably four are associated with Paul's mission *to the gentiles*. The presence of a handful of Jewish Christian missionaries to the gentiles would only affirm the gentile identity of the Roman congregations. To speak even of a Jewish minority in the Roman gentile congregations without serious qualification would be misleading. Paul therefore feels comfortable addressing the Romans as non-Jews.

This discussion of the names in Rom 16 may be of less value for the composition of the Roman churches than most scholars have realized. Terence Y.

---

ers differed between the diaspora's greater openness to God-fearers and the Holy Land's greater strictness and emphasis on full conversion to Judaism with circumcision.

189. *CIL* 6.9005: "Genio Coeti Herodian Praegustator Divii Augusti"; Lampe, *From Paul to Valentinus*, 177.

190. Lampe, *From Paul to Valentinus*, 177–78.

Mullins helpfully outlined how first-, second-, and third-person greetings function throughout ancient Greek letters. Authors typically employed the first-person form when they greeted their audiences. The third-person form relays to the addressee that a third party is greeting either the addressee or a fourth party. The second-person form, as employed throughout Rom 16:3–15, requests that the addressees greet someone on the author's behalf.[191] Mullins wrote that, by employing the indirect salutation of the second-person type rather than the first person, "the writer of the letter becomes the principal and the addressee becomes his agent in establishing a communication with a third party who is not intended to be among the immediate readership of the letter."[192] John White, in his study of ancient letters, concurred: "Letter writers began with some frequency, from the reign of Augustus onward, to extend greetings *to or from a third party (or parties)* in the letter closing."[193] Mullins concluded that Paul felt that he had a "close enough rapport" with the Roman congregation to request that they act on his behalf to greet those who were not in their midst.[194] So also Stanley Stowers: "Ancient letters frequently send salutations to individuals who are not the encoded readers."[195] Thorsteinsson elaborated on Mullins's point:

> This aspect of Paul's greetings in Romans 16:3–15 has been entirely overlooked by interpreters of the letter. If Paul's choice of salutary form is to be taken seriously it must be concluded that, instead of being descriptive of the letter's audience, these greetings suggest that the persons meant to be greeted should *not* be counted among those to whom Paul wrote the letter. In other words, the greetings in Romans 16 say nothing conclusive about the identity of Paul's implied audience.[196]

---

191. Terence Y. Mullins, "Greeting as a New Testament Form," *JBL* 87 (1968): 418–26.

192. Ibid., 420.

193. John L. White, *Light from Ancient Letters* (Philadelphia: Fortress Press, 1986), 202 (emphasis added).

194. Mullins, "Greeting as a New Testament Form," 425–26. Mullins (p. 421) also observed that second-person greetings are frequently used in letters for the addressees to greet other members of the family. Note again the metaphorical kinship language throughout Romans as well as in chap. 16.

195. Stowers, *Rereading of Romans*, 33. In private correspondence he clarified this remark: In ancient letters writers frequently request "someone to greet someone else." Esler, *Conflict and Identity*, 110–11, questioned whether ancient writers would have distinguished between their "encoded" readers (whom the text explicitly addresses) and the "empirical" readers (those who actually read the text). Esler's criticism is beside the point, since Stowers thinks that Paul is requesting greetings to *a third party*.

196. Thorsteinsson, *Paul's Interlocutors*, 98–99.

Mullins's analysis indicates that the second-person greetings of Rom 16:1–16 do not provide any evidence for the ethnic composition of Paul's audience. The names of those to be greeted would serve rhetorically to reinforce Paul's authority with the Roman congregations.

Further Evidence for Jews in the Audience

Several arguments bandied about in the debate over the ethnic identity of the Roman audience are even less conclusive. For instance, Paul speaks to the audience of his own people who do not believe in Christ (Rom 10:1–2; 11:23, 28, 31). He refers to Israel in the third person in 9:3–5. Do these passages prove a gentile audience? Paul also speaks of gentiles in the third person in 9:24, 30; 11:11–12. These verses therefore offer little help in identifying the addressees. Paul claims that his "gospel" (εὐαγγέλιον) is to the Jew first and to the Greek in 1:16. This claim need only imply that gentiles are included among the intended beneficiaries of the gospel message, and not that Jews are members of the Roman audience. Romans 1:16 remains subordinated grammatically to 1:13–15 in which Paul identifies the Romans as within the bounds of his apostolic ministry to gentiles. In Rom 9:24 Paul writes of "us whom [God] has called, not from the Jews only but also from the gentiles" (NRSV, mod.). In this verse or its context, however, the apostle is not describing his audience but is rather asserting that the "we" who believe in Jesus as Messiah includes both Jews and gentiles. Cranfield pointed out that the first-person plural yields its referent with difficulty. Paul is not always clear if he is referring to himself and his readers, or to Christians in general.[197] Christians in general are the most likely subjects in Rom 9:23.[198]

In Rom 4:1 Paul speaks of Abraham, the forefather of the Jewish people, as "our forefather according to (the) flesh" (τὸν προπάτορα ἡμῶν κατὰ σάρκα; cf. 9:10). Richard Hays thought that this verse offers strong evidence that the encoded audience included Jewish Christians: "Such a reference makes sense only if the question of 4:1 is addressed to a fellow Jew, a fellow descendant of Abraham 'according to the flesh.'"[199] Since gentiles could hardly claim Abraham as their forefather according to *the flesh*, the audience was therefore Jewish.

---

197. C. E. B. Cranfield, "Changes of Person and Number in Paul's Epistles," in *Paul and Paulinism: Essays in honour of C. K. Barrett* (ed. Morna D. Hooker and Stephen G. Wilson; London: SPCK, 1982), 283–87. Lampe, *From Paul to Valentinus*, 72 n. 12, agreed that the rhetorical first-person plurals do not necessarily identify the readers.

198. So also Thorsteinsson, *Paul's Interlocutor*, 117. Dunn, *Romans 9–16*, 570, noted the emphasis on "us."

199. Hays, "'The Gospel Is the Power of God,'" 36 (contra Stowers).

Paul, however, calls the Israelites in the wilderness "our fathers" in relation to his gentile Corinthian addressees (1 Cor 10:1, 14). As Cranfield pointed out, the first-person plural does not necessarily identify the addressees. Paul could be talking about Christians in general. That he is speaking more generally is confirmed by Rom 4:11–12 and 4:16–18 where he explains that Abraham is the (fore)father of *all* who have faith whether they are circumcised or not. Hays contended forcefully that 4:1 must be understood as a question: "Have we found Abraham to be our forefather according to the flesh?"[200] The sense of "according to the flesh" (κατὰ σάρκα) in Rom 4:1 remains unclear. While the phrase most likely modifies "our forefather," it may refer to physical descent or to *the manner* in which Abraham received fatherhood. Stowers translated 4:1: "What then will we say? Have we found Abraham to be our forefather by his own human efforts [that is, according to the flesh]? For if Abraham was justified by works, he has reason for boasting" (cf. 4:4–5).[201] Romans 4:1, for Stowers, maintains the diatribal style of the preceding chapters where the individual addressed remained the fictive Jew of 2:17.[202] Paul's sustained discussion with the fictive Jewish interlocutor demonstrates for his gentile audience that their justification does not depend on the Jewish Law lest God act like a local tribal deity rather than Lord of the nations. Even granting that Rom 4:1 refers to physical descent and that 4:1 does not continue the address to the fictive interlocutor, as Elliott wrote: "There are no grounds for restricting the address of this discussion to Jews. That gentile Christians were absorbed with the issue of their identity as Abraham's children should be expected on the basis of the promises in Gen 17 and 18 alone, and is given ample confirmation in Paul's letter to the Gentiles in Galatia."[203] Gentiles were taught to value incorporation into fleshly Abrahamic descent by means of the Law.[204]

Richard Hays wrote of Rom 15:7–9: "Most commentators see here a clear appeal for Jewish and Gentile Christians to 'welcome one another for the glory of God,' following the example of Christ, who welcomed Jews and Gentiles in order that they might join together in praising God.'"[205] Paul urged the Romans

---

200. Richard B. Hays, "'Have We Found Abraham to Be Our Forefather according to the Flesh?' A Reconsideration of Rom 4:1," *NovT* 27 (1985): 76–98.

201. Stowers, *Rereading of Romans*, 234, 241–42. Moo, *Romans*, 259–60, demonstrates that physical descent is viable in Rom 4:1 as Paul prepares for 4:12, 16–18, and in light of 3:29–30.

202. Stowers, *Rereading of Romans*, 231–37.

203. Elliott, *Rhetoric*, 158.

204. On the use of Abraham as a key figure for Jewish instruction of gentiles, see Das, *Paul and the Jews*, 22–23.

205. Hays, "'The Gospel Is the Power of God,'" 37.

to "welcome one another" and then spoke of Christ as the servant of the circumcised in order that the gentiles might glorify God for his mercy. Those admonished to welcome one another were presumably the Jewish circumcised and the gentile uncircumcised. James C. Miller, like Hays, considered this verse a serious problem for those, like Elliott and Stowers, who claimed that the audience was gentile: "How does one integrate the call for 'mutual' acceptance that concludes the letter-body in a letter designed to counter only Gentile Christian arrogance?"[206] Paul does not, however, identify his audience as Jewish or gentile in these verses. Stowers demonstrated the shortcomings in the assumption that the mutual welcoming must be between the Jews and gentiles, whom Christ welcomed:

> Again logic fails. To use a contemporary analogy, the fact that in writing to the Israeli government the secretary general of the United Nations mentioned Arab states and used Albania as an example for some point would not require the conclusion that the letter was also addressed to Arabs and Albanians.[207]

To conclude the presence of Jews in 15:7–9 would be analogous to concluding that Jews had to be in the audience of Romans because Paul spoke *about* Israel in Rom 9–11. If Christ welcomed both Jew and gentile, how much more should the non-Law-observant gentile strong welcome the Law-observant gentile weak? Paul's rhetoric in these verses would apply equally to a gentile context in which observances of the Jewish Law proved a dividing factor. These verses do not, then, militate against an all-gentile audience inclusive of God-fearers. Runar Thorsteinsson called attention to the frequently overlooked motif of glorifying God in 15:6–12 that further demonstrates a gentile audience. In v. 6 Paul prays that the Roman audience would with one voice glorify God (δοξάζητε). In 15:7 the apostle Paul urges his audience to welcome one another just as Christ welcomed them "*for the glory of God*" (εἰς δόξαν τοῦ θεοῦ). Then according to vv. 8–9, Christ has become "a servant of circumcision" in order to confirm God's promises to the patriarchs. The gentiles, on the other hand, are to "glorify" (δοξάσαι) God for God's mercy. The Scriptural citations which follow in vv. 9b–12 emphasize the glorification of God by the gentiles.[208] Thus the "you" (ὑμᾶς) welcomed by Christ for the glory of God are gentiles.

---

206. James C. Miller, "The Romans Debate: 1991–2001," *CurBS* 9 (2001): 339.

207. Stanley K. Stowers, *A Rereading of Romans*, 32–33.

208. Thorsteinsson, *Paul's Interlocutor*, 119 n. 102, noted the contrast with the gentiles who refused to glorify God in 1:21–25. The letter has come full circle.

Steve Mason pointed to Rom 15:16–19 as proof that Paul did not consider his audience to be gentiles. Since Paul claims that his gentile mission is complete (Rom 15:18–19), the Roman audience must not have included gentiles or else Paul's mission to the gentiles would have had to continue on to Rome.[209] Paul, however, does not claim that his *entire* gentile mission is complete. He claims only to have traveled from Jerusalem to the border of (or including) Illyricum (the lands of Albania and the former Yugoslavia). In v. 23 he explains that since his work in those regions is complete he is continuing on to the Romans and to Spain. This implies that Paul *does* include the Romans among the gentile recipients of his ministry. Mason also pointed out that in Rom 15:27 Paul spoke rather objectively of the offering owed by "the gentiles" to the Jerusalem church with no implication that the Roman readers were in any way likewise obligated.[210] On the other hand, Paul's subject in v. 27 remains the Macedonians and Achaians (from v. 26), who have shared their resources with Jerusalem. His comment about "the gentiles" grounds why it is appropriate for the Macedonians and Achaians to share in this way. The Romans are not numbered among "the gentiles" specified as residing in the East. Paul's point is simply that the collection project and its delivery has to that point hindered his plans to come to Rome. Paul will resume his westward path in due time.

The Weak of Romans 14:1 — 15:6

Romans 14:1 — 15:6, with its discussion of the "strong" and the "weak," has offered critics some of the strongest evidence for a Jewish constituency in the Roman congregations. The "weak" were seeking to keep Jewish customs from the Law of Moses. In Rom 14:5–6 the weak "observe the day." While non-Christian gentiles certainly observed special days, pagan calendrical observances would not be a point of contention between two factions *within the church*. These verses are most likely referring to Jewish sabbaths, feasts, and fast days. A regular, weekly insistence on Sabbath observance by a part of the congregation would have caused friction with those who did not honor the Sabbath.[211] In Rom 14:14 the weak see certain foods as "common" or "unclean" (κοινός;

---

209. Mason, "Paul," 211.

210. Ibid.

211. John M. G. Barclay, "'Do We Undermine the Law?' A Study of Romans 14.1 — 15.6," in *Paul and the Mosaic Law* (ed. James D. G. Dunn; Tübingen: J. C. B. Mohr [Paul Siebeck], 1996), 292. Again, the Jews were known in Rome for their practice of the Sabbath; see Barclay, pp. 296–99, for a discussion of the primary sources.

three times!), a classification derived from the Mosaic Law.[212] The word Paul uses for "unclean" (κοινός) is never used in Greek literature to express purity concerns apart from the influence of Judaism and the Mosaic Law.[213] In Rom 14:20 Paul declares all things "clean" (καθαρά), a term likewise used for ritual cleanliness in the Mosaic Law (see Acts 10:15; 11:9). The "weak" are avoiding meat and wine in favor of a diet consisting of vegetables and water (Rom 14:21; cf. 14:17). Historically, those observing Jewish customs would abstain from meat and wine in hostile circumstances where they had no control over their diet.[214] Some have questioned whether this is viable evidence the "weak" are Jews. The avoidance of meat on the part of Roman church members may reflect the same neo-Pythagorean influence that perhaps impacted the Colossian congregation.[215] The problem with a neo-Pythagorean rationale for the avoidance of meat and wine at Rome is that the weak are observing these practices "for the Lord" (14:6) and could lose their faith if forced to drop their customs (14:20). "It is hard to imagine Pythagorean vegetarianism being so closely wedded to Christian faith as to be an issue on which believers could feel their loyalty to God depended."[216] Pythagorean asceticism was a matter of personal choice. Why, then, would the weak consider their lifestyle a universal mandate for all and judge the "strong" in 14:2? Paul would certainly not be as accommodating of the weak if their views

---

212. See Mark 7:15–23; Acts 10:14, 28; 11:8; 1 Macc 1:47, 62; Josephus, *Ant.* 3.7.7 §181; 11.8.7 §346; 12.7.6 §320; 13.1.1 §4.

213. Dunn, *Romans 9–16*, 818–20; Ulrich Wilckens, *Der Brief an die Römer*, vol. 3 (2d ed.; EKKNT VI/1–3; Neukirchener-Vluyn: Neukirchener, 1989), 112–13.

214. Dan 1:8–16; Jdt 12:1–14; Esth 14:7, 17 [LXX]; Josephus, *Ant.* 4.6.8 §137; *Life* 3 §§13–14 (on captive Jewish priests' diet of "figs and nuts" in Rome). The Jews were known in Rome for their abstention from certain meats; see Barclay's discussion of the primary sources in "Do We Undermine the Law?" 294–95. On Jewish abstention from pagan, (likely) idolatrous meat and wine, see Philip F. Esler's excellent discussion in *Galatians* (New Testament Readings; London: Routledge, 1998), 92–116.

215. Col 2:15–23; Heinrich Schlier, *Der Römerbrief* (HTKNT 6; Freiburg: Herder, 1977), 403–6; Ulrich Wilckens, *Der Brief an die Römer*, 3.111–12.

216. As John M. G. Barclay has observed, ("Do We Undermine the Law?" 292). This objection would equally apply to Max Rauer's thesis in *Die "Schwachen" in Korinth und Rom nach den Paulusbriefen* (BibS[F] 21, 2/3; Freiburg: Herder, 1923) that the "weak" are adherents of Gnostic, Hellenistic mystery religions. This was taken up by Robert J. Karris, "Romans 14:1 — 15:13 and the Occasion of Romans," *CBQ* 25 (1973): 68 (repr. *The Romans Debate*, 65–84. [rev. and enl. ed.; ed. Karl P. Donfried; Peabody, Mass.: Hendrickson, 1991]), even though he disagreed with Rauer's overall conclusions. For a detailed critique of Rauer, see Nelio Schneider, *Die 'Schwachen' in der christlichen Gemeinde Roms* (Theologie 5; Münster: Lit, 1996).

were the result of gentile or pagan convictions (cf. the far less friendly approach in Colossians).[217] Romans 15:7–13 provides additional evidence that the weak Paul describes in the immediately preceding verses are observing Jewish customs. He urges Jews and gentiles to welcome one another as Christ has welcomed them. This explicit return to Jews and gentiles in Christ maintains the thread that has dominated the letter from its beginning in 1:16.[218] The "weak" appear, then, to be observing the Jewish customs from the very Law discussed at length throughout the letter.

Mark Nanos offered a novel approach to Rom 14:1 — 15:13. He suggested that the "weak" were actually non-Christian rather than Christian Jews.[219] Stanley Stowers's critique of Nanos's theory raised important questions not only for Nanos's approach but also for the usual identification of the "weak" as Christian Jews:

> My question is why Paul, who is quite capable of openly naming names and throughout Romans speaks boldly of Jews and gentiles, and even conjures up imaginary individuals who are explicitly identified as Jews and gentiles to make concrete his argument (e.g., 2:1–16; 2:17–24; 11:17–24), would be so allusive, to the point of being encoded, in Romans 14 and 15 when (per Nanos) he is supposed to be laying down the major directive of the letter? Could readers have actually understood that the "strong" were gentile Christians ..., and the "weak" were Jews. .... I am struck by the matter-of-fact and off-handed way that Paul introduces his language about the weak and strong, as if the meanings would be obvious to readers.[220]

Nanos's response was candid: "The short answer to why Paul is so allusive, perhaps coded, with reference to the *astheneis* and *dynatoi* of faith, is, of course: I do not know."[221] Proponents of the traditional approach (weak = Jewish Christian; strong = gentile Christian) have struggled with Paul's oblique and allusive handling as well. On the other hand, that the weak were observing the Jewish distinction between clean and unclean foods is clear, because the terminology Paul employs is unique to Judaism. The description is therefore not entirely

---

217. Barclay, "Do We Undermine the Law?" 293.

218. Paul has been explicitly discussing the relationship between Jews and gentiles throughout chaps. 2–3 and 9–11, and the same sorts of issues dominate the rest of the letter as well. In fact, Rom 14–15 builds on the preceding discussions. Paul's reprisal of "weak *in faith*" applies the notion of "faith" (πίστις) expounded throughout the letter.

219. See the detailed discussion of Nanos's theory in chap. 3, below.

220. Stanley K. Stowers, "An Assessment of Mark Nanos's *Mystery of Romans*," *CRBR* 11 (1998): 164.

221. Mark D. Nanos, "Response," *CRBR* 11 (1998): 175.

oblique or allusive. Stowers was not able to provide a viable alternative group in the Greco-Roman world that observed the combination of vegetarianism, a calendar, and the distinction between specifically Jewish "clean" foods and unclean foods.[222] He dismissed the evidence posed by κοινός by saying that this word *cannot* refer to the Jewish distinction or else Paul would be "destroying the whole of Jewish religion centered on the temple and its sanctity."[223] The answer to Stowers's critique comes from Stowers himself in his very next sentence: "I do not picture that Paul required any cultic purity of gentiles."[224] Precisely. Jewish observances are indeed in view, but as they are being practiced *by gentiles*. One may therefore accept Stowers's parallels to "weakness" (*astheneia*) in a Greco-Roman context. Cicero defined weakness as "unwholesome aversion and loathing for certain things." "The product of aversion moreover is defined as an intense belief, persistent and deeply rooted, which regards a thing that need not be shunned as though it ought to be shunned" (*Tusc.* 4.10–11 §§23, 26 [King, LCL]).[225] According to Stowers, Paul may well have been applying a psychagogic strategy in which the stronger should help bear those who displayed weakness.[226] For *gentile* Christians such observances would be matters of *indifference* and weakness. So Paul adopted the Greco-Roman strategy of becoming weak to the weak (1 Cor 9:22): "According to the common analogy used in the literature, the doctor has the responsibility to match the cure to each illness and to make sure that the attempted cure does not cause more harm than good."[227] In summary, the answer to the problem of Paul's apparent "obliqueness" in Rom 14:1 — 15:13 lies in recognizing (with Stowers against Nanos) that both the strong and the weak are *gentiles*, but (with Nanos against Stowers) that the weak are observing Jewish cultic practices. Because the weak are gentiles observing certain Jewish ritual observances, *of course Paul does not identify the strong as gentiles and the weak as Jews*, and of course, in view of his more than adequate description, Paul assumes the addressees will recognize who the weak and strong are. One of the major conundrums in the interpretation of this section of the letter is thus resolved.

Some scholars have concluded that the vegetarian practices of the weak require that they be Jewish. The Jews avoided the idolatrous meat and wine for

---

222. Stowers, "Assessment," 165.

223. Ibid.

224. Ibid.

225. Ibid., 164.

226. Stowers, *Rereading Romans*, 320–23; Clarence E. Glad, *Paul and Philodemus: Adaptability in Epicurean and Early Christian Psychagogy* (NovTSup 81; Leiden: Brill, 1995), 213–35.

227. Stowers, "Assessment," 164.

sale in the pagan marketplaces. How readily available non-idolatrous meat and wine were to the Jewish community would depend on the particular circumstances. While the Jews were known for their use of wine (Plutarch, *Quaest. conv.* 4.6.2; Persius, *Sat.* 5.179–84), the availability of non-idolatrous wine would depend upon the Jews being able to make their own libation. If they were unable to do so in particular circumstances, they would be forced to abstain. The sheer size of the Jewish community in Rome would place pressure upon members of their community and the population in general to provide access to appropriate meat and wine.[228] Josephus recorded an official resolution by the people of Sardis to restore Jewish "laws and freedom" as had "the Roman Senate and People" (*Ant.* 14.10.24 §§259–61). Since "suitable" (ἐπιτήδεια) food was sold in the official markets of Rome, it must therefore be made available in Sardis. Winter speculated that when the Jews were expelled from Rome under Claudius, official sanction of kosher meat was denied until Nero later revoked the decree and restored Jewish privileges. Winter's hypothesis questionably assumed a mass expulsion in 49 CE[229] Apart from an unusual, major action against the Roman Jewish population as a whole, ordinary Jewish privileges included access to their own meat and wine markets.[230] Peter Lampe thought that the Jews in Rome may indeed have experienced the lack of kosher meat even though he granted the presence of Jewish butchers in the city: "The renunciation of all meat is demonstrable in a Jewish milieu." "Some Jewish priests on a trip to Rome in the time of Nero ate only figs and nuts in order to avoid contact with meat offered to idols (Josephus, *Life* 3 §§13–14). They were not far in a time and place from the people presupposed in the letter to the Romans!"[231] This Josephus text does not support Lampe's claim since the Jewish priests were *not* in a situation comparable to other Jews in Rome who had access to their own meat markets. Lampe described them as visitors to the capital, an unfamiliar city, but they were actually *prisoners* sent "in bonds" by Felix to Claudius for judgment. Jews avoided meat and wine entirely when they received their food

---

228. Rightly C. K. Barrett, *A Commentary on the Epistle to the Romans* (2d ed.; BNTC; Peabody, Mass.: Hendrickson, 1991), 237. Whether Christians had equal access to these markets, contra Barrett, would depend on Christian-Jewish relations in general. Dunn, *Romans 9–16*, 801, wrongly assumed that Jewish meat and wine would *not* readily be available after the Claudius Edict when only small numbers of Jews had returned to Rome. This assumes a mass expulsion of Jews, which is rather doubtful (see chap. 4, below).

229. See the discussion of this point in chap. 4, below.

230. Bruce Winter, "Roman Law and Society in Romans 12–15," in *Rome in the Bible and the Early Church* (ed. Peter Oakes; Grand Rapids: Baker, 2002), 90.

231. Lampe, *From Paul to Valentinus*, 73.

from non-Jews (for example, Dan 1).[232] The sizeable Jewish population of Rome would not have been forced to adopt a vegetarian diet.

The observance of Jewish customs in Rom 14:1 — 15:13 does not require the presence of Jews in Paul's audience. The Jewish customs identified in Rom 14:1 — 15:13 are precisely the sort of customs observed by "God-fearers." Paul does not mention circumcision but rather food laws and the honoring of the day (for example, sabbaths). Josephus described many Hellenes observing Jewish Sabbath and food customs (πολλὰ τῶν εἰς βρῶσιν ἡμῖν οὐ νενομισμένων): "The masses have long since shown a keen desire to adopt our religious observances; and there is not one city, Greek or barbarian, nor a single nation, to which our custom of abstaining from work on the seventh day has not spread, . . . and [where] many of our prohibitions in the matter of food are not observed" (*Ag. Ap.* 2.39 §282 [Thackeray, LCL]).[233] Feldman observed with respect to this passage:

> The fact that Josephus singles out specific observances as having spread among non-Jews, citing as two of his four examples the laws pertaining to the Sabbath, apparently the most popular Jewish practice among the "sympathizers," and referring to *many* of the dietary laws (rather than *all* of them, the observance of which is required of converts) shows that we are dealing not with full proselytes but with "sympathizers."[234]

Philo claimed: "[Jewish customs] attract and win the attention of all, of barbarians, of Greeks, of dwellers on the mainland and islands, of nations of the east and the west, of Europe and Asia, of the whole inhabited world from end to end" (*Mos.* 2.4 §20).

Josephus and Philo were not inventing such sympathizers for their own purposes. Gentile authors likewise noted the popularity of Jewish customs. Seneca the Younger (4 CE–65 CE) lamented: "The customs of that most accursed nation [the Jews] have gained such strength that they have been now received in all lands. The conquered have given laws to the conquerors" (as cited by Augustine, *Civ.* 6.11 [*NPNF¹* 2:120–21]). Juvenal wrote of uncircumcised gentiles rigidly observing the Sabbath and food prescriptions, which included abstention from

---

232. For discussion along with several further examples from the Jewish literature of this period, see Philip F. Esler, *Galatians* (New Testament Readings; London: Routledge, 1998), 102–16.

233. See also *Ag. Ap.* 2.10 §§121–4 (and *Ant.* 3.8.9 §217, 3.15.3 §§318–9, 20.2.3 §34, 20.2.4 §41, 20.8.11 §195; *War* 2.7.10 §454; 2.8.2 §463; and Tertullian, *Nat.* 1.13.

234. Feldman, *Jew and Gentile*, 352.

pork (*Sat.* 14.96–106). Horace related gentiles observing the Jewish Sabbath (*Sat.* 1.9.68–72 [Fairclough, LCL]). Horace's friend claims he cannot converse since "to-day is the thirtieth Sabbath. Would you affront the circumcised Jews?" When Horace responds that he does not observe such customs, Fuscus jokes that he is "a somewhat weaker brother, one of the many." (Note the language of "weakness" in connection with gentile observance of Jewish customs; Fuscus's humor depends on the general perception that the Sabbath was a superstition common in the populace, especially among the ordinary and less educated.)[235] Ovid frequently mentioned the Sabbath (*Am.* 219–20). Ovid even granted a glimpse of the extent of Jewish influence on the general population when he noted how shops and businesses were closed on the Sabbath (*Ars* 1.413–16).[236] Seneca (*Ep.* 95.47) and Persius (*Sat.* 5.180–84) both lamented how some Romans light lamps on the Jewish Sabbath, a practice Josephus proudly mentioned along with the cessation of work in *Ag. Ap.* 2.39 §282.[237]

An inscription from an association at Elaiussa in Cilicia (southwest of Tarsus) identified the association as the "Sabbatists," who offered to the god "Sabbatistes" and who were establishing a "synagogue leader" (*synagōgos*). No evidence suggests "Sabbatistes" was a pagan deity. At the same time, the inscription does not identify the association as Jewish. "The most likely option remains that this is an association of Gentiles who engaged in practices relating to the Sabbath."[238] Irina Levinskaya and Stephen Mitchell identified another gentile association worshiping the Jewish God (σεβόμενοι θεὸν ὕψιστον) from the mid-second century CE at Tanais in the Bosporan kingdom north of Asia Minor.[239] The church fathers Epiphanius and Gregory of Nazianzus referred to "prayer houses" (*proseuchai*) of gentiles that were neither of Jewish ethnic origin nor Christian (that is, heretical). These associations worshiped the Jewish God as All-Powerful and adopted

---

235. John M. G. Barclay, *Jews in the Mediterranean Diaspora: From Alexander to Trajan (323 BCE–117 CE)* (Edinburgh: T&T Clark, 1996), 296–97; idem, "Do We Undermine the Law?" 297. For further examples of gentiles observing Jewish customs, see Cohen, "Crossing the Boundary," 20–21. Ovid assumed a general familiarity with the Jews' Sabbath in *Ars* 1.75–76.

236. Barclay, "Do We Undermine the Law?" 297; idem, *Jews in the Mediterranean Diaspora*, 296–97.

237. Barclay, "Do We Undermine the Law?" 298. For observers' perception of the Jewish Sabbath practice, see Gruen, *Diaspora*, 48–50.

238. Harland, *Associations*, 50.

239. Levinskaya, *Book of Acts*, 83–116; Stephen Mitchell, "The Cult of Theos Hypsistos between Pagans, Jews, and Christians," in *Pagan Monotheism in Late Antiquity* (ed. Polynmnia Athanassiadi and Michael Frede; Oxford: Clarendon, 1999), 81–148, esp. pp. 116–17. See also the older discussion by Lake, "Proselytes and God-Fearers," 90–96.

certain dietary customs and observed the Sabbath.[240] Feldman pointed to a similar association (σύνοδος) of Sabbath sympathizers (Σαμβαθική) in Egypt from an inscription at Naucratois:"They cannot be Jews, because, so far as we know, Jews never refer to their G-d as 'the G-d of the Sabbath'; and hence they are most likely 'sympathizers.'"[241] Twenty-nine Egyptian papyri from the early-first century CE to the fifth century spoke of the children born on the Sabbath called "Sambathion" by their parents. The papyri were located in villages that appear to be non-Jewish. That "Sambathion" was the only borrowed name suggests groups of gentile Sabbath observers. Interestingly, the numbers of those identified as "Sambathion" declined as Jews in Egypt became fewer.[242] These gentiles appeared to have been influenced by the Jewish population and adopted a Jewish custom as their own. Harland placed this sort of evidence for gentile communities honoring the Jewish God alongside the New Testament and early Christianity (for example, 1 Pet 1:14–19; 4:3–4; Eph 2:11–12).[243]

Conclusion

The content of Rom 14:1 — 15:6 is completely comprehensible if the audience included current or former God-fearers alongside non-Law-observant gentiles. Insofar as the former had adopted Jewish customs, the ongoing validity and role of Moses' Law and Israel's heritage would be at issue. Longstanding Jewish custom prevented the Law-observant from partaking of the meat and wine of non-Law-observant gentiles. This well-established custom was probably a safeguard to avoid anything that might have been sacrificed to the pagan deities.[244] Although in a Christ-believing context most participants in a meal would have had similar scruples with respect to food or drink sacrificed to idols, God-fearers would have been uncomfortable as well around non-God-fearers and their meat and wine.[245] This would have led to tensions.

---

240. Mitchell, "Cult of Theos Hypsistos," 92–97.

241. Feldman, *Jew and Gentile*, 359.

242. Ibid., 360.

243. Harland, *Associations*, 50.

244. See Philip F. Esler's discussion of this point in *Galatians*, 93–116, and his interaction with E. P. Sanders's *Jewish Law from Jesus to the Mishnah: Five Studies* (Philadelphia: Trinity Press International, 1990), 272–83, and E. P. Sanders, "Jewish Association with Gentiles and Galatians 2.11–14," in *The Conversation Continues: Studies in Paul and John in Honor of J. Louis Martyn* (ed. R. T. Fortna and B. R. Gaventa; Nashville: Abingdon, 1990), 170–88.

245. Or perhaps not, if 1 Cor. 8–10 is any indication, but Paul does not identify meat sacrificed to idols as an issue at Rome as he had in Corinth.

In the event that the Jews in Rome were distancing themselves from the emerging Christ-movement, Law-observant gentile Christians would have found themselves in a difficult quandary. Cut off from their former relationships with the Jewish quarter, Law-observant Christ-believing gentiles would have experienced difficulty obtaining non-idolatrous meat and wine. They would have been forced to avoid pagan meat and wine in the same way as Law-observant Jews deprived of access to kosher nourishment throughout Jewish history.[246] Gary Shogren pointed out that even if the deprivation were only for the short term, temporary difficulties and expediencies would have led to enduring habits.[247] Many Law-respectful God-fearers would have become accustomed to avoiding meals with those who did not practice the Law.

As an increasing number of non-Law-observant gentiles joined the Christian movement, these gentile God-fearers would have confronted new issues. The God-fearers would have faced increasing social pressure to relinquish their practices as they found themselves in the midst of the "strong."[248] Many newer converts probably shared the Roman populace's frequent disdain for Jewish customs. Paul therefore includes in his letter instructions on how Jews and gentiles are to relate to each other as well as on the role of the Mosaic Law among Christians: his goal is to facilitate a healthy relationship between the non-Law-observant gentiles and the Law-observant gentiles in the Roman Christian congregations.

---

246. Lampe, *Paul to Valentinus*, 73 n. 21, rightly asked, "Can one really imagine that Jewish butchers in Rome after the mighty conflicts leading to the edict of Claudius still would gladly serve Christian apostates at their stands?" Although Francis Watson's position suffers from the weaknesses of viewing the Romans as a mixed community of both Jews and gentiles, he rightly recognized an issue in gaining access to kosher markets that would be even more pronounced for observant gentile Christians (*Paul, Judaism, and the Gentiles*, 95).

247. Gary Steven Shogren, "'Is the Kingdom of God about Eating and Drinking or Isn't It?' (Romans 14:17)," *NovT* 42 (2000): 248–51. They may also have been emulating certain heroes of old, such as Daniel, who had been placed in similar circumstances. Shogren also noted the priests sent to Rome under arrest in Josephus (*Vita 3* §§13–14).

248. Horace (*Sat.* 1.9.68–72) offered an instance of a gentile seeking to observe the Jewish Sabbath. The gentile then describes himself as a "weaker brother."

Chapter 3

Former God-Fearers or Synagogue Subgroup?

Stephen Wilson's *Related Strangers* tracked the emerging split between Jews and Christians in the first two centuries. His review of second-century literature on both sides of the growing divide is one of the best introductions available. As for the first-century New Testament documents, Wilson surveyed the Gospels and Hebrews but, interestingly, chose not to review the letters of Paul — for the sake of sanity. He claimed that "little new" can be said.[1] Wayne Meeks, on the other hand, *did* include Paul among his snapshots of the "breaking away." Against the backdrop of John's Gospel, with its hostile references to "the Jews" along with the rupture from the synagogues vivid in the Johannine sect's memory, Meeks was struck by the general lack of such polemic in the undisputed Pauline epistles. He concluded:

> The main difference is this: the great issue in Pauline Christianity is not between "the synagogue" and the sect of the Christians, but within the Christian movement. The social context of Pauline groups is the private household provided by various patrons in each city. . . . [T]he Pauline groups were never a sect of Judaism. They organized their lives independently from the Jewish associations of the cities where they were founded, and apparently, so far as the evidence reveals, they had little or no interaction with the Jews.[2]

---

1. Stephen G. Wilson, *Related Strangers: Jews and Christians 70–170 C.E.* (Minneapolis: Fortress Press, 1995), xiv.
2. Wayne A. Meeks, "Breaking Away: Three New Testament Pictures of Christianity's Separation from the Jewish Communities," in *"To See Ourselves as Others See Us"*:

Although most would concur with Meeks on the social context of the Pauline congregations, Mark Nanos, a rare Jewish voice in Pauline scholarship, has heartily agreed with those specialists who date any split between "Christ-believers" and their non-Christ-believing peers to a later era. Nanos has contributed a reading of Paul's Romans that supports his thesis. As the apostle was active traveling, ministering, and writing letters, "Christianity" in his day was still a Jewish movement even for the Pauline communities. According to Nanos's unique approach, when Paul wrote Romans he realized that the letter would be read in the context of gentile subgroups of those who recognized Jesus as the Messiah *amidst members of the larger synagogue assemblies.*[3] Since the first "Christ-believers" were part of an intra-synagogue movement, those scholars who employ the term "Christian" for Paul's audiences, as if Christ-believers were distinguishable from other Jews, are guilty of an anachronism.[4] Nanos has therefore been able to account ingeniously for the gentile audience presumed by the letter as well as for the Romans' familiarity with the Jewish Scriptures.

The centerpiece of Nanos's approach is his interpretation of Rom 14:1 — 15:6. For Nanos's Paul, the synagogue Jews had not recognized the full significance of Jesus as Israel's Savior, the Messiah. They had not realized that, as foretold by the prophets, God was now including gentiles as equal participants in the new age of salvation. Nevertheless, while Christ was the full revelation of God, non-Christ-believing Jews were still "brothers and sisters" of "faith," even if "weak" in that faith. Thus the apostle urged the gentile Christ-believing "strong" to be respectful of non-Christ-believing Jews.[5] In their presence the gentiles should adopt a Law-respecting way of life as "righteous gentiles" to prevent the "weak in faith," the non-Christ-believing Jews, from stumbling and falling away from their faith in the same God. Far from excluding non-Christ-believing

---

Christians, Jews, "Others" in Late Antiquity (ed. Jacob Neusner and Ernest S. Frerichs; SPSH; Chico, Calif.: Scholars Press, 1985), 106.

3. Mark D. Nanos, *The Mystery of Romans: The Jewish Context of Paul's Letter* (Minneapolis: Fortress Press, 1996).

4. As I discuss the identity of the "weak" in relation to Nanos's argumentation, I will employ his terminology. If, however, the Roman churches were no longer meeting in the synagogues in the wake of a break, then one may be justified in using the term "Christian," with due recognition that this is *early* Christianity.

5. Certainly the strong are admonished as Christ-believers in 14:15: "Do not destroy with your food him for whom Christ died." Paul as a believer in Christ numbered himself among the strong in 15:1. The strong were not observing Jewish practices, since they ate all things (14:2) and did not regard the days (14:5) and drink wine. See also Nanos, *Mystery*, 95–96.

Jews, Nanos's Paul assumed their inclusion with believing gentiles in one united people. The Christ-believing gentiles should even submit to the Jewish synagogue leadership.

After decades of familiar and well-worn perspectives on the "Romans debate," Nanos's fresh and unusually original thesis caused quite a stir among biblical scholars and ecumenists. No study of the early relationship between Jews and Christians can afford to ignore his approach. *The Mystery of Romans* won the 1996 National Jewish Book Award in the category of Jewish-Christian Relations. The Society of Biblical Literature in 1997 devoted an entire session to the review of Nanos's *Mystery*.[6] In 1998 the annual meeting of the Catholic Biblical Association followed suit with its own full session of discussion. Nanos, a prolific writer and vigorous advocate, has furthered his Romans thesis with a compatible approach to the Letter to the Galatians.[7] He actively participates in and co-moderates the international "Corpus Paulinum" scholarly discussion group in which he regularly holds court and has been the center of attention for several years.

Robert A. J. Gagnon published the lone, sustained critique of Nanos's approach to Romans. Gagnon contends that the weak and the strong must be identified respectively as the righteous (or Torah-respectful) and the non-Law-observant within all-gentile assemblies which have already parted ways with the synagogues.[8] Nanos countered in 2000 with a lengthy and detailed rebuttal, which he subsequently updated and placed on his website in 2003.[9] Since Nanos's position remains influential and persuasive for many, his thesis merits consideration in a discussion of the situation in Rome behind Paul's letter. At

---

6. In fact, one of the reviewers at that meeting, a rather perceptive interpreter, has "converted" to Nanos's position on the weak as non-Christian Jews; see Neil Elliott's "Asceticism among the 'Weak' and 'Strong' in Romans 14–15," in *Asceticism and the New Testament* (ed. Leif E. Vaage and Vincent L. Wimbush; New York: Routledge, 1999), 235–39.

7. Mark D. Nanos, *The Irony of Galatians* (Minneapolis: Fortress Press, 2002). For a critique of Nanos's work on Galatians that complements the discussion of Romans in this chapter, see A. Andrew Das, *Paul and the Jews* (Library of Pauline Studies; Peabody, Mass.: Hendrickson, 2003), 23–29.

8. Robert A. J. Gagnon, "Why the 'Weak' at Rome Cannot Be Non-Christian Jews" *CBQ* 62 (2000): 64–82.

9. Mark D. Nanos, "A Rejoinder to Robert A. J. Gagnon's 'Why the "Weak" at Rome Cannot Be Non-Christian Jews.'" 37 pages. [Created 14 July 2000. Updated 20 June 2003. Cited 1 August 2005] Online: http://mywebpages.comcast.net/nanosmd/Gagnon-rejoinder-6-20-03.pdf.

issue is whether Paul was addressing gentile Christ-believers still assembling in the synagogues or whether these Christ-believers were meeting completely apart from non-Christ-believing Jews. Gagnon outlined nine key arguments in Nanos's reasoning. Nanos in his rebuttal followed Gagnon's outline. After reviewing Nanos's nine supporting arguments, a tenth section in this chapter will review *other* evidence that Nanos has cited in support of his thesis, evidence that Gagnon either omitted or reviewed only briefly without enumeration.

The Compatibility of Romans 14:1 — 15:13 with Jewish-Christian Relations in Rome

Mark Nanos believes that the relations between the "weak" and the "strong" in Romans 14:1 — 15:13 took place in the context of the synagogues. The "weak" "need not be Christian Jews."[10] The "faith" of the weak must have been faith in God quite apart from any reference to Christ (14:1).[11] Although Paul's instructions were primarily to the strong, with the exception of 14:3 and perhaps 15:7–9, Nanos is convinced that the "weak" were non-Christ-believing Jews who maintained institutional power within the Roman synagogues. Gagnon considers this unlikely, because Paul's instructions to the gentile "strong," who seem to be bearing the burden of responsibility for the relationship, would require that the gentiles were in a position of control in order to "welcome into your network of intimate relationships ($\pi\rho\sigma\lambda\alpha\mu\beta\dot{\alpha}\nu\epsilon\sigma\theta\epsilon$) the weak in faith, not for judgmental evaluations of positions" (14:1).[12] Gentile Christians would not have been in a position of control in the synagogues. Thus Gagnon concludes that the admonition for the gentile Christian strong to welcome the weak must be in the context of Christian house churches.

Nanos's response to Gagnon's briefly worded critique was quite lengthy.[13] "I argue rather that it is the 'weak/stumbling-in-terms-of-faith-in-Christ' who are in a position to 'judge' the 'strong/able-to-believe-in-terms-of-faith-in-Christ,' and not the other way around, as Gagnon suggests. He has turned by [sic] argument upside down, then attacked that misrepresentation."[14] Nanos contends that the "strong" and "weak" were labeled as such *not* on the basis of institutional power but on the basis of faith in Christ. Institutionally, however, the weak were in the

---

10. Nanos, *Mystery,* 110.

11. Ibid., 118–19.

12. Gagnon's translation; "'Weak' at Rome," 65.

13. Gagnon devoted less than a page of his nineteen-page article to this topic; Nanos devoted more than a quarter of his rather lengthy rejoinder in response.

14. Nanos, "Rejoinder," 3.

unique position of being able to judge the strong and to deny them the seal of approval as acceptable to God (14:18). The strong's welcoming and respect for the weak would, in turn, lead to the weak's welcoming and approving of the strong.

Nanos's response leaves several matters unattended. Certainly in 14:3 Paul admonished the weak not to *judge* the strong who eat, while he admonished the strong not to *despise* the weak. In v. 10 he again referred to the two groups' respective judging and despising. The distinction between the weak who judge and the strong who despise is easily explained without reference to the power structures within a synagogue gathering. The weak "judge" the strong in relation to the legal standard established in Moses' writings, whether they held positions of social authority or not. The strong "despise" the weak because the strong did not adhere to that same standard and may have found those who practice its customs worthy of contempt. The distinction between weak and strong in judging and despising, respectively, does not of itself offer proof of a synagogue setting. Gagnon considers the weak "Noahide" or Law-respectful gentiles who had previously associated with synagogue Jews but were now meeting along with other gentiles. The distinction between judging and despising is not a decisive factor in discerning between the differing reconstructions of the community setting proposed by Nanos and Gagnon.

Nanos makes much of the human approval in v. 18 (δόκιμος τοῖς ἀνθρώποις). He assumes that this verse refers to the weak, who were in a position of power within the synagogues, setting a seal of approval upon the strong. To maintain that the approval in v. 18 must reflect institutional authority simply goes beyond the language of the text. Although many commentators would agree with Nanos that the focus in v. 18 remains on the weak in relation to the strong, other interpreters take an approach that Nanos does not consider. They see a reference in v. 18 not to the weak but rather to people in general.[15] To appreciate why v. 18 may well refer to people in general, one must begin with v. 16. Immediately after admonishing the strong not to cause the ruin "of [the weak] one for whom Christ died" in v. 15, Paul concluded (οὖν) in v. 16: "So do not let your good be spoken of as evil," or literally "reviled," "blasphemed" (βλασφημείσθω).[16] Paul employed the verb "blaspheme"

---

15. Nanos, *Mystery*, 127–28, 130–31.

16. On "your good" as referring to the faith of the strong to eat all things, see Robert A. J. Gagnon, "The Meaning of ὑμῶν τὸ ἀγαθόν in Romans 14:16," *JBL* 117 (1998): 675–89. Thomas R. Schreiner, *Romans* (BECNT 6; Grand Rapids: Baker, 1998), would disagree. He notes that v. 17 supports the conclusion drawn in v. 16 rather than a conclusion from both vv. 15b and 16. "[I]t is improbable that the argument leaps over the οὖν in verse 16" (p. 727). Paul in v. 17 explicated "the good" in terms of "the kingdom of God," which "is not food and drink" but rather "righteousness and peace and

in Rom 2:24 for gentile observers who were reviling God's name because of the behavior of the Jews.[17] Since outside observers are reviling in Rom 2:24 (so also 1 Tim 6:1 and Tit 2:5), Rom 14:17 would include reference to outside observers of the conflict between the weak and the strong.[18] "Paul's primary concern, therefore, remains the glory of God. The 'strong' should not behave in a manner that brings unwarranted criticism against the gospel."[19] If this interpretation of v. 16 is correct, v. 18 is referring to the approval of outside observers of the relationships between the strong and the weak and not to the approval of the strong by the weak. The outside observers' approval in v. 18 would form a contrast to their potential reviling in v. 16. Verse 18 therefore provides doubtful support for Nanos's claim that the "weak" possess the power of approval and institutional authority.[20]

Although Nanos appeals to the admonitions in vv. 3 and 10 to the weak not to judge the strong in order to prove that the weak maintain institutional power, he ignores instances where Paul urged the strong not to judge the weak. Nanos himself translates 14:1 in such a way that the strong are to receive or welcome the weak "but not for the purpose of passing judgment on his opinions."[21] In this translation, Nanos follows many commentators in taking διακρίσεις as "passing judgment" and διαλογισμῶν as "doubts, scruples" or "thoughts, opinions" (an objective genitive). Διακρίσεις occurs once in the LXX (Job 37:16) and twice

---

joy in the Holy Spirit" as demonstrated in the strong's joyful and harmonious relations with the weak as wrought by the Spirit. Such righteousness and peace expresses itself in how the strong handle matters such as food and drink for the sake of the kingdom (pp. 739, 741).

17. Whereas in 1 Cor 10:30 "blaspheme" is used in connection with Christian liberty, in Rom 14:16 "the good thing" (τὸ ἀγαθόν) is despised rather than the "person" (as in 1 Cor 10:30). Schreiner, Romans, 740, concludes from this point that the parallel with 1 Corinthians is inexact and perhaps not as helpful as evidence within Romans itself. Gagnon ("The Meaning of ὑμῶν τὸ ἀγαθόν," 686–88), for his part, emphasizes the connections between Rom 14:16–18 and 1 Cor 10:30.

18. Stuhlmacher, Paul's Letter to the Romans, 227; C. K. Barrett, A Commentary on the Epistle to the Romans (2d ed.; BNTC; Peabody, Mass.: Hendrickson, 1991), 243 (but with no discussion).

19. Schreiner, Romans, 740.

20. Gagnon, "The Meaning of ὑμῶν τὸ ἀγαθόν, 686, maintains that the primary reference is to the weak's potential reviling the strong rather than the reviling of outside observers. He nevertheless agrees that 14:18 "stresses the widest possible reference for the revilers of 14:16, namely, both believers and unbelievers" (emphasis his). If the weak are included alongside outside observers (of the relations between weak and strong) in reviling and approving, then synagogue authority remains a non-factor.

21. Nanos, Mystery, 95. The participles are modifying προσλαμβάνεσθε, which requires that the subject of the participial action remains the strong.

in the New Testament and means "distinguishing, discerning" (1 Cor 12:10; Heb 5:14), but the discernment involves a passing of judgment.[22] The cognate verb means "pass judgment" in Acts 10:20; 11:2; Jude 9. The references to judging in the ensuing verses of Rom 14 further support translating διακρίσεις in v. 1 as "passing judgment."[23] Romans 14:1 would therefore be introducing that discussion as Paul admonished the strong not to judge the weak. While Paul urged the weak not to judge the strong in vv. 3 and 10, with v. 13, as commentators have recognized, he was expanding his admonition to include also the strong's potential judging of the weak: "Then let us no more pass judgment [κρίνωμεν] on one another."[24] Paul added: "But rather let us decide [κρίνατε] never to put a stumbling block or hindrance in the way of a brother." This stumbling block consists in vv. 14–21 of the strong's not eating what the weak judged as unclean in the weak brethren's presence: "it is right not to eat meat or drink wine or do anything that makes your brother stumble" (v. 21). Romans 14:13 offers further evidence that the strong were also judging.

Nanos contends that the weak's judging of the strong in Rom 14:1—15:13 proves that the weak maintained institutional power, but he downplays evidence that the strong may also judge the weak. In fact, the preponderance of Paul's admonitions were addressed to the strong, as Nanos recognizes. Gagnon is right to question whether gentile Christians could exert such control over the relationship with the weak in a synagogue setting as the admonitions to the strong assume. A *non*-synagogue environment therefore appears more likely.

The Credibility of Paul's Exhortations to Non-Christian Jews in Romans 14:1 – 15:13

Nanos believes that the implied audience of Romans is a gentile subgroup within the synagogues (the strong) and does not include the Jewish majority (the weak). Paul is not instructing the weak in Rom 14:1—15:13. "The statements

---

22. Clarence E. Glad, *Paul and Philodemus: Adaptability in Epicurean and Early Christian Psychagogy* (NovTSup 81; Leiden: Brill, 1995), 222–23.

23. On the translation of διάκρισις as "quarrels over scruples," see uncial D in Acts 4:32 and the discussion of Douglas J. Moo, *The Epistle to the Romans* (NICNT; Grand Rapids: Eerdmans, 1996), 836–37. Commentators remain divided.

24. See for instance, C. E. B. Cranfield, *A Critical and Exegetical Commentary on the Epistle to the Romans* (ICC; 2 vols.; Edinburgh: T&T Clark, 1975, 1979), 2:711–12; Glad, *Paul and Philodemus*, 222. Paul has been admonishing both groups in the preceding verses (note ἕκαστος in vv. 5, 12) and is drawing a conclusion in v. 13a (οὖν) for both groups (ἀλλήλων). Paul likely already hinted at mutual judgment in 14:1b.

that appear to be directed to the 'weak' may have been provided to frame Paul's weighty instructions to the 'strong.'"[25] The apparent instructions of the weak were provided for "balance."[26] Nanos minimizes their extent (for example, 14:3, 5). Gagnon counters that the apostle gave equal attention to both the strong and the weak in 14:2–13a. Although Paul began his exhortations admonishing the strong to welcome the weak in faith in 14:1, he concluded in 15:7 "welcome one another," which builds on the mutual admonitions in 14:13a, 19; 15:5, 14.[27] Nothing in the text suggests that these admonitions are only "apparently" and not actually addressed to the weak. Gagnon therefore asks by what authority Paul would be able to command and instruct the weak as non-Christ-believing synagogue Jews. The apostle recognized that his call was to serve as apostle of Christ to the *gentiles* (1:5–6, 13–15; 15:15–17; Gal 2:7–9). If the implied audience of the letter consisted exclusively of gentile Christians (1:5–6, 13–15; 11:13–14; 15:15–18; cf. 6:19 with 1:24; 13:11–14), then the "weak" must number among those gentile Christians.

Nanos contends in response that Gagnon confused the "encoded" or "implied" audience of the letter with the actual audience. Nanos agrees that the implied audience of the letter was gentiles but that the non-Christ-believing Jewish "weak" "ostensibly addressed" in Rom 14:1 — 15:13 were likely part of the *actual* audience of the letter.[28] Nanos's reasoning is flawed. The "implied" or "encoded" reader of a letter is a construct inferred from the letter itself. Rhetorical exigency certainly may require an author to address an encoded or target audience that differs in respects from the actual audience.[29] The problem for Nanos is that

---

25. Nanos, *Mystery*, 110.

26. Ibid., 146.

27. Nanos objects to concluding from the mutual exhortations throughout 14:3–13; 15:5–7 that the weak are members of the implied audience: "A call such as Paul's for mutual respect may be made to a target group without implying that the 'other' is also a part of the writer's/speaker's audience, that is, that the writer/speaker has the same authority or access to them as those to whom he writes/speaks" ("Rejoinder," 5). The rhetoric of mutual welcoming is directed toward the strong in order that the resultant behavior would lead in response to a corresponding welcome by the weak. The problem with Nanos's reasoning here is that he otherwise admits that Paul "ostensibly" is addressing the weak and not the strong at various points in this section of the letter. For admissions of "ostensible" address "to" the weak, see Nanos, *Mystery*, 108, 110, 144–47. See the admonitions to the weak not to judge the strong in vv. 3, 10 and Nanos's discussion of those verses in the preceding section above.

28. Nanos, "Rejoinder," 11.

29. Stanley K. Stowers, *A Rereading of Romans: Justice, Jews, and Gentiles* (New Haven: Yale Univ. Press, 1994), 33.

the "weak" and the "strong," whom Paul counseled and instructed *within the letter,* both figure into the letter's encoded audience.[30] Gagnon correctly reads the admonitions to the strong and the weak alongside Paul's identifications of the audience as gentiles elsewhere in the letter (for example, Rom 1:5–6, 13). Hence the weak who are respectful of the Law in Rom 14:1 — 15:13 must be gentiles (or for Gagnon, "Noahide Gentiles"). Paul's rather bold "ostensible" instructions to the "weak" would not be likely if he were addressing non-Christ-believing synagogue Jews.[31] Paul had no authority to issue instructions to the synagogues.

Nanos finds supportive of an intra-synagogue context that Paul should "frame his concerns" throughout the letter "in terms of Jewish conceptual and social space, not the pagan world of these gentiles' past and present lives."[32] On the other hand, the target audience *did* live, to an extent, in Jewish social space if a portion of the Christ-believing Roman congregations, the weak, at some point associated with the synagogues, adhered to its sacred texts and stories, and were maintaining a Law-respectful lifestyle as gentiles.[33] As the weak and the strong worshiped and socialized, they experienced problems that required Paul's intervention and an extended discourse on the gentiles' indebtedness to a Jewish heritage, a heritage the "weak" properly appreciated but the "strong" had discounted. The biblical quotations in Rom 15:9–12 remind the "strong" that they are spiritually indebted to the Jewish people. They should therefore be respectful of the "weak" and less hasty to scorn the Jewish heritage of their movement. Nanos is therefore unable to account for the inclusion of both the weak and the strong among the implied gentile readers of the letter.

"Your Brother," a Reference to Non-Christian Jews

In Rom 9:3 Paul called non-Christ-believing Jews his brothers.[34] Nanos contends on the basis of this verse that

---

30. Thus also Stowers (in private correspondence).

31. Nanos, "Rejoinder," 11, does not include the "weak" within the encoded audience of the letter, even though Paul clearly (or, for Nanos, "ostensibly") addressed the weak. Paul never signaled that his enjoinders to the weak in Rom 14:1 — 15:13 were only for the ears of the strong. That conclusion would not be "ostensible."

32. Ibid., 12.

33. See chaps. 2 and 4 in this volume.

34. "Brother" in the original Greek is, of course, intended to be inclusive of women. I follow Nanos and Gagnon in using the literal term "brother," but with this caveat noted.

> Jews were the historical community of the One God, whether they believed in Jesus as the Christ or not. Thus to be a Christian, whether Jew (which would be natural to Paul) or gentile (which was a wonderful new reality that had always been part of Israel's eschatological expectation), would have immediately made one a "brother" to all Jews, whether they were Christians or not.[35]

The apostle called the weak "brothers [and sisters]" in 14:10 even as he clearly identified non-Christ-believing Jews earlier in the letter as "brothers [and sisters]" (9:3–5). The rift between non-Christ-believers and Christ-believers would come later. In Paul's day the Jews remained "brothers," irrespective of faith in Jesus Christ. As further support for this claim, Nanos lists the various appellations Paul applied to Christ-believers in Rom 8:15–18, 28–29. In Rom 9 Paul applied most of these very appellations to non-Christ-believing Jews. Both Christ-believers and non-Christ-believing Jews are equally members of God's people.

Nanos, however, misses Paul's logic in Rom 8–9. What necessitates the discussion of non-Christ-believing Jews has been the incredible application of Israel's historic benefits as God's elect to *non-Jews*. The line of reasoning in Rom 8 culminates in God's election in which nothing can separate the Christ-believer from his or her Lord (v. 35). As commentators frequently note, this climactic application of Israel's blessings to Christ-believing gentiles posed a serious problem for Paul. How could gentile Christ-believers take comfort in their election as a people when another people are not benefiting from *their* election? This motivated the expression of anguish and distress regarding non-Christian Israel in Rom 9:3. Paul yearned to be "cut off" for the sake of his ethnic people even as Christ had been cut off from God on behalf of all humanity. Paul wanted to identify with the dire fate of his own people for their benefit. Nanos skips over the dire situation for ethnic Israel in 9:1–3 without comment.

"Brother" *can* be used for non-Christian Jews, as in Rom 9:3, but Gagnon notes in his response the unusual qualifications of "brothers" in this verse as "*my* brothers" (not "your" or "our") and "according to the flesh." He then contends that of the 108 unqualified references to "brothers" in the undisputed Pauline letters and of the twenty in the disputed Paulines, "brother" in each instance refers to Christians.[36] In 1 Cor 7:12–14 Paul gave instructions to the "brother" who "has an unbelieving wife" in the context of the "Lord" who has been raised by God (6:14). In 1 Cor 7:24 Paul spoke of brothers immediately after speaking of being a "slave of Christ" (v. 22). In 1 Cor 15:6 five hundred "brothers" at

---

35. Nanos, *Mystery*, 111.
36. Gagnon, "'Weak' at Rome," 67.

one point saw the resurrected Christ. When Paul spoke of the "brother" who was "weak" in Rom 14:15, 21, the closest parallel is in 1 Cor 8:11–13 where the apostle described the "weak" as "the brother for whom Christ died." The "strong" in 1 Cor 8 must not eat meat "in order that I may not cause my brother to trip" and thus "sin against Christ."[37] Romans 14:23 similarly warned the strong that they may pressure the weak to eat and thereby lead to the weak's condemnation, as well as to grief (14:15) and blasphemy.[38] While the weak in Rome apparently expressed stronger convictions about dietary scruples than the weak in 1 Cor 8, the linguistic connections between the two discussions are too numerous to dismiss as entirely irrelevant, and, as Gagnon adds, Paul was writing to Rome from Corinth![39]

Within Paul's letter to the Romans, in 1:13 Paul addressed the gentile "brothers and sisters" (ἀδελφοί) at Rome whose "faith is proclaimed throughout the world" (v. 8) and to whom he sent grace and peace also from the Lord Jesus Christ (v. 7). In Rom 7:4, 6 Paul spoke to "brothers and sisters" (ἀδελφοί) who "have died to the law through the body of Christ" and were thus "discharged" from it. The "brothers and sisters" in 8:12 were recipients of Christ's Spirit (v. 9) and "heirs with Christ" (v. 17). They were "conformed to the image of his Son" (v. 29). Paul distinguished the "brothers and sisters" of 10:1 from "them," Israel. The "brothers and sisters" addressed in 11:25 were the same gentiles of 11:13. The "brothers and sisters" of 12:1 were members of the one body of Christ in 12:3–8. In other words, Paul consistently employed "brothers and sisters" without qualification for Christ-believers in this letter.

Nanos has not been impressed by Gagnon's reasoning. He rightly notes that Gagnon's appeal to the differing context of 1 Cor 8 is not decisive in itself. He further adds:

> But this does not mean that there are no circumstances under which he might also address non-Christ-believing Jewish people as his brothers and sisters. Or in which he might address non-Christ-believing gentiles as his brothers and sisters apart from such qualification, or likewise as the brothers and sisters of Christ-believing gentiles, since they are such, for example, in terms of Paul's belief in the One Creator God of all humankind (3:29–30).[40]

Quite apart from what Paul *could* have expressed of his brothers and sisters according to the flesh — a possibility that is unverifiable — the decisive issue

---

37. Ibid., 68.
38. Ibid., 67.
39. Ibid.
40. Nanos, "Rejoinder," 14.

is whether Paul ever *did* refer to fellow Jews as his brothers and sisters apart from qualification. The unusual qualifiers in Rom 9:3 signal a *departure* from Paul's ordinary usage. Nanos would need to make a case that an unqualified use of "brother" in Romans or in Paul generally may refer to a Christ-believing Jew. Nanos asks: "Do we have a letter from Paul by which to disqualify, much less quantify Gagnon's universal proposition that Paul *could not* consider non-Christ-believing Jewish people the kin of Christ-believing gentiles?"[41] Questions of "could" or "could not" are impossible to answer since the interpreter does not have access to the apostle's mind apart from the writings he left behind. Gagnon rightly limits himself to the available evidence and argues for a consistent pattern from letter to letter. Paul's ordinary usage of "brother" for Christ-believers and the qualifying comments when he departed from that pattern in Rom 9:3 provide strong evidence that the "brothers" in Rom 14:1 — 15:13 must also be Christ-believers.

The Monotheistic Character of the Appeal to the "Weak"

Clearly Paul wanted the strong to follow the example of Christ, but Nanos notes that Paul nowhere asked the same of the weak.[42] Paul never mentioned Christ in connection with the weak, as he did with the strong (cf. 14:15). "Interestingly, in the first eight verses [of Rom 14] mention of Christ is completely absent; the focus is on 'God' and on 'the Lord' — phrases that are inclusive of non-Christian Jewish faith."[43] Nanos equates "God" (14:3, 6, 10, 11, [12]) and "Lord" (14:4, 6, 8, 11) as excluding Christ.[44] The weak were therefore non-Christ-believing.

Surprisingly, as Gagnon and other reviewers have noticed, Nanos in *Mystery of Romans* never cites Rom 14:9: "Christ died and lived . . . that he might be Lord (κυριεύσῃ) of both the dead and the living." Verse 9 unpacks living and dying "for the Lord" in v. 8. The "Lord" of v. 8 is therefore Jesus Christ. Verses 8–9 cast their shadow back upon the behavior of the weak in 14:6: "Those who observe the day, observe it in honor of the Lord, since they give thanks to God; . . . while

---

41. Ibid., 16.

42. Nanos, *Mystery*, 118. Paul does, however, speak of the weak as those "for whom Christ died" in 14:15. Ben Witherington, *Paul's Letter to the Romans: A Socio-Rhetorical Commentary* (Grand Rapids: Eerdmans, 2004), 331, believes: "[Romans] 14.15 is an insurmountable objection to Nanos' reading of this material."

43. Nanos, *Mystery*, 113.

44. For further development of the equation of Christ as "Lord" in Paul, see Das, *Paul and the Jews*, 84–85, 93–94.

those who abstain, abstain in honor of the Lord and give thanks to God." With the clear affirmation of Christ as Lord in 14:9, God and Christ may be distinguished only with difficulty, as Paul appeared to shift unconsciously between the two appellations.[45] In Rom 14:10–11 Paul described God as the one who judges, but in 2 Cor 5:11 Paul ascribed this activity to *Christ*. Likewise in Rom 14:11 every knee bows to God, but Paul cited the same Old Testament passage for every knee bowing to *Christ* in Phil 2:10–11. Gagnon claims that "Lord" always refers to Christ in the twenty-two unambiguous instances in Romans apart from Septuagintal quotations.[46] Romans 10:12–13 and 12:11 are ambiguous but likely refer to Christ as well. "Serving the Lord" in Rom 12:11 parallels "serving Christ" in 14:18 and 16:18. Since Rom 10:12-13 is grammatically subordinated to the expression of Christ as Lord in 10:9, Rom 10:13 does not likely allude to Rom 3:29–30's reference to God. Within the context of Rom 14:1 — 15:16, Paul says in 14:14: "I know and am persuaded in the Lord *Jesus*." In 15:6 he speaks of "our Lord *Jesus Christ*."

Nanos argues: "Also, there is an implicit recognition that the 'weak' and the 'strong' regard each other as serving different 'masters' (v. 4) that Paul challenges in making his point that they are wrong, for both are serving, and therefore accepted by, the same Lord."[47] What Paul actually said, though, was, "Who are you to pass judgment on servants of another? It is before their own lord that they stand or fall." In other words, the weak are servants of the Lord and are accountable before their Lord. The strong do not have the right to judge the weak as the Lord's servants, nor the weak the strong. Nowhere did Paul imply that the strong regarded the weak as serving a different Lord. Gagnon notes the reference in 14:18 to serving Christ as a slave, a clear parallel in language to the weak's serving the Lord in 14:4. The Lord of the weak again appears to be the same Lord as of the strong.

Although Nanos has not been entirely convinced by Gagnon's response, Nanos does not offer any counterarguments and concedes that "Paul and his target audience believe in Jesus Christ as Lord."[48] This concession poses a serious problem for Nanos's position, since he has mistakenly excluded the weak who

---

45. Gagnon, "'Weak' at Rome," 69. For a similar critique of Nanos (along with further argumentation), see Mark Reasoner, *The Strong and the Weak: Romans 14:1 — 15:13 in Context* (SNTSMS 103; Cambridge: Cambridge Univ. Press, 1999), 134.

46. Gagnon, "'Weak' at Rome," 69–70. Reasoner, *Strong and the Weak*, 134 n. 162, makes the very same point as Gagnon. The OT quotations of God as Lord are Rom 4:8; 9:28–29; 10:13, 16; 11:3, 34; 12:19; 14:11; 15:11.

47. Nanos, *Mystery*, 113.

48. Nanos, "Rejoinder," 18.

are addressed in Rom 14 from that target audience. The weak as members of Paul's audience agree with the strong that Jesus is Lord. The weak must therefore be Christ-believers.

Romans 14:22b–23 as Condemnation of the "Strong" for Eating in Doubt

Romans 14:22b–23 reads: "Blessed are those who have no reason to condemn themselves because of what they approve. But those who have doubts are condemned if they eat, because they do not act from faith; for whatever does not proceed from faith is sin." These verses appear to bless the strong and to warn the weak of condemnation should they eat with doubt. Nanos does not agree with most commentators that Paul was censuring the weak for their doubts regarding food in these two verses. He thinks that whatever weakness is in view throughout Rom 14:1 — 15:6 has nothing to do with food but rather with the weak's lack of faith in Christ. He translates Rom 14:22b–23:

> "Happy is he who does not condemn himself in what he approves. But he who doubts [διακρίνομαι] is condemned if he eats, because his eating is not from faith; and whatever is not from faith is sin."[49]

To clarify how Nanos's translation and interpretation differ from the usual view, Gagnon has helpfully inserted explanatory notes in brackets:

> "Happy is he [the 'strong' person] who does not condemn himself [bring down God's condemnation] in what he approves [by not asserting his rights in matters of diet and calendar]. But he who doubts [the 'strong' person who doubts in the sense of not judging himself correctly, here by insisting on his right to eat all things] is condemned if he eats, because his [the 'strong' person's] eating is not from faith [he does not trust God enough to give up his rights]; and whatever is not from faith is sin."[50]

For Nanos, Paul's concern in these verses was not with the weak but with the strong.

In his "Rejoinder" Nanos revises his position by pointing out that διακρίνομαι should not be translated "doubt" or "waver," as the BDAG lexicon suggests, but rather "dispute" or "criticize (someone)."[51] This would further support Nanos's contention that the strong are criticizing the weak rather than the weak doubting themselves with respect to food. In a helpful study of διακρίνω throughout the

49. Nanos, *Mystery*, 134–36.
50. Gagnon, "'Weak' at Rome," 71.
51. Nanos, "Rejoinder," 20.

New Testament, David DeGraff demonstrates that "doubt" is not a defensible translation of διακρίνω. In 388 non-biblical instances of διακρίνω, primarily from 200 B.C. to A.D. 100, διακρίνω never means "doubt."[52] For instance, in Philo's "On Dreams," "matters of doubt (τὰ ἐνδιαζομένα) are settled by an oath" (τῶν πραγμάτων ὅρκῳ διακρίνεται; *Somn.* 1.2 §12). "In this instance, then, the action denoted by διακρίνω is not that of being uncertain, but rather of making an uncertain thing *more* certain."[53] In the Septuagint, διακρίνω in its thirty instances, including the middle or passive forms, is almost always used for judging, judging between, or separating people.[54] What leads translators to take διακρίνω in the New Testament as "doubt" or "waver" is its usage alongside "faith." Διστάζω means "doubt" and is frequently contrasted with πίστις (for example, Matt 14:31). Διακρίνω, however, is not synonymous with διστάζω elsewhere in Greek literature. This leads DeGraff to suggest that the διακρίνω/πίστις contrast would suggest a different meaning of πίστις than "faith."[55] Πίστις, DeGraff contends, may involve a notion of faithfulness as expressed in the community. In the context of Rom 14:23, however, Paul was likely referring to a conviction regarding food. In Rom 14:23 DeGraff suggests the translation: "the divisive one [the strong] is condemned if he eats."[56] The strong remains the subject in v. 23, even as in v. 22. Were the weak in view in 14:23, the implication would be that they have been induced to eat what the strong are eating, but Paul does not say that.[57] The issue in this context is "not that people are violating their own scruples, but that people are allowing their differing opinions about a permissible diet to divide the community."[58]

These verses pose a serious problem for Nanos's contention that the "weak" are labeled such because they lack faith in Christ. Gagnon connects 14:22b–23's "faith" with the reference to "faith" in the preceding half-verse, 14:22a: "The faith that you have, have as your own conviction before God." Commentators concur with Gagnon that "faith" in 14:22a must include, if not be identified with, a conviction regarding certain foods. Douglas Moo speaks for the majority: "As in v. 1, 'faith' does not refer to general Christian faith but to convictions about

---

52. David DeGraff, "Some Doubts about Doubt: The New Testament Use of ΔIAKPINΩ," *JETS* 48 (2005): 735–36.

53. Ibid., 736.

54. Ibid., 737.

55. Ibid., 739.

56. The strong's divisive judging of the weak further undermines Nanos's contention that the weak were judging the strong because they were in a position of authority.

57. DeGraff, "Some Doubts about Doubt," 740.

58. Ibid., 741.

the issues in dispute in Rome that arise out of one's faith in Christ."[59] As Joseph Fitzmyer puts it: "Here [14:22–23] it is clear that *pistis* . . . expresses a conviction about food, drink and calendric observances. Essential Christian faith, rather, is something that one may, and sometimes may have to, parade before humanity; but this is not true of conviction about indifferent matters."[60] Fitzmyer also agrees with the many modern commentators who take "faith" in the maxim-like utterance at the end of v. 23 ("whatever is not from faith is sin") as a conviction with respect to indifferent matters (*adiaphora*), that is, food.[61] Nanos concedes that diet and calendar continue to figure in 14:22b–23. The eating-which-is-not-from-faith in 14:23 more likely refers primarily to a conviction regarding food and not trust in God (as Nanos's interpretation requires).[62] Indeed, the phrase "weak in faith" in 14:1 is qualified in 14:2 as "believes [has faith] *in eating anything.*" Clarence Glad thinks 14:1–2 and 14:22–23 are an *inclusio* that must be read alongside each other since Paul employs faith (πιστ–) language as well as διακρίνομαι in both.[63] This would strengthen the inference that "faith" in 14:22–23 must be understood as regarding food.[64] Nanos, in his own approach,

---

59. Moo, *Romans*, 861–62. He adds:

> Paul is not, then, telling the "strong" Christian to be quiet about his or her faith in Christ — a plea that would be quite out of place in the NT! Nor is he necessarily requiring "strong" believers never to mention their views on these matters or to speak of their sense of freedom before others. As the context suggests, the silence that Paul requires is related to the need to avoid putting a stumbling block in the way of the "weak." This will mean that the "strong" are not to brag about their convictions before the "weak" and, especially, that they are not to propagandize the "weak."

60. Joseph A. Fitzmyer, *Romans* (AB 33; New York: Doubleday, 1993), 698. Among recent commentators, Schreiner, *Romans*, 732, dissents from the majority in viewing "faith" here as trust in God, but even Schreiner includes in that trust conviction regarding certain foods (contra Nanos).

Although not ultimately decisive, as Nanos, "Rejoinder," 19–20, shows, Gagnon, "'Weak' at Rome," 70, nevertheless offers an interesting parallel from 1 Cor 10:25–30, where Paul vigorously affirms "the right of the 'strong' to eat in private settings and even in public when blissful ignorance operates," but not where there is potential for upsetting another individual's conscience.

61. Fitzmyer, *Romans*, 700; likewise Moo, *Romans*, 863; contra Schreiner, *Romans*, 737–38.

62. Trust in God would be secondary.

63. Glad, *Paul and Philodemus*, 218–19.

64. Nanos's artificial distinction, *Mystery*, 103–5, between weakness of *faith* and *opinion* misses the point that it is precisely an attitude toward food that results from and

awkwardly defines "faith" in 14:23 as the strong's not trusting God enough to give up their rights. This translation of "faith," if carried over consistently to the immediately following maxim ("whatever is not from faith is sin"), renders the maxim incomprehensible. Christological affirmations are only distantly related to Paul's concerns in these two verses.

Internal Consistency in Romans 1–11

Paul regularly refers to the Jewish people in Rom 1–11. Nanos, in identifying the "weak" in Rom 14:1 — 15:6 as non-Christ-believing Jews, links them to the non-Christ-believing Jews discussed earlier in the letter.[65] Gagnon, on the other hand, offers an alternative understanding of the relationship between chaps. 1–11 and 14:1 — 15:13 in which the "weak" are gentile Christians.[66] A "debt theology" dominates the overarching logic of chaps. 1–11. As God has acted graciously on behalf of Paul's audience, his audience must therefore attend to right conduct (for example, 6:1 — 8:17). Romans 12:1 is a conspicuous example of this sort of reasoning: "I exhort you . . . by the mercies of God." The same reasoning is at work in Rom 15:7: "Welcome one another, just as Christ has welcomed you to the glory of God." After all that God has done for the Roman community in Christ, they will surely not get mired in disputes over matters of food and days but will imitate God's gracious benefaction in their relationships with one another (8:12; 13:8; 15:1; cf. 1:14). Gagnon also notes the "layered trap" in chaps. 1–11. As soon as Paul demolished any potential Jewish ethnic superiority by refusing to exempt the "Jew" from God's judgment in chaps. 2–3, he turned around in 11:17–24 to warn gentile Christians that they too may be broken off from the olive tree of God's saving relationship with Israel if they do not continue in [God's] kindness. Nanos lodges no disagreement with Gagnon's approach but simply notes: "these observations do not 'require' the 'weak' to be non-Christian Jews," nor do they demonstrate that "the weak/stumbling 'cannot'

---

betrays a weakness in faith. That Paul defines the weak with respect to their behavior and not their failure to trust in Christ, see also Peter J. Tomson, Review of Mark D. Nanos, *The Mystery of Romans, JSJ* 28 (1997): 346.

65. Nanos, *Mystery*, 90, 107, 159; idem, "The Jewish Context of the Gentile Audience Addressed in Paul's Letter to the Romans," *CBQ* 61 (1999): 298–99.

66. Gagnon, "'Weak' at Rome," 73, begins by noting that Rom 1–11 does not give direct information about the "weak" in Rom 14:1 — 15:13, but Nanos, "Rejoinder," 23, sensibly counters that his reading does not require direct information about the "weak" in these chapters, only that chaps. 1–11 may be appealed to in order to inform the reading of 14:1 — 15:13. Romans 1–11 informs Gagnon's approach to Rom 14:1 — 15:13 as well.

be as I have proposed."[67] As Nanos recognizes, this particular line of thought is simply indecisive for determining the identity of the "weak."

The Incompatibility of Paul's Approval of the "Weak" and Their Observance of the Law

Nanos again claims that the "weak" are labeled as such for their failure to believe in Christ and not for their observance of Jewish customs and the Law. In support, he notes that Paul never required the weak to give up their adherence to Jewish customs. On the contrary "the 'strong' should change their *own* behavior and act like the 'weak.'"[68] Gagnon responds by distinguishing Paul's accommodation of the weak in their scruples from a commendation of those scruples. Paul doubly emphasized in Rom 14:14, 20 that "nothing is unclean in itself; but it is unclean for anyone who thinks it unclean. . . . Everything is indeed clean." Paul has relativized the legal distinction and left it as a matter of individual preference. "For the kingdom of God is not food and drink but righteousness and peace and joy in the Holy Spirit" (14:17). Gagnon rightly labels the distinction between clean and unclean foods a matter of indifference (an *adiaphoron*). God has not commanded Christ-believers to avoid certain foods as unclean, and so the strong are not commanded to do so. Rather, "we who are strong ought to put up with the failings of the weak, and not to please ourselves" (15:1). That means not eating meat in the company of those brothers or sisters who would be troubled by such eating (14:21). The matter of clean or unclean foods is not worth debating (14:1) or causing division (15:6).

Nanos, for his part, thinks that Paul was commending the weak for avoiding unclean meat "in honor of the Lord" (14:6–7), but, contra Nanos, the apostle never *admonished* the weak to continue their practices.[69] If a "weak" individual decided to abandon a prior conviction that certain foods are unclean, Paul would not have disagreed with their decision or urged them to return to a properly Law-observant lifestyle (14:14, 20). That individuals live their lives "for the Lord" in matters of indifference does not make those lifestyle choices somehow mandated. Gagnon is right to view the respectful actions of the strong in the presence of the weak a matter of accommodation. In light of the Mosaic Law's own distinctions, Nanos, in his desire for a consistently Law-observant Paul, does not appear to appreciate how explosive is the declaration in Rom 14:14, 20

---

67. Nanos, "Rejoinder," 25.
68. Nanos, *Mystery*, 117; cited also by Gagnon, "'Weak' at Rome," 75.
69. Nanos, "Rejoinder," 26.

that everything is clean.[70] One can only imagine such boldface declarations in the context of those who share Paul's Christ-centered convictions and certainly not in the context of synagogue Jews.

Nanos considers it questionable that Paul ever taught Christ-believing Jews to abandon their Jewish customs.[71] Gagnon responds that the audience of Romans was entirely gentile. So Paul was *not* teaching Jews to abandon their customs. Paul did, however, claim that the Law's ritual requirements are matters of indifference and not required for those who wish to enjoy God's favor. Nanos does not believe that shifting the audience to gentiles removes the difficulty of what he calls "Luther's trap."[72] Paul would be dismissing the value of Jewish identity and behavior for "gentiles who still claim to be identified in Jewish terms, as Noahide children of Abraham/righteousness."[73] Rhetorical appeals to "Luther's trap," however, should not determine the interpretation of Paul. The question is

---

70. Barclay, "'Do We Undermine the Law?'" 300–1; Daniel Boyarin, *A Radical Jew: Paul and the Politics of Identity* (Berkeley: Univ. of California Press, 1994), 9–10.

71. Nanos, *Mystery*, 117.

72. For Nanos, Luther made the mistake of concluding from Paul's comments in Rom 14–15 regarding the "weak" that the apostle was patronizing and judgmental with respect to the Jews and Judaism. This conclusion may therefore say more about Luther than the apostle. Paul, according to Nanos and contra Luther, respectfully affirmed the genuine faith of the weak (*Mystery*, 115, 119).

73. Nanos, "Rejoinder," 27. On the lack of evidence for Noahide laws prior to 100 CE, see Martin Goodman, *Mission and Conversion: Proselytizing in the Religious History of the Roman Empire* (Oxford: Oxford Univ. Press, 1994), 53. For a satisfying reading of the apostolic decree in Acts 15 that resolves the significance of the particular four elements mentioned, see Ben Witherington, III, *The Acts of the Apostles: A Socio-Rhetorical Commentary* (Grand Rapids: Eerdmans, 1998), 460–66. Witherington dispels any notion that Acts 15 is referring to much later Noahide gentile prescriptions in Rabbinic writings or that Lev 17–18 is in view (instructions for those dwelling *in* the land and only with regard to the eating of blood). See also E. Elizabeth Johnson, "A Critical Assessment of Mark Nanos, *The Mystery of Romans*," *CRBR* 11 (1998): 153–62, although her critique lacks the precision that Witherington brought to the debate. Witherington sees all four elements in Acts 15 pointing toward the proscription of idolatry in Christian circles (εἰδωλόθυτον is unique to Christian usage and unattested in Judaism). Further, all four activities are common to *pagan temples*, especially idolatry and sacred prostitution (e.g., 2 Macc 6:4–5). Likewise, pagan officiants would often choke the sacrifice or strangle it as an expression of transferring its life breath to the idol. The priest would sometimes taste the blood of the sacrifice. The pagan temple is not in view in Rom 14:1 — 15:13. The "apostolic decree" of Acts 15 and Paul in Rom 14:1 — 15:13 would be addressing entirely different situations.

whether *Paul,* insofar as he communicated his perspective in the Letter to the Romans, considered it a matter of indifference for gentiles to adopt a degree of Jewish identity and behavior. Again, Paul's bold declaration of all foods clean in Rom 14:14, 20 appears to answer this question.

Gagnon goes further to argue that the Mosaic Law is no longer a requirement and a matter of indifference also for Christ-believing Jews. Much of his discussion and Nanos's response delve (all too briefly) into Paul's view of the Law in general. For example, Gagnon considers the Law essentially "undoable."[74] Nanos disagrees, since, in agreement with Dunn's "new perspective," he contends that the Law itself provides for sin and failure.[75] In Gal 2:21 and 3:21, however, Paul emphasizes that Christ's death would have been unnecessary had the Law provided for sin. The sole basis for atonement and repentance for Paul was the death of Christ and not some instrument from the Law of Moses.[76] Gagnon is right in maintaining that Paul did not view the Law as *binding* for himself or other Jewish Christians insofar as God's salvation is "apart from the Law" and "without the works of the Law." Galatians 2:16 makes this very claim in the context of what Jewish Christ-believers all "know."[77] Galatians 3:10 and Rom 7 both support Gagnon's contention that Paul viewed the Law as "undoable" because mercy and forgiveness, in the face of human failure, are only available in Christ (cf. Gal 3:13; Rom 7:24–25).[78] Gagnon rightly appeals to the universal language of Rom 3:22 and 10:12, which explicitly included the Jewish people for the salvation available in Christ.[79] Gagnon concludes from 1 Cor 9:20 that Paul observed the Law for pragmatic reasons rather than as necessary for salvation. This Paul is the same Jewish Christ-believer who declared all foods clean in Rom 14:14, 20. In principle he had no problem with Jews putting aside distinctively Jewish aspects of Torah.

> At Antioch he could charge Cephas (or could wish he had charged Cephas) with tacitly admitting that the Law could not justify him yet making the

---

74. Gagnon, "'Weak' at Rome," 76.

75. Nanos, "Rejoinder," 28.

76. For full development of this point see chaps. 3–5 in A. Andrew Das, *Paul, the Law, and the Covenant* (Peabody, Mass.: Hendrickson, 2001), 70–144.

77. On the Jewish Christian identity of "we Jews" in 2:15–16a, see A. Andrew Das, "Another Look at ἐὰν μή in Galatians 2:16," *JBL* 119 (2000): 529–39.

78. For further discussion of the frustrating life "under the Law" and its demand in Rom 7, see Das, *Paul, the Law, and the Covenant,* 222–28. For Paul's assumption that no one does what the Law requires in Gal 3:10, see Das, *Paul, the Law, and the Covenant,* 145–70.

79. For God's impartial dealings with both gentile *and Jew* in judgment and salvation in Christ, see Das, *Paul and the Jews,* 86–88, 92–96.

Law a requirement by ceasing to eat with gentiles (Gal 2:11–14). It was not by "tearing down" the Law that Paul "commended himself" (ἐμαυτὸν συνιστάνω) as a transgressor but by "building up" the Law again (Gal 2:18). When he "died to the Law," he died to the Law itself as a power with binding jurisdiction over his life (cf. Rom 7:1–6), not in order to lead a sinful life but in order to "live for God" (Gal 2:19). To reinstitute the Law itself as a binding authority for Jewish or gentile believers would be tantamount to rejecting the grace of God and asserting that "Christ died for nothing" (Gal 2:21).[80]

Nanos responds that Paul's concern was a new age dawning in Christ with implications *for gentiles*.[81] Nanos leaves unaddressed the Pauline passages that employ universal language for the plight of humanity in sin with faith in Christ as the instrument of salvation for both gentile *and Jew*. He simply claims that Gal 5:3 proves that Paul himself was as fully Law-observant as any other Jewish Christ-believer.[82]

"Weak" as Meaning "Stumbling"

Nanos identifies the "weak" in faith in Rom 14:1 — 15:13 as those who are "stumbling" in Rom 9–11 because they recognize neither that Jesus is Lord nor that the gentiles must be included in God's saving plan.[83] Nanos observes that the Septuagint often translated the Hebrew verb "to stumble" (כשׁל) into Greek with "to be weak" (ἀσθενεῖν). If "weak" means "stumbling," the only people who have stumbled in Romans, outside of Rom 14:13, 20–21 (and 16:17), were the Jews who stumbled because of their unbelief concerning Christ in 9:32–33; 11:9, 11. Since the weak/stumbling are non-Christ-believing Jews in Rom

---

80. Gagnon, "'Weak' at Rome," 78 n. 12.

81. Nanos, "Rejoinder," 31. Nanos largely agrees with the thesis of Lloyd Gaston, *Paul and the Torah* (Vancouver: Univ. of British Columbia, 1987), that Paul adopted a particular understanding of Christ's significance for *the gentiles*. Gaston's thesis has been recently championed again by John G. Gager, *Reinventing Paul* (Oxford: Oxford Univ. Press, 2000). Nanos's Paul would hope and pray that the Jews come to recognize Jesus as the Messiah and Savior, especially through the behavior of Christ-believing gentiles. For a thorough critique of Gaston's approach to Paul, a critique that would apply equally to Nanos, see Das, *Paul and the Jews*, 96–106.

82. Nanos, "Rejoinder," 31–32. Paul's appeal in Gal 5:3 for the gentiles not to adopt the Law may be grounded just as well in Paul's presentation in Gal 1 of his fully Law-observant *past* when he considered the Law God's means of salvation; so also Phil 3:3–11.

83. Nanos, *Mystery*, 120–39, 157–59.

9:32–33; 11:9, 11, Nanos concludes that the weak/stumbling must be non-Christ-believing Jews in Rom 14:1 — 15:13. The strong should not give those who are stumbling "that little push [by eating offensive food] likely to cause them to continue to stumble until they have fallen and been 'destroy[ed].'"[84] Gagnon supportively adds that a disputed, lengthier variant of Rom 14:21 juxtaposes "stumbling" (προσκόπτει), "tripping" (σκανδαλίζεται) and "being weak" (ἀσθενεῖ) as synonymous.

Gagnon raises a series of objections for Nanos's proposal that have remained unanswered. Nanos has not demonstrated that Paul ever used words with the ἀσθεν- stem for "stumbling." In Rom 15:1 τὰ ἀσθενήματα are further described as "incapable" (τῶν ἀδυνάτων), which suggests "weakness" and not "stumbling" as the meaning. Nanos's specialized sense of the ἀσθεν- word group in Rom 14:1 — 15:13 remains unsupported. Nanos has not demonstrated that ἀσθενεῖν ever bears the sense of "stumble" elsewhere in Greek literature apart from the Septuagint. As for the Septuagintal usage, in 25 of the 56 instances of the verb ἀσθενεῖν, the meaning is *not* "to stumble" but rather "to be weak." The adjective ἀσθενής in the Septuagint *never* means "stumbling," and three of the five instances of the noun ἀσθένεια do not mean "obstacle" or "offense" in translating the Hebrew (מכשול). Gagnon also notes several Hebrew texts where the word for "stumbling" (כשל) means "weak" (2 Chr 28:15; Pss 31:10; 109:24; Lam 1:14; Zech 12:8).[85] Also, when "weak" is used in connection with "strong" (οἱ δυνατοί), "weak" and "strong" are clearly functioning as opposites and define each other. While Paul did indeed use the language of standing and falling (for instance, 14:4), *that* language, and not ἀσθενεῖν, signals the notion of stumbling.[86]

Even granting Nanos's translation of ἀσθενεῖν as inclusive of the notion of stumbling in Rom 14:1 — 15:13, Gagnon notes how the context of usage for "stumbling" in Rom 9:32–33 and 11:9, 11 does not match that of Rom 14:1 — 15:13:

> Although Paul insists that Israel has not "stumbled so as to fall" (11:11, but contrast 11:22, "those who fell"), he clearly regards it as already accursed (9:3), prepared for destruction (9:22), outside salvation (10:1) and a "remnant" (11:5) whose members are broken off from the olive tree "because of their unbelief" (11:19–24). None of this is hinted at as an added consideration regarding the "weak" in 14:1 — 15:13.[87]

---

84. Ibid., 125.
85. Gagnon, "'Weak' at Rome," 78–79 n. 15.
86. Contra Nanos, *Mystery*, 126.
87. Gagnon, "'Weak' at Rome," 79.

The "weak" of Rom 14:1—15:13 are "weak *in faith*" (τὸν ἀσθενοῦντα τῇ πίστει), but the "stumbling" of Rom 9–11 are *in unbelief* (τῇ ἀπιστίᾳ; Rom 11:20, 23; cf. 3:3).[88] Paul did not employ ἀσθενεῖν in Rom 9–11 in anticipation of his later discussion. He did employ ἀσθενεῖν in 1 Cor 8:7–13 but offered no contextual clue that the word should be taken as anything other than "weak." Nanos responds to Gagnon's case: "I can find no significant criticism of my proposal that ἀσθένεια is better rendered in this case as stumbling, rather than weak, or that it refers to non-Christ-believing Jewish people."[89] Nanos does not seem to appreciate that Gagnon has conceded the possibility (and certain attractive aspects) of Nanos's connection between these two passages but has strongly disputed its plausibility, especially on linguistic grounds. Apart from other considerations in favor of plausibility and in view of the differences in context, ἀσθενεῖν is best taken, as in other Greek literature of Paul's day, as "weak." The identification of the "weak" as non-Christ-believing Jews must be advanced on other grounds.

The Analogy of Abraham, Not Weak in Faith (Romans 4:19–21)

Nanos contends that Rom 14:1, 5, 23; 15:1, 6, and 9 echo Rom 4:19–21. In Rom 4 Abraham and Sarah's bodies were "dead." Yet Abraham "was credited with righteousness" (4:3) because of his steadfast faith in God's promise that he would become the father of many nations even if God had to raise an heir for him from the dead. Just as Abraham was commended for not wavering in unbelief or doubt that God would raise an heir from his dead body, so the weak's wavering or doubt in Rom 14:1—15:13 must be with respect to Jesus' resurrection from the dead (note the same word as in Rom 4:19; ἀσθενέω).[90] Further, even as the Law was not yet in existence in Abraham's day (Rom 5:13–14) and does not figure in Paul's discussion of Abraham in Rom 4:19–21, so the wavering or doubt of the weak must not be with respect to the Law, whether its dietary

---

88. Ibid., 78 n. 13; James D. G. Dunn, Review of Mark D. Nanos, *The Mystery of Romans, JTS* 48 (1997): 600. The stumbling of Rom 9–11 are *not* described as "weak *in faith.*" So also Angelika Reichert, *Der Römerbrief als Gratwanderung: Eine Untersuchung zur Abfassungsproblematik* (FRLANT 194; Göttingen: Vandenhoeck & Ruprecht, 2001), 274–75 n. 229.

89. Nanos, "Rejoinder," 33.

90. Nanos, *Mystery*, 142–44.

restrictions or calendar.[91] "Weakness" in Rom 14–15 must refer to something else. Nanos contends it refers to a non-Christ-believing status. Finally, just as Paul described Abraham's faith in the language of strength and weakness, he reprised the same language in Rom 14:1 — 15:13 for the "strong" in faith "who recognize God's righteousness as did Abraham" and "believe in the faithfulness of God to keep his promise in spite of appearances to the contrary . . . in Abraham's 'seed' (Jesus the Christ)."[92] Non-Christ-believing Jews are "weak in faith," in spite of their trust in God, because they stumble over Christ's resurrection and over the inclusion of the gentiles *as gentiles* in God's saving plan.

Usually interpreters have identified the object of Abraham's faith with less specificity as simply a God who is faithful to promises.[93] Gagnon agrees with Nanos that 4:19 and 14:1 — 15:13 are verbally linked, but Gagnon interprets the significance of the connection differently. Gagnon observes that Paul relied on the Abrahamic narrative throughout Rom 4, but the apostle was drawn especially to two points in that narrative: Gen 15:6 (in Rom 4:3; cf. Gen 12:2; 13:16) and Gen 17:7 (in Rom 4:19). In Gen 15:6 Abraham believed God's promise of descendants. In Gen 17:7 Abraham first contemplated the difficulty of conception because of his age. More than a decade, then, separated Abraham's first serious consideration of his age from his initial belief in the promise (Gen 15:6; 17:7). Gagnon therefore concludes that Rom 4:19 concerns someone who *already* believed in the "promise." Already in Rom 4:24 Paul compared Abraham's faith to that of the Christian who believes "in the one who raised Jesus from the dead." So, given the connections between Rom 4 and 14–15, the weakness and wavering of Rom 14:1, 23; 15:13 must characterize those who are *already* believers in the fulfilled promise of Jesus Christ, whom God raised from

---

91. Nanos, *Mystery*, compares Abraham's "weakness" and "wavering" (both used together) in Rom 4:19–21 to the wavering/doubt of the weak in Rom 14:22–23. In his "Rejoinder," p. 20, he corrects himself with respect to 14:22–23 that "waver" or "doubt" should be replaced by "dispute" or "criticize" in relation to *the strong* and *not* the weak. He unwittingly creates a difficulty for an argument based on the parallels between Rom 4 and 14. DeGraff, "Some Doubts about Doubt," 755, thinks διακρίνω in Rom 4:19–21 has a *different* sense ("be disloyal") than in Rom 14:22–23 ("be divisive").

92. Nanos, *Mystery*, 142.

93. Mark Reasoner, *Strong and the Weak*, 134, notes that in 4:20 the "strong" in faith give glory to God; he believes that Paul is implying that if Abraham were "weak" in faith he would not have given glory to God. On the other hand, in Rom 14:6 and 15:5–6 the "strong" and the "weak" *both* give glory to God. Conceptual differences between the two passages hinder such strained conclusions from the verbal parallels.

the dead. They were *not* non-Christ-believing Jews.[94] Gagnon even wonders if Paul offered a veiled compliment to the weak in faith in Rom 14:1 — 15:13 for their trust in the promise of God regarding Christ in spite of their wavering in matters of diet and calendar. Perhaps Paul was even encouraging the weak to continue on that firm path of faith in Christ as the fulfillment of the Abrahamic promise by recognizing that all things were now clean. At the same time, the strong must not alienate the weak in a matter of indifference and thereby hurt those who would "give glory to God" (4:20; cf. 15:6). Like Abraham the strong and the weak must join together in "hoping against hope" (4:18; cf. 15:13).[95] Gagnon's reading demonstrates that the connections with Rom 4:19–21 do not prove that that the "weak in faith" were not Christ-believing. They could just as well have been believers in Christ.[96]

---

94. Gagnon qualifies that the analogy is not exact, since "weak" in 14:1 — 15:13 refers to diet and calendar and not Jesus' messianic identity. He notes that Abraham did not implement the Law's requirement of circumcision until Gen 17:18, *after* the earlier moments of trust and potential wavering.

95. Gagnon, "'Weak' at Rome," 78–81.

96. Nanos in his response, "Rejoinder," 35, calls Gagnon's arguments "strained throughout." He poses a series of questions. First, "Why does Gagnon grant that weakness to regard Jewish diet as appropriate is still regarded by Paul as a matter of *faith*, when Gagnon has concluded that Paul no longer considered the practice of Law an expression of faith, since it was now obsolete for the Christ-believer? Is continued Law-observance then not sin, since 'whatever is not of faith is sin' (14:23)?" The Law, however, may not be obsolete for Paul. Rather, its distinctions of food and days are matters of indifference for Paul's gentile audience. No sin is involved as long as the weak do not begin to judge the strong or consider the legal practices necessary for the enjoyment of God's saving activity. Nanos also asks, "If continued Law-observance is not commensurate with the practice of faith in Christ, one wonders in what way the weak/stumbling may be described by Gagnon as those who 'have proven themselves "strong" with respect to 'the promise of God' concerning Christ' (80)." Gagnon grants for the sake of argument that the strong trust in "the promise of God concerning Christ" but actually thinks "weak" in faith refers in this passage to food and days. Schreiner may have a stronger approach when he contends that weak in faith refers *primarily* to food and days, but not to the exclusion of the promises of God. The point is that, granting Nanos's connections to 4:19–21, the conclusion that the "weak" are non-Christ-believing does not necessarily follow. Nanos continues, "Why should such faith be esteemed strong/able by Gagnon's Paul if it remains Torah-observant, and thus opposed by Paul as not-faith?" However, an interest in the Mosaic Law is *not* an expression of "not-faith" unless such observances are deemed necessary. Nanos again: "One might wonder why Gagnon's indifferent Paul thought that this extensive instruction about respecting the sensibilities of the weak/stumbling in faith, even if calculated by themselves to be in the service of the Lord, was

Other Evidence That the Weak Are Non-Christ-Believing

No Separate Christ-Believing Churches or "Ekklesia"?

Nanos makes several additional points in support of his contention that the Roman synagogue Jews and the gentile Christ-believers had not yet parted ways at the time of Paul's letter.[97] Nanos observes that Paul did not describe the Romans as meeting in their own church or churches (ἐκκλησία).[98] He concludes from this that the letter must come from a time prior to the split when Christians were still worshiping in the synagogues. Paul, however, did in fact greet an ekklesia meeting in the home of Prisca and Aquila in 16:5.[99] Paul's Philippians offers a parallel to Romans in only incidentally referring to the audience toward the end of the letter as an ekklesia (4:15).

The "Weak" as Neighbors of the Christ-Believing Subgroup

Paul described the "weak" in Rom 15:2 as "neighbors" to the strong. Nanos concludes that the "weak" must be outsiders to the Christ-believing subgroup.[100] On the other hand, in 13:9 Paul urged those within the community of Christ-believers to love their "neighbor." The commandment to love one's neighbor supports Paul's admonition to the gentile Christ-believing audience in the preceding verse to "love one another" (so also 1 Thess 3:12). The use of the word "neighbors"

warranted, instead of calling for the strong/able to teach the weak/stumbling to recognize, by word and example, that the Law is obsolete and opposed to God's purpose, since its continued practice weakened or sickened faith" (Nanos, "Rejoinder," 35–36). In a gentle way, Paul *did* encourage the weak to become strong by not being so worried about days and food, which are ultimately clean. Paul even numbered himself among the strong but — as a matter of indifference — did not press the point but instead urged the strong to accommodate the weak as they both give glory together to God. Nanos thinks that such accommodation of the Jewish practices of the weak would entice and endanger the strong, but that is hard to imagine in the Roman church where it is precisely a respect for the Jewish heritage that is at issue in the first place.

97. These are arguments to which Gagnon either did not respond or mentioned very briefly in passing.

98. Nanos, *Mystery*, 115.

99. As the first gathering greeted, one may infer that the other gatherings greeted in 16:10, 11, 14, and 15 are likewise "churches" (comparable to Gal 1:2); thus Lampe, "Roman Christians," 229–30.

100. Nanos, *Mystery*, 114.

therefore does not mandate the conclusion that the weak are outsiders to the community of the strong.

Overlap of the Roman Christ-Believers with the Jews of Rome

Nanos notes the extensive overlap of physical territory within which Christians and Jews worked and resided in Rome. They labored in common trades. They shared remarkably similar burial customs, locations, and materials. The available evidence suggests that Jews and Christians enjoyed significant social interaction.[101] From their shared social location and interaction, Nanos concludes that Jews and Christ-believers still worshiped together. The evidence Nanos marshals for this contention is far too circumstantial. Christians were coming to Rome as immigrants, entrepreneurs, and slaves, as had the Jews. Newcomers would naturally migrate toward those quarters of Rome where immigrants, including the Jews, typically lived. James C. Walters surmises that the Jews and Christians "shared a common social context — that of Rome's immigrant poor — as well as certain religious customs," but to claim that Jews and Christians must (still) be worshiping together would be pressing the evidence too far.[102] Nero's actions against the Christians, as distinct from the Jews, suggest a split by 64 CE.[103]

The Jealousy Motif

Nanos touts the jealousy motif in Romans as powerful proof of his thesis.[104] Paul wrote in Rom 11:11, 13–14 that he hoped to make the Jews jealous of his success as a missionary among the gentiles. If the Christ-believers had already gone their separate path and were meeting apart from the synagogues, why, Nanos asks,

---

101. Mark D. Nanos, "Jewish Context," 285–86; idem, *Mystery*, 69–72. Gagnon does not identify or respond to this argument.

102. James C. Walters, "Romans, Jews, and Christians: The Impact of the Romans on Jewish/Christian Relations in First Century Rome," in *Judaism and Christianity in First-Century Rome* (ed. Karl P. Donfried and Peter Richardson; Grand Rapids: Eerdmans, 1998), 179 n. 17 (comments made in response to John Elliott's critique of Peter Lampe, who also rightly recognized that this evidence does not demonstrate that the Christians were still worshiping in synagogues).

103. Walters, "Romans, Jews, and Christians," 179–80. Nanos, "Jewish Context," 288, does not seem to recognize the seriousness of this problem for his position. Nero did not make this distinction apart from external influences on the court; see the discussion in chap. 4, below.

104. Nanos, *Mystery*, 247–55.

would the Jews be jealous of what Paul was doing in a different community?[105] The apostle appears to assume "firsthand knowledge of the response of these gentiles" on the part of the Jews.[106] "If Paul's ministry is not taking place within the confines of the Jewish community, then they would neither know about it nor really care, at least not enough to provoke the kind of extensive and positive reaction Paul intends."[107] It would be a different matter if Paul had been attracting more gentile worshipers *into the synagogues* through his message about Christ. Then non-Christ-believing Jews may have been jealous of Paul's ministry in their midst and would wish to emulate it. The problem with Nanos's reasoning, however, is that Christ-believers meeting separately from the synagogues could still claim Israel's heritage. A good portion of the general Roman population continued to confuse Christians with Jews well into the second century.[108] After all, they lived in the same quarters of the city, buried their dead in the same places, worked in similar trades, and appealed to the same Jewish Scriptures. Rapid growth in the Christian communities, which also claimed Israel's heritage, could easily have become a source of jealousy among the Jews, and such jealousy, as Paul hoped, could lead them to reconsider their position regarding Christ.[109] Many Jews in Paul's day looked forward to a mass turn of the gentiles in the last days to the worship of Israel's God.[110] The apostle may very well have been reasoning that if the Jews recognized the fulfillment of their own eschatological expectations

---

105. Nanos, "Jewish Context," 303; idem, "Rejoinder," 17–18.

106. Nanos, *Mystery*, 251.

107. Ibid., 251.

108. Lucian, *Peregr.* 11; Acts 16:20–21; *Ps.-Clem.* H 4.7.2: A pagan reproaches the novel's protagonist for thinking and acting "after the manner of the *Jews*" because of Peter's influence (cf. Epictetus, *Diatr.* 2.9.20–21). See Nanos, "Jewish Context," 288, on this point as well, although he presses the evidence too hard in trying to counteract Nero's stunning ability to distinguish Christians and Jews. On Lucian, see Hans Dieter Betz, *Lukian von Samosata und das Neue Testament: Religionsgeschichtliche und Paränetische Parallelen* (TUGAL 76; Berlin: Akademie, 1961), 8.

109. *Paul* was assuming that his ministry was in a close enough proximity to the Jews to evoke a reaction. What the Jews actually thought was a different matter, assuming they were aware of Paul's ministry. See the discussion of Acts 28:21–22 in chap. 4, below.

110. See, for instance, Mic 4:1–5; Tob 14:5–7; *Pss. Sol.* 17:21–46 [cf. 11:1–9]. Terence L. Donaldson, "Proselytes or 'Righteous Gentiles'? The Status of Gentiles in Eschatological Pilgrimage Patterns of Thought," *JSP* 7 (1990): 3–27; Paula Fredriksen, *From Jesus to Christ: The Origins of the New Testament Images of Jesus* (New Haven: Yale Univ. Press, 1988): 149–51; E. P. Sanders, *Jesus and Judaism* (Philadelphia: Fortress Press, 1985), 213–18; idem, *Judaism: Practice and Belief 63 BCE–66 CE* (Philadelphia: Trinity Press International, 1992), 280–98.

among the Christian communities in their midst, thanks to his own ministry and efforts, they would reconsider and recognize Jesus Christ's significance for themselves as Jews.[111] Nanos writes: "Paul expects these Jews to recognize in his ministry that *their own* positive hopes and expectations for a successful ministry with gentiles at the end of time are being realized, though without their expected participation."[112] Again, Nanos writes in his earlier work:

> Yet the fact that gentiles are becoming coparticipants in the eschatological blessings through *Paul's* ministry as Israel's representative and *not their own* quenches the rejoicing, for it bears witness against them. It signifies that *they* are those suffering the eschatological curse ("hardened": vv. 7–10 from Deut. 29:4; Isa. 29:10; Ps. 69:22–23), that *they* are standing outside the promised blessings, while *Paul* is fulfilling Israel's eschatological privilege of bringing light to the gentiles. They are among those whom the prophets warned of hardness of heart. . . . Thus Paul hopes their jealousy toward his ministry will awaken them to the reality of the times so that they will "not continue in unbelief" (Rom. 11:23), so that he might "save some of them" (v. 14), indeed, so that the fullness of the blessings (the resurrection? 11:12, 15, 26) may come.[113]

Nanos's cogent reasoning would remain equally applicable for communities that may not have worshiped together but were otherwise proximate.

---

111. On the OT background to the jealousy motif in Deut 32, see Richard H. Bell, *Provoked to Jealousy: The Origin and Purpose of the Jealousy Motif in Romans 9–11* (WUNT 2, 63; Tübingen: J. C. B. Mohr [Paul Siebeck], 1994), 39–42, 108–18, 156–66, 200–85 (esp. pp. 271–72).

112. Nanos, "Jewish Context," 302. In other words, one may grant much of what Nanos has to say about the jealousy motif without assuming that the Christians were still gathering alongside the Jews.

113. Nanos, *Mystery*, 250. Against those who think that the end-times restoration of the Jews will take place entirely by God's supernatural action, Nanos cites William Campbell, *Paul's Gospel in an Intercultural Context: Jew and Gentile in the Letter to the Romans* (Studies in the Intercultural History of Christianity 69; Frankfurt am Main: Peter Lang, 1991), 92–93 who writes: "As we have noted, this outcome [the final conversion of Israel] is generally taken to be by the direct action of God Himself—but the jealousy motif suggests that it is in fact the winning of the representatives from the nations which causes Israel's restoration." See on this point also Das, *Paul and the Jews*, 109–11.

Nanos, *Mystery*, 258, notes that Paul's jealousy motif poses a serious problem for those who think that Israel will be saved by a separate path independently of the Christ (contra Stendahl, Gaston, and Gager).

Parallels in Language with Other Pauline Letters

Gagnon follows many commentators in enumerating the various parallels in language and terminology between Rom 14:1 — 15:13 and other Pauline letters where the Christ-believing contexts are clearer.[114] Nanos rightly questions the strength of this sort of evidence. These parallel texts must be properly interpreted *on their own terms* before drawing any conclusions regarding their implications for the specific situation at Rome. Surely evidence from Romans itself must be given priority.[115] At the same time, proceeding to the other extreme, as Nanos appears to do, of divorcing parallel language in one letter from other letters likely written from the same period in Paul's ministry and likely from/to the same location is not valid either. An interpretation in which the apostle used shared terminology similarly in both letters should not be discounted. Gagnon's incorporation of parallels in language between Rom 14:1 — 15:13 and Paul's other letters has merit. The Christ-believing contexts of these other letters suggest the same for Romans.

Acts 28:21–22

On the basis of Acts 28:21–22, Nanos doubts whether the Christians had separated from the Jewish synagogues:

> [The local leaders of the Jews] replied [to Paul], "We have received no letters from Judea about you, and none of the brothers coming here has reported or spoken anything evil about you. But we would like to hear from you what you think, for with regard to this sect we know that everywhere it is spoken against."

Luke was describing events somewhere between 58 and 62 CE, when Paul was under house arrest in Rome. The Jewish leaders appeared to be aware of the Christian movement and were concerned about this "sect," but they did not display any personal hostility toward it. The lack of hostility seems (to Nanos) inconceivable if the Claudius edict had violently disrupted the Jewish community in 49 CE The Jewish leaders would have had "*firsthand, extensive, and extremely negative* knowledge of the gospel and its proclaimers and the situation in Rome upon Paul's arrival" [Nanos's emphasis].[116] These Jewish leaders would have been those personally affected by the expulsion from Rome that the Christians had

---

114. For a listing, see Gagnon, "'Weak' at Rome," 70–71.
115. Nanos, "Rejoinder," 18–19.
116. Nanos, *Mystery*, 375.

caused.[117] These leaders were aware of the "sect," and yet they did not know why it was "spoken against everywhere," nor had they heard of Paul's message. Luke mentioned the expulsion in Acts 18:2.[118] Had such an expulsion taken place according to Acts, Nanos contends that Luke, given his pattern (as scholars have traced it), would surely have woven the resultant hostility into his account of Jewish rejection in Acts 28.[119] A violent disruption of the Roman Jewish community therefore had not taken place.

Mark Reasoner has not found Nanos's reasoning compelling:

> It is an argument from silence that questions why Luke doesn't present the Jewish leaders as more familiar with Christianity and negative toward it. . . . [A]ll that these two verses picture is some Jewish leaders in Rome who do not know Paul but know that Christianity is ubiquitously in ill repute claiming that they want to hear Paul. Luke is painting with broad strokes here. The portrait could fit a situation of complete polarization, or one in which Christians are still in the synagogue ambit.[120]

The Jewish leaders may have understated their knowledge of Christianity as they sought what Paul himself had to say. Ben Witherington contends that Acts 28:21–22 militates *against* Nanos's thesis that Christians were still meeting within the synagogues: "The split between the two communities came well before Paul wrote Romans, and Acts 28 does not suggest anything to the contrary. In fact, it suggests that the synagogue officials in Rome know little about what is going on with Christians, including those in their own city."[121] Had the Christians still been a part of the synagogues (as Nanos supposes), the leaders would have been better informed. Their lack of knowledge about the new "sect"

---

117. Nanos was dependent on Stephen Benko, "The Edict of Claudius of A.D. 49 and the Instigator Chrestus," *TZ* 25 (1969), 417–18, for this argument from Acts 28 against the usual interpretation of Claudius's edict.

118. While Luke mentions Claudius's order, he does not indicate how extensively this order was executed *in practice* beyond its impact on Prisca and Aquila. Nanos, *Mystery*, 376, did not consider this. When Nanos, *Mystery*, 378, questioned why Paul's accusers before Felix, Agrippa, or others did not mention that Paul's movement had already caused a major stir in Rome under Claudius (had it happened) he again assumed a mass expulsion. His objection loses its force if Claudius's action was far less severe and involved only the ringleaders in the conflict.

119. Nanos, *Mystery*, 379–80.

120. Reasoner, *Strong and the Weak*, 135. Reasoner (p. 136) was convinced that a separation between church and synagogue had already occurred.

121. Witherington, *Romans*, 331.

would be understandable if they were visiting Paul ten to fourteen years after the separation of Christians from the synagogues.

Synagogue Authorities in Romans 13:1–7

Nanos thinks that Paul urged Christ-believers to submit to the ruling authorities *in the synagogues* in Rom 13:1–7. Nanos's reading of Rom 13:1–7, if correct, would confirm his approach to Rom 14:1 — 15:13 as referring to intra-synagogue relations. Few, if any, have found Nanos's approach persuasive. Nowhere else in Paul's writings did he ask the church to submit to synagogue rule. Nanos must take the reference to the sword in 13:4 metaphorically for the power of the synagogue rulers or perhaps for the word of God (cf. Heb 4:12). He takes τέλος to refer to Jewish "customs" or "behavior," even though the word is used alongside φόρος and must therefore refer to paying tribute. These are the terms for direct and indirect taxes.[122] Nanos dismisses the parallels to other passages in the New Testament urging obedience to the secular government (Tit 3:1; 1 Pet 2:13–17). The early Christian respect for the secular government is indebted to Jewish tradition. The Jews regularly ascribed the source of the ruler's dominion as from the God who raises up and brings down governments and nations (for example, 2 Sam 12:8; 1 Chr 29:11–12; Jer 27:5–6; Dan 2:21, 37–38; Sir 10:4,8; Wis 6:1–3; *Let. Aris.* 219, 224; 4 Macc 12:11).[123] Nanos ignores the technical vocabulary that others have noted in this passage; here, for example, is Ben Witherington:

> In regard to technical vocabulary here, the following can be noted: *exousiai* and *tetagmenai* are terms for prominent Roman officials; *leitourgos* refers to an authorized representative of an administrative body such as the Senate, the proverbial "public servant"; *archē* refers to a municipal or city official; the phrase *tou theou diatagē* was used to characterize the state's power, which was given divine authority to establish order; *kalos* and *agathos* characterize politically good conduct; and wearing the sword was characteristic of the emperor but also of various deputies beneath him in the power structure.[124]

---

122. See Bruce Winter, "Roman Law and Society in Romans 12–15," in *Rome in the Bible and the Early Christian Church* (ed. P. Oakes; Grand Rapids: Baker, 2002), 83–85.

123. The Wisdom reference helps resolves Nanos's quandary (*Mystery*, 297) over secular authorities being "ordered" or "appointed" by God; David Winston, *The Wisdom of Solomon* (AB 43; New York: Doubleday, 1979), 152–53.

124. Witherington, *Romans*, 310. Winter, "Roman Law and Society," 82, compares the note of "praise" from the authorities in Rom 13:3 with inscriptions of civic recognition. Likewise, the "reverence" (φόβος) and "honor" (τιμή) Paul enjoins in 13:7 agrees with what is due rulers (Winter, "Roman Law and Society," 84).

Nanos may offer alternative interpretations of individual words, but it is the *cluster* of political terminology that proves decisive.[125] Alternatively, Paul never employed in Rom 13 distinctively Jewish vocabulary for the authorities (e.g., ἀρχισυνάγωγος). James D. G. Dunn struggles to understand how the "sword," in the context of the *Roman* destination of the letter and diaspora attitudes toward foreign rulers, could mean anything other than the Roman government. Dunn notes: "Even if the alternate suggestion that 'sword' stood for Scripture had merit, would Paul indeed have encouraged the Gentile converts to look to the synagogue authorities for a proper wielding of that sword/interpretation of the Scripture?"[126]

The advantage of the more common reading of Rom 13:1–7 as a reference to Roman power is the correspondence of this paragraph to events taking place in the mid-50s in Rome. Tax riots broke out under Nero in 58 CE Tacitus recorded that such an outcry from the masses against the excessive greed and exploitation of the revenue collectors caused Nero to consider complete abolishment of indirect taxes. Several senators discouraged him by warning that an abolition of indirect taxes would lead to popular demand to abolish the direct taxes as well. The uprising forced Nero to overhaul the entire taxation system (Tacitus, *Ann.* 13.50–51). The Letter to the Romans is normally dated two or three years prior to Nero's actions during the period of popular protest. Paul appeared to be alluding to this crisis when he referred to both φόρος, direct taxes collected by government officials, and τέλος, indirect taxes collected by the Roman equestrian order such as harbor fees or duties on imports and exports.[127] Paul may have been urging the Roman Christians to avoid drawing attention to themselves in the midst of the public turmoil especially since the Christians had been at the center of another conflict less than a decade earlier under Claudius.[128]

---

125. Neil Elliott, "'*Paulus Contra Gentiles*': Comments on Mark Nanos, *The Mystery of Romans*," *CRBR* 11 (1998), 151, comments, "Unfortunately, the case made for the *plausibility* of [Nanos's] view is not supported by any refutation of the conventional reading of these terms as part of the Hellenistic rhetoric of civic politics."

126. Dunn, review of Mark D. Nanos, *Mystery of Romans*, 601; e.g., Rom 10:1–4; 1 Cor 2:14; 2 Cor 3:14–16.

127. Johannes Friedrich, Wolfgang Pohlmann, and Peter Stuhlmacher, "Zur historischen Situation und Intention von Rom 13, 1–7," *ZTK* 73 (1976): 156–59. See, however, Neil Elliott's important qualifications of Friedrich, Pohlmann, and Stuhlmacher's thesis in *Liberating Paul: The Justice of God and the Politics of the Apostle* (Sheffield: Sheffield Academic, 1995), 219, 223–25.

128. Nanos, along with others, expresses doubt about the usual reconstructions of this earlier conflict under Claudius. See the discussion of Claudius's edict and expulsion in chap. 4, below.

Evaluation

Mark Nanos is proving to be one of the most creative and original Pauline interpreters of his generation. No work on the Romans situation can ignore his labors. The central issue is the *plausibility* of his thesis that the Christ-believers were still meeting within the synagogues at the time Paul wrote to the Romans. Unfortunately, several of Nanos's arguments summarized above prove indecisive, especially regarding the internal consistency of Rom 1–11, the overlap of Roman Christ-believers with the Jews of Rome, the jealousy motif, and his interpretation of Rom 13:1–7. Other avenues of inquiry that Nanos initially proposed actually demonstrate the strong probability that the Roman Christians were *no longer* meeting in the synagogues (the interpretation of Rom 14:1 — 15:13 in the first two sections above, his view of Rom 14:22b–23 and Acts 28:21–22, and his comments on separate Christ-believing churches at Rome at that time). Moreover, several other avenues of inquiry discussed above indicate that the weak were Christ-believing. A decisive split had taken place between the Jews and the Christ-believers by the time Paul wrote. The Christians were meeting separately in their own house churches.

Chapter 4

Claudius's Edict of Expulsion: The External Evidence

Paul's letter to the Romans reflects an intriguing and unique situation in early Christianity. His audience consisted of gentiles — but rather atypical gentiles. These gentiles were familiar with the Jewish Scriptures, Israel's heritage, and the customs necessary for respectful behavior in the presence of Jews. Clearly, some of the Roman gentile Christians had benefited from synagogue instruction. At the same time, the vegetarian habits of some of the gentile Christians in a city with a sizeable Jewish population suggests that they were no longer associating with the synagogues. The letter bears every indication that the gentile Christians had begun to worship separately. Many of the gentile Christians, nevertheless, maintained a Law-respectful lifestyle in the face of newer gentile converts who did not share the same scruples. This chapter moves beyond the evidence of the letter itself to consider possible corroborative evidence from the historians and other sources of the period.

In his *Lives of the Caesars*, Suetonius, the second-century Emperor Hadrian's secretary, described a conflict that had taken place in the Jewish community over "Chrestus," a conflict that required imperial intervention. Emperor Claudius responded, Suetonius related, by expelling the Jews from Rome. Although debate continues to rage on almost every aspect of Suetonius's brief note, "Chrestus" remains most likely a reference to "Christus," that is, Jesus Christ. Claudius's expulsion most likely took place in 49 CE Jewish followers of Christ were those primarily impacted by the decree, and their departure paved the way for a separation between Christ-followers and the Jewish community — a separation confirmed by Nero's prescient recognition in 64 CE of Christians as distinct from Jews. The historians of the period therefore provide independent external

149

evidence that confirms the thesis, derived from the Letter of Romans itself, for a gentile audience meeting separately from the Jewish communities. The external evidence, however, also explains *why* the Christians had broken away from the synagogues to meet in their own house churches.

Suetonius: *Chrestus/Christus?*

In his biography of the Caesars, Suetonius mentioned that Claudius "expelled the Jews who were making constant disturbances at the instigation of Chrestus" (*Claudius* 25.4). Suetonius may have confused the name "Christus," or Christ, with the name "Chrestus." "Christus" was virtually unknown as a proper name in Rome at the time, and the two names were pronounced the same way. The confusion of the names "Chrestus" and "Christus" would continue well into the following centuries. One of the major Greek manuscript witnesses to the New Testament text, the Sinaiticus, spells "Christian" in Acts 11:26, 26:28, and 1 Pet 4:16 as "Chrestianos" (Χρηστιανός).[1] Even when the proper spelling was better known, the defenders of Christianity lamented that their opponents would misspell the word for Christian as "Chrestianos" in order to imply that the founder of the new movement, or "superstition," bore the name of a common slave (Justin, *1 Apol.* 4.5; Tertullian, *Apol.* 3 [*Christianus vero... sed et cum perperam Chrestianus pronuntiatur a vobis*]; *Nat.* 1.3.9 [*Etiam cum corrupte a uobis Chrestiani pronuntiamur*]; Lactantius, *Inst.* 4.7).[2]

Suetonius's report implied that "Chrestus" was actually present in Rome, an absurd claim if referring to Jesus Christ. William Lane responded to this observation: "The notorious confusion displayed in the words *impulsore Chresto* suggest a contemporary police record. It is well known that Suetonius merely

---

1. For deliberate play with the spelling in early Christian writings, see Stephen Benko, "The Edict of Claudius of A.D. 49 and the Instigator Chrestus," *TZ* 25 (1969): 410. In other words, while non-Christians may have been confused, Christians generally were not. As for the popular confusion and interchange of "Chrestus"/"Christus" and "Chrestianos"/"Christianos," the most thorough discussion remains Helga Botermann, *Das Judenedikt des Kaisers Claudius: Römischer Staat und Christiani im 1. Jahrhundert* (Hermes-Einzelschriften 71; Stuttgart: Franz Steiner, 1996), 72–95.

2. See also William L. Lane, "Social Perspectives on Roman Christianity during the Formative Years from Nero to Nerva: Romans, Hebrews, 1 Clement," in *Judaism and Christianity in First-Century Rome* (ed. Karl P. Donfried and Peter Richardson; Grand Rapids: Eerdmans, 1998), 205. Suetonius's spelling may have been a deliberate aspersion; thus Rainer Riesner, *Paul's Early Period: Chronology, Mission Strategy, Theology* (Grand Rapids: Eerdmans, 1998), 165.

reproduced his sources without attempting to evaluate them carefully. . . ."[3] Helga Botermann agreed that Suetonius was conservatively relaying the wording of an actual edict.[4] Suetonius, had he made the connection to the Christian movement, would not necessarily have felt any impulse to modify the report with its implication of an actual, living "Chrestus" in Rome, since the Christians were known for their claim of a living, resurrected Christ; Suetonius's near contemporary, Pliny, in his letter to Trajan, reports Christians' singing hymns to Christ as to a god.[5] If, on the other hand, the confusion of the name were indeed on the part of Suetonius rather than a source, the confusion would still be understandable, since he did not otherwise reveal any concrete knowledge about the person and life of Christ when he wrote vaguely of the *christiani* in *Nero* 16.2.[6] Over seventy years after the events he narrated, Suetonius may have mistakenly assumed that Christ had actually been present in Rome at the time.

Tacitus, on the other hand, was better informed about the Christians and knew that Christ had been crucified under Tiberius's reign (*Ann.* 15.44). Yet, in view of the manuscript tradition, even he may not have known the correct spelling of "Christ" or "Christian" (*Chrestianos* in the manuscript tradition). The

---

3. Lane, "Roman Christianity," 204–5.

4. Botermann, *Das Judenedikt*, 95–102. She argued that Suetonius was drawing upon the archives of the Caesars and would often preserve the original document's wording. Suetonius's account therefore preserved the confusion of the day over this new movement and its claim that Jesus had risen from the dead and was still present. Suetonius did not narrate the beginning of the Christian movement until the time of Nero, well after the "Chrestus" edict.

5. Ibid., 100–102.

6. "Punishment was inflicted [by Nero] on the Christians, a class of men given to a new and mischievous superstition" (Rolfe, LCL). Contra H. Dixon Slingerland "Chrestus: Christus?" in *The Literature of Early Rabbinic Judaism: Issues in Talmudic Redaction and Interpretation* (New Perspectives on Ancient Judaism 4; ed. Alan J. Avery-Peck. Lanham: University Press of America, 1989; repr. and rev. in *Claudian Policymaking and the Early Imperial Repression of Judaism at Rome* [SFSHJ 160; Atlanta: Scholars Press, 1997), 133–44, Suetonius did not appear to know much about the Christians and could have been unaware of the exact nature of the events during Claudius's expulsion. Runar Thorsteinsson's judgment, *Paul's Interlocutor in Romans 2: Function and Identity in the Context of Ancient Epistolography* (ConBNT 40; Stockholm: Almqvist & Wiksell, 2003), 95 n. 24, that Suetonius was "well familiar" with the Christians, while possible, remains unsupported by the text itself. Thorsteinsson noted Suetonius's close personal acquaintance with Tacitus and Pliny the Younger, who were aware of the Christians, but it is sheer supposition that friendship with these men demonstrates that Suetonius knew what they did of the Christians.

manuscripts of Suetonius and Tacitus were conveyed through Christian scribes, who were tempted and often succumbed to correcting (or introducing) misspellings.[7] The failure to change "Chrestus" to Christ in Suetonius's reference to the Claudian action against the Jews — or perhaps even a deliberate change *to* "Chrestus" — may have reflected scribal interpretation that Suetonius could not have meant Jesus, since he had not been in Rome at the time and was not such a troublemaker.[8] In short, the brevity and ambiguity of the "Chrestus" comment in Suetonius permits reference to the "Christ movement" in Rome.[9]

"Chrestus" was a very common name for slaves and freedmen in Rome.[10] Stephen Benko therefore concluded that an extremist ("zealot") leader was inciting the problems in the Roman Jewish community. He pointed to Jewish riots in Alexandria, Philadelphia, Samaria, and the unrest that led to the Jewish revolt against Rome in 66 CE and suggested similar unrest may have taken place in Rome.[11] In 44 CE Claudius had abolished the Jewish state, which led to increasing tensions with the Jews in their homeland. Benko even speculated that the Jewish community set the fire in Rome and then pressed Nero to blame the Christians.[12] Harry J. Leon, in his important study on the Jews in Rome, listed 550 Jewish names, and "Chrestus," while common elsewhere, was not in the list.[13] Rainer Riesner added that no evidence exists even *outside* of Rome

---

7.   Irina Levinskaya, *The Book of Acts in Its Diaspora Setting* (*The Book of Acts in Its First Century Setting* 5; ed. Bruce W. Winter; Grand Rapids: Eerdmans, 1996), 179–81, and esp. p. 179 n. 53, regarding *Codex Mediceus* 68.2 with its scribal alterations.

8.   Mark D. Nanos, *The Mystery of Romans: The Jewish Context of Paul's Letter.* Minneapolis: Fortress Press, 1996), 378–79, did not account for scribal activity when he argued firmly from Suetonius's and Tacitus's use of *christiani* and not *chrestiani* for the Christian movement. Thus Nanos, following E. A. Judge and G. S. R. Thomas, "The Origin of the Church at Rome: A New Solution?" *RTR* 25 (1966), 85, cannot juxtapose the Suetonius references to "chrestus" and "christiani" as proof that "Chrestus" is not Christ.

9.   Riesner, *Paul's Early Period*, 166.

10.   For Chrestus as a Roman name, see *CIL* 6. 668, 880, 975, 1929, 3555, 11707, 14058, 14433, 14805, 20770, 21531, 22837, 26157, 28324, 28659, 37672, 38735.

11.   Stephen Benko, "Edict of Claudius," 413–18; idem, *Pagan Rome and the Early Christians* (Bloomington, Ind.: Indiana Univ. Press, 1984), 19. Benko lacks such evidence from Rome. Judge and Thomas, "Origin," 87, preferred a conflict over a messianic pretender, whose identity has since been lost.

12.   Benko, *Pagan Rome*, 19–20.

13.   Harry J. Leon, *The Jews of Ancient Rome* (Updated ed.; Peabody, Mass.: Hendrickson, 1960), 93–121. Botermann, *Das Judenedikt*, 58, observed, "Für Juden begegnet

for a Jew named "Chrestus."[14] It is difficult to imagine that an actual or former slave could have caused such an uproar within the Jewish community in Rome.[15] Nor is there any corroborating evidence for a Jewish rabble-rousing extremist at Rome named Chrestus.[16] Had the Jewish community been disturbed by an otherwise completely unknown figure, Suetonius would likely have written instead "at the instigation of *a certain* Chrestus" (*impulsore Chresto quodam*).[17] The most plausible understanding of Suetonius's reference, then, is that there had been an uproar in the Jewish community in Rome as a result of those promoting "Chre/istus" or Christ. Apparently some in the Jewish community were opposing others who accepted Jesus as Messiah. The resulting conflicts were severe enough to warrant an imperial banishment of the Jews from Rome.[18]

Thaddée Zielinksi and Marcus Borg proposed variations on the "rabble-rouser" hypothesis, describing either a Jewish messianic pretender in Rome or an anti-Roman, Jewish nationalist movement which originated from an agitated

---

er allerdings nur einmal, und zwar in der *weiblichen* Form Chreste" (emphasis added; *CIJ* 1.683, line 5 — Χρήστη — a Bosporan inscription).

14. Riesner, *Paul's Early Period*, 165. This poses a problem for Dixon Slingerland's hypothesis, "Chrestus: Christus?" 133–44, that Chrestus was a non-Christian Jew stirring up trouble in the Jewish community, as well as for those who followed Slingerland, such as Nanos, *Mystery*, and Lloyd Gaston, "Reading the Text and Digging the Past: The First Audience of Romans," in *Text and Artifact in the Religions of Mediterranean Antiquity: Essays in Honour of Peter Richardson* (ed. Stephen G. Wilson and Michel Desjardins; SCJ 9; Waterloo, Ont.: Wilfrid Laurier Univ. Press, 2000), 35–44.

15. Slingerland, *Claudian Policymaking*, 179–201, however, demonstrated that while this was a common slave name in the western part of the empire and Rome, the name was also used for free and freedpersons, especially in the East. He even identified a few upper-class Romans in Claudian circles with the name.

16. Contra Slingerland, "Chrestus: Christus?"

17. Henri Janne, "Impulsore Chresto," *Annuaire de l'Institut de philologie et d'histoire orientales et slaves* 2 no. 1 (1934): 540–41; F. F. Bruce, "Christianity under Claudius," *BJRL* 44 (1961): 316. Slingerland recognized the limits of this argument ("Chrestus: Christus?" 141). Slingerland thought that "Chrestus" was an otherwise well-known figure not needing further identification for Suetonius or his audience, and yet not connected in any way to Christianity. See the critique of this position below.

18. George Howard, "The Beginnings of Christianity in Rome: A Note on Suetonius, Life of Claudius XXV.4," *ResQ* 24 (1981): 177, pointed to the late fourth century Syriac *Doctrine of Addai* as further evidence (complementing Orosius) that the early Christians recognized the expulsion of Claudius as a result of conflict between the Jews of Rome and Christians. On the date of the Syriac document, see T. D. Barnes, "Legislation against the Christians," *JRS* 58 (1968): 32–50.

homeland (along with its zealotic, messianic hopes).[19] Unlike Benko, Zielinski and Borg took the evidence that "Chrestus" referred to a messianic figure or movement seriously. They were unable, however, to cite Roman sources that corroborated the presence of a messianic pretender or a growing nationalist fervor in the local Jewish community. No one doubts the turmoil and unrest in Judea under Roman rule, but without further evidence from the primary sources, a messianic figure or movement *in Rome* would be difficult to envision.[20] Messianic expectations in the Second Temple period were rather diverse. The attested messianic, revolutionary leaders were Palestinian Jews in a location where resentment against foreign, Roman rule was at its peak. One can only speculate whether such apocalyptic, messianic fervor reached the distant capital in the heart of the gentile, *Roman* world. Botermann observed that no great Jewish thinker or leader emerged in Rome. Roman authors may have commented on Jewish customs and observances, but never on the Roman Jews as a major political movement.[21] Further, the situation of the Roman Jewish population cannot be determined by a preconception about overall Jewish hostility to Roman rule. Jewish relations with neighbors varied from city to city and from location to location.[22] Botermann pointed out that the Roman Jews had no single organizational structure or a leading figure. They were not positioned for a revolt.[23] The notion of an otherwise unknown messianic pretender or movement in Rome lacks evidence and plausibility.

Dixon Slingerland proposed in his more recent monograph that "Chrestus" should be understood as an influential figure in the imperial household rather than in the Jewish community. Following Sejanus's precedent when he encouraged Tiberius's action against the Roman Jews, "Chrestus" "instigated" yet another imperial action against the Jewish community.[24] There is, however, no corroborating evidence for the existence of this hypothetical prominent figure in Claudius's

---

19. Thaddée Zielinksi, "L'empereur Claude et l'idée de la domination mondiale des Juifs," *RUB* 32 (1926–27): 128–48; Marcus J. Borg, "A New Context for Romans xiii," *NTS* 19 (1972–73): 209–13.

20. Rightly Botermann, *Das Judenedikt*, 64–65.

21. Ibid., 66–67.

22. Rightly Botermann, *Das Judenedikt*, 68. See discussion of this point later in this chapter.

23. Ibid., 69. She also debunked the notion that the Roman Jews were getting into trouble right and left for zealous proselytizing (pp. 69–70).

24. Slingerland, *Claudian Policymaking*, 163–68. Slingerland's thesis has gained adherents. See, for instance, Neil Elliott, "Disciplining the Hope of the Poor in Ancient Rome," in *Christian Origins* (PHC 1; ed. Richard A. Horsley; Minneapolis: Fortress Press, 2005), 186–87.

household. Furthermore, Suetonius's practice was to introduce to the readers figures not well known in the second century.[25] An otherwise unknown figure in the court would require introduction, whereas Christ would not (Suetonius referred to the "Christians" elsewhere). Finally, as Erich Gruen pointed out, Slingerland's hypothesis "founders on philological grounds. The ablative absolute in Suet. *Claud.* 25.4 occurs within the participial phrase, bracketed by *Iudaeos* and *tumultuantis.* Suetonius cannot be taken to mean that *impulsore Chresto* modifies the verb."[26] A reference to Christ remains the most likely explanation of "Chrestus."

Acts 18:2 offers corroborating evidence that Suetonius was referring to a disturbance caused by followers of Christ. In Corinth Paul "found a Jew named Aquila . . . who had recently (προσφάτως) come from Italy with his wife Priscilla, because Claudius had ordered all the Jews to leave Rome." The couple had been forced to leave Rome because of an edict of Claudius regarding the Jews. Gerd Luedemann noticed that in Acts 18:2–3 Luke did not describe the couple as Christians. He supposed that they were converted to Christianity at Corinth, although Luke never recorded their conversion whether by Paul's influence or otherwise.[27] Peter Lampe responded that the silence in Acts with respect to the couple's Christian identity would match Luke's redactional tendencies. Luke celebrated Paul as the *founder* of Christianity in various cities. So Luke glossed over the couple's potential work in Corinth prior to Paul's arrival. Note that in Acts 18:26 only *after* Paul's own missionary work at Ephesus in 18:19–21 did Luke refer to the activity of the couple.[28] Aquila and Priscilla most likely left Rome for Corinth as Christians. Paul's first convert in Greece was Stephanas and not the couple (1 Cor 16:15). Paul converted Lydia in Philippi (Acts 16:14–15). Paul had baptized the household of Stephanas as well as Gaius and Crispus in 1 Cor 1:14–16. Amid mention of these various "first converts," Aquila and Priscilla, for all their prominence in the narrative, were conspicuously never included.[29] Yet

---

25. Slingerland, *Claudian Policymaking,* 169–77.

26. Erich S. Gruen, *Diaspora: Jews amidst Greeks and Romans* (Cambridge, Mass.: Harvard Univ. Press, 2002), 272 n. 155.

27. Gerd Luedemann, *Early Christianity according to the Traditions in Acts: A Commentary* (trans. John Bowden; Minneapolis: Fortress Press, 1989), 198, 201–2. So also Slingerland, "Chrestus: Christus?" 139; Benko, "Edict of Claudius," 413; Nanos, *Mystery,* 376–77.

28. Peter Lampe, *From Paul to Valentinus: Christians at Rome in the First Two Centuries* (trans. Michael Steinhauser; Minneapolis: Fortress Press, 2003), 13.

29. Botermann, *Das Judenedikt,* 46–47. The description of Stephanas's household as the "firstfruits (ἀπαρχὴ τῆς Ἀχαΐας) of Asia" may, on first glance, appear to contradict Aquila and Priscilla's Christian identity. If they were present in Corinth prior to Paul's arrival and were Christians, then how can Stephanus's household be the "firstfruits" or

according to Acts 18:3 Paul lived and worked with Aquila and Priscilla from the very beginning of his stay in Corinth.[30] As a Christian missionary, Paul's early association with them would be more likely if he had known them as already baptized. If Priscilla and Aquila were expelled from Rome because they had been involved as non-Christ-believing Jews in disturbances within their community, they would not likely have risked associating with and offering hospitality to Paul, a missionary known for stirring up conflict in the synagogues of Asia Minor and Greece.[31] If Priscilla and Aquila had been expelled from Rome for their non-Christian messianic or revolutionary convictions, an abandonment of their costly prior convictions in favor of Jesus Christ when they met Paul would be unlikely.[32] Peter Lampe also observed that had the couple been expelled from Rome as leaders of the *opposition* to the followers of Christ in the Jewish community, an association with Paul in Corinth from the very beginning would be unlikely.[33] Priscilla and Aquila were not non-Christian participants in a general

---

first Christians in Achaia. On the other hand, as Willi Marxsen, *Introduction to the New Testament: An Approach to Its Problems* (trans. G. Buswell; Philadelphia: Fortress Press, 1968), 99, pointed out, Priscilla and Aquila were not the first *Achaian* Christians.

30. Peter Lampe, *From Paul to Valentinus*, 11–2 n. 2, argued at length that Paul's early association in Corinth with Aquila and Priscilla is based on reliable traditions in Acts: (1) 1 Cor 4:12; 9:4, 6–7, 12; 2 Cor 11:7–8; 12:13 corroborate Luke's presentation of Paul as a tradesman working his craft; (2) 1 Cor 16:19 matches Acts 18:2–3, since the couple knew the Corinthians personally, were in Ephesus with Paul, and could have met him in Corinth; (3) "Pontus" and "staying with a fellow craftsman" are without Lukan parallel and appear to be non-Lukan; (4) The apparently compressed statements in Acts 18:2–3 may reflect varying traditions; and (5) Oral tradition may be present in Acts 18:3, because of the use of the *hapax legomena* ὁμότεχνος and σκηνοποιός. Lampe also doubted that ἐργάζομαι is Lukan.

31. Raymond E. Brown and John P. Meier, *Antioch and Rome: New Testament Cradles of Catholic Christianity* (New York: Paulist, 1983), 100; so also Philip F. Esler, *Conflict and Identity in Romans: The Social Setting of Paul's Letter* (Minneapolis: Fortress Press, 2003), 100.

32. So Botermann, *Das Judenedikt*, 71:

> Der Gipfel einer solchen Kette von Zufällen wäre allerdings, daß *Prisca und Aquila*, die prominenten Missionare der ersten Generation, Rom als Anhänger dieses unbekannten falschen Christus namens Chrestus verlassen hätten und in Korinth Anhänger von Jesus Christus gewesen wären. Angesichts dieser Anhäufung unwahrscheinlicher Zufälle kann man den "unbekannten Aufrüher" zu den Akten legen und sich den Problemen zuwenden, die durch die *Gleichsetzung von Chrestus mit Jesus Christus* entstehen.

33. Lampe, *From Paul to Valentinus*, 12.

Jewish disturbance. Nor were they participants in a messianic movement or opposed to Roman Christianity. The edict of Claudius appears to have impacted this couple *as Christ-believing* Jews.[34] "Jew" ($\text{'Iου}\delta\alpha\hat{\iota}\text{ος}$), as used in Acts 18:2, may include Jewish Christians in view of Luke's usage of the word elsewhere.[35] A conflict in the synagogues of Rome over the significance of Christ would parallel the pattern of conflict in the synagogues elsewhere in the Book of Acts.[36] If Luke is right, such conflict at Rome took place *early on* in the development of Christianity.[37]

Dixon Slingerland questioned whether Acts 18:2 and Suetonius referred to the same expulsion under Claudius or actually referred to two *separate* events.[38] Slingerland's hypothesis of two separate events would require the expelled Jews to have risked returning to Rome in Claudius's lifetime only to be expelled a *second* time.[39] Certainly Aquila and Priscilla had returned to Rome by the time Paul wrote (Rom 16:3–5), but their return was most likely under Nero, who had promised early in his reign to rule by Augustan precedent which had been favorable for the Roman Jewish population (Suetonius, *Nero* 10). The simplest and most satisfactory understanding of the evidence would equate the expulsion referred to in Acts 18:2 with Suetonius's expulsion.[40] The fourth century writer Orosius independently dated Claudius's expulsion to the same

---

34. Contra also Slingerland, "Chrestus: Christus?"

35. See Acts 16:1, 20; 21:39; 22:1; 22:3, 12 (cf. Acts 9:10), including Paul himself; contra Slingerland, "Chrestus: Christus?" 139. He speculatively suggested that the appellations for Aquila were chronological but did not provide evidence from Luke's writings for such an approach.

36. Acts 6:9–15; 13:45, 50; 14:2, 5; 14:19; 17:1–9; 18:12–17. Slingerland, "Chrestus: Christus?" 140, assumed without evidence that Luke fabricated this pattern. Such conflict is consistent with Paul's own account. See, for instance, 2 Cor 11:21–26; Gal 1:13, 23; 1 Thess 2:14–16. For a demonstration of the authenticity of 1 Thess 2:14–16, see A. Andrew Das, *Paul and the Jews* (Library of Pauline Studies; Peabody, Mass.: Hendrickson, 2003), 129–39.

37. The evidence that the expelled Aquila and Prisca were Christians prior to meeting Paul militates strongly against theories that the "Chrestus" dispute in the Jewish community at Rome was not over the significance of Jesus Christ; contra especially Borg, "A New Context," 212.

38. Dixon Slingerland, "Suetonius, Acts 18, and Orosius' *Historiarum Adversum Paganos Libri VII*: Dating the Claudian Expulsion(s) of Roman Jews," *JQR* 83 (1992): 133–36.

39. Slingerland backed off his claim in his more recent work: "I no longer find [the analogies used to support more than one expulsion] to be credible" (*Claudian Policymaking*, 120 n. 35).

40. Esler, *Conflict and Identity*, 99.

time period as the Acts 18:2 expulsion, further evidence that the two expulsions are one and the same.

The Date: 49 CE

Orosius dated Suetonius's expulsion under Claudius to 49 CE (*Adv. Pag.* 7.6.15–16). Unfortunately, Orosius is not the most reliable source.[41] He claimed that he found the date in Josephus's history, but Josephus's extant works nowhere mentioned the expulsion under Claudius, let alone its date.[42] Orosius's date, however, is corroborated by further considerations.[43] First, Acts 18:2 independently suggests a date of 49 CE.[44] Scholars vary in their assessments of the overall

---

41. He wrongly claimed (7.4) that the persecution under Tiberius of the Jews was really a persecution of Roman Christians, and that Helene of Adiabene, the famous Jewess, was really a Christian (7.6). His history is of value only when it can be confirmed by other evidence. On the philosophy of history behind his work, see Glenn F. Chestnut, "Eusebius, Augustine, Orosius, and the Later Patristic and Medieval Christian Historians," in *Eusebius, Christianity, and Judaism* (ed. Harold W. Attridge and Gohei Hata; Detroit: Wayne State Univ. Press, 1992), 697–69.

42. Some have thought that the actual source of Orosius's information may have been Julius Africanus (who drew upon Josephus); for this suggestion from Harnack, see Kirsopp Lake, "The Chronology of Acts," in *The Acts of the Apostles* (*The Beginnings of Christianity* 1; ed. F. J. Foakes Jackson and Kirsopp Lake; Grand Rapids: Baker, 1979), 5:459; and Riesner, *Paul's Early Period*, 184–85. On the other hand, Harnack's attribution of Orosius's claim to Julius Africanus is "highly conjectural"; rightly Slingerland, "Suetonius, Acts 18, and Orosius," 137–39. Slingerland, *Claudian Policymaking*, 124, noted that Orosius's knowledge of Josephus appears to be secondhand through Suetonius and Eusebius. Slingerland added that a dating of the expulsion to 49 CE may well have dovetailed with Orosius's own apologetic tendencies ("Suetonius, Acts 18, and Orosius," 139–42). While such apologetic tendencies *may* be a factor in Orosius's dating of the events, Slingerland has only demonstrated the possibility of such tendencies playing a role, and that Orosius's date should be corroborated with further data.

43. See Slingerland, "Suetonius, Acts 18, and Orosius," 127–32, for a thorough review of the lack of evidence for placing the expulsion in 41 CE. Hostile actions toward the Jews early in Claudius's reign need not have been limited to those early years, and sentiments toward the Jewish nobility did not translate into actions toward the Jewish masses. When Philo spoke of Augustus *not* expelling Jews (*Legat.* 23 §157), he may just as well have been contrasting Augustus's positive actions with the expulsion under Tiberius rather than events in the 40s. Further, Dio Cassius firmly denied that an expulsion took place in 41 CE (see the evidence below for dating the ban on meetings in lieu of an expulsion to that year).

44. While Orosius's dating of the expulsion to 49 CE was based on a source other than Josephus, this other source was not Acts 18. On the independence of Orosius and

historical accuracy of Acts.[45] Nevertheless, this particular section of Acts has proved especially reliable when compared with Paul's own letters or extrabiblical evidence.[46] Paul's period in Corinth in Acts 18, when he met Aquila and Priscilla, can be fairly precisely dated. During Paul's eighteen-month stay in Corinth, according to Acts 18:12–17, he met the proconsul Gallio. An inscription dates Gallio's tenure in Achaia and Corinth in all probability to the summer of 51 CE.[47] Priscilla and Aquila's departure from Rome in 49 CE, if dated according to Orosius, would neatly dovetail with Paul's meeting of the couple in Corinth not long thereafter.[48] As Peter Lampe remarked: "The coincidence between the Orosius tradition and the Acts 18 chronology is amazing."[49] Second, 47–52 CE was a period in Claudius's reign when he was actively engaged in a campaign to curb the growth of foreign cults and to reestablish the old Roman religious rites.[50] "We need not postulate deep-felt religiosity. The image of the regime

---

Acts, see Riesner's argumentation in *Paul's Early Period*, 182–86. Acts 18:2 does not cite a 49 CE date, but that date is derived in conjunction with the Gallio inscription (see the following discussion). Orosius and Acts 18 are therefore both independent witnesses to an expulsion in 49 CE Robert Jewett, *A Chronology of Paul's Life* (Philadelphia: Fortress Press, 1979), 38, called the agreement between Orosius's date and an Acts dating based on the Gallio inscription a "striking correlation."

45. For a more critical assessment of the historicity of Acts, see Paul J. Achtemeier, *The Quest for Unity in the New Testament Church* (Philadelphia: Fortress Press, 1987), esp. pp. 67–74. For a defense of Acts' historicity, see Colin Hemer, *The Book of Acts in the Setting of Hellenistic History* (ed. Conrad H. Gempf; Winona Lake, Ind.: Eisenbrauns, 1990).

46. Abraham J. Malherbe, *The Letters to the Thessalonians* (AB 32B; New York: Doubleday, 2000), 55–71; Rainer Riesner, *Paul's Early Period*, 29–31, 412–15.

47. Jerome Murphy-O'Connor, "Paul and Gallio," *JBL* 112 (1993): 315–17; idem, *Paul: A Critical Life* (Oxford: Oxford Univ. Press, 1996), 15–22, followed by Riesner, *Paul's Early Period*, 207. Murphy-O'Connor's discussion of the dating of Gallio's tenure is perhaps the most thorough available.

48. On the other hand, if the couple had not gone directly to Corinth from Rome, the date of their departure from Rome prior to these additional travels may have been earlier than the late 40s. An earlier dating would not dovetail as well with Orosius. Luke, however, gives the impression that they had "recently" (προσφάτως) arrived *from Italy*; contra Levinskaya, *Book of Acts*, 174–75.

49. Lampe, *From Paul to Valentinus*, 14. Slingerland considered Orosius's date entirely fictitious, since it matched his tendencies ("Suetonius, Acts 18, and Orosius," 136–42; idem, *Claudian Policymaking*, 123–29).

50. Lake, "The Chronology of Acts," 460; Lane, "Roman Christianity," 205; Riesner, *Paul's Early Period*, 194–201; A. D. Nock, "Religious Developments from the Close of the Republic to the Death of Nero," *The Cambridge Ancient History* (ed. S. A. Cook,

was what mattered. Religion, politics, and publicity were intertwined."[51] In 47 CE Claudius provided a Roman alternative to eastern astrology by restoring the college of Haruspices (Tacitus, *Ann.* 11.15). In 48 CE he promoted several men to the patriciate in order to guarantee the priestly colleges the necessary number of members (Tacitus, *Ann.* 11.25). In 49 CE he restored the *Salutis Augurium*, the augury for determining when prayers on behalf of the state should be offered. He also extended the *pomerium*, the area where only Roman gods could be worshiped (Tacitus, *Ann.* 12.23). In the subsequent years, Claudius had several people prosecuted for consulting astrologers, and in 52 CE he expelled the astrologers from Rome (Tacitus, *Ann.* 12.22; 12.52; 12.59).[52] A Jewish expulsion in 49 CE would not be out of character for Claudius during these years. Josephus portrayed Claudius's actions toward the beginning of his reign in 41 CE as quite often favoring the Jews. For instance, his establishment of a system of redress for adherents of the Jewish religion in Alexandria in 41 CE may have strengthened the status of Jews throughout the empire generally (*Ant.* 19.5.2 §§279–285, to Alexandria and Syria, and 19.5.3 §§286–291, to the rest of the empire).[53] Such favorable actions may render a decree as extreme as expulsion more likely later in Claudius's reign. Certainty is not possible, since Josephus's own interests may belie a less friendly environment.[54] Claudius's extant letter to the Alexandrians expressed a dislike for the Jewish people who "stir up trouble throughout the whole world."[55] He warned them against seeking further privileges or enlarging their community lest it arouse his "greater suspi-

---

F. E. Adcock, and M. P. Charlesworth; Cambridge: Cambridge Univ. Press, 1934), 10:499–500.

51. Gruen, *Diaspora*, 39.

52. Vincent M. Scramuzza, *The Emperor Claudius* (HHS 44; Cambridge: Harvard Univ. Press, 1940), 145–52; Gruen, *Diaspora*, 39–41.

53. On the other hand, even in the midst of Claudius's more favorable actions, the emperor still expressed a dislike for the Jewish people. Claudius's attitude toward the Jews was not necessarily particularly positive, irrespective of his close dealings with Agrippa (H. Dixon Slingerland, "Suetonius *Claudius* 25.4 and the Account in Cassius Dio," *JQR* 79 [1989]: 308–12; repr. and rev. in *Claudian Policymaking and the Early Imperial Repression of Judaism at Rome* [SFSHJ 160; Atlanta: Scholars Press, 1997]). The harsher actions of the late 40s are understandable.

Against the theory that the Jews enjoyed legal privileges since Julius Caesar, see Ben Witherington III, *The Acts of the Apostles: A Socio-Rhetorical Commentary* (Grand Rapids: Eerdmans, 1998), 541–44, and the discussion later in this chapter.

54. Slingerland, *Claudian Policymaking*, 99–101.

55. P. Lond. 1912, lines 98–100. Original text available in E. Mary Smallwood, *Documents Illustrating the Principates of Gaius, Claudius, and Nero* (London: Cambridge Univ. Press, 1967), 99–102. Translation provided by Molly Whittaker, *Jews and*

cions."[56] On the other hand, Claudius was in this instance attempting to settle a serious conflict between two parties and admonished *both* severely.[57] As Gruen concluded, "The year 49 has ancient attestation, not to be lightly dismissed. And that year has its relevant episodes: extension of the *pomerium*, revival of the *salutis augurium*, and the resort to expiatory sacrifices that date back to the regal period of hoary antiquity."[58] Third, to return to the matter of dating, the fact that Orosius attributed his date to a source indicates that he himself was not the source. Fourth, a date in the late 40s is more likely than the early 40s, since Christian movement and evangelization beyond Palestine would have been likely on a smaller scale before the mid-40s.[59] Finally, the expulsion must have come *after* the early part of Claudius's reign since Dio Cassius indicated that Claudius did *not* expel the Jews at that time.[60] This evidence cumulatively points to the late 40s for Claudius's expulsion of the Jews and would suggest that Acts 18 and Suetonius were referring, indeed, to the same event.[61]

Christians: Graeco-Roman Views (CCWJCW 6; Cambridge: Cambridge Univ. Press, 1984), 99–100.

56. P. Lond. 1912, lines 88–98 (trans. Whittaker); see also Slingerland, *Claudian Policymaking*, 101. Claudius's attitude with respect to the Alexandrian Jewish situation should not be generalized without further evidence. Tensions ran high between the Jews of Alexandria and the Greek population as a result of favorable Roman actions toward the Jews. Greek hostility toward the Jews was fueled in part by a resentment of the Romans; John G. Gager, *The Origins of Anti-Semitism* (Oxford: Oxford Univ. Press, 1983), 42–54.

57. Slingerland, *Claudian Policymaking*, 144–47. This imperial action because of a disturbance contradicts Slingerland's view that Claudius was generally hostile toward the Jewish religion as such. Order in the empire was the priority, and the Jewish religion a matter of indifference or scorn but not outright animosity.

58. Gruen, *Diaspora*, 41.

59. E. Mary Smallwood, *The Jews under Roman Rule: From Pompey to Diocletian* (SJLA 20; Leiden: E. J. Brill, 1976), 211.

60. See reference and discussion to follow as well as the discussion in Slingerland, *Claudian Policymaking*, 112–14. He also refuted (pp. 114–16) Karl Wieseler's highly conjectural and problematic attempt to date the expulsion to 52 CE (*Chronologie des apostolischen Zeitalters bis zum Tode der Apostel Paulus und Petrus* [Göttingen: Vandenhoeck und Ruprecht, 1848]).

61. Dixon Slingerland suggested that Suetonius and Acts 18 may be referring to two separate expulsions under Claudius, but he offered no real evidence for this claim and had to ignore the cluster of evidence pointing to the same general time in the late 40s for an expulsion and thus *the same* expulsion ("Suetonius, Acts 18, and Orosius," 133–36). The equation of Suetonius and Acts 18 is not a mere assumption.

The Expulsion of the Entire Jewish Population of Rome?

Several commentators have supposed that Claudius expelled *all* or the majority of the Jews from Rome.[62] They would translate Suetonius, *Iudaeos impulsore Chresto assidue tumultuantis Roma expulit:* "Since the Jews were constantly making disturbances at the instigation of Chrestus, he expelled them from Rome." If Claudius expelled all the Jews (or at least the vast majority) from Rome, then the Jewish Christian presence would have been decimated, and the absence of Jewish Christians would have forced a complete social restructuring of the Roman Christian community. Gentile adherents of Christ in the synagogues would have been forced to meet on their own. In the ensuing years of Claudius's reign, Jews would have trickled back into Rome with the pace of return quickening after Nero's accession in A D 54. The Jewish Christians, who had originally been the backbone of the Christ movement in Rome, would now have been unwelcome among fellow Jews. They would have found themselves in the minority in the separate Christian assemblies. Most scholars agree that there was a gentile majority and a Jewish minority in Rome's churches.[63] The tensions between these

---

62. For example, Wolfgang Wiefel, "The Jewish Community in Ancient Rome and the Origins of Roman Christianity," in *The Romans Debate*, 93 (rev. and enl. ed.; ed. Karl P. Donfried; Peabody, Mass.: Hendrickson, 1991; repr. from "Die jüdische Gemeinschaft im antiken Rom und die Angänge des römischen Christentums," *Judaica* 26 [1970]: 65–88). More recently (and a random sampling), Gary Steven Shogren, "'Is the Kingdom of God about Eating and Drinking or Isn't It?' (Romans 14:17)," *NovT* 42 (2000): 243; N. T. Wright, "Romans and the Theology of Paul," in *Pauline Theology 3: Romans* (ed. David M. Hay and E. Elizabeth Johnson; Minneapolis: Fortress Press, 1995), 35; A. Katherine Grieb, *The Story of Romans: A Narrative Defense of God's Righteousness* (Louisville: Westminster John Knox, 2002), 7: "[Claudius] threw them all out."

63. For instance, William Sanday and Arthur C. Headlam, *A Critical and Exegetical Commentary on the Epistle to the Romans* (5th ed.; ICC; Edinburgh: T&T Clark, 1902), xxxiii–xxxiv; C. K. Barrett, *Romans*, 6–7, 23, 235; Leon Morris, *The Epistle to the Romans* (Grand Rapids: Eerdmans, 1988), 5; James D. G. Dunn, *Romans 9—16* (WBC 38B; Dallas: Word, 1988), xlv, liii; Douglas J. Moo, *The Epistle to the Romans* (NICNT; Grand Rapids: Eerdmans, 1996), 9–13; Mark A. Seifrid, *Justification by Faith: The Origin and Development of a Central Pauline Theme* (NovTSup 68; Leiden: Brill, 1992), *Faith*, 201–6; Joseph A. Fitzmyer, *Romans* (AB 33; New York: Doubleday, 1993), 32–33. In fact, Thomas R. Schreiner, *Romans* (BECNT 6; Grand Rapids: Baker, 1998), 13 n. 25 judged the position that the Roman church was exclusively gentile, as advocated by Johannes Munck, *Paul and the Salvation of Mankind* (Atlanta: John Knox, 1959), 200–209, and Stanley K. Stowers, *A Rereading of Romans: Justice, Jews, and Gentiles* (New Haven: Yale Univ. Press, 1994), to be simply "wrong."

two groups would have motivated Paul's discourse on the relation between Jews and gentiles in Rom 9–11 which includes the warning against gentile arrogance in 11:13–21 and 12:3–4. Paul especially wants, these scholars reason, to urge the gentile strong to accept the Jewish Christians' observances regarding food and drink and various days in 14:1 — 15:13. The reason Paul primarily addresses the gentile majority throughout this letter is because of their pride over against the Jews in their midst. As easily as God had grafted the gentiles onto the olive tree — representing Israel's heritage and benefits — where Israelites had been cut off, Israel could just as easily be grafted back in (11:17–24).[64]

The assumption of a complete expulsion of the Jews under Claudius is fraught with insurmountable problems. The Roman historian Tacitus never mentioned an expulsion of the Jews in his record of this period (*Ann.* 12), nor did the Jewish historian Josephus ever mention such an expulsion. The only corroborating evidence for an expulsion of Jews from Rome is the reference in Acts to the arrival of Priscilla and Aquila in Corinth from Rome. Dio Cassius, another Roman historian, likewise nowhere mentioned the mass expulsion to which Suetonius referred, but he did record an earlier action by Claudius to ban the Jews from meeting. Dio Cassius indicated that Claudius had taken this action because he *could not* expel them (*Hist.* 60.6.6). The Jews in Rome, a population estimated between 20,000 and 50,000, were simply too numerous to be expelled.[65] By way of contrast, the historians all recorded the expulsion by

---

64. The classic expression of this still common view is by Marxsen, *Introduction to the New Testament*, 95–109. See also Wiefel, "The Jewish Community in Ancient Rome," 92–96. More recently, see William L. Lane, "Roman Christianity," 198–202.

65. The practice of naming synagogue assemblies after contemporary benefactors, as attested in the literary remains, has led to the conclusion that as many as thirteen synagogues are first century CE in origin, with several even earlier in origin (Augustus, Agrippa, Herod, Volumnia [a Syrian official in 9–7 BCE]). "The Synagogue of the Hebrews" and "The Synagogue of the Vernaculars" are likely among the first Roman synagogues (cf. the "Synagogue of the Hebrews" in an inscription at Corinth). Peter Richardson concludes from this evidence that at least four or five Roman synagogues were in existence prior to and at the beginning of the first century CE (*Building Jewish in the Roman East* [Waco: Baylor University Press, 2004], 120–24). The presence of several synagogues in first century Rome and the mention in Tacitus of four thousand draftable age Jewish men in 19 CE contribute to the estimates of the overall Jewish population. For the derivation of these estimates, see especially John M. G. Barclay, *Jews in the Mediterranean Diaspora: From Alexander to Trajan (323 BCE–117 CE)* (Edinburgh: T&T Clark, 1996), 295; Leon, *Jews of Ancient Rome*, 135–36; and the overview in Karin Hedner-Zetterholm, "The Jewish Communities of Ancient Rome," in *The Synagogue of Ancient Ostia and the Jews of Rome: Interdisciplinary Studies* (ed. Birger Olsson, Dieter Mitternacht, and Olof Brandt; Stockholm: Svenska Institutet i Rom, 2001), 132–3.

the emperor Tiberius of four thousand Jewish men of draftable age in 19 CE.[66] If *tens of thousands* of Jews had been expelled, one would expect such an event to have left an even greater imprint in the pages of the historians. Such is not the case. The Romans were constantly "expelling" people, whether astrologers, fortune-tellers, or cult leaders. The emperor or senate would issue a decree of expulsion and then the commanders of the army would or would not enforce it. Expulsions were haphazard affairs.[67] As one commentator put it: "Administrative action required both policy and the will to act on it. Rome's will to act in such cases was motivated by civil disturbances or the lobbying of concerned parties (for example, informants)."[68] Erich Gruen noted that expulsions were traditionally acts of political "posturing," symbolic gestures with little practical effect. In 161 BCE the Roman praetor M. Pomponius managed to orchestrate a senatorial ban on philosophers and rhetors from the city (Suetonius, *Rhet.* 1.2; Gellius, 15.11.1). The decree would have been highly impractical with Rome's educational needs, and Athenian philosophers were on record lecturing to captivated audiences in 155. In 154 Epicurean philosophers were expelled, even though Epicureans remained active and influential in the city thereafter (Athenaeus, *Deipn.* 12.547a; Aelian, *Var. hist.* 9.12).[69] Gruen: "Action by the regime in Rome under Claudius, as under Tiberius and in the Republic, came only when it might benefit the government's image—and even then it was largely performance and ceremony."[70] Tacitus made a telling comment in his *Annals*: "The expulsion of the astrologers from Italy was ordered by a drastic and *impotent* decree of the senate" (emphasis added).[71] So when Luke claims in Acts 18:2 that the Jews were "ordered" out of Rome, such an order would not by any means result in an *actual* mass eviction of the Jews. As Gruen surmised from the history of expulsion orders in Rome, "And the exodus (such as it was) in each instance had few par-

---

66. Josephus, *Ant.* 18.3.5 §§83–84; Tacitus, *Ann.* 2.85; Suetonius, *Tib.* 36; Dio Cassius, *Hist.* 57.18.5.

67. Tacitus, *Hist.* 1.22 (astrologers); Ramsay MacMullen, *Enemies of the Roman Order: Treason, Unrest, and Alienation in the Empire* (Cambridge: Harvard Univ. Press, 1966), 125–26, 132–33. Slingerland inexplicably assumed that decrees of expulsion automatically brought about "the expulsion of whole populations" (*Claudian Policymaking*, 120 n. 35).

68. James C. Walters, *Ethnic Issues in Paul's Letter to the Romans: Changing Self-Definitions in Earliest Roman Christianity* (Valley Forge, Pa.: Trinity Press International, 1993), 43.

69. Gruen, *Diaspora*, 17–18.

70. Ibid., 41.

71. Tacitus, *Ann.* 12.52 (Jackson, LCL).

ticipants and was of brief duration. The gesture alone mattered. The continuity of Jewish communities in Rome seems largely uninterrupted."[72]

Josephus's omission of an expulsion of the Jews under Claudius is very telling for other reasons as well. Although not presenting Claudius in the best light, Josephus nevertheless characterized Claudius as supportive of the Jews. The Jewish ruler Agrippa I was raised in Rome as a child and socialized with the future emperors Gaius and Claudius (*Ant.* 18.6.1 §§143–6; 18.6.4 §§165–6). Agrippa I undertook perilous negotiations with the Roman senate in order to gain its endorsement of Claudius as the new emperor (*Ant.* 19.4.1 §§236–47; cf. 19.5.1 §§274–5). Josephus related that Claudius issued edicts confirming Judean rights in the empire and Judean civic status in Alexandria (*Ant.* 19.5.2 §§278–91; cf. 19.6.3 §§302–11). Josephus even narrated how Claudius overruled his governors in favor of the Jews (*Ant.* 15.11.4 §407//20.1.2 §§7–14; *War* 2.12.7 §245//*Ant.* 20.6.3 §136).[73] A mass expulsion of the Jews, had such an incredible event taken place, would have contradicted Josephus's overall portrayal of Claudius and required some explanation. For the benefit of his Roman audience, Josephus's habit was to explain away as the fault of other groups what might have reflected badly on the Jews. Josephus would not only have had to explain away such an expulsion in light of his depiction of Claudius, but he would also have wanted to exonerate the Jews, lest such an expulsion offer an obvious counter-example to his favorable portrayal of his own people.[74]

The Suetonius text itself need not be translated to suggest such a large-scale action. Suetonius may have been saying that it was the Jews actually involved in the Chrestus disturbance who were expelled from Rome ("He expelled from Rome the Jews constantly making disturbances at the instigation of Chrestus").[75] In other words, Suetonius's reference to "the Jews" being expelled may very well have referred to a small-scale action involving only those actually involved in the

---

72. Gruen, *Diaspora*, 53. Tongue in cheek, he added: "It would certainly be wrong to imagine that Roman Jews lived in perpetual insecurity, with bags packed and departure vehicles at the ready."

73. Steve Mason, "'For I Am Not Ashamed of the Gospel' (Rom. 1.16): The Gospel and the First Readers of Romans," in *Gospel in Paul: Studies on Corinthians, Galatians and Romans for Richard N. Longenecker* (ed. L. Ann Jervis and Peter Richardson; JSNT-Sup 108; Sheffield: Sheffield Academic, 1994), 265; Benko, "The Edict of Claudius," 407–8.

74. On Josephus's pattern of exoneration of the Jews in general, see Steve Mason, *Josephus and the New Testament* (Peabody, Mass: Hendrickson, 1992), 53–84.

75. William L. Lane, *Hebrews 1—8* (WBC 47; Dallas: Word, 1991), lxiv–lxv; idem, "Roman Christianity," 204; Smallwood, *Jews under Roman Rule*, 216.

conflict — the "Chrestus" people.[76] Even Orosius thought only the ringleaders were expelled. A smaller-scale action would explain why Tacitus did not mention it.[77] Luke, for his part, does assert in Acts 18:2 that "all the Jews" had been expelled from *Italy* (!), but he often employs the word "all" in a non-literal, exaggerated sense.[78] Further, "all" ($\pi\hat{\alpha}\varsigma$) may well be in the predicate position, in which case Luke is not referring to the totality of Jews in Rome (as had it been in the attributive position).[79] The expelled group in Acts 18:2 would simply have been those involved in the conflict to which Claudius's edict had been directed, and the verse need not imply that every Jew in Italy was expelled. Luke may also be referring to the actual wording of the edict itself rather than to the execution of the edict. As for the expulsion from *Italy* as opposed to Rome, Luke is in good company. Tacitus had a habit of recording expulsions from Rome as expulsions from all Italy (*Ann.* 2.32; 4.14; 13.25; *Hist.* 2.62). So he described Tiberius's expulsion of the Jews in 19 CE as involving Italy (*Ann.* 2.85). Josephus (*Ant.* 18.3.5 §§83–4) and Suetonius (*Tib.* 36) spoke only of Rome. Such an action on Claudius's part, even if more limited than a mass expulsion, could still have violently disrupted the population of Christians in the Roman synagogues.

---

76. Slingerland countered that Suetonius employed "Iudaeus" "inclusively" and not restrictively (*Claudian Policymaking*, 117–18). He cited the "inclusive" usage of Lycians, Rhodians, Trojans, Germans, and Druids in the immediate context of *Claudius* 25.3–5. He contended that Suetonius employed "Iudaeus" inclusively elsewhere in his *De vita caesarum* (*Tiberius* 36, *Vespasian* 4.5; 8.1; *Julius* 84.5; *Augustus* 76.2). The "Jews" in *Vespasian* 4.5 and 8.1, however, are not the Jewish people as a whole but those residing in the homeland. *Julius* 84.5 refers only to those Jews "who even flocked to the place [of Caesar's funeral] for several successive nights." *Tiberius* 36 refers only to "Jews" (in Rome) "of military age." An inclusive reading, the Jews as a people, makes little sense in *Claudius* 25.4 since Suetonius has already restricted "Jews" in this context to those who resided in Rome. Even as *Tiberius* 36 restricted the Jews expelled to those "of military age," *Claudius* 25.4 may well be limited to those Jews causing the tumult.

77. Contra Esler, *Conflict and Identity*, 99, who recognized that Tacitus's omission only argues against a large-scale expulsion. Dio Cassius's work is only partially extant for 49 CE.

78. See, for instance, Acts 2:5, 47; 3:9, 11, 18; 4:21; 5:11, 34; 8:1, 9–10; 9:35; 10:12, 22, 41; 19:10; contra Slingerland, *Claudian Policymaking*, 117. For further examples of Luke's hyperbolic use of "all," see Thorsteinsson, *Paul's Interlocutor*, 95 n. 27; Botermann, *Das Judenedikt*, 48.

79. Robert G. Hoerber, "The Decree of Claudius in Acts 18:2," *CTM* 31 (1960): 692–93.

Dio Cassius Versus Suetonius:
Two Separate Actions

The expulsion of the Jews under Claudius to which Suetonius referred should not be confused with another, earlier action by the emperor.[80] In Dio Cassius's chronological record of the year 41 CE, Claudius ordered the Jews "not to hold meetings" (60.6.6–7; "the next year" begins in 60.9.1).[81] The historian added that it was impossible for Claudius to expel the Jews because of their number, a statement at odds with Suetonius's claim that an expulsion *did* happen. These two assertions are contradictory only if they refer to the same event, as Gerd Luedemann contended (along with a 41 CE date).[82] Suetonius claimed that there were Jewish tumults; Dio only spoke of the potential of tumult. Suetonius

---

80. Contra Levinskaya, *Book of Acts*, 174.

81. The ban on meetings took place according to Dio Cassius in the same year that Claudius gave land to Agrippa I and Herod. The gifts of land were in 41 CE according to Josephus (*Ant.* 19.5.1 §§274–7). In his chronological listing of events, Dio Cassius began "the next year" in 60.9.1; Dixon Slingerland, "Suetonius *Claudius* 25.4 and the Account in Cassius Dio," 307–8. Suetonius, on the other hand, wrote in a topical rather than annalistic style. Slingerland (pp. 308–16) refuted various challenges to the 41 CE date. He observed that one should not confuse a general toleration of the Jews early in Claudius' reign with a "friendly" disposition toward them. Actions taken on behalf of Jewish aristocracy do not necessarily imply that Claudius would not act against Jewish populations in general should there be a threat to the welfare of the empire. Much of the rest of Slingerland's article dispels the connections between Suetonius's *Chrestus* incident and Dio Cassius as evidence for a later dating of Dio Cassius's events. Elsewhere, Slingerland demonstrated that Philo's *Flaccus* and *Legatio* (dated to 41 CE) describe actions Augustus did *not* do as if in contrast to actions taken specifically by Claudius early in his reign in 41 CE (*Claudian Policymaking*, 90–96). See Slingerland's refutation (*Claudian Policymaking*, 102–5) of attempts to overturn the 41 CE date by Benko and Seston.

82. Gerd Luedemann, *Paul, Apostle to the Gentiles: Studies in Chronology* (trans. F. Stanley Jones; Philadelphia: Fortress Press, 1984), 164–66, 187–88. Nanos, *Mystery*, 381 n. 31, wrote, "It seems a curious negative comment for Dio at this point. Why would he note what did not happen when writing the history of what did happen unless he was challenging another version of the event(s) at this point?" The key assumption is "at this point." Dio Cassius may have been contrasting what took place in 41 CE with *other* expulsions of the Jews. Rightly Reasoner, *Strong and the Weak*, 135 n. 164. In fact, Slingerland, "*Claudius* 25.4 and Cassius Dio," 320, contended that Dio Cassius was comparing what took place under Claudius, when the Jews' numbers had increased considerably, with the expulsion that took place under Tiberius, which Dio Cassius himself recorded earlier (hence the numbers of the Jews "again" increased). Reasoner

said that Claudius acted against the Jews; Dio said that he acted against Jewish institutions. Suetonius mentioned "Chrestus"; Dio did not.[83] Suetonius showed no awareness of the sort of ban on meetings that Dio mentioned. "In reality, until it has been demonstrated that [Dio Cassius and Suetonius] refer to the same event, no disagreement exists between the two accounts. In other words, such argumentation is circular."[84]

What motivated Luedemann's argumentation was his belief that Dio was correcting a source that both he and Suetonius had used.[85] Dio Cassius did not, however, appear to be correcting a source. Lampe observed:

> But this hypothesis does not bother with Dio's context. Dio is not correcting a source: οὐκ ἐξήλασε, "he did not expel," needs to be completed with "as Tiberius had done." Dio refers here quite clearly back to his own context, to Tiberius' great expulsion of the Jews from Rome (πλεονάσαντας αὖθις; "they had *again* grown in numbers"!), which he had described in 57.18.

Even if Luedemann were right that Dio Cassius and Suetonius had been refer-ring to the same event, Lampe was puzzled that Luedemann would prioritize the chronology of Dio Cassius's account over Acts 18, which comes from a hundred years earlier than Dio Cassius.[86]

No doubt Dio Cassius is correct that Claudius acted against the Jews in Rome in 41 CE. Not long after Claudius became emperor, Philo reported that Claudius's illustrious predecessor Augustus did not expel the Jews from Rome or

---

(p. 135) pointed out that Claudius had to address early on Jewish unrest, which he had inherited from Caligula.

83. Dio's reference to *hetaireiai*, or private societies, does not single out or describe Christians; Judge and Thomas, "Origin," 91.

84. Dixon Slingerland, "Acts 18:1–17 and Luedemann's Pauline Chronology," *JBL* 109 (1990): 688–90. For further argumentation, see Slingerland, "*Claudius* 25.4 and Cassius Dio," 316–22. Riesner, *Paul's Early Period*, 176–79, provided additional evidence why Dio Cassius and Suetonius could not be referring to the same event.

85. Luedemann, *Paul*, 164–66, 187–88. For a further refutation of the flawed reasoning involved in seeing Dio Cassius as a correction of Suetonius, see Slingerland, "*Claudius* 25.4 and Cassius Dio," 318–20, and the discussion in Slingerland, *Claudian Policymaking*, 105–9.

86. Lampe, *From Paul to Valentinus*, 15. He added that if the two historians were referring to the same set of events, then Suetonius would be referring only to the expul-sion of the ringleaders in the conflict, and Dio Cassius would be narrating the fate of those left behind. Lampe thought the prohibition on meetings would force the Jewish Christians out of the synagogues and to their own underground assemblies.

prevent them from meeting (*Legat.* 23 §157).[87] Philo may have been presenting Augustus as a sort of counter-model for the new emperor.[88] Claudius's *Letter to Alexandria* from late 41 warned the Alexandrian Jews of imperial wrath for their nuisance-making throughout the empire. His March 41 CE letter had been much milder and friendlier in tone. Claudius's reference in his later letter to Jewish troubles elsewhere in the empire may have referred to the events in Rome of 41 CE. Dio Cassius reported that Claudius temporarily had banned synagogue meetings in 41 CE. E. Mary Smallwood speculated that Agrippa I may have drawn on his friendship with Claudius to soften the action against the Roman Jews. But, as Claudius himself put it in his *Letter to Alexandria* (*P. Lond.* 1912 lines 88–104), the rights of the Jews as a privileged people were dependent upon their behavior.[89] So Smallwood, along with many others, theorized that, since Claudius's ban on meetings in 41 CE did not calm the Jewish community, he took the more drastic measure in 49 CE of expelling Jews from Rome when yet another disruption took place, in this instance over Chrestus, or Christ.[90]

Helga Botermann even hypothesized that *Christian* activity in Rome required an imperial response already in 41 CE.[91] Such a scenario might explain why Claudius affirmed the Jews' ancestral traditions even while forbidding them from meeting. Christian activity in the Jewish community did not cease with the action in 41 CE. With the continued threat to the Jews' ancestral customs, the emperor acted again later in the decade. While Botermann's proposal is possible, little

---

87. On the dating of the document, see *Legat.* 30 §206, where Claudius executed one of Gaius's freedmen, an action that likely took place early in his reign; Smallwood, *Jews under Roman Rule*, 213–14 n. 38.

88. Thus Smallwood, *Jews under Roman Rule*, 214. Smallwood pointed out that this would explain Philo's silence about Tiberius's role in the expulsion of 19 CE. Philo emphasized, instead, Sejanus's anti-Jewish actions, which allowed Philo to cast Tiberius in a more pro-Jewish light. Philo also referred to Tiberius's defense of the Jews in a letter ostensibly from Agrippa I to Gaius (*Legat.* 37–38 §§298–305, 39 §308) — a letter that may reflect Philo's own handiwork.

89. Original text in Smallwood, *Documents*, 99–102.

90. Among the scholars who support this conclusion, see Smallwood, *Jews under Roman Rule*, 213–16; Francis Watson, *Paul, Judaism, and the Gentiles: A Sociological Approach* (SNTSMS 56; Cambridge: Cambridge Univ. Press, 1986), 91–93; A. J. M. Wedderburn, *The Reasons for Romans* (Edinburgh: T&T Clark, 1988), 57; Dunn, *Romans 8–16*, xlviii–xlix; Wiefel, "The Jewish Community in Ancient Rome," 93; F. F. Bruce, "The Romans Debate—Continued," in *The Romans Debate*, 175–94 (repr. from *BJRL* 64 [1981–82]: 334–59); Fitzmyer, *Romans*, 31–34; Walters, *Ethnic Issues*, 50–52.

91. Botermann, *Das Judenedikt*, 131–32.

is available in the primary sources to confirm this reconstruction of the events. Botermann pointed to the conflicts in the Jewish communities throughout the Book of Acts over Jesus Christ and Paul's own rather harsh reception among fellow Jews throughout the Empire (2 Cor 11:24–25).[92] That Christians are not singled out as the cause of the Roman tumult in 41 CE is explainable by the placement of these events so early in the Christian movement before they had an identity distinct from the rest of the Jews. She even conceived of Peter in Rome under Claudius, but she was unable to explain both Luke's and Paul's failures to mention Peter's visit. Instead she preferred the much later and less viable accounts of Eusebius and the *Kerygma Petri*.[93]

A 49 CE date for the expulsion of the Jews who had been involved in the "Chrestus" conflict would agree with Aquila's and Priscilla's "recent" arrival in Corinth from Rome (in Acts 18), an account which cannot be dated as early as 41. If this interpretation of Suetonius's record of Claudius's decree is correct, the implication would be that the Roman Christians had not severed their ties with the Jewish synagogues prior to the expulsion. Jews, both Christian and non-Christian, had been associating with each other in the synagogues. Suetonius represented the dispute as an *intra*-Jewish conflict. If Claudius expelled only the ringleaders in the conflict, then most certainly the Jewish advocates of "Chrestus," who had caused the stir, would have been among those expelled. The Jewish Christian presence in Rome would have been decimated.

After drawing the attention of the Roman imperium, the Jewish synagogues would likely have taken measures to distance themselves from the emerging Christian movement.[94] Certainly relations between Christ-believing and non-Christ-believing Jews with(in) the synagogues, strained prior to the Claudian edict, would have worsened as a result of the edict. James Walters wrote in his analysis of the early Roman church: "The edict in effect drove a wedge between [Christ-believers and non-Christian Jews in Rome] by dramatically communicating—especially to non-Christian Jews—that it would be in their best interests to go their separate ways."[95] If the Roman Christians were previously

---

92. Ibid., 132–37.

93. Ibid., 136–40.

94. Too much discussion of the Roman situation has remained fixated on the return of Jewish Christians to Rome after the expiration of the expulsion edict. A more plausible reconstruction of the situation at Rome prior to Paul's letter must account for the immediate aftermath of the expulsion of Jewish Christians.

95. James C. Walters, "Romans, Jews, and Christians: The Impact of the Romans on Jewish/Christian Relations in First Century Rome," in Donfried and Richardson,

indistinguishable from ordinary synagogue members, where would Christians worship after the expulsion necessitated a split? While Claudius's edict likely expelled the Jewish Christian instigators, and perhaps a few of the more prominent gentile Christian God-fearers involved in the conflict, no doubt other gentile Christians would have remained behind.[96] Those Christians left behind after the expulsion would become the core of a new church in Rome. For the first time, Christianity in Rome would become a gentile phenomenon. Christians would no longer have been welcome to meet in the Jewish synagogues. They would have had to form their own house churches.

Christ-Believing God-Fearers Expelled?

Outsiders may not have been able to distinguish between Jews and their gentile sympathizers.[97] Some in the Greco-Roman world employed the word "Jew" (Ιουδαῖος) not only for Jews and their proselytes but also for those who adhered to Jewish customs, quite apart from circumcision. For Epictetus, one who "adopts the attitude of mind" of a Jew "both is a Jew in fact and is called one" (καλεῖται Ἰουδαῖος).[98] Dio Cassius (37.17.1) wrote: "The country has been named (ὠνόμα-δαται) Judaea, and the people themselves Jews (Ιουδαῖοι). I do not know how this title (ἐπίκλησις) came to be given them, but it applies also to all the rest of mankind (καὶ ἐπὶ τοὺς ἄλλους ἀνθρώπους), although of alien race (ἀλλοεθνεῖς) who affect

---

Judaism and Christianity in First-Century Rome, 178. On the possible expulsion of gentile God-fearers in the conflict, see Walters, *Ethnic Issues,* 58–59.

96. For an overview of the issues and evidence for "god-fearers," see chap. 2, as well as Scot McKnight, *A Light among the Gentiles: Jewish Missionary Activity in the Second Temple Period* (Minneapolis: Fortress Press, 1991), 110–15; and Alan F. Segal, *Paul the Convert: The Apostolate and Apostasy of Saul the Pharisee* (New Haven, Conn.: Yale Univ. Press, 1990), 93–96.

97. For a detailed discussion of gentile sympathizers or God-fearers in the Jewish community, see chap. 2. For further helpful summaries of the evidence, see McKnight, *Light among the Gentiles,* 90–101, 108–14; Magnus Zetterholm, *The Formation of Christianity in Antioch: A Social-Scientific Approach to the Separation Between Judaism and Christianity* (London: Routledge, 2003): 121–29.

98. Arrian, *Epict. diss.* 2.19–21; Menahem Stern, ed. and trans., *Greek and Latin Authors on the Jews and Judaism* (3 vols.; Jerusalem: The Israel Academy of Sciences and Humanities, 1974), 1:542–44. See also the discussion of this text in Shaye J. D. Cohen, "'Those Who Say They Are Jews and Are Not': How Do You Know a Jew in Antiquity When You See One?" in *Diasporas in Antiquity* (ed. Cohen and Ernest S. Frerichs; BJS 288; Atlanta: Scholars Press, 1993), 33–34; repr. in Cohen, *The Beginnings of Jewishness: Boundaries, Varieties, Uncertainties* (Berkeley: Univ. of California Press, 1999), 60.

[strive for] their customs" (ὅσοι τὰ νόμιμα αὐτῶν ζηλοῦσι).[99] Plutarch classified anyone who abstained from pork a "Jew."[100] The term "Jew," for these authors, went beyond proselytes and the natural born to include even those observing only elements of Jewish custom.[101] A handful of scholars have therefore doubted whether the Claudius edict impacted only Jews and not also their gentile sympathizers. Thorsteinsson reasoned that the Romans would not have been able to distinguish "gentile Christians" and "Jewish Christians," and would have expelled adherents of Christ indiscriminately.[102] Walters likewise contended that since the gentile Christians were associating with the synagogues and would have been considered Jews to outside observers, they too would have been expelled.[103]

On the other hand, identifying gentile sympathizers of Judaism from other gentiles would have perhaps been more difficult than distinguishing gentiles from Jews. Josephus and Philo both mentioned the widespread observance of various Jewish customs among the gentiles (Philo, *Mos.* 2.4 §§17–24; *Hypoth.*; Josephus, *Ag. Ap.* 1.22 §§162–67; 2.39 §§281–84). Seneca concurred: "The customs of this accursed race have gained such influence that they are now received throughout all the world. The vanquished have given laws to their victors."[104] As Shaye Cohen wrote:

> Even people assembled in a synagogue or present in a Jewish neighborhood were not necessarily Jews themselves. In the Roman diaspora social mingling between Jews and gentiles was such that, without inquiring or checking, you could not be sure who was a Jew and who was not.[105]

Even the observance of Jewish customs did not guarantee that an individual considered himself or herself a Jew.[106] Because of their observance of Jewish customs and their association with synagogues, some gentiles might then have been mistaken as Jews.[107] The frequent interaction of Jews and gentiles would make it difficult for observers trying to single out which gentiles were God-fearers.

---

99. Cary, LCL, as modified by Thorsteinsson, *Paul's Interlocutor*, 203.

100. *Quaest. conv.* 5.1–3; Stern, *Greek and Latin Authors*, 1:550–59.

101. See also the discussion of this text in Cohen, "'Those Who Say They Are Jews and Are Not,'" 31–32; *Beginnings of Jewishness*, 149–50.

102. Thorsteinsson, *Paul's Interlocutor*, 96.

103. Walters, *Ethnic Issues*, 58–64; idem, "Romans, Jews, and Christians," 177.

104. Augustine, *Civ.* 6.11 as trans. by Green, LCL; see also Stern, *Greek and Latin Authors*, 1:431–32.

105. Cohen, "'Those Who Say They Are Jews and Are Not,'" 30.

106. Ibid., 34–35.

107. Ibid., 39–40.

Ultimately, from the standpoint of those in the empire's capital, circumcision served as *the* marker of Jewish identity.[108] "Roman authors give the impression that circumcision was known in Rome as a uniquely Jewish characteristic, such that a man's circumcision could alone prove his Jewish origin."[109] Suetonius (*Dom*. 12.2) described how a man could be physically examined in a Roman court for the mark of circumcision in order to determine if he was liable for the *fiscus Iudaicus*. Petronius satirized men who disguise themselves with the appearance of circumcision in order "to look like Jews" (*ut Iudaei videamur*; *Satyricon* 102.14 [Rouse, LCL]). Petronius recognized the vast distinction between a sympathizer and a full convert: "The Jew may worship his pig-god and clamour in the ears of high heaven, but unless he also cuts back his foreskin with the knife, he shall go forth from the people and emigrate to Greek cities, and shall not tremble at the fasts of Sabbath imposed by the law."[110] The Roman author Tacitus thought that Jews adopted circumcision "to distinguish themselves from others by this difference" (*ut diversitate noscantur*; *Hist* 5.5). John Barclay concluded from this evidence: "In the Roman environment, then, circumcision constituted, for males, a practically unambiguous token of Jewish identity."[111] Outsiders would have recognized Jews and proselytes as committed members of the Jewish community since the entry rite publicly signaled their priorities and social ties. Whereas gentile Christians may have sought to distance themselves from the synagogues in the midst of a conflict growing all too serious with the emperor's involvement, the Jews and proselytes involved would have identifiably stood out from the rest of the populace by reputation from both synagogue involvement and the public baths.[112] Jewish Christian instigators of the "Chrestus" conflict would have been more easily identified and targeted. This, of course, assumes that the Romans would exert the energy to identify the members of the Jewish community.

Mark Nanos's concerns were more nuanced:

---

108. Note the texts listed and discussed in ibid., 12–18. Augustine, *Civ*. 6.11.

109. Barclay, *Jews in the Mediterranean Diaspora*, 438; so also Shaye Cohen, *Beginnings of Jewishness*, 40–44.

110. Fragment 37 (Poem 24 in Heseltine, LCL); cited as fragment 50 (*AL* 696, Bu 47) in R. Bracht Branham and Daniel Kinney, eds. and trans., *Petronius* (Berkeley: Univ. of California Press, 1996), 163. Dietary observances and worship of the high God are not enough. One must also *be circumcised* and observe the Sabbath.

111. Barclay, *Jews in the Mediterranean Diaspora*, 438.

112. Walters, *Ethnic Issues*, 58–64, and Nanos, *Mystery*, 383, did not consider that Jewish Christians and proselytes were more readily identifiable than gentile Christians by virtue of their circumcision.

Could [the Romans] distinguish Christians from Jews at any level? Would they even bother to try? If so, this would suggest a heightened discriminatory policy on the part of the Romans toward Jews and Judaism, a viewpoint that modern scholarship has challenged. Further, it necessitates a far more extensive knowledge of the Christian movement than even the proponents of this construct otherwise suggest.[113]

The concern of Roman imperial policy was for good order and the avoidance of subversive disturbances. When a disturbance emerged in the Jewish community over "Chrestus," the rabble-rousers would be the concern rather than the entire Jewish population. How would the Romans have identified the rabble-rousers? The most outspoken and active troublemakers would likely have been recognizable even to outsiders. As for the rest, the authorities would surely have had to rely on information from the synagogues themselves where the conflict had erupted.

The synagogues, in pointing fingers, would have been more concerned with the threat posed by fellow community members rather than with those who were less integrated into their community, such as gentile sympathizers or God-fearers. The issue is not who would be considered Jewish from a gentile Roman standpoint, but who would be considered members of the Jewish community from an *internal* standpoint. Nanos wrote: "In other words, it follows logically that if the Jews were expelled, so too were the Christian gentiles, who would most likely have been classified at this time as Jews or semi-Jews (Judaized gentiles) by both the synagogue leaders and Roman officials."[114] Nanos is correct only insofar as the opinion of the synagogue leaders would be far more critical. As the Jewish leadership identified troublemakers, gentile sympathizers would *not* be at the top of the list of people in a position to cause difficulties for the Jewish community. As Shaye Cohen observed in his work on the social boundary between Jews and gentiles: "A gentile who engaged in 'judaizing' behavior may have been regarded as a Jew by gentiles, but as a gentile by Jews."[115] "From the Jewish perspective, without social conversion — that is, without the integration of a gentile into Jewish society — there is no conversion at all; the gentile remains a gentile."[116] A gentile male had to be circumcised to join the Jewish community. Cohen: "No matter what its import, circumcision was essential; without it social

---

113. Nanos, *Mystery*, 383.

114. Ibid., 383. So also Vincent M. Scramuzza, "The Policy of the Early Roman Emperors towards Judaism," in Foakes Jackson and Lake, *The Acts of the Apostles* 5:296, who thought that Christians were also expelled as ringleaders in the conflict.

115. Cohen, *Beginnings of Jewishness*, 14.

116. Ibid., 168.

conversion for men was impossible."[117] "[N]o Jewish community in antiquity (including Philo's) accepted as members proselytes who were not circumcised." Cohen faulted those who emphasize the possibility of being a righteous gentile (a category drawn from Philo and Josephus). While such uncircumcised gentiles might find favor before God, "none of this implies 'social conversion' — that is, the integration of the convert into the Jewish community."[118] Terence Donaldson concurred: "Any males wanting to be accepted as full proselytes to Judaism needed to be circumcised."[119]

Neil J. McEleney in an important study voiced his disagreement that circumcision was *the* mark of a Jewish proselyte and argued that the Jews prior to 70 CE considered uncircumcised gentiles full proselytes in many instances.[120] McEleney pointed to a passage in Philo, *QE* 2 §2: "the (true) proselyte [προσή-λυτος] is one who is circumcised not in the foreskin but in lusts and desires and other passions of the soul" (see also *Somn.* 2.4 §25; *Spec.* 1.66 §§304–6). He then extrapolated from his interpretation of this passage as referring to uncircumcised "proselytes" to every other usage of the word "proselyte" (προσήλυτος) in Philo and concluded that circumcision was not necessary for proselyte status. John Nolland disputed McEleney's interpretation of this particular text. Philo presupposed that his readers would assume the necessity of the circumcision of proselytes: "Even if he is to be understood as standing over against this demand, his formulation presupposes its existence."[121] In other words, even if Philo did

---

117. Ibid., 169. This does not mean that the Jewish community would check visitors for circumcision. On the other hand, rabbinic Jews frequented the Roman baths. How much more likely would diaspora Jews? See the discussion in Cohen, "'Those Who Say They Are Jews and Are Not,'" 20–21.

118. Cohen, *Beginnings of Jewishness*, 219. This was the problem, for Cohen, with the study by Neil J. McEleney, "Conversion, Circumcision and the Law," *NTS* 20 (1974): 319–41, esp. pp. 328–33. See also John J. Collins, "A Symbol of Otherness: Circumcision and Salvation in the First Century," in *"To See Ourselves as Others See Us": Christians, Jews, "Others" in Late Antiquity* (ed. Jacob Neusner and Ernest S. Frerichs; SPSH; Chico, Calif.: Scholars Press, 1985), 163–86.

119. Terence Donaldson, *Paul and the Gentiles: Remapping the Apostle's Convictional World* (Minneapolis: Fortress Press, 1997), 59; see the full discussion on pp. 57–59, which agrees with Cohen.

120. McEleney, "Conversion," 328–33.

121. John Nolland, "Uncircumcised Proselytes?" *JSJ* 12 (1981): 175. Martin Hengel and Anna Maria Schwemer, *Paul between Damascus and Antioch* (Louisville: Westminster John Knox, 1997), 72, concurred regarding the interpretation of this text: "[I]t would be wrong to read out of this text, which has been so much discussed, that Philo knew the possibility of 'uncircumcised proselytes.'" So also Thomas M. Finn, "The God-fearers Reconsidered," *CBQ* 47 (1985), 82 (the proselyte language was simply that of the text

believe that a proselyte need not be circumcised, he demonstrated from his very statement how widespread the requirement was in his day. Nolland further noted that Philo did not typically dispute the Jewish customs of his day or assume minority positions. His pattern was to allegorize what he assumed to be normal Jewish practice. The disputed passage in *Quaestiones et solutiones in Exodum* was therefore most likely another instance of the allegorizing of a Jewish custom or physical rite. Philo explained elsewhere that as one obeyed the literal law of circumcision, one attuned the body to the mind.[122] Such an allegorical approach to the text was warranted, for Philo, by the surprising use of "proselyte" in the text for the Israelites in Egypt ("You were sojourners in the land of Egypt" [LXX: προσήλυτοι]). Nolland paraphrases Philo's introductory question to *QE* 2 §2: "What deeper sense to proselyte (than one who has entered Judaism by circumcision) can be discovered from the juxtaposition in the text of the mention of proselytes with the mention of the Israelites as proselytes in Egypt?"[123] In other words, the real proselyte was one who was circumcised in mind. The point of comparison was not a negative one — the Israelites' lack of circumcision — but rather the Israelites' true proselytism in comparison to true proselytism in Philo's own day. Opposition to circumcision was simply not a factor in this particular passage from Philo.[124] Martin Goodman agreed with Nolland's approach to this Philonic text. By explicitly noting that the Israelites were not circumcised, Goodman reasoned, Philo implied that one would have expected them to be circumcised. His main point, however, was the importance of turning to God for salvation.[125] To claim that Philo did not consider circumcision necessary, even in certain cases, would be to ignore the allegorical interpretive approach that he employed.[126] Elsewhere Philo disagreed sharply with those who had abandoned the literal rite of circumcision (*Mig.* 16–18 §§89–105).[127]

Philo was commenting upon). Hengel and Schwemer concluded that Philo, as other Jews of his day (e.g., Ananias to Izates), was leaving the door open for God-fearers and sympathizers (not proselytes) to dispense with circumcision in certain instances.

122. Nolland, "Uncircumcised Proselytes?" 175–76.

123. Ibid., 177.

124. Ibid., 177–79.

125. Goodman, *Mission and Conversion*, 73.

126. Ibid., 81–82.

127. Collins, "Symbol of Otherness," 171–73, concluded from Philo's concept of a twofold circumcision of both the inner and the outer that he considered only the inner circumcision to be of ultimate significance: "Philo does not treat circumcision as a central symbol of ethnic or religious identity" (pp. 172–73). McKnight, *Light among the Gentiles*, 146 n. 14, faulted Collins's conclusion for not properly accounting for *Mig.* 16 §92 "regardless of how spiritual Philo wanted the rite to be in its deepest sense."

McEleney cited Epictetus's *Diatr.* 2.9.20–1 (c. 55–130 CE) as evidence that one could convert to Judaism with baptism alone:

> Why, being Greek, do you pretend to be Jewish? Do you not see why each is called Jew, Syrian, or Egyptian? When we see someone play it both ways, we usually say, 'He is not Jewish, but pretends to be Jewish.' But when he takes up the mentality of the baptized and of the adherents, then he is really Jewish and one calls him Jewish. Thus it is with us imposters, 'Jews' in speech, but in deed something quite other in discord with our speech, far removed from practicing the doctrines we expound, those doctrines we pride ourselves on knowing.[128]

Nolland faulted McEleney for misconstruing Epictetus's reasoning that commended the true Jew as one who did not merely pretend to be a Jew but who actually was one in practice. Epictetus was not, then, suggesting a Jew who was merely baptized but not circumcised. Rather, Epictetus spoke of the Jew who fulfilled *all* that the name required. He used baptism as his example instead of circumcision, Nolland reasoned, because baptism was more amenable for universalizing to the true Epicurean and to the true Stoic rather than just to the true Jew. Baptism was a practice among many non-Jews, and, as a literary decision, allowed for more general application.[129] Goodman again agreed with Nolland that Epictetus may have been taking a part of the Jewish initiation as a figure for the whole — assuming, of course, that Epictetus was not confused regarding Jewish customs.[130]

Finally, McEleney pointed to Josephus's account of King Izates' conversion (*Ant.* 20.2.4 §§38–46). When the king and his mother were concerned that his subjects would not tolerate the rule of a circumcised Jew, Ananias posed to the king the compromise of stopping short of circumcision. Josephus wrote: "To be a devoted adherent of Judaism . . . counted more than circumcision" (§41). "God would pardon him" (§42). Nolland responded:

> But even there the failure to be circumcised is presented as understandable or forgivable rather than as right. Ananias is providing Izates with a justification for remaining at a penultimate stage of commitment to Judaism rather than claiming that this penultimate commitment will make Izates a Jew.[131]

---

128. As cited by McEleney, "Conversion," 332. McEleney provides the original Greek and his translation is clearer in English than Oldfather's in the LCL.

129. Nolland, "Uncircumcised Proselytes?" 180–82.

130. Goodman, *Mission and Conversion*, 81.

131. Nolland, "Uncircumcised Proselytes?" 193.

Nolland has also observed that Josephus presented Ananias as a man very interested in self-preservation: "He was afraid that if the matter became universally
known, he would be punished, in all likelihood, as personally responsible" (§41).
Eleazar is strict περὶ τὰ πάτρια (when it came to the ancestral laws) (§43)
whereas Ananias considered circumcision to be distinct from τὰ πάτρια, at
least by his advice in this case. Nolland emphasized the unique nature of this
incident since it involved a special dispensation to a ruler who could experience
serious loss of property, life, and position by receiving circumcision. Nolland also
demonstrated that McEleney misinterpreted several passages in the Talmud in
arguing his case (for example, b. Pesah. 92a; b. Hul. 4b; b. Yebam. 46b).[132]

The requirement of circumcision remained a major stumbling block for
gentile God-fearers. Martial in the late first century CE (7.82; cf. 7.30) satirized
a man who, while exercising in public, had tried (unsuccessfully) to conceal his
circumcision. Juvenal recognized circumcision as the crucial final step in moving
from paganism to Judaism (Sat. 14.96–9). He distinguished those who revered
(metuentem) the Sabbath and avoided pork from the next generation who went
all the way and accepted circumcision (14.96–9). Petronius distinguished sympathizers of the "pig god" from those who were also circumcised and who obeyed
the Sabbath.[133] Feldman commented on this passage: "When Petronius says, as
he does here, that the former group 'shall go forth from the people,' he means
that such individuals cannot be accepted as full Jews unless they accept the entire
law, including circumcision."[134] Philo introduced as "an object of ridicule among
many people, namely the circumcision of the genital organs" (Spec. 1.1 §2).
He nevertheless treated circumcision as a "vestibule" or portal through which
one might understand the rest of the commandments (Spec.1.1–2 §§1–11). In
Josephus's account of Izates' conversion (Ant. 20.2.4 §§38–9), Izates' mother
Helena rightly recognized that his reception of circumcision would result in
disaffection from the populace. Ananias felt that God would overlook Izates'
failure to be circumcised, in these harsh circumstances, and would treat him as
a full (πάντως) Jew (Ant. 20.2.4 §41). Eleazar, however, explained to him that
he had to be circumcised to become a Jew (Ant. 20.2.4 §43). The Herodians
insisted that non-Jews be circumcised when marrying into their family (Ant.
16.7.6 §225; 20.7.1 §139, 20.7.3 §145). Josephus (War 2.18.2 §463) described
the massacres in Syria prior to the first-century CE Jewish revolt against Rome.
The Syrian cities considered the Jews a "mixed lot" (μεμιγμένον), with some in

---

132. Ibid., 182–92.

133. Fragment 37 (Poem 24) in Heseltine, LCL.

134. Louis H. Feldman, Jew and Gentile in the Ancient World: Attitudes and Interactions from Alexander to Justinian (Princeton, N.J.: Princeton Univ. Press, 1993), 346.

their midst of "doubtful" Jewish identity (ἀμφίβολον). The Syrians hesitated to kill those who were mere "sympathizers."[135]

Sociologists D. A. Snow and R. Machalek described both "membership status" and "demonstration events" as necessary accompaniments of conversion for the insider to accept the outsider. As for "membership status," "Students of both mainstream religious traditions and new religious movements frequently treat shifts in organizational affiliation as indicators of conversion — e.g., denominational switching . . . and changes of the rite of passage variety whereby a nonmember becomes a member."[136] With respect to the second factor, "demonstration events," "These activities are essentially public displays of conversion that function as status confirmation rituals. They ostensibly provide dramatic evidence both to oneself and to others. . . ."[137] Whether nothing more than a form of "compliance behavior," the rite of circumcision remained necessary as a signal of entry into the Jewish community. The uncircumcised God-fearer had not yet crossed the social boundary to become a full member of the Jewish community and, by their refusal to be circumcised, confessed their continued allegiance, at some level, to other communities and traditions.

The case of proselytes confirms the social distance of the God-fearer from the Jewish community. Josephus called proselytes Ἰουδαῖοι. When Hyrcanus conquered the Idumeans in second century BCE, Josephus narrated that he permitted them to stay in their country "so long as they had themselves circumcised and were willing to observe the laws of the Jews....And from that time on they have continued to be Jews (Ἰουδαίους)" (*Ant.* 13.9.1 §§257–58).[138]

---

135. Feldman, *Jew and Gentile*, 155, wrote, "The very fact that Paul decided not to require circumcision of Christian proselytes and to interpret circumcision allegorically may well have been influenced by the general hostility of the Graeco-Roman world to this practice; and there is reason to believe that circumcision was a major stumbling block that kept 'G-d-fearers' from converting completely to Judaism."

136. David A. Snow and Richard Machalek, "The Sociology of Conversion," *Annual Review of Sociology* 10 (1984): 171.

137. Snow and Machalek, "Sociology of Conversion," 171–72. They wrote of a third factor in the conversion process: rhetorical indicators, the change of discourse that comes with the conversion as the convert asserts his or her new social identity by acting "to further the group's cause or mission" (p. 174). Both authors, in a separate article, emphasized that these factors are, nevertheless, imperfect indicators of conversion (David A. Snow and Richard Machalek, "The Convert as a Social Type," *Sociological Theory* 1983 [ed. Randall Collins; The Jossey-Bass Social and Behavioral Science Series; San Francisco: Jossey-Bass, 1983], 259–89). A more fully satisfactory theory of the sociology of conversion has not yet been articulated.

138. Cohen, *Beginnings of Jewishness*, 17–18, 81–82, 110–29; *Ant.* 20.2.4 §§38–39.

Origen wrote: "The noun *Ioudaios* is the name not of an *ethnos* but of a choice (in the manner of life). For if there be someone not from the nation of the Jews, a gentile, who accepts the ways of the Jews and becomes a proselyte, this person would properly be called a *Ioudaios*."[139] On the other hand, proselytes frequently did not achieve equal status with those born as Jews: "In the eyes of outsiders a proselyte or convert was a gentile who became a Jew. But in the eyes of (some?) Jews, a gentile who converted to Judaism became not a Jew but a proselyte—that is, a Jew of a peculiar sort."[140] The ethnic definition of a Jew was supplemented by the religious definition but not replaced by it. Since converts did not have the native-born blood lineage, they could not become the same as full Jews.[141] The *Fragments of a Zadokite Work* (14.5–6) from the Dead Sea Scrolls placed proselytes into their own category. In the Mishnah, proselytes ranked low on the social ladder and could not call the fathers of Israel his fathers. Only an emancipated slave had a lower status (*m. Hor.* 3:8; *m. Bik.* 1:4; *m. Yebam.* 6:5).

God-fearers, for their part, were far less integrated into the Jewish community since they also maintained strong social ties with non-Jews. As Zetterholm rightly observed: "For some Gentiles, however, having the position of god-fearer would be a very attractive alternative, since this could mean having the best of both worlds: that is, maintaining a Gentile social and religious identity but at the same time reckoning on being embraced by the salvation of the god of Israel."[142] God-fearers, including gentile Christians, would have had varying degrees of commitment to the Jewish synagogues. Jewish communities were often not the only social group they frequented — hence their decision not to become proselytes. Proselytes faced harassment from gentiles and were subject to synagogue discipline (*b. Yebam.* 47a, b). The same could not be said for God-fearers. God-fearers and sympathizers, provided they ceased attending the synagogues, would pose no threat to the Jewish communities. Faced with the threat of imperial intervention, God-fearers could leave the synagogues and blend into other communities. Jewish and proselyte troublemakers, on the other hand, were identified primarily by their membership in the synagogue and, as

---

139. As cited in ibid., 134.

140. Ibid., 162.

141. Thus Cohen, *Beginnings of Jewishness*, 132–33, 137, 162, 169; Feldman, *Jew and Gentile*, 338–41; Thorsteinsson, *Paul's Interloctor*, 203 noted an inscription from Rome in which a convert is called "Iudeus proselitus." An epitaph identified a God-fearing proselyte. The distinction remained between the convert and the full member of the community.

142. Zetterholm, *The Formation of Christianity in Antioch*, 127–28.

full members of the community, would more likely be singled out for Roman attention.[143] The Romans wanted the disturbance to the peace in Rome quieted. In carrying out the decree of expulsion, the Romans would have had to rely on information from the Jewish community in order to isolate the troublemakers, and less integrated God-fearers would not have been at the top of the list.

Separate Christian Assemblies

Imperial Restrictions on Religious Societies

With the crisis over "Chrestus" escalating because of imperial intervention, Christ-believing God-fearers would not have been welcome in the synagogues and would have distanced themselves from the conflict. They would have begun worshiping in their own assemblies. Mark Nanos objected that gatherings of Christ-believers independent of the synagogues would have been impossible. Julius Caesar had forbidden religious societies in Rome with the exception of the Jews.[144] He had dissolved all *collegia* "except those of ancient foundation" (Suetonius, *Jul.* 42.3; cf. Josephus, *Ant.* 14.10.8 §§213–16, 18.3.5 §§83–84). Likewise, Suetonius narrated how Octavian disbanded all *collegia*, "except such as were of long standing and formed for legitimate purposes" (*Aug.* 32.1–2). Once Christ-believers began meeting apart from the Jews, they could no longer claim the legitimacy of antiquity. But would they have been considered illegal as Nanos supposed? Esler: "Caesar's decree seems not to have been enforced in relation to the category of *collegia* most relevant to Romans."[145] As G. La Piana explained: "The collegia domestica were very numerous in the time of Augustus, and it is probable that the law governing associations was not applied to them, and that they were not dissolved. But whether they were assimilated to the collegia tenuiorum and required authorization we do not know." The absence of evidence for the authorization of the household *collegium domesticum* suggests that such authorization was not generally required.[146] The Christians likely

---

143. On the difficulties in identifying who should be expelled, see, for instance, Leonard Victor Rutgers, "Roman Policy toward the Jews: Expulsions from the City of Rome during the First Century C.E.," *CA* 13 (1994): 64–66; repr. in *Judaism and Christianity in First-Century Rome* (ed. Karl P. Donfried and Peter Richardson; Grand Rapids: Eerdmans, 1998), 104–6.

144. Nanos, "Jewish Context," 186–87, citing Josephus, *Ant.* 14.10.8 §§213–16. See also Nanos, *Mystery*, 73–75, 384.

145. Esler, *Conflict and Identity*, 105–6.

146. George La Piana, "Foreign Groups in Rome during the First Centuries of the Empire," *HTR* 20 (1927): 275.

avoided trouble with the authorities because their gatherings were indistinguishable from a *collegium domesticum*.[147]

More fundamentally, the actions of Julius Caesar, Octavian, or other Roman
authorities against various associations were specific responses to political unrest
and were of a more limited nature than has generally been recognized. When
Julius Caesar dissolved all *collegia* "except those of ancient foundation" (Suetonius, *Jul.* 42.3; cf. Josephus, *Ant.* 14.10.8 §§213–16, 18.3.5 §§83–84) he was
acting against groups threatening his tentative grip on power, especially associations organized more recently to stir up political opposition and unrest. He was
not trying to establish a law to control associations throughout the empire.[148]
Roman officials were not opposed to associations as such, since associations
were a vibrant part of the empire.[149] When Suetonius narrated how Octavian
disbanded all *collegia*, "except such as were of long standing and formed for
legitimate purposes" (*Aug.* 32.1–2 [Rolfe, LCL]), Octavian was not instituting
a law or *lex Iulia*.[150] Octavian was attempting to control gangs of brigands who
were roaming the countryside and committing crimes (so also Appian, *Bell. civ.*
5.132). So Suetonius had Octavian disbanding all *collegia* in the same breath
as stationing military guards and inspecting workhouses. These alleged *collegia*
were really subversive gangs tied to local leaders who were trying to subvert
Octavian's efforts to stabilize Rome after the "legacy of the civil wars." "Nothing
in the passages in Suetonius or Appian implies that Octavian was initiating
some comprehensive law that involved control of ordinary guilds and associations in Italy, let alone the empire, henceforth."[151] As Walters admitted, *collegia*

---

147. Esler, *Conflict and Identity*, 107.

148. Jerzy Linderski, *Roman Questions: Selected Papers* (HABES 20; Stuttgart:
Steiner, 1995), 217–23, 649–50. Linderski's argumentation was helpfully unpacked
by Zwi Yavetz, *Julius Caesar and his Public Image* (Ithaca, N.Y.: Cornell Univ. Press,
1983), 85–96.

149. Philip A. Harland, *Associations, Synagogues, and Congregations: Claiming a Place
in Ancient Mediterranean Society* (Minneapolis: Fortress Press, 2003), 164–65.

150. As Jean-Pierre Waltzing claimed in *Étude historique sur les corporations professionnelles chez les Romains depuis les origins jusqu'à la chute de l'empire d'Occident* (Bologna:
Mémoires couronnés et autres mémoires publiées par l'Académie Royale des Sciences,
des Lettres et des Beaux-Arts de Belgique 50, 1895), 1:115–16. Walters, *Ethnic Issues*,
15–6, who was influenced by Waltzing, wrongly concluded that this passage from Suetonius proves that there had been "a lapse in the enforcement of the [Julian] ban." This
interpretation assumes evidence not available, that such a ban had been in force in the
intervening period.

151. Harland, *Associations*, 166.

proliferated in Rome and throughout the empire with little official involvement or intervention under Augustus:

> The number of such groups was so large that no measures were taken to disband them unless disorderliness drew attention to their presence. This is what Peter Garnsey has called "tolerance by default," groups allowed by Rome to exist because there was no way of stamping them out, or at least a lack of resolve to do so.[152]

Thus civil unrest or disruption typically would be necessary to motivate official intervention against an association.

The authorities in the first century CE conformed to the same pattern of action with regard to associations. Tacitus (*Ann.* 14.17) recorded an incident at a gladiatorial show in Pompeii in 59 CE that is also reflected on a wall painting from the city's ruins. Spectators erupted into a battle with one another. The Roman Senate responded by banning gladiatorial shows at Pompeii for ten years and by dissolving the associations involved. As was the case with both Julius Caesar's and Octavian's actions, the ban was for the sake of maintaining public order. Harland concluded: "[I]ntervention occurred only when associations were caught up in broader disorderly incidents that were not adequately dealt with locally. Incidents like this one do not reflect consistently enforced control of associations as such by Roman authorities in Rome or Italy, let alone the provinces."[153]

Some have cited Marcian, the early third-century jurist, as proof of a much earlier law (Augustan? A *lex Iulia*?) controlling associations in Italy and the provinces:

> By the Decrees of the Emperors, the Governors of provinces are directed to forbid the organization of corporate associations, and not even to permit soldiers to form them in camps. The more indigent soldiers, however, are allowed to put their pay every month into a common fund, provided they assemble only once during that time, for fear that under a pretext of this kind they may organize an unlawful society, which the Divine [Septimius] Severus stated in a Rescript should not be tolerated, not only at Rome, but also in Italy and the provinces.[154]

---

152. Walters, *Ethnic Issues*, 16; Peter Garnsey, "Religious Toleration in Classical Antiquity," in *Persecution and Toleration* (PEHS; ed. W. J. Sheils; Oxford: Blackwell, 1984), 9.

153. Harland, *Associations*, 166.

154. *Digest* 47.22.1, as cited in *The Civil Law Including The Twelve Tables, The Institutes of Gaius, The Rules of Ulpian, The Opinions of Paulus, The Enactments of Justinian, and The Constitutions of Leo* (trans. S. P. Scott; Cincinnati: Central Trust, 1932), 11:10–1.

The passage, however, concerns primarily the army. Harland chided scholars for ignoring what follows in Marcian's passage: "To assemble for religious purposes is, however, not forbidden if, by doing so, no act is committed against the decree of the senate by which unlawful societies are prohibited."[155] Religious associations were generally *permitted*. The particular senatorial decree referred to by Marcian is not clear, but may have been one attested in several Italian inscriptions. For instance, a Lanuvian inscription cited a senatorial decision which the group in question then proceeded to violate by meeting more than once a month for reasons other than burial or cult (*CIL* 14.2112; c. 136 CE). In other words, the Lanuvian association did not feel particularly compelled to act strictly by the senatorial decision.[156] The sixth-century collection of Roman legal sources called the *Digest* quoted a document attributed to the early second-century Gaius that relied on the precedent of the Greek law of Solon (sixth century BCE) to the effect that associations could exist and were "authorized to make whatever contacts they may desire with one another, provided they do nothing in violation of public law" (*Digest* 47.22.4).[157] As long as associations did not stir up civil unrest against the state, Roman policy was typically tolerant. In a rather detailed study, Harland offered imperial practice in Asia Minor as further evidence of the occasional and limited nature of official intervention.[158]

Walters suggested that Rome may have acted against eastern religions for reasons other than civil unrest. He highlighted proselytism as the cause of the expulsion of Jews under Tiberius.[159] This was not an either-or matter. Rome had no official policy as such against religious practice or proselytism, but if a religious movement generated controversy and conflict within the population, such controversy may have necessitated an official response. For instance, Claudius's early actions on behalf of the Jews of Alexandria was likely out of concern for order in the empire's breadbasket.[160] Josephus identified the theft of some "purple and gold" from a wealthy female convert as the cause of the

---

On associations, see also *Digest* 47.22.2–4 in *Civil Law*, 11:11, and *Digest* 3.4.1–10 in *Civil Law*, 3:30–33.

155. Harland, *Associations*, 168.

156. The date of the Marcian text needs to be considered as well. The late second-century reign of Septimius Severus witnessed several radical changes in how the state handled associations (e.g., compulsory membership in occupational guilds).

157. As quoted in Harland, *Associations*, 169.

158. Ibid., 169–73.

159. Walters, "Romans, Jews, and Christians," 181, and especially n. 24, questioning Rutgers's conclusions.

160. Slingerland, *Claudian Policymaking*, 100–101. He noted (p. 101 n. 39): "This is why the emperor insisted upon personal control of the city through his own prefect."

mass expulsion under Tiberius (*Ant.* 18.3.5 §§83–84). Leonard Rutgers noted that the response was entirely disproportionate. Thus Josephus's explanation is questionable. Why punish the entire community for the behavior of a few, and why punish to the extent of issuing a special *senatus consultum*?[161] Tacitus traced the cause of Tiberius's expulsion to the practice of "Egyptian and Jewish rites" but did not mention any proselytizing activity (*Ann.* 2.85.4–5). Dio Cassius explained that Jewish proselytizing was on too grand a scale (57.18.5a), but little evidence exists for such a large-scale effort or success in Roman proselytization by the Jews.[162] The sources are simply not consistent on the cause of Tiberius's expulsion of the Jews, and it would be difficult to draw any firm conclusions.[163] A viable hypothesis lies somewhere between Dio Cassius's explanation and that of Josephus. Jewish practitioners apparently found themselves engrossed in a conflict with certain upper-class Romans, and a serious enough disturbance ensued that official intervention was required.

Judaism as Religio Licita?

Some have supposed that the Romans had established a "charter of rights" or a "Magna Carta" for the practice of Judaism as a *religio licita* that the first Christians, if they met separately from the synagogues, would not enjoy.[164] Josephus recorded several actions by emperors, consuls, proconsuls, and others on behalf of the Jewish people (for example, *Ant.* 16.6.7 §§172–3). He freely admitted that his purpose in narrating such accounts was to encourage further benefaction toward the Jews to assure the free expression of their religion (*Ant.* 14.10.1 §§186–9; 14.10.26 §§265–7; 16.6.8 §§174–8). Tessa Rajak questioned at length the notion of a Jewish charter.[165] Likewise Harland: "The privileges found in the decrees that Josephus records do not represent some sort of legally defined

---

161. Note that Josephus traces the Jews' expulsion not to the proselytizing of an upper-class woman but rather to the criminal activity that followed ("stealing the 'purple and gold' Fulvia wanted to send to the Temple in Jerusalem"); Rutgers, "Roman Policy," 63; repr. 102.

162. See also Goodman, *Mission and Conversion*, 69–90; McKnight, *Light among the Gentiles*; Leonard Victor Rutgers, "Attitudes to Judaism in the Greco-Roman Period: Reflections on Feldman's *Jew and Gentile in the Ancient World*," *JQR* 85 (1995): 361–95.

163. See the discussion of the sources in Rutgers, "Roman Policy," 60–66; repr. 98–105.

164. For example, Smallwood, *Jews under Roman Rule*, 128; Nanos, *Mystery*, 73–75.

165. Tessa Rajak, "Was There a Roman Charter for the Jews?" *JRS* 74 (1984): 107–23. She wrote (p. 107):

Magna Carta protecting the Jews, nor an acknowledgment of their official status as a legally recognized religion (*religio licita*). Rather, these were ad hoc responses to requests or complaints that were standard procedure under Roman rule."[166] Even in the expulsions of the Jews under Tiberius and Claudius, Rome was acting to stem general unrest since Roman law never penalized non-Roman religious practices per se with expulsion. Consequently, the authorities did not act against the Jewish religion elsewhere in the empire.[167] These actions (*senatus consulta*) were generally limited in scope to resolving specific disputes between Jews and Greeks in particular cities, although these individual measures did provide precedent for governors and even emperors in handling Jewish rights in other cases.[168] Josephus speaks of the expulsion of the Jews in 19 CE along with the expulsion of adherents of the Isis cult (*Ant.* 18.3.3 §§63–4). Isis cult devotees were repeatedly expelled in the first centuries BCE and CE in times of *political unrest* — but *not* because the cult was an un-Roman religion. In 58 BCE Clodius manipulated the Isis cult for the purpose of causing strife (Dio Cassius 53.2.4 [28 BCE]). In response, Isis worship was forbidden inside the *pomerium*, but no restrictions were placed on the Isis cult outside the *pomerium*. Isis practitioners were not singled out or persecuted.[169] Similarly, astrologers were expelled in times of political turmoil. Yet no edict was ever issued to forbid astrologers in the empire prior to Diocletian. Roman actions in the midst of unrest and disturbance simply followed a standard formula that was traceable to the Bacchanalia affair in 186 BCE. After public disturbances which included murder and other crimes, the senate punished those responsible in the Bacchanalian cult and discouraged the practice of its religion although cultic practice remained possible in certain circumstances (Livy 39.18.7–9). Livy expressed a Roman

---

One way — the traditional way — of depicting the situation is to say that the Jews happened to be protected by a special legal status, first conferred by Julius Caesar and then regularly renewed for over a century. On this view, Judaism was put in a supposed formal category of *religio licita* (the term originates with Tertullian), and the Jews had their privileges (or rights) enshrined in a charter. . . . However, for the Roman world, this model is inappropriate. We shall see that, as a matter of fact, such a charter did not exist. But it is also in the nature of the situation that Jews did not require it.

166. Harland, *Associations*, 222.
167. Rutgers, "Roman Policy," 60–66; repr. 98–106.
168. Ibid., 57–59; repr. 94–96.
169. Ibid., 69; repr. 109.

bias and concern that "vile and alien rites" might well lead "to every crime and lust" (39.15.3). Rutgers concluded:

> All the elements one later encounters in Rome's actions against Jews, Isis worshipers, and astrologers are thus present in Livy's account of the Bacchanalia affair: when law and order were disturbed, Roman authorities interfered because they feared the possible political consequences of such disturbances. The scope and actual effectiveness of the measures tended to be limited. Interventions were most likely to occur in periods of general civil unrest. Religious concerns played only a subordinate role, that is, intervention was not generally aimed at suppressing religious practices as such, but was usually carried out because specific criminal offenses that could be formally prosecuted had been committed.[170]

Rutgers added: "Rome was interested in keeping the urban masses under control and in checking initiatives of too political a nature. For the rest, Roman authorities just let people be."[171] "The most salient feature of [Roman] policy . . . was that Rome did not have a standard policy toward the Jews: Roman magistrates responded to situations."[172] When the First Jewish Revolt broke out in 66 CE, Rome acted against the insurgents but took no measures against Jews in the diaspora. Measures outside of the Jewish homeland were simply unnecessary.

When Josephus recorded actions on behalf of the Jews, he was relaying various benefactor-beneficiary exchanges rather than an official, far-reaching policy enactment. Such a policy enactment was unnecessary since the Jews had already enjoyed a general freedom to assemble and practice their religion. The Romans were not being tolerant; they were simply indifferent.[173] The same general freedom in the face of Roman indifference would apply to the Christ-followers.[174]

---

170. Ibid., 70; repr. 110.

171. Ibid., 71; repr. 111.

172. Ibid., 59; repr. 96.

173. Ibid., 71–72; repr. 112. At the same time the Romans confirmed Jewish privileges, they would often verbally run down the Jewish community.

174. When Pliny brought the issue of the Christians to the attention of Emperor Trajan, he responded that it was impossible to lay down a general rule that could be applied as a fixed standard to every case involving a Christian (Pliny, *Ep. Tra.* 10.97). Christians as such were not to be sought out and prosecuted, but rather, Trajan advised, they should be dealt with on a case by case basis when accusers brought a charge. Trajan's response substantiates the passive administrative stance the Romans had taken toward the Christians (and other sects). As Walters, *Ethnic Issues*, 45, summarized:

> Roman toleration of foreign religions should not be taken to mean that the Romans steered clear of cults when the interests of the state were thought

Official policy did not exist that would deter Christ-followers from meeting in their own homes apart from the synagogues.[175] As Gerhard Krodel rightly recognized some time ago: "Irrespective of the feelings of Roman aristocrats concerning the intrinsic worth of 'foreign superstitions,' Roman pragmatism tolerated, or even encouraged the practice of their respected religions by its subjugated peoples." He added that the Romans freely permitted participation in foreign cults on the part of citizens "not by official decree but by actual practice" as witnessed to by

> the absence of official religious tests, in the lack of evidence of legal proceed-
> ings against citizens for participation in foreign cults, and in the absence
> of sections in the Roman civil and penal laws dealing with membership of
> citizens in foreign cults. The concept of "*religio licita*" did not exist during
> this period. Rome did not possess a department of religious affairs which
> licensed foreign cults, but it tolerated them and in this sense they were
> "lawful."[176]

When conflict and trouble broke out between Jews and Greeks or between Jews and other ethnic groups, the claim of a friendly or relevant edict of support might aid the Jewish community should the authorities intervene.[177] Jewish

---

to be jeopardized by some religious group's conduct. However, action was prompted by destabilizing behavior among reckless members of a cult or through the lobbying of opponents hostile to the cult. Crackdowns were not the result of routine audits conduced by officials with responsibility of keeping tabs on cults according to well-articulated guidelines. A catalyst was required to trigger Roman intervention; nevertheless, during times of high tension regarding Oriental religions small catalysts could occasion disproportionate reactions.

175. The same line of reasoning would argue against Mark D. Nanos's crucial contention that the Galatian gentiles would have wanted to be associated with Jewish synagogue gatherings lest they suffer as a *religio illicita* (*The Irony of Galatians* [Minneapolis: Fortress Press, 2002], 257–67).

176. Gerhard Krodel, "Persecution and Toleration of Christianity until Hadrian," in *Early Church History: The Roman Empire as the Setting of Primitive Christianity* (ed. Stephen Benko and John J. O'Rourke; London: Oliphants, 1971), 256. He cited Pliny as introducing a new approach to handling Christians rather than attesting to any sort of established policy. He also noted how the Jews were allowed to practice their religion even in the midst of three armed rebellions against Rome. So also Gruen, *Diaspora*, 26.

177. The problem was that sometimes the local authorities would ally themselves against the Jewish population.

diplomats and representatives lobbied for such benefaction and support from city officials, provincial governors, the emperor, or even (in one case) a *senatus consultum* in case of conflict with their neighbors.[178] Josephus' various documents in support of the Jews represented his attempt at apologetics for his people. He exaggerated these documents' legal power and scope.[179] As Rajak observed: "To strengthen his case, Josephus at times introduces documents with something of a flourish, *as though* they concerned Jewish status universally; for example, at [*Ant.*] XIV, 228ff. he writes, 'these then are the favours which Dolabella granted to our people when Hyrcanus sent an envoy to him.' But what is in the texts often belies the sweeping introduction." Josephus then explained the favor as a rather limited exempting of Ephesian Jews who were Roman citizens from military service. Even Caesar's infamous ban on *collegia*, which permitted the free expression of Judaism as a religion of ancient foundation, referred *only to the city of Rome* (*Ant.* 14.10.9 §215). Josephus's record of the *senatus consultum* in *Ant.* 14.10.10 §221 remains vague as to its extent (περὶ ὧν . . . ὑπὲρ Ἰουδαίων

---

178. Rajak observed:

> First, the frequent alienation of Jews from their neighbours served only to strengthen the natural ties between Diaspora communities, and those ties facilitated the effective diffusion of texts and encouraged appeal to precedent. Secondly, the Jews in the cities were constantly dependent upon Roman support in any struggle to hold their own against Greek authorities whose attitude was often hostile. A vicious circle was soon no doubt created, in which renewed appeal to Roman intervention served to incur further local hostility. Thus their eyes were directed Romewards more than those of other groups. This was especially so during periods of political instability in Roman politics, when they will have reacted to the threat of losing their protection, and that is in part the explanation for the burgeoning of grants of privilege during the civil war and triumviral periods when Rome might have been expected to be more, rather than less, neglectful. Third, this tripartite relationship meant that Roman directives could well go by default. It is to be expected that the cities would sometimes slide out of their obligations, and the evidence suggests that they did, for we have instances both of recalcitrant recipients and of trouble recurring in one and the same place. ("Roman Charter," 118)

179. As a helpful corrective to Josephus's and Philo's spin on Jewish relations with the emperors, Slingerland demonstrated that quite often the same writers betray between the lines hostile actions on the part of the emperors toward Jewish communities at various points, including Augustus (*Claudian Policymaking*, 65–87). Slingerland went too far to suggest that religion alone motivated these actions apart from local influences (i.e., disturbances and lobbying).

ἔκρινε καὶ εἰς τὸ ταμιεῖον οὐκ ἔφασεν ἀνενεχθῆναι).[180] Augustus permitted the Jews to follow their own customs in accordance with their ancestral laws, including observance of the Sabbath and respect for their holy books (*Ant.* 16.6.2 §§162–6). His decree was a direct response to the Asian Jews who had lodged a complaint and not a universal edict for the Jews in general.[181] These actions, nevertheless, provided Josephus precedents for encouraging Romans to treat his co-religionists similarly elsewhere.

As Josephus highlighted difficulties in Jew-gentile relations in making his case, he ironically magnified an impression of conflict.[182] Relations between Jews and their neighbors were often well-disposed. The same positive dynamic would likely have applied to fledgling Christian communities. As long as they did not draw excessive negative attention to themselves by provoking unrest, they would have enjoyed calm and peace. However, when the Christian communities found themselves embroiled in conflict with their neighbors, they lacked the supportive official gestures that the Jews had enjoyed. Apart from occasional conflicts with their neighbors that prompted official intervention, Christians would have enjoyed the same freedom to practice their religion as the Jews. Christians could therefore freely form their own worshiping communities without concern for having separated from Judaism as a supposed "*religio licita.*"

Synagogue Buildings Versus House Churches

The Jews in Rome assembled in official meeting places or buildings, called προσευχαί (*proseuche*). Philo employed the same word προσευχαί for the buildings in which the Alexandrian Jewish population met, as opposed to οἰκίαι, which were considered "private" (ἴδιος, ἰδιωτικός; *Legat.* 18–20 §§121–35; *Flacc.* 7–9 §§44–62, 14 §§122–23). So when he referred to προσευχαί in Rome (*Legat.* 23 §§156–57), he was speaking of buildings dedicated to Jewish assemblies: "Augustus therefore also knew that they [the Jews/Judeans] have προσευχαί and meet in them, especially on the Sabbath when they are publicly instructed. . . . [Augustus] introduced no changes into their προσευχαί, he did not prevent them from meeting for the exposition of the Law, and he raised no

---

180. Rajak, "Roman Charter," 113.

181. For a more complete discussion of Josephus's record of such actions, see Rajak, "Roman Charter." These examples are merely representative.

182. Rajak, "Roman Charter," 122.

object to their offering of the 'first-fruits.'"[183] L. Michael White, in his work on ancient church and synagogue architecture, thought that the Jews converted their first-century private *insulae* into public synagogues at a significantly later point in time. The evolution of public space in Judaism would parallel, for White, the same shift in Christianity from private homes for worship and assembly in the first century to larger, public structures in subsequent centuries.[184] Other studies have overturned White's conclusions. For instance, the original structure of the Ostian synagogue is from the first century CE, perhaps even as early as the reign of Claudius.[185] Anders Runesson demonstrated an east-west orientation in the earliest structure compatible with an official site of worship.[186] Binder: "As with his treatment of the synagogue at Delos, White never compares the earliest phase of the Ostia synagogue with local examples of domestic architecture. Had he done this, he would have been hard-pressed to show any simi-

---

183. That προσευχή is definitely a Jewish designation for their places of worship, even to the point of using that fact to *identify* ancient inscriptions as Jewish, see Levinskaya, *Book of Acts*, 213–25. On the evidence that the Jews were meeting in official sites, see Esler's summary in *Conflict and Identity*, 88–97. Esler relied, as do I, on the important studies by Donald D. Binder, *Into the Temple Courts: The Place of Synagogues in the Second Temple Period* (SBLDS 169; Atlanta: Society of Biblical Literature, 1999); Anders Runesson, "The Synagogue at Ancient Ostia: The Building and Its History from the First to the Fifth Century," in *The Synagogue of Ancient Ostia and the Jews of Rome*, 29–99; and Runesson, "A Monumental Synagogue from the First Century: The Case of Ostia," *JSJ* 33 [2002]: 171–220). See also Anders Runesson, *The Origins of the Synagogue: A Socio-Historical Study* (ConBNT 37; Stockholm: Almqvist & Wiksell, 2001), 429–36.

184. L. Michael White, "Synagogue and Society in Imperial Ostia: Archaeological and Epigraphic Evidence," in *Judaism and Christianity in First-Century Rome* (ed. Karl P. Donfried and Peter Richardson; Grand Rapids: Eerdmans, 1998), 43–52; idem, *The Social Origins of Christian Architecture* (HTS 42; Valley Forge, Pa.: Trinity Press International, 1997), 1:69–71; 2:379–91. On Nanos's assumption that the Jews were worshiping in private homes, see *Mystery*, 42–43.

185. See the evidence provided by both the masonry techniques and the brick-stamps in Runesson, "Synagogue at Ancient Ostia," 81–82.

186. Runesson, "Synagogue at Ancient Ostia," 37–40. (White had argued for a north-south orientation.) Runesson and Donald Binder both have disputed White's handling of the Mindus Faustus inscription; Binder, *Into the Temple Courts*, 326–331(who decisively refuted White's translation of private rooms being dedicated for public service); Runesson, "Synagogue at Ancient Ostia," 85–89 (who wondered if the inscription had been moved to its Ostian location from elsewhere).

larities between the two types of structures. There is simply no comparison."[187] Runesson demonstrated that the earliest phase of the Ostian synagogue was indeed a functional public site.[188] The Jews were therefore assembling in official meeting sites, προσευχαί/*proseuchae*. Runesson asserted flexibility in the use of terminology in the ancient sources, but he granted that προσευχαί/ *proseuchae* referred to buildings dedicated to public use.[189] The archaeological support for Jewish *proseuchae* is limited to the structures at Ostia and Delos, only two examples, with neither from Rome itself. Rome, however, did possess a larger, more established, and wealthier Jewish population. As Binder wrote with respect to the smaller synagogue structure at Ostia: "It must have been fashioned at least partly in imitation of other synagogues from nearby Rome, which may have been built to an even grander scale."[190] Also, the use of public facilities by the Jews does not mean that they did not also use homes for worship where no building was available.[191] At the same time, Philo regularly employed προσευχαί for the buildings that served as meeting sites. Even non-Jews would

---

187. Binder, *Into the Temple Courts*, 331. See also Runesson, "Synagogue at Ancient Ostia," 83–85. Ostia is significant for the interpretation of the Roman synagogues because of parallels between Ostian remains and those found in the Roman Jewish catacombs.

188. Runesson, "A Monumental Synagogue," 171–220. Problems of definition, imprecision, and constant revisions or corrections plague White's work at Ostia. Runesson (p. 181) even noted how White has of late conceded that the original building "might have contained a collegial hall." Gruen, *Diaspora*, 112, drew attention to the colonnaded gateway, the lack of parallels with Ostian private dwellings, and the similarity of the original ground plan to the later ground plan that was clearly for public use.

189. Howard Clark Kee argued against the notion that *synagōgē* referred to public buildings prior to 70 CE. The *sole* exception he noted was Luke 7:5; "Defining the First-Century C.E. Synagogue: Problems and Progress," in *Evolution of the Synagogue: Problems and Progress* (ed. Howard Clark Kee and Lynn H. Cohick; Harrisburg, Pa.: Trinity Press International, 1999), 11–23. James F. Strange disagreed, citing an inscription from Berenice of Cyrenaica; "Ancient Texts, Archaeology as Text, and the Problem of the First-Century Synagogue," in *Evolution of the Synagogue*, ed. Kee and Cohick, 30–31. The attestation for Jewish public buildings as *synagōgē* (as opposed to *proseucha*) is therefore rare. The term was usually employed for the gathered. Paul does not speak of *synagōgē* in Rom 14–15 either (or *oikema*, *sabbateion*, *hieros peribolos*, *eucheion*). See also Richard A. Horsley's discussion in "Synagogues in Galilee and the Gospels," in *Evolution of the Synagogue*, ed. Kee and Cohick, 48–55.

190. Binder, *Into the Temple Courts*, 336.

191. Thus Esler, *Conflict and Identity*, 97, but, as he also pointed out, the evidence for house-synagogues in Rome is entirely lacking, quite unlike the archaeological and literary evidence for *proseucha*.

refer to Jewish synagogue structures as *proseuchae*. Juvenal's Umbricius in his *Satires* asked: "In what *proseucha* am I to seek you?" referring to a recognized, public site (3.296).[192] The first Jewish public buildings in Egypt for cultic and community use (third through first centuries BCE) are regularly labeled in the ancient inscriptions *proseuchai* (*CIJ* 1432; 1433; 1440; 1441; 1442; 1443; 1444; 1449; *CPJ* I.129; I.134). One Egyptian papyrus even distinguishes the *proseuchē* (προσευχή), as the building, from the *synagōgē* (συναγωγή), as the people assembled (*CPJ* I.138).[193] The likely presence of *proseuchae*/προσευχαί in Rome renders conspicuous the absence of reference to them in Paul's letter to the Romans and suggests a break from Judaism and its buildings of worship had indeed taken place.[194] The Christians in Rom 16:5 were assembling in private homes (τὴν κατ᾽ οἶκον αὐτῶν ἐκκλησίαν) and not the official, public Jewish προσευχαί/*proseuchae*.

Popular Anti-Judaism and the Evolving Roman Christian Community

By the time Aquila and Priscilla returned to Rome (presumably after Nero's death in 54 CE), the Roman churches would have existed apart from the synagogues for over five years. While some of the Roman Christians had learned of Christ as God-fearers several years before in the synagogues, the rest would now consist of gentiles who had joined the movement after the separation from the synagogues. The constitution of the gentile Christian population, which had originally met alongside Jewish Christ-believers, would now be changing. The Jewish Christ-believers were gone, and new converts, who had never associated with the Jewish religious assemblies, would not have had the same appreciation for Judaism as the first gentile Christians in Rome. While some in the first century found Judaism and its rites attractive, prejudice against the Jews was widespread even in Rome.[195]

The list of ancient writers who express anti-Jewish sentiments reads like a syllabus from a classics course: Cicero, Tacitus, Martial, Horace, Juvenal, Per-

---

192. Esler, *Conflict and Identity*, 94, cited an inscription from the first or second century CE that likewise used *proseucha* for a public landmark.

193. For a discussion of these inscriptions, see Richardson, *Building Jewish*, 115–16.

194. Esler, *Conflict and Identity*, 88–97, 102–7.

195. On the attraction of Judaism to some in the Greco-Roman world, see chap. 2, above.

sius, Dio Cassius, Marcus Aurelius, Apuleius, Ovid, Petronius, Pliny the Elder, Plutarch, Quintilian, Seneca, Suetonius.[196] Cicero labeled the Jewish faith a "barbaric superstition" (*Flac.*28.66–9). Seneca called them an "accursed race" (*De Superstitione*).[197] Martial despised "the lecheries of circumcised Jews" (*Epigrammata* 7.30).[198] Nevertheless, these Roman literary sources may well reflect upper-class, elitist attitudes along with traditional and conservative political interests that were in part a reaction to the attraction of eastern superstitions. In some instances the negative attitudes were a function of the genre of satire while in other cases the harsh language was a function of a changed environment in the wake of the Jewish revolt in 66–70 CE.[199] Sympathetic strands are sometimes ignored in the very passages considered representative of the traditional, antagonistic stance.[200] John Gager found the frequent dismissal of material more sympathetic toward Judaism problematic as he contended for the opposite extreme: that Judaism enjoyed great popularity in the first century.[201] Gager, in demonstrating that many Romans favored the Jewish people, has not dispelled the obvious fact that many also disliked them.[202] Such animosity would be understandable since the Jews were notorious for maintaining a separate and distinct identity.[203] Their avoidance of the idolatry that was so woven into the fabric of Greco-Roman society, their observance of the Sabbath, their avoidance of pagan meat and wine, and their practice of circumcision would have been strange to non-Jews and left the Jews vulnerable to ridicule.[204]

---

196. John C. Meagher, "As the Twig Was Bent: Antisemitism in Greco-Roman and Earliest Christian Times," in *Anti-Semitism and the Foundations of Christianity* (ed. Alan T. Davies; New York: Paulist, 1979), 6; see esp. pp. 3–12. See also the helpful, although much briefer, overview of the sources in Sten Hidal, "The Jews as the Roman Authors Saw Them," in *The Synagogue of Ancient Ostia and the Jews of Rome*, 141–44. Hidal rightly recognized (p. 144) that these sources are generally limited to an upper-class perspective.

197. Stern, *Greek and Latin Authors*, 1:431.

198. Original text and translation provided by Stern, *Greek and Latin Authors*, 1:525.

199. Gager, *Origins of Anti-Semitism*, 55–66.

200. Walters, *Ethnic Issues*, 23; contra Meagher, "As the Twig." See Tacitus, *Hist.* 5.4–5; Juvenal, *Sat.* 14.96–106; Horace, *Sat.* 1.9.60–78; Ovid, *Am.* 217–20.

201. Gager, *Origins of Anti-Semitism*, 59–61, 67–88.

202. So also Robert Goldenberg, review of John G. Gager, *The Origins of Anti-Semitism*, RSR 11 (1985): 335–37.

203. Walters, *Ethnic Issues*, 24.

204. Meagher, "As the Twig," 5–6.

James Walters helpfully suggested that the relations between Jews and non-Jews should be evaluated on a regional or local basis. For instance, hatred toward Jews was widespread in Alexandria because of unique circumstances in the city. In Sardis, on the other hand, the Jews appeared to be rather influential.[205] Many in Rome, such as Cicero or Nero, publicly spoke of Judaism as a "barbarous superstition" (Cicero, *Pro Flacco*) as they likely drew upon a strong "reservoir of anti-Jewish sentiment in the city."[206] Walters cataloged anti-Jewish sentiments in a lengthy list of Roman writers and concluded that "the separateness of the Jewish community, its foreign character, alien cult, and the negative reactions on the part of some Romans to the attraction of other Romans to Jewish religion and/or customs" led to "anti-Jewish views in Rome." "Roman administrative actions against the Jewish communities were not limited to Roman authors. Such administrative actions did not stem from the opinions of a few intellectuals nor were these views read only by the elite and literate."[207]

Many non-Jews resented the Jews' outright contempt for other deities besides their own. Juvenal (*Sat.* 14.97) mocked the Jews for worshiping nothing but the clouds and the divinity of the heavens. Apion (in Josephus, *Ag. Ap.* 2.6 §§65, 68, 73) judged the stubborn Jewish insistence on monotheism as unpatriotic and subversive.[208] Petronius seized on Jewish avoidance of pork to claim that they worshiped a pig-god.[209] Pliny the Elder (13.9 §46) labeled the Jews "a race remarkable for their contempt for the divine powers." Louis Feldman documented a similar hostility toward the Jewish rite of circumcision, the Sabbath, and the food laws.[210] Feldman discerned a popular animosity corresponding to that demonstrable in the intellectual sources behind Cicero's rhetoric in 59 BCE in *Flac.* 28.67. Because of the short supply of gold in Italy, the Roman Senate acted to forbid the export of gold out of Italy. Flaccus acted to forbid the Jews

---

205. Walters, *Ethnic Issues*, 23.

206. Neil Elliott, *The Rhetoric of Romans: Argumentative Constraint and Strategy and Paul's Dialogue with Judaism* (JSNTSup 45; Sheffield: Sheffield Academic, 1990; Fortress Press edition, 2006), 51 n. 2.

207. Walters, *Ethnic Issues*, 40; see pp. 37–40.

208. See also the discussion in Feldman, *Jew and Gentile*, 151. Gruen, *Diaspora*, 43–46, has demonstrated that the Jews were not considered menacing or subversive in any way to the empire, but he conceded throughout his discussion dislike for the Jews, especially for their separatism.

209. Fragment 37 (Poem 24 in Heseltine, LCL).

210. Feldman, *Jew and Gentile*, 153–70. He qualified his conclusions by noting that not all intellectuals were hostile toward the Jews and their insistence on monotheism, despite the frequency of the attacks (pp. 152–53).

from sending their gold to Jerusalem, which had been the custom "on the Jews' account from Italy and all our provinces" (MacDonald, LCL). Although Flaccus had been acting primarily against the Jews of Asia Minor, Cicero suggested similar bitterness against the Jews in Rome: "Who is there, gentlemen, who cannot genuinely applaud this measure?"[211] Jewish insistence on circumcision as well as their refusal to venerate other gods or eat meat from the marketplace increased the Jews' cultural separation.

Jewish separatism was a major cause of gentile hostility. Josephus cited Apion's malicious description from the first century CE that the Jews took an oath to show no goodwill to any alien (*Ag. Ap.* 2.10 §121). Quintilian (3.7.21), at the end of the first century CE, credited Moses as the creator of the Jewish "superstition" and of a people who are bent on the destruction of others. In the early second century CE, Tacitus, in his long list of reasons for displeasure with the Jews (*Hist.* 5.5), described the Jews as hating the rest of humanity as their enemies (*adversus omnis alios hostile odium*). Juvenal satirized the Jews for not showing the way to a fountain spring to anyone except fellow Jews (*Sat.* 14.103–4). Aelius Aristides in the second century CE described how the Jews "seceded from the Greeks or rather from all the better people."[212] Philostratus in the third century (*Vit. Apollonii* 5.33) described the Jews as those who "cut themselves off long ago, not only from the Romans, but from all mankind, since [they are] people who have devised an unsociable way of life, with no meals, libations, prayers, or sacrifices in common with other men, [and] have moved further away from us than Susa, Bactria, and the Indians beyond that" (Jones, LCL). These statements reflected the general populace's resentment against Jewish aloofness and separation.

Nanos offered a balanced review of the evidence:

> In summary, it is fair to say that the prevailing attitudes among the gentiles of Rome to Jews and Judaism, while no doubt mixed, were often negative. Despite the general intention of kindness observed above on the part of Jews toward their gentile neighbors, the implicit, when not explicit, judgment on pagan practices made it difficult for Romans not to take offense. Nor is it likely that all Romans overlooked the political and military problems associated with the Jews of Palestine in the development of their opinions about Jews in Rome. While no doubt some gentiles were attracted to Jew-

---

211. Ibid., 109–10. Feldman, pp. 107–13, emphasized the economic motivation behind popular animosity against the Jews in the Roman world. On popular hatred against the Jews in Alexandria, Feldman, pp. 113–17, noted the attack that took place in 38 CE. Alexandria and Caesarea both witnessed violent, popular assaults against the Jews in 66 CE as likewise Antioch at a later point (Feldman, *Jew and Gentile*, 117–22).

212. *Or.* 46 (*De Quattuorviris* 309); Stern, *Greek and Latin Authors*, 219–20.

ish people and the faith and practice of Judaism as well as the philosophies Jews embraced, the general views, unlike the reverence occasionally noted in some Greek cities, were for Romans apparently mixed with resentment and prejudice.[213]

As an increasing number of gentiles joined the Roman Christian gatherings, many of these converts would not have had the same appreciation for Judaism as the original members who had attended synagogue gatherings.[214] The changing constitution of the Roman Christian communities would likely have led to tension, if not outright conflict. An identity crisis would have developed over the necessity and extent of Christianity's ties with Judaism.

A word of caution: Paul provides no evidence that the "strong" constituted the majority of the Roman churches or that the "weak" were in the minority. Similarly, nothing can be assumed regarding how many of the Roman Christians had or had not participated in the synagogues or their relative proportion in relation to each other. Paul provides no evidence for the overall size of the Roman Christian population in Rome. These questions may be unanswerable. If, however, God-fearers were meeting in their own assemblies in the wake of Claudius's edict, many newer members would not have had the same experiences in the synagogues as the God-fearers.

Separation of Jews and Christians: Claudius to Nero

Between Claudius's edict in 49 CE and Nero's persecution of the Christians in 64 CE, the new movement had grown. Suetonius recognized the Christians as a distinct "class of men" by Nero's time (*Nero* 16.2 [Rolfe, LCL]). Tacitus narrated a variety of violent public spectacles suffered by the "vast numbers" of confessed Christians during Nero's persecution (*Ann.* 15.44 [Jackson, LCL]). *First Clement* 6:1 described "a great multitude" (πολὺ πλῆθος) tormented and tortured. New members joining the ranks of the gentile Christian movement

---

213. Nanos, *Mystery*, 67–8.

214. Nanos, *Mystery*, 385–86, noted the later evidence for positive Christian-Jewish interaction and traced this to a Christianity that was still within the synagogues in the first century. One may just as easily suggest that Christianity had separated from the synagogues, but Paul's letter, in its call for an appreciation of the Jewish roots of Christianity, had yielded a positive effect. The interaction between Christians and Jews in Rome was not, however, uniformly positive, and the nonbiblical evidence is lacking to reconstruct with any great precision Christian-Jewish relations in Paul's day.

from the general populace would have raised new issues for Roman Christianity, not the least of which would have been the role of the Jewish Law and Jewish customs. Tensions would have arisen over Christianity's Jewish heritage and identity. Many or most of the gentiles who had previously associated with the synagogues prior to the expulsion may have preferred a Law-observant lifestyle as God-fearers while newer members were likely uncomfortable with or cared little for such practices. They may even have scorned them or been outspoken against them. That Paul's letter addresses the relationship between Christianity and its Jewish heritage is hardly surprising as the gentile Christian churches were facing an identity crisis.

The separation process, which began in the synagogues as the aftermath of the Claudian edict, likely continued as the Jews were distancing themselves from the Christians.[215] Whereas Suetonius did not distinguish the Jewish followers of "Chrestus" from other Jews under Claudius in 49 CE, "Christians" were apparently a distinct and recognizable group to many in Rome by the time of Nero's persecution.[216] Such a rapid change in perception from 49 to 64 CE was most likely not only a result of the Christian movement's growth. In the wake of the Claudian edict, some of the Jews had likely lobbied to distinguish themselves from the Christians. The Jews would have wanted to avoid further negative attention from the imperium.[217] The persecution of Christians under Nero may even have been a side-effect of this attempt at differentiation. The Jews had strong ties to Nero's court. The emperor was married in 62–65 CE to Poppaea

---

215. Judge and Thomas, "Origin," 86, questioned whether the Claudius expulsion as recorded by Suetonius involved Christians: "Yet if the common interpretation of *impulsore Chresto* is correct, we have to suppose that the Jewish lobby completely missed a unique opportunity of settling their account with the Christians by laying the blame firmly where it belonged. They failed to have the Christians as such named as political agitators, and at the same time allowed to pass into the record the title that implicitly conceded to Jesus the status they were at most pains to deny." The Jews *may very well* have lobbied, as best they could in their troubled circumstances in the face of imperial agitation. The problem was that outsiders to the Jewish movement could not yet comprehend the distinction. More explanation (and lobbying) was required and *was successful*. The lobbying one would expect after the Claudius edict apparently *did* take place.

216. Suetonius, *Nero* 16.2. Walters, *Ethnic Issues*, 62, wrote: "Nero's persecution presupposes that Roman administrators could distinguish between Christians and Jews when sufficiently motivated to do so."

217. Rightly Walters, *Ethnic Issues*, 62. Walters also thought that Christianity would be in "danger of Roman censorship as a superstitious, non-national foreign cult of recent origin with riotous tendencies." Such censorship, when it took place, should be regarded as an occasional response motivated by particular circumstances.

Sabina, a "God-fearer" who, according to Josephus, would have been sympathetic to Judaism.[218] During this period two Judean embassies were successful with Nero even though they made requests contrary to Roman interests. Josephus traced the positive results to Poppaea's mediation (*Ant.* 20.8.11 §§189–96; *Life* 3 §§13–6; Tacitus, *Ann.* 16.6).[219] Josephus also credited a Jewish actor in the court, who was a favorite of Nero and who had access to Poppaea.[220] Jewish lobbying against the Christians may explain the emperor's prescient recognition of Christians as a distinct movement from the Jews.

Despite her designation as "God-fearer" (θεοσεβής) by Josephus, Poppaea's interest in or loyalty to the Jewish community is difficult to pinpoint with any precision. E. Mary Smallwood, in an important exchange with Margaret Williams, highlighted Poppaea's instigation of the murders of Agrippina and Octavia in order to become empress. Such actions would contradict an interest in Judaism and its Law, which had clearly forbidden murder.[221] She was promiscuous, at least prior to her marriage to Nero (Tacitus, *Ann.* 13.45–6). Did not the Jewish Law forbid adultery? Williams responded that Tacitus's description of Poppaea's nefarious actions was dubious, especially since he was asserting a motive for the murder of Nero's mother. Due recognition of Tacitus's redactional interests should suggest caution in painting too dark a picture of the historical Poppaea.[222] Even if Tacitus's charges were true, Poppaea would not be the first "God-fearer" who was less than consistent in adhering to Judaism. Berenice, whom Josephus otherwise described as seriously devoted to Judaism, often flouted Jewish laws and entered into an adulterous affair with Titus (Josephus, *War* 2.15.1 §§313–14; *Ant.* 20.7.3 §§145–46; Tacitus, *Hist.* 2.2; Dio Cassius 65.15.3–4).[223] Smallwood asked whether a true Jewish sympathizer would have consulted astrologers (Tacitus, *Hist.* 1.22).[224] Williams agreed that Poppaea was

---

218. *Ant.* 20.8.11 §195.

219. Arguing in favor of Jewish influence in Nero's court, see also Feldman, *Jew and Gentile*, 98, 491 nn. 39, 40.

220. Vincent M. Scramuzza, "The Policy of the Early Roman Emperors towards Judaism," in *The Acts of the Apostles*, 5:296–7. So also Smallwood, *Jews under Roman Rule*, 217–19; Stephen Benko, *Pagan Rome*, 20. Scramuzza also thought that Epaphroditus, Josephus's patron and perhaps Nero's secretary, was a Jewish proselyte, but Scramuzza recognized the evidence for Epaphroditus as imperial secretary is debatable.

221. E. Mary Smallwood, "The Alleged Jewish Tendencies of Poppaea Sabina," *JTS* 10 (1959): 332.

222. Margaret H. Williams, "'θεοσεβὴς γὰρ ἦν': The Jewish Tendencies of Poppaea Sabina," *JTS* 39 (1988): 102.

223. Ibid., 102–3.

224. Smallwood, "Alleged Jewish Tendencies," 332.

involved in official, pagan rites, but such duties necessary to her office did not rule out an interest in Judaism. Williams pointed to Cornelius, the "God-fearer" in Acts 10, whose duties as a Roman centurion included pagan rites. Julia Severa was the high priestess of the imperial cult at Akmonia in Phrygia, and yet she was also an active supporter of the Jewish community.[225] Smallwood traced Poppaea's positive actions toward the Jews to a general sense of religiosity rather than to a particularly Jewish interest. She may have acted on behalf of Josephus because of his ties to other Roman leaders and not because of any love for Judaism.[226] On the other hand, as Williams pointed out, "God-fearer" in Josephus normally *did* indicate an attachment to Judaism at some level. The few exceptions to the rule force the interpreter to pay particular attention to the context of usage. In the case of Poppaea, the sense of "God-fearer" as mere benefactor is unlikely. The natural interpretation is that her intervention on behalf of the Jews should be attributed to her status as one who respected the Jewish God. Williams judged Smallwood's suggestion that Poppaea's intervention was merely out of respect for others' religious scruples "dubious and anachronistic." Josephus invoked a Jewish actor as intermediary and referred to other positive actions she took on behalf of Jews. Williams also noted the interest in Judaism on the part of upper class Roman women, but wisely refrained from claiming anything more specific with regard to Poppaea's connections to Judaism.[227]

Poppaea may indeed have been a factor in Nero's recognition of the Christians as a group distinct from the Jews. Certainty in the matter is not possible. Perhaps Nero's persecution of the Christians was the result of *indirect* pressure from the Jewish community.[228] Jewish influence in and on the court, whether by Poppaea or more indirectly, may have helped lead to the targeting of Christians as distinct from Jews — or at least as distinct from *legitimate* Jews.[229] If the Christians, as a potentially dangerous foreign cult, were active proselytizing, the Jews likely would have wanted to distance themselves from the attention this activity would draw.[230] Clement of Rome, writing a generation after the events in 95 CE, traced the persecution under Nero to people close enough to the

---

225. Williams, "Jewish Tendencies," 103–6.

226. Smallwood, "Alleged Jewish Tendencies," 333–34.

227. Williams, "Jewish Tendencies," 106–8, 110–11. Josephus did *not* describe her as "Judaizing" (ἰουδαΐζειν), i.e., adopting Jewish customs.

228. W. H. C. Frend, *Martyrdom and Persecution in the Early Church* (Oxford: Basil Blackwell, 1965), 164–65; T. D. Barnes, "Legislation against the Christians," *JRS* 58 (1968): 48–49.

229. On the frequent Jewish lobbying of the authorities, see also Tessa Rajak, "Was There a Roman Charter for the Jews?" *JRS* 74 (1984): 107–23.

230. Walters, "Romans, Jews, and Christians," 181–83.

Christian movement to experience "jealousy and envy," that is, members likely of the Jewish community (*1 Clem.* 5.2, 4, 5). Melito of Sardis in the middle of the second century likewise attributed Nero's persecution of the Christians to his having been "persuaded by certain calumniators" who were making "slanderous accusations" (*Hist. eccl.* 4.26.9–10 [*NPNF*² 1:205–6]). Religious divisions could lead to public unrest.[231] Although the believers in Christ at Rome were not called "Christians" until 70 CE, they were recognized by many in Rome as a group distinct from the Jews in the mid-sixties CE during a period of intense persecution.[232]

Summary

A disturbance in the Jewish community in the late 40s CE required Claudius's intervention and the expulsion of Jews from the capital. The expelled were the ringleaders in a conflict over "Chrestus" or Christ. Among those expelled were Paul's eventual companions Priscilla and Aquila as attested by Acts 18:2. Christ-believing God-fearers, on the whole, were not among those expelled. The Roman authorities lacked the resolve or means to determine who were members of the synagogues and who were not. Apart from the more vocal troublemakers, the authorities would have had to rely on information provided by the synagogues themselves.

From the standpoint of observers in the Roman capital, circumcision not only marked members of the Jewish community but also remained what sociologists call a "demonstration event." Gentiles who submitted to circumcision had identified themselves with the Jews. God-fearers, on the other hand, maintained strong social ties not only with the Jewish community but also with those outside the Jewish community. God-fearers remained on the margins of synagogue life. Christ-believing God-fearers would not have posed the same threat to the Jewish community's self-identity as natural-born Jews and proselytes who had accepted and were promoting Jesus as the Christ. The synagogues would have marked Christ-believing Jews and proselytes for Claudius's expulsion. The Christ-believing God-fearers remaining in Rome were forced to recognize that they were no longer welcome in the Jewish community and would have begun meeting separately for worship. As the dramatic change in public perception from 49 to 64 CE attests, Jews were distancing themselves from the Christ-move-

---

231. Proselytism is cited as a factor in Tiberius's expulsion of the Jews by some of the historians. See Josephus, *Ant.* 18.3.5 §§83–84; Dio Cassius, 57.18.5a.

232. Acts 11:26; Tacitus, *Ann.* 15.44; Suetonius, *Nero* 16.2; *1 Clem.* 5:1; 6:1.

ment. Nero, as a result of direct or indirect lobbying, blamed the Christians, not the Jews, for the fire in Rome.

Over time, the constituency of the gentile Christian churches shifted. As other gentiles joined the Christ-movement, many newer converts did not share the same appreciation for Judaism or its customs as the original Christ-believers who frequented the synagogues. Many gentiles shared with their culture a disdain for Judaism as an eastern religion, a religion of the conquered and occupied. Such a crisis of identity and tension over the relationship between Christ-believers and Judaism is the very issue that Paul addresses in the Letter to the Romans. In other words, a plausible reconstruction of the events based on the limited available external evidence independently confirms what may be surmised from the letter itself.

Chapter 5

Reading Romans with the Encoded Audience: Romans 7:7–25 and Romans 11:25–26

Most interpreters approach the Letter to the Romans through the lens of a presumed audience consisting of both Jews and gentiles. From that standpoint Paul understandably appeals to the Jewish Scriptures. He speaks of judgment and salvation for both "Jew and Greek" (1:16–17; 2:9–10). He turns to "the Jew" in Rom 2:17 and notes the habit of the "weak" of avoiding "unclean" food in favor of the "clean" (14:1 — 15:6). He desires that the Roman Christians welcome one another (15:7). If Paul is writing instead to a Christ-believing audience of God-fearers and other gentiles without the same appreciation for Judaism, the elements of the letter deemed relevant for an audience inclusive of Jews would function rather similarly. Paul would still have to tackle the relationship of faith in Christ to its Jewish roots. He would still have to place Jewish customs, such as observance of the Law, circumcision, food laws, and the Sabbath, into a larger framework. If God-fearers and non-Law-observant gentiles are to welcome one another in Christ, who "has become a servant of the circumcised . . . in order that the gentiles might glorify God and praise his mercy" (15:7–9, NRSV mod.), then Jewish customs should not divide them. A thoroughly gentile audience, on the other hand, places certain sections of the letter into even starker relief. For instance, Rom 11:26 assumes a greater role in the letter if directed to an audience of gentiles. A gentile audience also helps unravel otherwise difficult passages such as Rom 7:7–25.

Romans 7:7–25: Resolving Perennial Conundrums

Romans 7:7–25 has proved to be a perennial mystery. Whom does Paul describe when he speaks of the "I" who was "once alive apart from the Law" (7:9)? Who is the individual who proves unable to do what he wants because of the greater power of sin? The "I" who fails in the struggle against the flesh in Rom 7 is not a Christian. The longstanding popularity of interpreting the "I" as a Christian may be traced through Martin Luther to Augustine in the fourth century. Krister Stendahl, Harvard's Lutheran professor emeritus of New Testament, has observed that the "dilemma of the introspective conscience" in the interpretation of Paul does not emerge until Augustine's later years: "It is, however, with Augustine that we find an interpretation of Paul which makes use of what to us is the deeper layer in the thought of the great Apostle."[1] Augustine melded Platonism with his newfound Christian beliefs. In the Platonic tradition the physical world takes second place to the world of ideas, the soul, and hidden realities. Historian of philosophy Phillip Cary titled his book *Augustine's Invention of the Inner Self: The Legacy of a Christian Platonist.*[2] A millennium later, in Luther's day, "Penetrating self-examination reached a hitherto unknown intensity."[3] Luther, who had struggled with the medieval system of penance in his search for a gracious and forgiving God, naturally gravitated to Augustine's "introspective conscience." The dark and difficult struggle of Paul's "I" with sin resonated with the Reformer. Stendahl, in his widely recognized essay, urged modern readers to reach behind the fourth and sixteenth century interpretations of Rom 7:7–25 to an approach that fully accounts for the first century context: "We should venture to suggest that the West for centuries has wrongly surmised that the biblical writers were grappling with problems which no doubt are ours, but which never entered their consciousness."[4]

Romans 7:14–25

The difficulties of reading Rom 7:7–25 with the later Augustine and Luther as a description of a Christian remain numerous and unresolved. In Rom 7:14

---

1. Krister Stendahl, "The Apostle Paul and the Introspective Conscience of the West," *HTR* 56 (1963): 204; repr. in *Paul among Jews and Gentiles and Other Essays* (Philadelphia: Fortress Press, 1976). On the evolution of Augustine's interpretation of Rom 7:7–25, see Paula Fredriksen, "Paul and Augustine: Conversion, Narratives, Orthodox Traditions, and the Retrospective Self," *JTS* 37 (1986): 20–28.

2. Phillip Cary, *Augustine's Invention of the Inner Self: The Legacy of a Christian Platonist* (Oxford: Oxford Univ. Press, 2000).

3. Stendahl, "Apostle Paul," 203.

4. Ibid., 214.

Paul describes the "I" as "of the flesh (ἐγὼ δὲ σάρκινος), sold into slavery under sin" (εἰμι πεπραμένος ὑπὸ τὴν ἁμαρτίαν). This verse presents at least three discrete challenges to a Christian interpretation of the "I." First, Paul never describes believers in Christ as "under" (ὑπό) the forces of the old era. Those who rely on the works of the Law are "under (ὑπό) a curse" in Gal 3:10. "Now before faith came, we were imprisoned and guarded under the law (ὑπὸ νόμον) until faith would be revealed" (Gal 3:23). With Christ's arrival, the Galatians are no longer "subject to a disciplinarian" (ὑπὸ παιδαγωγόν; 3:25). Until the date set by the father, minors are "under guardians and trustees" (4:2), "enslaved to the elemental spirits" (ὑπὸ στοιχεῖα τοῦ κόσμου; 4:3). God's Son was born "under the law, in order to redeem those who were under the law" (ὑπὸ νόμον; 4:4). Paul chastises those who "desire to be subject to the law" (οἱ ὑπὸ νόμον; 4:21). On the contrary, "if you are led by the Spirit, you are not subject to the law" (5:18). So also in Rom 6:14–15: "You are not under law but under grace" (οὐ γάρ ἐστε ὑπὸ νόμον ἀλλὰ ὑπὸ χάριν). Romans 7:14, on the other hand, describes the "I" as "under sin."

Paul's description of the "I" as "sold into slavery" poses a second problem for a Christian interpretation of the "I." The Christian of Rom 6 and 8 is consistently described as "freed" from slavery under sin and the Law. The baptized of Rom 6 has "died to sin" (v. 2). The "old self was crucified with him so that the body of sin might be destroyed, and we might *no longer* be enslaved to sin. For whoever has died is freed from sin" (vv. 6–7). "Sin will have *no dominion* over you" (v. 14). "You, having been *set free* from sin, have become slaves of righteousness. For just as you *once* presented your members as slaves to impurity . . . , so now present your members as slaves to righteousness for sanctification" (6:18–19). "When you *were* slaves of sin, you were free in regard to righteousness" (6:20). "You have been freed from sin and enslaved to God" (6:22). In the immediate context of 7:6: "But now we are discharged from the law, dead to that which held us captive, so that we are slaves not under the old written code but in the new life of the Spirit." In 8:2, immediately *after* 7:7–25: "For the law of the Spirit of life in Christ Jesus has *set you free* from the law of sin and death." The Christian is therefore decidedly *not* sold into slavery under sin as the "I" of 7:14 or "captive to the law of sin" (7:23).[5]

---

5. See especially Paul J. Achtemeier, "'Some Things in Them Hard to Understand': Reflections on an Approach to Paul," *Int* 38 (1984): 265; Werner Georg Kümmel, *Römer 7 und das Bild des Menschen im Neuen Testament* (TB 53; Munich: Chr. Kaiser, 1974), 97–98; Herman Ridderbos, *Paul: An Outline of His Theology* (trans. John Richard De Witt; Grand Rapids: Eerdmans, 1975), 126–27; Mark A. Seifrid, *Justification by Faith: The Origin and Development of a Central Pauline Theme* (NovTSup 68; Leiden: Brill, 1992), 232, 236.

Finally in Rom 7:14, Paul contrasts the "spiritual" (πνευματικός) Law with the "fleshly" "I."[6] This description of the "I" as "fleshly" (ἐγὼ δὲ σάρκινος) stands in tension with Rom 8:9: "But you are *not* in the flesh; you are in the Spirit, since the Spirit of God dwells in you" (ὑμεῖς δὲ οὐκ ἐστὲ ἐν σαρκὶ ἀλλὰ ἐν πνεύματι).[7] "Anyone who does not have the Spirit of Christ does not belong

---

6. Seifrid, "The Subject of Rom 7:14–25," *NovT* 34 (1992): 319–20, commented: "Although careful exegetes who apply the text to the Christian, such as Cranfield and Dunn, argue that Paul describes only one aspect of Christian existence here, the absolute statement of 7:14 . . . seems to prohibit taking the passage as expressing a conflict within the believer between the two epochs of Adam and Christ." The *Law* is "spiritual," not the "I." On the other hand, in 1 Cor 2:13, 15; 3:1; 14:27, Paul refers to "Spirit people"; John M. G. Barclay, "Πνευματικός in the Social Dialect of Pauline Christianity," in *The Holy Spirit and Christian Origins: Essays in Honor of James D. G. Dunn* (ed. Graham N. Stanton, Bruce W. Longenecker, and Stephen C. Barton; Grand Rapids: Eerdmans, 2004), 161: Πνευματικός "describes people not through analysis of their human constitution but in relation to their new status as graced by the Spirit of God."

7. Even if a distinction could be maintained between being "in the flesh" (8:7), which is clearly antithetical to Christian existence, and being "fleshly" (7:14), Paul does not grant without qualification that Christians are "fleshly"; contra L. Ann Jervis, "'The Commandment which is for Life' (Romans 7.10): Sin's Use of the Obedience of Faith," *JSNT* 27 (2004): 201. His description of the Corinthians as "fleshly" in 1 Cor 3:1 is embedded in the rhetoric of that letter. Rather ironically, the "spiritual," who have overlooked or denied the bodily resurrection (15:12), prove to be "fleshly." Paul recognizes that the Corinthians are, in fact, "spiritual" (2:12). The problem is that their behavior is on a par with those who are truly "fleshly," that is, those who do *not* possess the Spirit. Paul is trying to shock his readers to the realization that they are thinking and living in a fashion that is antithetical to who they really are as spiritual people. Paul writes with a genuine hope that his harsh words will stimulate his audience to the proper response (cf. Gordon D. Fee, *The First Epistle to the Corinthians* [NICNT; Grand Rapids: Eerdmans, 1987], 122–24). Such a possibility does not exist for the "I" of Romans 7. This approach to 1 Cor 3 agrees with Rom 7:5–6, the immediate context of 7:7–25, in which Paul stresses that "living in the flesh" is a former state in contrast to the "now" of the "new life of the Spirit." See also David Wenham, "The Christian Life: A Life of Tension? A Consideration of the Nature of Christian Experience in Paul," in *Pauline Studies: Essays Presented to Professor F. F. Bruce on his 70th Birthday* (ed. Donald A. Hagner and Murray J. Harris; Grand Rapids: Eerdmans, 1980), 82–83, who contends (against James D. G. Dunn's belief in a continuing fleshly state of Christians) the lack of evidence for a morally negative use of σάρξ in contrast to πνεῦμα for Christians. So also Robert H. Gundry, "The Moral Frustration of Paul Before His Conversion: Sexual Lust in Romans 7:7–25," in Hagner and Harris *Pauline Studies*, 236–37. The one place where Paul speaks of Christians in clear relation to a morally negative σάρξ is Gal 5:17–24, a passage where the Spirit gives the willing Christian the confident ability to defeat the flesh, much as Paul assumes remains possible for his readers in 1 Cor 3, despite their prior failures.

to him" (8:9). "Possession of the Spirit is a *sine qua non*" for a Christian.[8] The Spirit nowhere factors into the struggles of the "I" against sin in 7:7–25 (cf. 7:6!). The absence is conspicuous and renders likely the conclusion that Rom 7:5–6 functions to an extent as a thesis for both 7:7–25 and 8:1–17: "While we were living in the flesh [cf. 7:14], our sinful passions, aroused by the law, were at work in our members to bear fruit for death [7:7–25], but now [cf. 'now'; 8:1] we are discharged from the law, dead to that which held us captive, so that we are slaves not under the old written code [as in 7:7–25] but in the new life of the Spirit" [thus 8:1–17]. A new era has opened up and stands in full view. With the emphatic "now" of Rom 8:1 (echoing the turn in 7:6) the Christian no longer experiences condemnation or "death" (cf. 7:10, 13).[9]

The absence of the Spirit in Rom 7:7–25 proves a decisive difference from the Pauline texts that refer to the struggle in the Christian life.[10] No one denies that the Christian is caught up in the transition from the present age, which is characterized by the ongoing activity of sin, to the full manifestation of the age to come. The imperatives of Rom 6 and 8 are necessary because of sin's continuing influence on the believer, but those imperatives follow from the indicative of a changed status in Christ. The contrast between Rom 7:7–25 and Rom 8 could not be more striking. Nineteen times Paul mentions the Spirit in chap. 8! The contrast between these two sections of the letter is therefore intentional. In Gal 5:16–18, by way of comparison:

> Live by the Spirit, I say, and do not gratify the desires of the flesh. For what the flesh desires is opposed to the Spirit, and what the Spirit desires

---

8. Robert Jewett, "The Question of the 'Apportioned Spirit' in Paul's Letters: Romans as a Case Study," in Stanton, Longenecker, and Barton, *The Holy Spirit and Christian Origins*, 196.

9. Kümmel, *Römer 7*, 69–70; Günther Bornkamm, "Sin, Law and Death: An Exegetical Study of Romans 7," in *Early Christian Experience* (New York: Harper and Row, 1969) 88–89. As Gundry, "Moral Frustration," 238, wrote: "The emphatic 'Now then' and the back reference to release from condemnation for those who are in Christ Jesus at the start of ch. 8 (cf. 3:19 — 5:21) seal the exclusion: Paul is no longer talking about his pre-Christian self, captured by sin and condemned under the law, but about all those who are free from the law and justified in Christ." Gundry also distinguished between "the body is dead because of sin" in 8:10, which speaks of physical death with respect to the believer, from "the body of *this* death" in 7:24 that refers to the *experience* of sin's springing to life (7:10, 11, 13) and the "dying" "I" who is incapable of doing good. The "body" of 8:10 will therefore be raised (8:11) and redeemed (8:25). For the contrary position, see especially Timo Laato, *Paul and Judaism: An Anthropological Approach* (trans. T. McElwain; SFSHJ 115; Atlanta: Scholars Press, 1995), 116.

10. Kümmel, *Römer 7*, 104–6.

is opposed to the flesh; for these are opposed to each other, to prevent you from doing what you want. But if you are led by the Spirit, you are not subject to the law."

"What you want" (ἃ ἐὰν θέλητε) in v. 17 does not have as its subject both the Spirit and the flesh. If both the Spirit and the flesh were hindering each other, then they would be acting as equal forces. Paul does not envision a stalemate between the flesh and the Spirit (thus his comments in v.16). The believer always has the power by virtue of the Spirit to choose and to act contrary to the flesh (Gal 3:3; 5:22–24). The same positive expectations would prevent taking "what you want" as Spirit-prompted desires that are successfully *stymied* by the flesh. In this context, "what you want" should be taken as the flesh's negative desires, which are defeated by the Spirit. The problem, however, is that "what you want" in Rom 7:15 (the same phrase) expresses *God-pleasing* intentions. In an unfortunately neglected study, Ronald Lutjens contended that Gal 5:17 includes a parenthetical remark: "For what the flesh desires is opposed to the Spirit (and what the Spirit desires is opposed to the flesh; for these are opposed to each other) to prevent you from doing what you want."[11] This punctuation maintains a positive sense for "what you want" *and* the Spirit's preeminence over the flesh. Paul can barely countenance the flesh's opposition of Spirit-prompted desires without immediately qualifying in a parenthesis that the flesh's actions are countered by the overwhelming power of the Spirit to which the Christian has immediate access. He can therefore admonish the freed Christian (5:1, 13) with the expectation of fulfillment in Gal 5:16: "Live by the Spirit, I say, and do not gratify the desires of the flesh."[12] Christians have a power available to them that is not accessible through Moses' Law. In Rom 7:7–25 that decisive power of the Spirit is conspicuously absent. The characteristic Christian struggle between the Spirit and the flesh is nowhere to be found. The "I" is unable to do what it wants and is only able to express the sinful desires of the flesh: "I do not understand my own actions. For I do not do what I want, but I do the very thing I hate….I can will what is right, but I cannot do it. For I do not do the good I want, but the evil I do not want is what I do" (Rom 7:15, 18–19). Sin is still waging a campaign against the Christian in Rom 6 and 8—hence the exhortations against sin (especially 6:12; 8:10–13, 23).[13] The baptized,

---

11. Ronald Lutjens, "'You Do Not Do What You Want' What Does Galatians 5:17 Really Mean?" *Presbyterion* 16/2 (1990): 103–7.

12. Contra the slave of sin in Rom 7; Bornkamm, "Sin, Law, and Death," 100–101.

13. James D. G. Dunn, "Rom. 7,14–25 in the Theology of Paul," *TZ* 31 (1975), 264–73, was right to stress the already-not yet tension throughout Rom 6 and 8. The

Spirit-empowered Christian, unlike the "I" of Rom 7:7–25, is able to *stop* sinful desires from expressing themselves in action.[14] The Christian not only wills but also is empowered to *do* (Phil 2:13; Rom 8:4; Rom 12:1–12).[15] As Paul explains in Rom 7:4, the power that hold sways over an individual expresses itself by that individual's *fruit*.[16] The "I" without Christ and the Spirit is unable to produce the righteous deed.[17]

---

problem is that Dunn deprives the indicative of its force in his emphasis on the imperative (rightly Douglas J. Moo, *The Epistle to the Romans* [NICNT; Grand Rapids: Eerdmans, 1996], 449 n.18). The issue in Romans 7 is that sin is *victorious* in the struggle and the "I" completely imprisoned and unable to avoid the bad; rightly Gundry, "Moral Frustration," 238. In other words, the "already" as expressed by Paul's indicative statements of freedom from slavery to sin's rule throughout Rom 6 and again in 8:2 are *absent* in Rom 7:7–25. Paul's discussion remains more narrowly focused in this section on whether the Law is sin (7:7). After the negative statements on the enslaving character of the Law in 7:1–6 that paralleled what Paul says about sin in the preceding chapter, the question is understandable. The Christian must die to sin and the Law (6:2; 7:4) in order to be freed from their enslaving power (6:7, 18; 7:3, 6) and in order to experience the "new life of the Spirit" (7:6), the "newness of life" (6:4).

14. Paul never claims that sin and the desires of the flesh are completely overcome, only that the Christian has available decisive power. This contra Laato, *Paul and Judaism*, 144–45, who incomprehensibly affirmed a "deep pessimism" in Gal 5:16–17 and concluded: "The situation of the Christian does not look any better than that of the 'I.'"

15. Gundry, "Moral Frustration," 235, 237–38. Gundry stressed against those who emphasize an apparently renewed mind in Rom 7:14–25 that even a Christian mind must be exhorted to renewal (Rom 12:1–2). "The mind as such does not imply regeneration. Even pagans recognize God's righteous edict that sinners deserve to die (Rom. 1:32); so it should not surprise us that the unrenewed mind of a nomistic Jew agrees with and delights in God's law." Again, it is the ability to *do* the Law that distinguishes the regenerate. Paul's distinction between the actions of the "I" in the flesh and the will of the "I" in the mind, far from identifying a Christian, is precisely what allows him to characterize the unregenerate nomist; rightly Gundry, "Moral Frustration," 235.

16. Glenn S. Holland, "The Self against the Self in Romans 7.7–25," in *The Rhetorical Interpretation of Scripture: Essays from the 1996 Malibu Conference* (ed. Stanley E. Porter and Dennis L. Stamps; JSNTSup 180; Sheffield: Sheffield Academic, 1999), 262. Jervis, "Sin's Use of the Obedience of Faith," 210–12, strangely concluded that the Law is actually *done* with no struggle by people "prior to faith in Christ," whereas Christians struggle to obey Christ's command of righteousness with great "angst" and mixed results. Cf. A. Andrew Das, *Paul, the Law, and the Covenant* (Peabody, Mass.: Hendrickson, 2001), 185–86 n. 49.

17. In order sustain his interpretation of the Christian "I," Martin Luther was forced to deny what Paul actually says. Instead of "I do what I do not want," Luther amended the biblical text to read what he thought Paul *meant* to say: "he does not do the good as often and to such an extent and as readily as he would like." As Achtemeier, "Some

"The law is spiritual" (Rom 7:14). "I delight in the law of God in my inmost self" (κατὰ τὸν ἔσω ἄνθρωπον; 7:22). In Rom 7:16 the "I" agrees that "the law is good" and wants to do what is good, but in Rom 8:5–8: "For those who live according to the flesh set their minds on the things of the flesh, but those who live according to the Spirit set their minds on the things of the Spirit. . . . For this reason the mind that is set on the flesh is hostile to God; it does not submit to God's law — indeed it cannot, and those who are in the flesh cannot please God." Elsewhere the apostle maintains that spiritual matters are only discerned by the Spirit's presence (1 Cor 2:14–15). Is there a contradiction between the "I" of Rom 7:22 that recognizes and delights in the goodness of God's Law and the fleshly mind of 8:5–8 that is hostile to God? Some have concluded that the "I" of Rom 7:22 must be regenerate because of the apparent contrast with 8:5–8. The Spirit, again, is rather prominent in the life of Rom 8's believer, whereas *the Law* is "spiritual" in Rom 7, not the "I." Further, the "I" who delights in God's Law in Rom 7:7–25 is not at all inconsistent with how Paul describes *unbelievers*. Some are actually *zealous* for God's Law.[18] In Rom 9:31–32 Israel strives for the righteousness that is based on the Law. In 10:2–3, "I can testify that they have a zeal for God" and are "seeking to establish their own [righteousness]." When Paul adds "They have not submitted to God's righteousness" (10:3), the failure to submit recalls the mind set on the flesh in 8:7: "It does not submit to God's law — indeed, it cannot." In other words, a mind set on the flesh (8:7) can still be a Jew with great zeal for God's Law.[19] The "Jew" of Rom 2:17–20 knows, relies on, and boasts in the Law of God. Paul never disagrees with the Jew's claim to "know [God's] will" and to be "instructed in the law." He criticizes the Jew for not producing works consistent with that knowledge (2:17–29).[20] The gentile who is a Jew inwardly and who has received the circumcision of the heart will by his or her *actions* put to shame the outward Jew (2:25–29). The gentile who has been inwardly renewed and transformed will produce the works that the

---

Things," 266, commented: "These verses therefore do not speak of my moral dilemma as a Christian. The way out of a moral dilemma is 'Try harder,' or 'Learn better to know the good.' But neither of those apply here. The passage speaks not of a moral dilemma but of an absolute imprisonment; it speaks not of intentions, and thus subjectively, but of actions, and thus objectively." The imprisoned, enslaved "I" requires *rescue* by a power greater than sin.

18. The mind of the "I" in Rom 7 differs from the "mind" of Rom 1 in that the "I" is aware of Moses' Law.

19. Gundry, "Moral Frustration," 236.

20. Paul contrasts "the Jew" with the gentile whose works in keeping the Law put to shame "the Jew." These gentiles have what the Law requires written on their hearts as their defending *and accusing* consciences will attest (2:15).

Jew who relies on and boasts in the Law lacks. Inner, spiritual transformation expresses itself in god-pleasing action.[21] Disobedience is the criterion indicating the absence of regeneration. The "I" of Rom 7 knows God's will but does not produce works consistent with that knowledge. In Gal 1:14 Paul describes himself before his encounter with Christ as having been "zealous for the traditions of my ancestors." Or in Phil 3:6: "as to zeal, a persecutor of the church; as to righteousness under the law, blameless."[22] A genuine zeal for God's Law may therefore characterize the unregenerate Jew even though that individual's striving for righteousness does not achieve the desired result — indeed it cannot. Zealous Jews have misunderstood the Law's ultimate goal/end in Christ (10:1–4).[23] Zeal for God's Law does not obviate the need for the mind and the will to be renewed for there to be right conduct (Rom 12:2; the conduct absent in Rom 7:7–25). Only by such a renewal of the mind will the inability to do the good in Rom 7:14–25 — the very same inability of the fleshly mind in Rom 8:8 — be overturned.

At first glance, the emphasis on the "inmost self" or "inner person" of Rom 7:22 may indicate regenerate existence (cf. 2 Cor 4:16). Robert Gundry, in his study of Pauline anthropology, explained that "inner man" should not be equated with "new man" (Eph 2:15; 4:24; Col 3:10) and "outer man" should not be equated with "old man" (Rom 6:6; Eph 4:22; Col 3:9).[24] "New man" and "old man" are always hamartiological in usage signifying the presence or absence of regeneration. The "old man" parallels existence "in Adam" as opposed to "in Christ," two contrasting ages (Rom 5:12–21; 6:6). The "old man" must therefore

---

21. That Paul is anticipating in Rom 2:25–29 his discussion of Christians in what follows, see the fuller discussion in Das, *Paul, the Law, and the Covenant*, 185–86, n. 49.

22. Brian Dodd, *Paul's Paradigmatic "I": Personal Example as Literary Strategy* (JSNTSup 177; Sheffield: Sheffield Academic, 1999), 223, followed others in claiming that Phil 3:6 describes how Paul thought about his accomplishments *before* he was a Christian. Such a claim overlooks the literary function of Phil 3 in a line of thought that has developed since early in Phil 2. The boasts of Phil 3:6 are *legitimate* boasts. Paul does not avail himself of legitimate prerogatives as a blameless Jew for the sake of his gentile audiences in a parallel fashion to Jesus' not availing himself of divine prerogatives for the sake of all humanity (cf. 2:5–11).

23. Knowledge of Moses' Law *distinguishes* the mind of the "I" from the mind of the idolater in Rom 1:18–32. The positive claims for the "I" do not, then, contradict Rom 1 and align better with Rom 2.

24. Robert H. Gundry, Soma *in Biblical Theology with Emphasis on Pauline Anthropology* (SNTSMS 29; Cambridge: Cambridge Univ. Press, 1976), 135–40. He is, of course, using the language in a generic sense; note the alternate language of the NRSV.

be crucified in order to neutralize the body of sin and to *free* an individual from sin's enslavement (Rom 6:6). The "new man" is God's special creation in the new age in Christ (Eph 2:15–16) and must be "put on" (Eph 4:24). The "outer man," on the other hand, simply wastes away (2 Cor 4:16). The "outer man" is an "earthly tent" that is subject to weakness and decay. The "outer man" will be destroyed and replaced by a "building from God" (2 Cor 5:1–2). Even as the "outer man" refers to the body, the "inner man" of Rom 7:22 is associated with the "mind" and stands opposite the "members," "flesh," and "body."[25] Likewise the "inner man" of Eph 3:16 strengthened by the Spirit is parallel to the "hearts" indwelt by Christ in v. 17.[26] Paul is contrasting in Rom 7 the inner mental functions with the outer bodily. "In this context, it is much more likely that 'inner person' has its well-attested anthropological meaning than a questionable soteriological meaning."[27] Nothing in this description of the "I" requires a regenerate Christian.

Some claim that the qualification of Rom 7:18, "that is, in my flesh," would be unnecessary for a non-Christian.[28] On the contrary, to interpret Christian existence from this qualification would be to overextend the text. Paul is certainly contrasting the mind and the members (7:22–25), but a human being nevertheless remains a unified entity with respect to salvation. In Rom 7:14 the "I" is fleshly. In 7:23 the "I" *as a whole* is "captive to the law of sin." With Moo: "While Paul's anthropology is essentially 'monistic' rather than dualistic — that is, he usually regards people as wholes, in relationship to other things, instead of, as the Greeks did, as divided into two distinct 'parts,' body (or flesh) and soul (or spirit, or mind) — there is an undeniable element of anthropological dualism as well."[29] "Flesh" is therefore parallel to the "members" of v. 23 as opposed to the

---

25. Ibid., 137. So also Moo, *Romans*, 462; contra Michael Paul Middendorf, *The "I" in the Storm: A Study of Romans 7* (St. Louis: Concordia Academic Press, 1997), 106. Philo, *Plant.* 42: the mind is "the real man in us"; *Congr.* 97: the mind is the "man within the man" [Colson et al, LCL]).

26. As Harold W. Hoehner wrote in his commentary on Eph 3:16: "In the present context it is the innermost being of the believer which is to be strengthened with God's power. That innermost being corresponds with the heart of the believer in the following verse. It does not . . . refer to Jesus Christ himself or to the "new" person mentioned in 2:15 but rather to the innermost part of individual believers" (*Ephesians: An Exegetical Commentary* [Grand Rapids: Baker, 2002], 479; cf. 377–80, 609–10 on "new person").

27. Moo, *Romans*, 462.

28. Middendorf, *"I" in the Storm*, 96–7, 193. Middendorf's book is the most thorough and comprehensive case available for the traditional reading of Rom 7:14–25 as Christian existence.

29. Moo, *Romans*, 459; relying on Gundry, Soma *in Biblical Theology*.

"mind." Paul's qualification of the flesh in v. 18 places emphasis on the bodily members as the *instrument* of the sinful actions of the "I."[30]

Paul shifts in Rom 7:14–25 from past tense verbs (imperfect and aorist) of 7:7–13 to present tense verbs. This change in tense should not be taken as a shift from pre-Christian to Christian existence as is often thought. Present tense verbs do not necessarily indicate action in the present. Stanley Porter, in his study of Greek tense and aspect, contended that present tense verbs do not convey time.[31] Present tense verbs grammaticalize the imperfective aspect, and aorist verbs grammaticalize (that is, represent a meaning by choice of word-form) the perfective. The contrast between the two categories is between narrative (perfective) and descriptive (imperfective).[32] Those who stress that the present tense must describe Paul's Christian existence ignore the *absence* of temporal markers at the level of the larger grammatical or conceptual units of Rom 7:14–25.[33] Temporal markers in the context of Phil 3:3–6 are precisely what permit Paul to describe his non-Christian *past* with present tense verb forms. Without temporal markers in the context of Rom 7:14–25, the tense of the verbs does not of itself indicate a setting in the present. Paul has shifted from his narration of life under the Law in 7:7–12 to a description of the condition or state of that

---

30. Seifrid, "Subject of Rom 7:14–25," 320 n. 17; 330 n. 51; contra, e.g., Laato, *Paul and Judaism*, 122–23.

31. Stanley E. Porter, *Idioms of the Greek New Testament* (2d ed.; Sheffield: Sheffield Academic, 1994), 20–49; Stanley E. Porter, *Verbal Aspect in the Greek of the New Testament, with Reference to Tense and Mood* (New York: Peter Lang, 1989), 76–83, 105–7, 198–208. Against those (including Buist Fanning) who think that ancient authors used the present tense to lend a sense of vividness to past action, Porter wrote: "[I]t must be rejected because of its outdated view of tense functions, the lack of indication in the text of such a perspectival shift, and the resulting clumsiness in perspective when tenses are seen as shifting so quickly" (p. 30). He highlighted Mark 5:35–42 with nine present verbs, three aorist, and one imperfect as "unlikely evidence indeed that events are shifted temporally for vividness" (p. 30).

32. Porter, as summarized by Seifrid, "Subject of Rom 7:14–25," 321–22. Or with Porter himself (*Idioms*, 31): "[D]ifferent tense-forms can obviously be used in similar temporal contexts, and that the imperfective verbal aspect (present tense-form) is used whenever one wishes to draw added attention to a given event," or the action to which the present form refers. In the context of Rom 7:7–25 the present tense forms amplify the experience of the "I."

33. K. L. McKay, one of the leading specialists in verbal aspect, seconded Porter's observations regarding tense when considered by itself: "[I]t is clear that time is not morphologically expressed, but is determined by context" ("Time and Aspect in New Testament Greek," *NovT* 34 [1992]: 226).

person. The unfolding state of the slave to sin is conveyed through the present tense.[34] Romans 7:14–25 is therefore best taken as describing the experience of a non-Christian "I" under the power of sin and the Law.[35]

Romans 7:7–12

Scholars tend to agree that Rom 7:7–12 is describing a non-Christian. This paragraph, however, raises yet a new set of issues. Some have detected allusions to Genesis. Others have detected allusions to the history of Israel. Robert Gundry, in a novel approach, suggested that Paul is describing his adolescent experience after instruction in the Law. Gundry translated Rom 7:7: "You shall not lust." Sexual desire sprang to life in Paul at the time of his bar mitzvah. Paul had once been alive "apart from the Law" (7:9), that is, apart from the Law from the point of view of its command against sexual lust. With puberty he began to experience moral frustration.[36] Philo described a sort of "age of innocence": "The infant from the day of its birth for the first seven years, that is through the age of childhood, possesses only the simplest elements of soul . . . and has not yet received any impression of good or evil" (*Her.* 59 §294 [Colson and Whitaker, LCL]). In *m. Avot* 5:21: "At five years old [one is fit] for the Scripture, at ten years for the Mishnah, at thirteen for [the fulfilling of] the commandments."[37] Gundry was too specific in his interpretation when he limited Rom 7:7 to sexual desire. Paul's wording (οὐκ ἐπιθυμήσεις) exactly matches Rom 13:9 with its list

---

34. Thus Seifrid, *Justification by Faith*, 234; followed by Thomas R. Schreiner, *Romans* (BECNT 6; Grand Rapids: Baker, 1998), 386–87. Wenham, "Christian Life," 86–7, noted the shift in topic accompanying the change of tense. Whereas in vv. 7–12 Paul defended the Law, he does not really elaborate on the malignant influence of sin as *experienced* by the "I" until 7:14–25. The present tense, as Porter explained (*Verbal Aspect*, 106–7), is employed for describing an action as it unfolds.

35. On the order and relationship of v. 25a and v. 25b from the vantage point of a non-Christian "I," see Gundry, "Moral Frustration," 240; Paul W. Meyer, "The Worm at the Core of the Apple: Exegetical Reflections on Romans 7," in *The Conversation Continues: Studies in Paul and John in Honor of J. Louis Martyn* (ed. Robert T. Fortna and Beverly R. Gaventa; Nashville: Abingdon, 1990), 79.

36. Gundry, "Moral Frustration," 232–33.

37. As translated by Danby. Gerd Theissen, *Psychological Aspects of Pauline Theology* (ed. John P. Galvin; Philadelphia: Fortress Press, 1987), 223, 230–1, therefore modified Gundry's approach and claimed instead that Paul is referring more generally to a time prior to full acquaintance with the Law and then a dawning consciousness. This is not the most natural sense of "apart from the law."

from the Decalogue.[38] Paul therefore has the Tenth Commandment in mind. The "desire" should not be limited, then, to sexual lusts. The Tenth Commandment was frequently cited in Jewish literature without an object in order to function in a generalizing manner (4 Macc 2:4–6; Philo, *Decal.* 28 §§142–53; 35 §173). Romans 7:7 conforms to the pattern of generalization as Paul explains in v. 8 that he is speaking of "*all kinds of*" desire in v. 8 (πᾶσαν ἐπιθυμίαν). Gundry ignored v. 8 without comment. "Every kind of desire" cannot be limited to the sexual desires after puberty. No other instance of the noun or verb of "desire" (ἐπιθυμία; ἐπιθυμεῖν) in the Septuagint or the New Testament ever refers to sexual desire unless the specific context requires it.[39] Also, no firm evidence exists that the bar mitzvah was practiced in Paul's day.[40] "Early Talmudic times," as per Gundry, would be at least a hundred and fifty years later. The Jews never spoke of themselves as "apart from the law" in the sense of the Mosaic Law.[41] The Jewish people considered themselves under the Law from infancy. Philo could therefore describe the Jews as "trained as they were we may say even from the cradle, by parents and tutors and instructors and by the far higher authority of the sacred laws and also the unwritten custom" (*Legat.* 16 §115). Or a little later in the same document: "For all men guard their own customs, but this is especially true of the Jewish nation. Holding that the laws are oracles vouchsafed by God and having been trained in this doctrine from their earliest years, they carry the likenesses of the commandments enshrined in their souls" (*Legat.* 31 §210). Similarly Josephus: "The result, then, of our thorough grounding in the laws from the first dawn of intelligence is that we have them, as it were, engraven on our souls" (*Ag. Ap.* 2.18 §178). The circumcision of a child means, for Paul, that the child is under the Law (Gal 5:3; Phil 3:5). Paul denies any possibility of childish innocence. In Rom 5:12 all people from Adam experience death because of sin. In Rom 3:19–20, 23 he emphatically denies that anyone is without sin or unaccountable. Romans 7:7–12 simply does not

---

38. Douglas J. Moo, "Israel and the Paul in Romans 7.7–12," *NTS* 32 (1986): 123.

39. J. A. Ziesler, "The Role of the Tenth Commandment in Romans 7," *JSNT* 33 (1988): 45–46. Exod 20:17 and Deut 5:21 do not limit desire to sexual lust.

40. Kümmel, *Römer 7*, 82–83. The tradition that a boy was exempt from the commandments until puberty is attested in *m. Nid.* 6; *b. Nid.* 52; *b. B. Qam.* 44a, 88a. J. A. Ziesler, "The Role of the Tenth Commandment in Romans 7," *JSNT* 33 (1988), 45, considered it *possible* that Rom 7:9 is an earlier witness to this later tradition but "not likely." Ziesler contended persuasively in his article that Paul picked the Tenth Commandment because of the Jewish tradition of the day that traced all sin from this initial desire.

41. So Origen concludes that Paul must speaking of natural law in *Comm. Rom.* 6.8 (1082).

specify a particular time in Paul's life when desire was aroused. Few have found Gundry's approach convincing.

Ernst Käsemann in his Romans commentary quipped: "There is nothing in the passage which does not fit Adam, and everything fits Adam alone."[42] For Käsemann, Rom 7:9, "I was once alive apart from the law," could only describe Adam in the Garden prior to the command not to eat of the tree. No one after Adam was "*living*" (in its full theological sense) before the arrival of the Law (thus Rom 5:12–19). Eve experienced "desire" in the garden (Gen 3:6) as Satan — like the personified Sin of Rom 7:7–12 — "deceived" her.[43] "I died" would describe Adam's experience after violating the command (Gen 2:17; 3:3, 19).[44] An allusion to the Garden of Eden, however, faces serious difficulties. Adam, Eve, the serpent, and the tree with its fruit are never mentioned in Rom 7:7–11 (cf. Rom 5:12–19; 1 Cor 15:45). In other words, the allusion to Adam in the garden is not obvious. Paul, for his part, emphasizes *Eve's* deception in 2 Cor 11:3 and not Adam's (so also 1 Tim 2:14). Adam, then, was not powerless to resist sin and so was held accountable (Rom 5:12–19).[45] The language Paul uses in v. 7 (οὐκ ἐπιθυμήσεις) refers to the Decalogue of Moses (note the same language in Rom 13:9).[46] Little evidence presents itself from the Second Temple era that Adam was ever entrusted with the Torah of Moses in an as yet unwritten form.[47]

---

42. Ernst Käsemann, *Commentary on Romans* (Grand Rapids: Eerdmans, 1980), 196. See the fuller explication of this position in S. Lyonnet, "L'historie du salut selon le chapître VII de l'épître aux Romains," *Bib* 43 (1962): 117–51; also Theissen, *Psychological Aspects*, 202–11.

43. ἀπατᾶν in Gen 3:13; ἐξαπατᾶν in Rom 7:11; cf. 2 Cor 11:3; 1 Tim 2:14.

44. Paul also shifts from speaking of the Law (νόμος) to the "command" (ἐντολή). Not eating from the tree would preserve life, even as the command in Rom 7:10 is εἰς ζωήν. So specialists frequently find the echoes to Adam (and Eve) persuasive, e.g., Edward Adams, "Paul's Story of God and Creation: The Story of How God Fulfils His Purposes in Creation," in *Narrative Dynamics in Paul: A Critical Assessment* (ed. Bruce W. Longenecker; Louisville: Westminster John Knox, 2002), 27–28.

45. Gundry, "Moral Frustration," 231–32.

46. Moo, "Israel and Paul in Romans 7.7–12," 123. Jervis, "Sin's Use of the Obedience of Faith," 193–96, 206–7, contended that the reference to the Mosaic "commandment" disqualifies Adamic references in 7:7–12 only to abandon any reference to a Mosaic commandment (which actually is more natural after the citation of a specific commandment of the Decalogue in v. 7) in favor of a reference to the "commandment of Christian righteousness."

47. *Tg. Neof.* 1 on Gen 2:15; 3:9, 22 interprets Adam as entrusted with the Law's commands in the Garden, but this tradition postdates Paul by several centuries; contra S. Lyonnet, "L'historie du salut," 137–38. Peter Stuhlmacher, *Paul's Letter to the Romans: A Commentary* (trans. Scott J. Hafemann; Louisville: Westminster John Knox, 1994),

Although the Septuagint does not employ the ἐπιθυμία (desire) word group in Gen 3, the Jews of Paul's day did, on occasion, interpret the command in the garden as a prohibition against "desire" along the lines of the later Tenth Commandment.[48] For instance, 4 Ezra 7:11 speaks of desire in relation to Gen 3:5–6 (but not ἐπιθυμία).[49] After outlining the potential evidence for a connection between the Garden of Eden and the Tenth Commandment, J. A. Ziesler immediately qualified: "The evidence is not extensive, and for reasons of geography as well as dating, we cannot be sure that Paul used or even knew this tradition."[50] Even if the traditions that claimed that Adam and Eve were in possession of the Law could be securely dated to the first century and if these traditions were known to Paul, he would not have agreed with them. In Rom 5:13–14 the era from Adam to Moses was *"before* the law." The Law entered *between* Adam and Christ (Rom 5:20). In Gal 3:17 Moses' Law came four hundred thirty years *after* the promise to Abraham. Gerd Theissen, who favored a connection between Adam and the Law, conceded: "Paul, in contrast to the rabbinic tendency to consider the law eternal attributes great significance to its secondary and historical character . . . , and that retrojection of the law into paradise contradicts his theological interests."[51] For the author of the *Apocalypse of Moses* (19:3), the serpent sprinkled on the fruit the evil poison of desire (ἐπιθυμία), the root of all sin. Paul's own logic in 7:8 is the exact opposite: sin produces desire, or with Leander Keck: "For Paul, the culprit is not sin-producing desire, but desire-producing sin."[52] Also, the Adam figure, if even present in Rom 7:7–12, is an *inclusive* figure for human experience in general, but the description of being

---

107, traces this tradition to *L.A.E.* (32 + 37), Josephus, *Ant.* 1.1.4 §§41–7, 4 Ezra 3:7; 7:11; Philo *Leg.* 1.29–31 §§90–7. Josephus explicates the "commandment of God" as the injunction against touching the tree and not with reference to an unwritten Mosaic Law. 4 Ezra 3:7 and 7:11 also appear to be referring to the command with respect to the tree. Philo certainly allegorizes the command regarding the tree but never implies that the entire Law had been entrusted to Adam. A. J. M. Wedderburn, "Adam in Paul's Letter to the Romans," in *Studia Biblical 1978: III* (ed. E. A. Livingstone; Sheffield: JSOT, 1980), 420, cites *b. Sanh.* 56b with its discussion of the commandments given to Adam.

48. Ziesler, "Tenth Commandment," 47, Theissen, *Psychological Aspects*, 204–6, and Wedderburn, "Adam in Romans," 420–21, have cited texts in support of the fusion of the commands not to eat and not to covet (or *lust*): *b. Sabb.* 145b–146a; *Yebam.* 103b; *Abod. Zar.* 22b; *Apoc. Mos.* 19:3; *Apoc. Ab.* 23:1–14; Philo, *QG* 1.2 §§47–48; and perhaps *Opif.* 56 §§157–60; *Leg.* 2.18 §§72, 74.

49. Theissen, *Psychological Aspects*, 203 n. 3.

50. Ziesler, "Tenth Commandment," 47.

51. Theissen, *Psychological Aspects*, 203 n. 3.

52. Leander E. Keck, *Romans* (ANTC; Nashville: Abingdon, 2005), 183.

"apart from the Law" only fits Adam as a unique historical figure. In fact, in Rom 5:12–19 Paul contrasts Adam as a unique historical figure with Jesus Christ. Further, with the command, sin "revived" (ἀναζάω; v. 9). Gundry commented on this choice of wording:

> When the commandment came, sin sprang to life. It was already dwelling within the "I." But the serpent was external to Adam and did not confront him, but Eve. Paul recognizes that sin was not dwelling within Adam before the Fall, for he explicitly says that "sin entered the world" at the Fall (Rom 5:12). ἀνέζησεν (Rom 7:9) is inappropriate to the entrance of sin."[53]

The "I" of Rom 7:7–12, unlike Adam, is already under sin's influence prior to the command's fully impacting the consciousness.[54] God also issued to the still sinless Adam the command not to eat *right after* his Creation and not after a significant interval (Gen 2:15–17; so also Sir 17:7, 11–12).[55] So even Adam in the Garden was never "apart from the law."[56] Finally, the "I" of Rom 7:7–12 remains the same "I" in Rom 7:14–25, and nothing in vv. 14–25 alludes to Adam. The inner struggles and emotions of 7:7–25 are not characteristic of Adam's portrayal in Jewish literature.[57] Romans 7:7–12 does not primarily refer, then, to the experience of the first human. Paul is developing a topic from Rom 7:1–6, the enslaving character of Moses' Law. The Law is not sinful, but sin has hijacked the Law (7:7). If Adamic motifs are present, as most commentators have thought, they have been "woven into the fabric of [Paul's] argument."[58] Adamic

---

53. Gundry, "Moral Frustration," 231.

54. D. J. W. Milne, "Romans 7:7–12, Paul's Pre-Conversion Experience," *RTR* 43 (1984): 11.

55. Gundry, "Moral Frustration," 231, who added: "If by some trick of the imagination it could be thought there was such an interval, its extreme brevity militates against Paul's making it a discrete period of salvation-history and describing life during it with a imperfect tense, which implies some duration of action (ἔζων)."

56. Had Paul intended Adam as the referent of the "I," why use "apart from *the Law*" and not remain consistent with "apart from *the commandment*"? "The commandment" would fit Adam better and would still permit Paul's application to the Mosaic Law.

57. Gundry, "Moral Frustration," 229. Sin in Rom 7:7–25 is depicted in terms of "inner processes" whereas Adam was tempted from without; Theissen, *Psychological Aspects*, 203.

58. Dodd, *Paul's Paradigmatic "I,"* 226. Dodd denied Adam as the referent of the "I" since too many traits of the "I" go beyond what fits Adam. Dodd favored, breathtakingly, a "composite" of Adam's story, Paul's experience, Jewish experience, and the experience of Christian believers (p. 230).

echoes would strengthen the plausibility of a gentile audience for Rom 7. The Adam-like experience of the "I" would apply to *all* children of Adam as they encounter the command. Paul is developing an understanding of the Law in a manner that would be appropriate for gentiles.

Others, especially Douglas J. Moo, have proposed that the "I" refers to Israel's reception of the Law at Mount Sinai (vv. 7–8: pre-Sinai; vv. 9–11: Sinai), Israel's violation of the Law, and their subsequent experience of death.[59] Although sin existed in the world before the Law, with the Law sin becomes transgression, a willful violation (Rom 4:15). The Law incited transgression (5:20). Romans 7:7–12 therefore describes the increase of sin after Mount Sinai (so also 1 Cor 15:56; Gal 3:19–22). This reading has its difficulties as well. Paul does not explicitly identify Israel as the subject in vv. 7–13. Romans 7:14–25 does not parallel the description of the "Jew" in 2:17–29 with the mistakenly robust conscience or "Israel" in 9:30 — 10:5. Paul even identifies gentiles without the Law as conscious of sin as their consciences also "accuse" (Rom 2:12–16).[60] Sin was not "dead" or dormant but "reigned" from Adam to Moses (Rom 5:12–14). Moo conceded that "I died" referred to the "condemnation resulting from sin," "death as eschatological penalty."[61] He claimed that this is the condemnation of Israel as a collective whole.[62] Moo noted that "life" does not often refer to spiritual life in Paul. Of fifty-nine instances of ζάω, only nine probably refer to spiritual life.[63] Thomas Schreiner responded to Moo's reasoning by observing that Paul contrasts "I was living" (ἔζων) in v. 9 with "I died" (ἀπέθανον) in v. 10, even as "life" (ζωή) functions as an antonym to "death" (θάνατος) in v. 10. The interpretation of "life" must therefore form a natural antithesis to "death." Schreiner: "If 'death' refers to Israel's eschatological death in the fullest sense, then it must follow that Israel had eschatological life previous to the covenant with Sinai. Only in this

---

59. Moo, "Israel and the Paul in Romans 7.7–12"; Andrea van Dülmen, *Die Theologie des Gesetzes bei Paulus* (SBM 5; Stuttgart: Katholisches Bibelwerk, 1968), 102, 109–10; Mark W. Karlberg, "Israel's History Personified: Romans 7:7–13 in Relation to Paul's Teaching on the 'Old Man,'" *TJ* 7 (1986): 65–74; Walt Russell, "Insights from Postmodernism's Emphasis on Interpretive Communities in the Interpretation of Romans 7," *JETS* 37 (1994): 521–23; Brendan Byrne, *Romans* (SP 6; Collegeville, Minn.: Liturgical, 1996), 218.

60. Middendorf, *"I" in the Storm*, 138.

61. Moo, "Israel and the Paul in Romans 7.7–12," 125.

62. Ibid., 127–28.

63. Ibid., 132 n. 29: Rom 1:17; 6:13; 8:13; 10:5; 2 Cor 8:4 (?); Gal 2:19; 3:11; 3:12; 5:25.

way can the two verbs be interpreted consistently."[64] Paul, however, sees the era from Adam to Moses as an era of death and condemnation.

> Thus it is difficult to believe — if the verbs bear their full theological meaning — that Paul could say Israel "lived" before the era of the Mosaic law. One could perhaps understand Paul to say that they received life upon entering the Sinai covenant, but this is not what the text says. He uses the construction ἔζων (imperfect verb) . . . ποτέ, which most likely indicates ongoing action in past time.[65]

Moo nuanced his position in his subsequent work by saying that "life" and "death" should be understood in "relative theological terms." Sin simply possessed greater destructive power after the coming of the commandment at Mt. Sinai.[66] Moo contended that Paul is writing about the "redemptive-historical" role of the Law for the Sinaitic generation who initially received it in vv. 7–13.[67] The more personal tone of 7:14–25 expresses Paul's experience as well as that of "all Jews under the Law" *since* Mt. Sinai.[68] The bifurcation between the Sinaitic generation (vv. 7–13) and all subsequent Jewish generations (vv. 14–25) creates an unnecessary division in the "I." The identity of the "I" does not change between vv. 7–13 and vv. 14–25.[69] Interpreters have frequently remarked on the experiential tone not just of vv. 14–25 but *also* of vv. 7–12.[70] Moo took vv. 7–12 as the

---

64. Schreiner, *Romans*, 362–63. The contrast between "death" and "life" renders Jervis's praise for the beneficial results of sin-induced "death" incomprehensible ("Sin's Use of the Obedience of Faith," 198–99).

65. Schreiner, *Romans*, 363

66. Moo, *Romans*, 429–30, 437.

67. Moo, "Israel and the Paul in Romans 7.7–12," 124; idem, *Romans*, 448–49.

68. Moo, *Romans*, 448.

69. Kümmel, *Römer 7*, 85.

70. Moo, *Romans*, 430, 438, therefore countered that Paul is speaking *objectively* of Israel. Paul, however, speaks of sin's producing "*in me* all kinds of covetousness" and sin's "working death *in me* through what is good in order that sin might be shown to be sin" (vv. 8, 13). Likewise, the experiential tone of the "I" in vv. 14–25 casts its shadow back on vv. 7–12. The "body of death" from which the "I" yearns to escape is the very body that "died" in vv. 7–12. In 7:7: "I would not have *known* sin" had it not been for the Law. The claim of these verses' "objective language" seems forced. As Moo himself elsewhere recognized: "But we should probably go further, and conceive this 'understanding' of sin [in v. 7] not in a purely noetic way but in terms of actual experience: through the law, 'I' have come to experience sin for what it really is. Through the law sin 'worked in me' all kinds of sinful desires (v. 8), and through the law sin 'came to life' and brought death (vv. 9–11). It is through this actual experience of sin, then, that 'I' come to understand the real 'sinfulness' of sin" (*Romans*, 433–34). And is it not that very "actual experience" what Paul elaborates on in vv. 14–25?

Jew in solidarity with the Sinaitic generation. The problem is that neither Paul nor any other Jew ever experienced life "apart from the Law" as did the Sinaitic generation.[71] The Jews did not elsewhere employ the phrase "apart from the Law" to describe their existence prior to the experience of a commandment. Verses 7–12 would be describing the experience of a *different* "I" than vv. 14–25. On the other hand, would not the experience of *gentiles* encountering the Mosaic Law bear a resemblance to the wilderness generation's experience as sin was converted at Mount Sinai into transgression? Moo's position may be more effective in accounting for the experiential dimensions of the passage if modified for those who actually were "apart from the Law."[72] The gentile's sins were not "reckoned" (Rom 5:13) prior to the encounter with the Law, but with exposure to the Law the God-fearer's sins are "charged" as "trespasses" (Rom 5:13; Gal 3:19).[73] The gentile God-fearer experiences God's wrath (Rom 4:15), imprisonment (Rom 7:6; Gal 3:22–23), and death (2 Cor 3:7) as the indwelling sin expresses itself with power through the Law. A God-fearer's experience would match the experience of a unified "I" throughout Rom 7:7–25.

A popular explanation for Rom 7:7–12, if not also 7:14–25, is that Paul is describing his pre-Christian past from the vantage point of his Christian existence. Many readers have remarked on the tone of Rom 7:7–25. In v. 24: "Wretched man that I am! Who will rescue me from this body of death?" Schreiner: "The emotion expressed here would be melodramatic, artificial, and incredibly theatrical if Paul were not describing his own experience."[74] James D. G. Dunn emphasized

---

71. Jewish experience of the Law in Paul's day was decidedly post-Sinaitic, as Moo showed with respect to Paul himself ("Israel and the Paul in Romans 7.7–12," 125–26).

72. The relative theological sense that Moo proposed would still be applicable for the God-fearer, but alongside the experiential dimension. The God-fearer experiences the full destructive power of sin through the Law; cf. the lesser accusing force of the conscience in Rom 2:14–16.

73. Moo interpreted Rom 5:13–14 as the history *of Israel*, but Rom 5:13–14 describes the experience of those "in Adam." The entry of the Law is placed on a world stage suitable for the gentile God-fearer.

74. Schreiner, *Romans*, 363, drawing upon J. I. Packer, "The 'Wretched Man' in Romans 7," in *SE 2: Papers Presented to the Second International Congress on New Testament Studies Held at Christ Church, Oxford, 1961*, part 1: *The New Testament Scriptures* (ed. F. L. Cross; TU 87; Berlin: Akademie,1964), 623 ("artificial"; "theatrical"); Gundry, "Moral Frustration," 229 ("poignant anguish and pathetic frustration"); Dunn, "Rom. 7,14–25," 260; C. E. B. Cranfield, *A Critical and Exegetical Commentary on the Epistle to the Romans* (ICC; 2 vols.; Edinburgh: T&T Clark, 1975, 1979), 1:345.

the "existential anguish and frustration."[75] D. J. W. Milne described a "highly charged personal and confessional tone."[76] So when Paul speaks in 7:7–12 of being "alive" apart from the Law and then "death" with the Law's entry, he is speaking not theologically but experientially. And Schreiner asserts: "Thus when he says 'I was living formerly apart from the law,' he reflects on his own consciousness before receiving the law. When the law intruded on his consciousness with the prohibition against coveting, he died (that is, he experienced separation from God through his transgression)."[77] Michael Middendorf, in agreement, translated χωρὶς νόμου (v. 9a) as "living apart from the heightened awareness of the nature of sin and its consequence."[78] If that is what Paul indeed meant, he did not choose the most natural way of expressing it. The notion of the Law's providing a greater awareness of the nature of sin is a notion conveyed by *the context* of the phrase "apart from the law" and not the phrase itself. A non-literal interpretation of "apart from *the law*" in Rom 7:9, as Schreiner's and Middendorf's approach requires, would be at odds with Paul's discussion of the Tenth Commandment and the Law of Moses in 7:7–12, which suggest a more literal understanding of νόμος. Although the "confessional" and "personal" tone leads many interpreters to accept an autobiographical referent for the "I," a more viable explanation is available.

In 1974 Werner Kümmel argued that the "I" in Rom 7 is rhetorical and not autobiographical.[79] The "I," for Kümmel, refers to all people in general and not specifically to Paul, Adam, or Israel. He pointed to several passages where he thought Paul was using the first person singular and plural rhetorically (Rom

---

75. Dunn, "Rom. 7,14–25," 260.

76. Milne, "Romans 7:7–12," 12. A literary comparison with other ancient texts that employ a "highly charged personal and confessional tone" would have been helpful (cf. Seifrid).

77. Schreiner, *Romans*, 364. Schreiner further explained: "But Paul in this text refers to the law's impinging on his consciousness. One can receive moral instruction when young, and yet the meaning and import of such moral norms may not strike home. In this text Paul reflects on the time when the prohibition against coveting impinged on his consciousness, and it is unlikely that this occurred in his childhood days" (pp. 364–65). He immediately qualified that he does *not* subscribe to Gundry's position that sexual lust is in view. Although Schreiner's understanding of Paul's meaning is defensible from the context of 7:7–12, he has not provided the most natural way to interpret the phrase "apart from the law" itself.

78. Middendorf, *"I" in the Storm*, 80, 168; following Bandstra. It is inconceivable that a supremely Law-observant and educated individual such as Paul, as he now describes his Jewish past in Phil 3:3–9 and Gal 1:13–14, would be saying in Rom 7:9: I was once living a life *"without the full knowledge and awareness of what the Law actually says"* (ibid., 169).

79. Kümmel, *Römer 7*.

3:5, 7; 1 Cor 6:12, 15; 10:29; 11:31–32; 13:1–3, 11–12; 14:11, 15; Gal 2:18). Critics have objected that in most of these instances Paul is including himself, and his experience is therefore typical.[80] In a stronger example in 1 Cor 10:29, the "strong" are personified as an "I" who *objects* to Paul's admonition to defer to the weaker brother's scruples.[81] In Rom 11:29 Paul identifies his gentile audience (the engrafted branches) as an "I."[82] N. M. Watson identified a rhetorical "I" in Jewish literature (Pss 44:5; 129:1–3; Isa 12:1–2; 40:27; 49:14, 21; Jer 10:19–20; Lam 1:19–22; 3:1–21; Mic 7:7–10; 2 Bar 4:1–7).[83] The problem with Kümmel's reasoning, as Dunn noted, is that any claim that the "I" refers to all people in general cannot, by definition, exclude Paul himself.[84]

The Gentile God-Fearer's Experience of Life "under" the Law

Stanley Stowers has challenged the autobiographical interpretation of the "I" with a vigorous case that the "I" refers to *gentile* experience. With respect to the "personal and confessional" elements of the passage, Stowers chided scholars for anachronism in failing to recognize how Rom 7:14–25, *including* its use of the first person singular and the tone, would have been heard in a first century context.[85] "I do not understand my own actions. For I do not do what I want, but I do the very thing I hate" (Rom 7:15). "For I do not do the good I want, but the evil I do not want is what I do" (Rom 7:19). Commentators have long recognized that such sayings were common in the Greco-Roman world, and the widespread parallels may be traced to Euripides' *Medea*, a character whose desire for revenge leads her, against her better judgment, to kill her children: "I am being overcome by evils. I know that what I am about to do is evil but passion [wrath] is stronger than my reasoned reflection and this is the cause of the worst evils for humans" (*Med.* 1077–80).[86] Phaedra said in Euripides' *Hippolytus*: "What we

---

80. Gundry, "Moral Frustration," 229; Moo, "Israel and Paul in Romans 7.7–12," 128–29; Middendorf, *"I" in the Storm*, 148–57; Theissen, *Psychological Aspects*, 191–201.

81. Theissen, *Psychological Aspects*, 193–94.

82. He signals the rhetorical "I" with "You will say." Other contextual cues signal the rhetorical "I" in Rom 7. See the discussion of Stowers's thesis, which points to the rhetorical question of 7:7 and the change from direct address in 7:1–6 ("you") to 7:7–12 where the "I" comes to the fore and the direct address disappears.

83. N. M. Watson, "The Interpretation of Romans VII," *ABR* 21 (1973): 28–29.

84. Dunn, "Rom. 7,14–25," 260–61; followed by Schreiner, *Romans*, 364; so also Gundry, "Moral Frustration," 229.

85. Stanley K. Stowers, *A Rereading of Romans: Justice, Jews, and Gentiles* (New Haven: Yale Univ. Press, 1994), 260, following Theissen, *Psychological Aspects*, 211–19.

86. As translated by Stowers, *Rereading of Romans*, 260.

know and understand to be noble we fail to carry out" (*Hipp.* 377–83; [Kovacs, LCL]). Plato's Socrates thought that most people do something other than what they know is best (*Prot.* 352d). Aristotle distinguished the impulsive lack of self-mastery from failure that is deliberate and self-aware (note the lengthy discussion in *Eth. nic.* 7). The Stoics asserted that the lack of self-mastery is the result of ignorance and false beliefs. Precedent may be found in earlier authors such as Xenophon who contended that "he who is ignorant of them [the wise and beautiful] *cannot do them,* and even if he tries, will fail" (*Mem.* 3.9.5 [March-ant, LCL]). The wise and prudent will be empowered by that knowledge to do what is beautiful and good. Chrysippus therefore reinterpreted Euripides' *Medea* character from a Stoic standpoint.[87] Seneca, Paul's contemporary, wrote his own *Medea* in which the central character cries out "What, wretched woman, have I done?" as she reflects on the overpowering of her will by anger (a repeated ex-clamation; for example, 1016, 1280: ταλαῖν; cf. 952, 991). Seneca's Phaedra: "I know that what you say is true, nurse; madness [*furor,* one of the passions] forces me to follow the worse path" (*Phaed.* 177–79 [Fitch, LCL]). Epictetus, another contemporary of Paul, reflected on Euripides' *Medea.* Just before introducing her character, Epictetus remarked: "I want something, and it does not happen; and what creature is more wretched than I? I do not want something, and it does happen; and what creature is more wretched than I?" (*Diatr.* 2.17.18; cf. 26 [Oldfather, LCL]). Elsewhere Epictetus wrote:

> For since he who is in error [ἁμαρτάνων] does not wish to err, but to be right, it is clear that he is not doing what he wishes [θέλει]. . . . He, then, who can show . . . and clearly bring home to him how he is not doing what he wishes, and is doing what he does not wish. . . ." (*Diatr.* 2.26.1–4 [Old-father, LCL])

The Platonists opposed the Stoic thinkers by emphasizing the battle that takes place in the soul. Galen contended against the Stoics that the distinct powers of the soul are always struggling against each other (*Hippoc. et. Plat.* 4.2.10–18). So Medea's irrational passion overcame her rational reason (*Hippoc. et. Plat.* 3.4.23–27; 4.2.27; 4.6.19–22).[88] Galen commended education in Greek phi-losophy as the means of empowering the rational faculties to overcome the passions (*Hippoc. et. Plat.* 3.3.13–18: Medea was an uneducated barbarian). In

---

87. See texts and translations in Theissen, *Psychological Aspects,* 214–25.

88. The numbering system and translation are from *Galen: On the Doctrines of Hippocrates and Plato* (ed. and trans. Phillip De Lacy; Corpus Medicorum Graecorum 5.4.1; Berlin: Akademie, 1984).

Diatr. 4.1.147 Epictetus ascribed the inner impulses to divine forces struggling against each other:

> And, indeed, when a man out of passionate love is under the compulsion to do something contrary to his opinion, all the time seeing the better thing but lacking the strength to follow, one might be all the more inclined to regard him as deserving pity, because he is in the grip of something violent, and, in a manner of speaking, divine (Oldfather, LCL).

Likewise Plutarch quoted Euripides: "Wretched I am, this evil comes to men from God, when one knows the good but does it not" (Euripides, frg. 841).[89] Even apart from the debates between the Stoics and their adversaries, Medea's dialogue was frequently quoted in letters and public orations. Ovid (*Met.* 7.17–21): "Come, thrust from your maiden breast these flames that you feel, if you can, unhappy girl [*infelix*]. Ah, if I could, I should be more myself [*sanitor*]. But some strange power draws me on against my will. Desire persuades me one way, reason another. I see the better and approve it, but I follow the worse" (Miller, LCL).[90] Stowers noted how common the cry of despair, "Oh, wretch that I am," was throughout the tragedians and comedians.[91] Euripides' tragedies were prime fodder for the anthologies of quotations used for the instruction of schoolboys in rhetoric (Quintilian, *Inst.* 10.1.67–9; Dio Chrysostom, *Dic. exercit.* [*Or.* 18] 6–7).[92] The original source of the saying was often forgotten once incorporated into the anthology (with respect to Euripides, see Acts 5:39; 26:14; 1 Cor 15:33). In reviewing the Greco-Roman topos of self-mastery, Stowers and others have provided the most direct parallels to Paul's language in Rom 7:14–25 in the use

---

89. As translated by Stowers, *Rereading of Romans*, 272. Plutarch finds pitiable the individual who knows better and yet, because of a lack of self-mastery (ἀκρασία), is influenced by pleasure (*Mor.* 33F). He chides the person who surrenders proper judgment in acquiescing to the pleasures (*Mor.* 446A).

90. Diodorus Siculus (1.71.3): "Oftentimes some who realize that they are about to commit a sin nevertheless do base acts when overpowered by love or hatred or some other passion" (Oldfather, LCL). The Vulgate translates ταλαίπωρος in Rom 7:24 with *infelix*, the same word used by Ovid; Stowers, *Rereading of Romans*, 271–72.

91. Stowers, *Rereading of Romans*, 271–72. For additional parallels to Rom 7:7–25 that also illustrate the Greco-Roman struggle with self-mastery and wrongdoing, see Peder Borgen, "The Contrite Wrongdoer: Condemned or Set Free by the Spirit? Romans 7:7 — 8:4," in Stanton, Longenecker, and Barton, *The Holy Spirit and Christian Origins*, 181–92. Unfortunately, Borgen appeared to be unaware of Stowers's prior work.

92. Abraham J. Malherbe, *Social Aspects of Early Christianity* (2d ed.; Philadelphia: Fortress Press, 1983), 42–43. Malherbe also noted the popularity of Euripides (and Menander) in the ancient papyri.

of the first person, the language of misery and wretchedness, the language of powerful, compelling forces, and the inner conflict with the passions.[93]

Romans 7:7–25 would not have been perceived by first-century readers primarily as an autobiographical or confessional statement but rather as an expression of the lack of self-mastery as transitory desires hinder people's long-term commitments, in this particular case a commitment to the Law of Moses.[94] Apart from the rhetorical use of the "I," the apostle never actually claims in this text that he is speaking of himself. The pathos of the "I" does not correspond to Paul's clearly autobiographical descriptions elsewhere (Phil 3:3–9; Gal 1).[95] Rather Paul is illustrating by the experience of the "I" that the Mosaic Law, far from providing power against the passions, only enhances sin's influence in the flesh. While the language Paul employs is widespread and parallels his larger Greco-Roman context, the situation of Paul's "I" stands in sharp contrast to those very parallels. Whereas Epictetus was confident that the solution for a person who was not doing what he wished lay in increased self-knowledge (*Diatr.* 2.26.1–4), for "Paul, the problem is neither ignorance of the good nor lack of will to do it, but the inability to do the willed good that is known through the law. In other words, he rejects the already-ancient Greek view that knowledge of the good leads to doing the good."[96] Paul is much more pessimistic in his anthropology than his Greco-Roman peers. While the plight of the "I" as Paul describes it parallels language from the tragedians, the "I" is an even more lamentable, desperate figure. The Jewish Law is of no help against the power of sin. The only solution for the gentile who has experienced such life under the Law is in Jesus Christ (v. 25).[97]

---

93. Stowers has been seconded by Thomas H. Tobin, *Paul's Rhetoric in Its Contexts: The Argument of Romans* (Peabody, Mass.: Hendrickson, 2004), 228–38. His review of the Greco-Roman topos of self-mastery supplements that of Stowers. He also reviewed the topos of self-mastery as it was employed by Jewish writers influenced by Hellenism.

94. Stowers, *Rereading of Romans*, 280.

95. Advocates of an autobiographical interpretation offer otherwise valid explanations for the difference in tone, e.g., Das, *Paul, the Law, and the Covenant*, 233. The literary point remains, though, that the pathos itself is absent from Paul's explicitly autobiographical descriptions.

96. Keck, *Romans*, 188. See also the detailed comparison of Paul with these Greco-Roman antecedents provided by Reinhard von Bendemann, "Die kritische Diastase von Wissen, Wollen und Handeln: Traditionsgeschichtliche Spurensuche eines hellenistischen Topos in Römer 7," *ZNW* 95 (2004): 35–63.

97. Romans 7:25 employs an "overlap" technique. Verse 25a introduces the perspective of chap. 8, whereas v. 25b concludes the previous section. Quintilian explains that,

Romans 7:7 must not be minimized in its role as a thesis statement for the rest of the chapter.[98] As Paul Achtemeier helpfully explained, Rom 5:20–21 sets the agenda for the ensuing chapters: the relationships between the Law, sin, and grace. These are quasi-personified cosmic forces that "exercise dominion" and hold people captive (for example, 6:12–22; 7:6). Paul tackles the relationship between sin and grace in 6:1, between Law and grace in 6:15, and he turns to the Law and sin in 7:7. The question Rom 7:7–25 answers is whether the Law is itself sinful, not Paul's own pre-Christian or Christian experience as such. Paul makes claims about the Law that parallel what he just said in the preceding chapter regarding sin. The Law rules over people, holds them captive, and enslaves as does Sin in chap. 6. One must be delivered from captivity "under the old written code" by death, even as baptism in chap. 6 frees the individual from Sin. Paul must therefore explain in 7:7–12 that the Law is not sinful, but Sin simply uses the Law for its own nefarious ends. The power (or lack thereof) of the Law remains the central point, and Paul draws on language that would resonate with his gentile readers in their first-century cultural context. Ben Witherington rightly observed, "The language here is strong, bordering on a concept of being possessed. But Paul says nothing of demons here, only of sin and its power over fallen human beings."[99] What a contrast with the indwelling of the Spirit in chap. 8!

That Paul is not describing his own experience is signaled by the sharp contrast between Rom 7:7–25 and the surrounding paragraphs. Origen noted the contradictions between Rom 7:14–25 and what Paul says of himself elsewhere in his writings (including especially Rom 6 and 8) and concluded that "the discourse has different characterizations [*prosōpopoiiai*] and the sections conform to various qualities of characters [*prosōpa*]."[100] Jerome and Rufinus both agreed with Origen's reasoning and conclusion.[101] *Prosōpopoiia* was introduced

---

like "men who link hands to steady their steps, and lend each other mutual support," the overlap is helpful "wherever it is essential to speak with force, energy, and pugnacity" (*Inst.* 9.4.126–30 [Butler, LCL]). A proper appreciation of the ancient techniques of rhetoric may calm the hearts of commentators who have agonized over the non-linear ABAB pattern in this verse and its context (so also Ben Witherington, with Darlene Hyatt, *Paul's Letter to the Romans: A Socio-Rhetorical Commentary* (Grand Rapids: Eerdmans, 2004), 196.

98. Achtemeier, *Romans*, 102.

99. Witherington, *Romans*, 200.

100. Stowers, *Rereading of Romans*, 267. See Origen, *Comm. Rom.* 6.9 (1085) on the contradictions between Rom 7:7–25 and its surrounding context. He continues the discussion of *persona* in the following discussion of Rom 7:7–25.

101. Likewise also the Greek fragments. See the extended discussion of the primary sources in Stowers, *Rereading of Romans*, 266–68.

in the ancient *progymnasmata*, the preliminary rhetorical exercises practiced by schoolboys. The fourth century BCE *The Rhetoric of Alexander* referred to these rhetorical exercises. Cicero in the first century BCE and the anonymous *Rhetoric for Herennius* reflected knowledge of the exercises.[102] Quintilian in the first century CE referred to "speech-in-character": "When we pretend that the persons concerned themselves are speaking, the personal note adds to the emotional effect."[103] Suetonius in the second century CE described the rhetorical exercises practiced in the early first century CE, including characterization (*Gramm.* 4; *Rhet.* 1). All the extant handbooks of rhetoric—by Aelius Theon (first century CE?), Hermogenes (second century CE), Aphthonius, Nicolaus the Sophist, and John of Sardis—describe *prosōpopoiia* or "speech-in-character" (*ēthopoiia* in the later rhetorical tradition).[104] Theon: "Personification [Gk. *prosōpopoeia*] is the introduction of a person to whom words are attributed that are suitable to the speaker and have an indisputable application to the subject discussed."[105] The young student of rhetoric in the grammar school would compose poetry or prose to be recited. Students grew accustomed to identifying through the speaking voice the particular character. As Stanley Stowers explained:

> In every passage the student had to ask, "who is speaking." Homer, for example, was the favorite text for elementary instruction although many others were also used. Sometimes Homer speaks in the authorial voice; sometimes one character or another speaks but often without the poet specifically indicating that such-and-such has begun to speak except by keeping the words in character with the speaker. The problem of identifying speakers occurs in most types of literature. . . .[106]

---

102. Cicero, *Inv.* 1.19 §27; 1.52 §§99–100; *Part. or.* 16 §55; 17 §57; *De or.* 3.53 §205; *Rhet. Her.* 1.8 §12; 4.43 §§56–57; 4.53 §66 ("language . . . appropriate to its character").

103. *Inst.* 6.1.25–27 (Butler, LCL); see also on *prosōpopoiia* 1.8.3; 3.8.49–54; 4.1.28, 69; 9.2.29–39; 11.1.39–41.

104. George A. Kennedy, *Progymnasmata: Greek Textbooks of Prose Composition and Rhetoric* (WGRW 10; Atlanta: SBL, 2003), 47–49, 84–85, 115–17, 164–66, 213–17. Aelius Theon's was made available with a critical text, English translation, and notes by James R. Butts, "The Progymnasmata of Theon: A New Text with Translation and Commentary" (Ph.D. diss., Claremont Graduate School, 1986).

105. Kennedy, *Progymnasmata*, 47.

106. Stowers, "Romans 7.7–25 as a Speech-in-Character (προσωποποιία)," in *Paul in His Hellenistic Context* (ed. Troels Engberg-Pedersen; Minneapolis: Fortress Press, 1995), 183. Aristarchus of Byzantium attempted to solve the contradictions in Homer by properly distinguishing Homer's voice from the voice of his characters (Stowers, *Rereading Romans*, 18–19). The Greek translations of the Psalms and Song of Solomon proved especially difficult in identifying speakers. Although skilled in basic apostrophe

Ps-Longinus in the first century CE instructed his readers with reference to Homer:

> Again sometimes a writer, while speaking about a person [περὶ προσώπου] suddenly turns and changes into the person himself [αὐτοπρόσωπον]. A figure of this kind is a sort of outbreak of emotion:
>
> > Hector lifted his voice and cried afar to the Trojans
> > To rush back now to the galleys and leave the blood-splattered booty.
> > Whomsoever I see of his own will afar from the galleys,
> > Death for him there will I plan." [*Il.* 15.346–9]
>
> There the poet has assigned the narrative to himself as his proper share, and then suddenly without any warning attached the abrupt threat to the angry champion. To insert "Hector said so and so" would have been frigid. (*On the Sublime*, 249–51; Fyfe, LCL)

Readers of ancient written texts were used to recognizing without any punctuation or explicit signal the change of voice as the author conveyed the character of a person (*prosōpon*).[107] The persona would fit a recognizable stock type, usually

---

and προσωποποιία, no one has claimed that Paul had advanced rhetorical training. On this question and the false dichotomy between Paul's receiving advanced rhetorical training or none at all, see Stanley K. Stowers, "Apostrophe, Προσωποποιία, and Paul's Rhetorical Education," in *Early Christianity and Classical Culture: Comparative Studies in Honor of Abraham J. Malherbe* (ed. John T. Fitzgerald, Thomas H. Olbricht, and L. Michael White; NovTSup 110; Leiden: Brill, 2003), 367–69. Stowers noted that προσωποποιία appeared "in many forms of ancient literature and in literature and writings of people from various social, economic, and ethnic contexts" ("Apostrophe," 362). David Daube, in a widely recognized article, demonstrated the influence of Greco-Roman rhetoric upon Jewish authors and teachers ("Rabbinic Methods of Interpretation and Hellenistic Rhetoric," *HUCA* 22 [1949]: 239–62).

107. Quintilian, *Inst.* 1.8.3: "Neither is it good, like some teachers to indicate speech-in-character in the manner of a comic actor, even though one ought to make use of some modulation of voice [when reading] in order to distinguish speech-in-character from where the poet is speaking in his own person" (as translated by Stowers, "Apostrophe, Προσωποποιία, Rhetoric," 354). The poet's voice was read one way and the character's another in order to distinguish them. Similarly Quintilian 9.2.36–7:

> We may also introduce some imaginary person without identifying him, as we do in the phrases, "At this point some one will interpose," or, "Some one will say." Or speech may be inserted without any mention of the speaker, as in the line: "Here the Dolopian host camped, here the fierce Achilles pitched his tent." [Virg. *Aen.* 2.29] This involves a mixture of *figures*, since to *impersonation* [προσωποποιία] we add the *figure* known as *ellipse*, which

from Greek and Roman drama.[108] Pathos, or great emotion, would be necessary for the speech of certain characters. Stowers pointed out: "Instances where the poet or speaker seem to contradict themselves or speak out of character may mean that the words have been attributed to the wrong person."[109] The ancient grammarians therefore taught at length that the words attributed to a person must be appropriate to that person's character. Dissonance from preceding speech was one signal of a change in the character speaking. Nilus of Ancyra, therefore, independently of Origen, recognized Rom 7:7–25 as an instance of "speech-in-character" or, what he called with the later rhetorical tradition, *ēthopoiia*: "God forbid! The divine apostle does not say concerning himself that 'I see another law in my members taking me captive through sin.' Rather these things are uttered by a person [ἐκ προσώπου] representing those who are troubled by fleshly passions [σαρκικῶν παθῶν]" (*Ep.* 1.152 [*PG* 79:145–6]).[110] Nilus also wrote:

> It is easy to grasp that the apostle is employing characterization [ἠθοποιία] when a voice says, "But I was once living without the law." And truly there is never any time when a person has respite without the law of Moses; for from a young age he was closely brought up in the law by Gamaliel. Moreover, the person [τὸ πρόσωπον] is to be understood as belonging to those who have lived outside the law of Moses. (*Ep.* 1.153 [*PG* 79:145–6])[111]

For Nilus, the "I" must be someone who was "outside" the Law of Moses and subsequently came under it. The "I" must be *a gentile God-fearer*.

Works employing *prosōpopoiia* were popular in Rome in Paul's day. For instance, Ovid's *Heroides* consisted of imaginary letters by legendary women.[112] Stowers pointed to numerous instances of apostrophe and προσωποποιία in

---

in this case consists in the omission of any indication as to who is speaking (Butler, LCL).

Stowers commented: "Ancient readers were accustomed . . . to read/hear προσωποποιία and related techniques, but . . . we are not" ("Apostrophe, Προσωποποιία, Rhetoric," 356).

108. J. Albert Harrill, *Slaves in the New Testament: Literary, Social, and Moral Dimensions* (Minneapolis: Fortress Press, 2006), 18–30, has drawn attention to the "slave" persona in the handbook tradition as most directly relevant for the interpretation of the *prosopoiia* in Rom 7:7–25.

109. Stowers, "Romans 7.7–25," 184.

110. As translated by Stowers, *Rereading of Romans,* 268. So also Didymus of Alexandria.

111. As translated by Stowers, *Rereading of Romans,* 268.

112. Ibid., 271.

Philo and Epictetus, near contemporaries of Paul.[113] Paul's abrupt change in voice to the first person after a rhetorical question would help signal the shift to *prosōpopoiia* in v. 7. The grammarians and rhetoricians labeled such a change in voice ἐναλλαγή or μεταβολή. Ancient audiences would then listen for διαφ-ωνία, a difference in characterization from the authorial voice, which is exactly what one finds in 7:7–25 with the slavery and helplessness of the "I" *under* the Law.[114] Paul describes a past without the Law (7:7–8), the present misery, and a future plight (7:24). The monologue fits a speech-in-character. In their rhetorical handbooks for students of *prosōpopoiia*, Hermogenes and Aphthonius recommended elaborating on the past, present, and future experience of the character. Aphthonius's Niobe began in the present bemoaning the loss of her children, shifted to the past and the origin of the predicament, and then reflected on future possibility. Such emotion-laden speeches were typical in the handbook illustrations of speech-in-character.[115] The tragic speeches that served as models for speeches-in-character usually employed the *first person singular*. The use of the first person pronoun therefore offers little or no support for the traditional autobiographical approach as opposed to speech-in-character.

Advocates of an autobiographical "I" have struggled with "I was once alive apart from the law" (v. 9). When was a Jew such as Paul ever "apart from the law"?[116] Jewish children learned the Law of Moses from early on (2 Tim 3:15; Josephus, *Ag. Ap.* 2.18 §178; Philo, *Legat.* 16 §115; 31 §210). Even Origen observed that "apart from the law" did not fit a Jew (*Comm. Rom.* 6.8 [1082]). The Jews never describe themselves as "apart from the Law." For whom would such a statement apply if not a gentile? Gentile God-fearers experienced life apart from the law as pagans, but upon exposure to its precepts they experienced its condemnation of death.[117]

The slavery to the passions and desire, as experienced by the "I," is characteristic for Paul of *gentile* existence. In 1 Thess 4:4–5: "Each one of you [must] know how to control your own body in holiness and honor, not with lustful passion, like the gentiles who do not know God" (NRSV, mod.). Paul is not

---

113. Stowers, "Apostrophe, Προσωποποιία, Rhetoric," 364–65.

114. Stowers, *Rereading of Romans*, 269–70.

115. Aphthonius: Hecuba and Achilles to Patrocles; Niobe's speech.

116. Kümmel, *Römer 7*, 76–77, 81.

117. Holland, "Self against the Self," 265, thought "apart from the law" militates against Stowers's thesis as well. Holland wrongly assumed a moral interpretation of "living" that does not work in Rom 7:7–12, since no one was alive in that sense prior to the Law, except Adam and Eve (for Holland). Without that assumption, the objection dissipates. Schreiner helpfully demonstrated that an experiential understanding of "life" and "death" makes the most sense of Rom 7:7–9.

alone in this regard. Second Temple Jews typically viewed slavery to the passions as characteristic of the gentiles. In the *Letter of Aristeas* 152:

> For the vast majority of humans pollute themselves by promiscuous inter-course, committing great wickedness, and entire countries and cities pride themselves on such things. For they not only have intercourse with men, but they pollute the mothers who bore them and even their daughters. But we have kept our distance from these sins.[118]

In light of the Second Temple Jewish traditions about the gentiles, Paul under-standably never describes the Jews as captive to their appetites and desires. God hands over the idolaters in Rom 1:24 to the "desires" (ἐπιθυμία) of their hearts to practice "impurity" (ἀκαθαρσία). They dishonor their bodies in passion (εἰς πάθη ἀτιμίας; v. 26). So in Rom 7:8 sin works all kinds of "desire." In ancient literature, the "slave to the passions" was typically the ethnic "other" or barbarian. Galen described Euripides' *Medea* as an uneducated barbarian in whom anger prevailed over reason.[119] Stowers wrote:

> One reason the figure of Medea gained such continuing popularity appears in connection with purity of citizenship and ethnicity ("nationality"). Medea stood for foreigners who corrupted the purity of the citizen body, and her saying about *akrasia* connoted the moral degeneracy that mixing with for-eigners would supposedly bring. I find great irony in the fact that Paul the Jew resonates these allusions back to Greeks and Romans who apparently now see themselves as gentiles, outsiders to Judaism described as immoral foreigners.[120]

The "I" is therefore

> A person . . . caught between two cultures. Like Medea, he cannot submit to a foreign law because his gentile passions will not allow it. Rom 7:7–25 represents the judaizing gentile's ambiguous status. Neither fully Jew nor fully Greek, he is torn between the passions of an idolater and the law of the one true God.[121]

The "I" is a gentile God-fearer.

---

118. So Philo promoted the Jewish Law of Moses as the ultimate instrument for gaining mastery over the passions and desire (e.g., *Virt.* 34 §§180–82; *Spec.* 4.15–25 §§92–132).

119. *Hippoc. et Plat.* 3.13.13–18; cf. barbarians as slaves of their desires in 3.3.6; 3.7.14.

120. Stowers, *Rereading of Romans*, 271.

121. Ibid., 278.

Paul identifies the Tenth Commandment in Rom 7:7–12. Not coinciden-
tally, the last time he mentioned the Ten Commandments was in the context
of the Jewish teacher of gentiles in Rom 2:21–22. Stowers corrected the usual
translation of the command from "you shall not covet" to "you shall not desire."[122]
The Septuagint employed ἐπιθυμία in translating the Hebrew original. Many
Second Temple Jews drew on the Septuagintal translation to argue a convergence
between the Law of Moses and the emphasis in Greek moral philosophy on the
passions and desire. Philo, for instance, wrote of the Tenth Commandment:
"The last commandment is against covetousness or desire which he knew to be
a subversive and insidious enemy. For all the passions of the soul which stir and
shake it out of its proper nature and do not let it continue in sound health are
hard to deal with, but desire is hardest of all" (*Decal.* 28 §142 [Colson, LCL]).[123]
The Tenth Commandment "blocks that fountain of injustice, desire [ἐπιθυμία],
from which flow the most iniquitous actions, public and private, small and great,
dealing with things sacred or things profane, affecting bodies and souls and what
are called external things. For nothing escapes desire, and as I have said before,
like a flame in the forest, it spreads abroad and consumes and destroys everything"
(*Decal.* 32 §§173–4 [Colson, LCL]). For Philo, the Jewish Law, because of its
prohibition of desire, was superior to any other set of laws: "The law holds that
all who conform to the sacred constitution laid down by Moses must be exempt
from every unreasoning passion and every vice in a higher degree than those
who are governed by other laws" (*Spec. Leg.* 4.9 §55 [Colson, LCL]). Likewise 4
Macc 2:4–6 interpreted the Tenth Commandment as a prohibition against desire. Second Temple Jews would therefore enthusiastically promote Moses' Law
to the gentiles as an effective instrument of self-mastery to combat desire (for
example, Philo, *Virt.* 33 §§175–9, 34 §182; Josephus, *Ag. Ap.* 2.23 §195, 2.31–32
§§221–35; see also Sir 15:15).[124] This background fits Rom 7 well, since Paul is
arguing *against* any notion that the Law can serve as an instrument for combating
sinful desire. He instead describes the bankruptcy of the Law.

Paul directly addresses his readers and describes their experience with the
Law in Rom 7:1–6 (7:1: ἀδελφοί and second person plural). The last time Paul
addressed the audience as brothers and sisters, he was including them among
the gentiles (1:13).[125] The readers are gentiles (6:19: ἀκαθαρσία; ἀνομία) who

---

122. Ibid.

123. Stowers, *Rereading of Romans*, 60–61, clarified that a "revolutionary" novelty
was negative in this age where antiquity was prized.

124. On this point along with a discussion of the primary sources, see ibid.,
58–64.

125. Ibid., 277.

have come to "know the law" (7:1).[126] Stowers observed that Paul increasingly identified himself with his audience from 4:23 through 6:23 until he reached a sort of apex in 7:1–6 when he addressed them as "brothers" again.[127] He signals the readers again in 7:7 and 7:14 with the first person plural (note: 7:14, "we know"; 7:18, "I know"). Paul does not identify with the Jew until 9:1–5, and he makes this shift in rhetorical identification clear: "my kindred according to the flesh." Paul may be able to relate to the plight of the "I," but the *primary* referent is the gentile God-fearer.[128] The "I" as the gentile encoded reader's experience under the Law in 7:7–25 would fit Paul's rhetorical pattern in the letter.[129] The "I" of Rom 7:7–25 is illustrating the statement of Rom 7:5: "While we [the audience] were living in the flesh, our sinful passions, aroused by the law, were at work in our members to bear fruit for death." Every aspect of the audience's description in v. 5 is unpacked in vv. 7–25: "living," "flesh," "sinful," "passions," "the law," "members," "death." The "I" of 7:7–25 is describing Paul's readers as they find themselves as God-fearers under sin and the Law. Paul therefore responds to the plight of the "I" in Rom 8:2: "For the law of the Spirit of life in Christ Jesus has set *you* free from the law of sin and death."[130]

In his monograph defending the traditional view of the "I" as Paul's Christian experience, Michael Middendorf tellingly conceded in a footnote:

> In the case of Paul's readers who had formerly been Gentile unbelievers and had then come to know the Law through the synagogue before conversion to Christianity, many of the difficulties involved in determining when or in what manner the "I" was live "apart from the Law" and then experienced a coming of the commandment readily vanish (v. 9). . . . It was admitted that

---

126. On Rom 6:19 as evidence for the gentile identity of the addressees, see chap. 2, above.

127. Stowers, *Rereading of Romans*, 277.

128. Holland, "Self against the Self," 268–71, argued that Paul is identifying himself with the gentile "I." If correct, the gentile would, for the reasons enumerated, remain the primary referent of the "I." It is difficult to conceive of Paul characterizing a blameless Jew such as himself as a slave to desire in a manner analogous to gentile existence.

129. Holland, "Self against the Self," 263; cf. p. 268, therefore wrote: "Significantly, this direct address ['brothers'; 7:1, 4] appears just before Paul's identification with his readers in their past and present situation as described in Rom. 7.5–6. Within this context, Rom. 7.7–25 may be seen as a reiteration and expansion of ideas introduced and explored in the previous chapters, using the first-person singular in place of the first-person plural."

130. The Alexandrian and Western witnesses converge in reading σε. See Bruce M. Metzger, *A Textual Commentary on the Greek New Testament* (Stuttgart: United Bible Societies, 1971), 516. The "I" is therefore not autobiographical.

the interpretation adopted here did not take the most literal sense of χωρὶς νόμου in verses 8–9. If the literal sense is insisted upon, the meaning of this phrase could be applied literally to Paul's Gentile readers whose role Paul is at least partially adopting through the "I."[131]

With Stowers: "All Paul's rhetoric . . . makes sense if we suppose that Paul's literary audience represents something like those who have traditionally been called godfearers in modern scholarship. From beginning to end, Romans presupposes an audience that consists of gentiles who had or still have a lively interest in Judaism."[132] The contrast between the "I" who is fleshly and "under sin" in 7:14 with Rom 6:1 — 7:6 and 8:1–17 is comprehensible since Paul is personifying gentile God-fearers' experience under the Law. The "I" was once "apart from the law," but upon encountering the Mosaic commandments, experienced a sort of death. Although the gentile "I" treasured the newfound Law, as did the Jews, it found itself helpless against the sinful desires ruling the flesh. As in both the popular and literary cultures of the day, the "I" could will the good but was unable to accomplish it. The "I" experienced the wretched misery of a Medea-like character with no control over the passions. The answer to this inability to control the passions of sin is not the Law but rather Jesus Christ (7:25a).[133] A gentile audience, including a number of God-fearers, would solve the various conundrums of Rom 7:7–25.

Romans 11:25–26: New Emphases

Reading Romans in light of its gentile audience will draw greater attention to certain passages. For instance, in Rom 11:26 Paul declares: "All Israel will be saved." Romans 11:25–26 is a difficult passage that has been interpreted in variety of ways, but the reception by its original hearers must be considered. One attractive approach to these verses in a modern age of interreligious dialogue contends that, whereas Christ is the savior of the gentiles, Israel will be saved by its own special path. John Gager attempted to reinvigorate this approach in his book *Reinventing Paul*.[134] True to its title, the book proved to be a reinvention of Paul — not Paul in his original context. Gager relied extensively on the prior work of Lloyd Gaston as well as his own *The Origins of Anti-Semitism*.

---

131. Middendorf, *"I" in the Storm*, 239–40 n. 23.

132. Stowers, *Rereading of Romans*, 277.

133. Seifrid, "Subject of Rom 7:14–25," 313–23, found parallels for Paul's language in Jewish penitential prayers and confessions. These prayers would likewise resonate with a God-fearer's experience under the Law.

134. John G. Gager, *Reinventing Paul* (Oxford: Oxford Univ. Press, 2000).

The approach of Gager and Gaston has been criticized at length through the years and has gained few adherents.[135] As N. T. Wright commented: "If Paul has indeed, while writing the letter, received as some have suggested a fresh revelation to the effect that the whole Jewish race will at the last day be saved by some special means, he did the wrong thing by adding it to what he had previously written. He would have done better to put the previous eleven chapters on the fire."[136] Paul goes out of his way to say the exact opposite: there is *no* special path or means for gentiles *or Jews.* "All Israel will be saved" in 11:26 parallels "all (who call on the name of the Lord) will be saved" in 10:13.[137] Israel's salvation can be in no other manner than by the faith in Christ articulated in 10:9–13. Both Jews and gentiles have the same Lord (10:9). God acts impartially by judging Jews and gentiles the same way (Rom 2:1–29) and by saving them the same way (1:16; 3:21–31; 10:9–21: note the emphasis in both passages on "all"). Romans 11:26 is by no means contradicting or abandoning Paul's repeated claims that there is no special path to God apart from faith in Christ.

"All Israel" as the Church: N. T. Wright

In his 2002 Romans commentary N. T. Wright has championed the most compelling and articulate case to date that the words "all Israel will be saved" (Rom 11:26) refer to the believing Jews and gentiles of the Church.[138] Wright's position represented a change of mind; he formerly held that Paul envisioned a future conversion of the bulk of ethnic Israel. The whole family of Abraham in the present age, whether Jews or gentiles, will come to Christian faith through

---

135. For two of the more detailed critiques, see Das, *Paul and the Jews,* 96–106, and E. Elizabeth Johnson, *The Function of Apocalyptic and Wisdom Traditions in Romans 9–11* (SBLDS 109; Atlanta: Scholars, 1989), 176–205. See also Lisa Wang, "Jesus as Messiah in Galatians and Romans: A Response to John Gager's *Reinventing Paul,*" *TJT* 19 (2003): 173–82; Reidar Hvalvik, "A 'Sonderweg' for Israel: A Critical Examination of a Current Interpretation of Romans 11.25–27," *JSNT* 38 (1990): 87–107; Bruce W. Longenecker, "Different Answers to the Different Issues: Israel, the Gentiles and Salvation History in Romans 9–11," *JSNT* 36 (1989): 95–123.

136. N. T. Wright, "The Letter to the Romans: Introduction, Commentary, and Reflections," in *NIB* 10 (Nashville: Abingdon, 2002), 689.

137. Das, *Paul and the Jews,* 104; Wright, "Letter to the Romans," 690.

138. Wright, "The Letter to the Romans," *NIB* 10. See also idem, *Climax of the Covenant: Christ and the Law in Pauline Theology* (Minneapolis: Fortress Press, 1991), 249–51; Hervé Ponsot, "Et ainsi tout Israel sauvé; Rom., XI, 26a," *RB* 89 (1982): 406–17.

a "steady process." If Wright were correct, Rom 11:26 would express the very point Wright had been making for the entirety of Paul's letters, and indeed for the New Testament as a whole. God's historic people in the Christ would now include the gentiles. A Church consisting of both Jew and gentile is "the new people of God." Paul does not articulate a future conversion of ethnic Israel earlier in Romans, nor, for that matter, elsewhere in his letters. For Wright, the explanatory scriptural citations in Rom 11:26b–27 say nothing more than Rom 9:24–26 and 10:6–13: God has incorporated the gentiles into "all Israel."[139] He sarcastically (and rather humorously) scoffed at "the last-minute version of the 'favored nation clause,'" a reference to the majority position that envisions a future for ethnic Israel.[140] The question is the *plausibility* of Wright's reading of Rom 11:26.

Wright argued for the Church as Israel on the basis of Rom 9:6:

> In particular, 9:6 gives the lie to the constantly repeated assertion that one cannot make "Israel" in 11:26 mean something different from what it means in 11:25. "Not all who are of Israel are in fact Israel"; Paul opened his great argument with a clear signal that he was redefining "Israel," and here [in 11:26] that argument comes full circle.[141]

As attractive as Wright's position is, he has not resolved the difficult exegetical hurdles. Wright explained that Paul in Rom 9:6 — 11:25b has consistently distinguished between two categories of Israel: the believing remnant and the unbelieving majority. Wright therefore translated the hardening ἀπὸ μέρους in 11:25a as a hardening "*in part*" (parallel to Rom 15:15; rather than "for a while" as in Rom 15:24). "While one part of 'Israel' constitutes the 'remnant,' the other part of 'Israel according to the flesh' — the great majority — has been 'hardened.'"[142] He further commented on this phrase in 11:25a and the distinction between the part and the remainder:

> Following 11:7, it [ἀπὸ μέρους] implies a division between the Israel that is hardened and the Israel that has become the "remnant": "the remnant obtained it, but the rest were hardened." This reminds us that from the very beginning of the discussion Paul made it clear that there were two categories of Abraham's children (9:7–8), and indeed two categories of "Israel" itself.[143]

---

139. Wright, "Letter to the Romans," 691.
140. Ibid., 693.
141. Ibid., 690.
142. Ibid., 688.
143. Ibid.

In Wright's discussion of Rom 9:6 and the redefinition of Israel, he conceded (perhaps without realizing?) that Paul in these chapters never includes gentiles in "Israel." Wright recognized that Paul limits the true Israel to those *within* ethnic Israel who believe. Paul explains in Rom 9:6–29 that God always distinguished between the descendants of Abraham as a whole and a believing remnant subgroup. The statement in Rom 9:6 that "not all Israel is Israel" is not, then, a reference to gentiles. Likewise the contrast in Rom 11:1–7 is between the majority of ethnic Israel and a remnant within ethnic Israel (esp. v. 7). By "Israel" the apostle always means either the Jewish people as an ethnic group or a believing remnant within that people. In Rom 9:4–5 Paul speaks of Israelites as *his kindred according to the flesh* to whom belong the covenants, the giving of the Law, and the fathers. Here he is speaking of ethnic Israel as a whole (so also 11:1–2). The entity of Israel is contrasted with the gentiles in 9:30–31. In 11:28 he refers to ethnic Israel as the object of hope: they are beloved for the sake of the fathers as regards election, even though they are enemies of God as regards the gospel. In other words, while the apostle certainly applies the term "Israel" with different senses throughout Rom 9–11, he *never* includes gentiles in an entity called "Israel."[144] Paul is absorbed in these chapters with the fate of his own people.

Paul rhetorically addresses "you gentiles" in Rom 11:13 and distinguishes them with second-person pronouns from Israelites for whom he employs third-person pronouns. He maintains a strict distinction between "you [gentiles]" and "those [Israelites]" throughout his ensuing discussion of the grafting of gentiles onto the olive tree representing Israel. "You" are the wild olive shoots while "they" are the natural branches (11:17–24). Paul continues to speak consistently of "Israel" as a group *distinct* from the gentiles in v. 25. In 11:28: "As regards the gospel *they* are enemies of God for *your* sake; but as regards election *they* are beloved, for the sake of *their ancestors*" (emphasis added). The subject of v. 28's "enemies with respect to the Gospel" remains unexpressed and *assumes the same subject as in vv. 26–27*. Even as the "enemies" of v. 28 refers to ethnic Israelites, as distinguished from the gentiles, so also must "all Israel" in 11:26 refer to ethnic Israelites. This

---

144. As Gottlob Schrenk, "Was bedeutet 'Israel Gottes'?" *Judaica* 5 (1949): 81–82, pointed out, Paul never signals a change of referent from what preceded in Rom 9–11: "Liest man die voranstehenden thematischen Verse Röm. 9, 4–6, vergleicht dann besonders 9,27–29 und 11,1–8 und muß feststellen, daß in diesen 3 Kapiteln durchweg der Sprachgebrauch ganz einhellig ist: Israel = die Juden als Gottesvolk — so erscheint es von vornherein als ganz unwahrscheinlich, daß einmal 11,26 Israel in einem ganz neuen Sinne auftreten sollte, ohne jede Erläuterung."

consistent distinction in 11:11–32 is a continuation of the pattern throughout Rom 9–10. Israel and the gentiles are contrasted in Rom 9:30—10:21. In 10:1 Paul addresses his audience as "brothers and sisters" and then speaks of Israel in the third person in 10:1–3 (see also 9:30–32). Nothing in Rom 11:26's "Israel" signals a change from Paul's consistent pattern of distinguishing "you" gentiles and "them" (Israel). Paul has, in fact, maintained a consistent distinction between Jew and gentile throughout the entire letter (for example, Rom 1:16; 3:1–2; 4:11–12; 15:8–9).

The logic of the olive tree imagery in Rom 11 requires that "Israel" remain exclusive of the gentiles. Israel represents the natural branches of an olive tree, but some of the natural branches are broken off and wild (gentile) branches are engrafted. Paul warns the wild branches that the natural branches may just as well be grafted back in and restored. The imagery proceeds from Israel (natural branches) to gentiles (engrafted wild branches) back to Israel (removed natural branches restored). The wild and natural branches always remain distinct in their identities. Verses 25–26 build on this discussion and maintain the same progression: Israel (a hardening upon part of Israel) — gentiles (the full number) — Israel (will be saved). The gentiles are benefiting *as gentiles* from what God is doing for his historic people Israel.

"All Israel" is a phrase with ample precedent in the Hebrew Bible and Greek Septuagint. Wright granted that "all Israel" in the Hebrew Bible normally refers to "the great majority of Jews alive at the time," but he noted that in Mal 3:22 the phrase refers to "the whole nation through time."[145] Either usage supports taking "all Israel" in Rom 11:26 as a reference to the bulk of ethnic Israel. "All Israel" is a corporate expression that does not mean every Israelite who ever lived or even every Israelite at the time when "all Israel" is saved. Joseph Fitzmyer pointed out that the 148 instances of "*kol-Yisrael*" in the Old Testament refer invariably to "historic, ethnic Israel."[146] Paul's "all Israel," then, does not likely include gentiles.[147]

---

145. Wright, "Letter to the Romans," 689 n. 455. On the other hand, Wright does not mention that this diachronic usage of "all Israel" is exceedingly rare in the Hebrew Bible. Of the 148 instances of the Hebrew phrase, only three are diachronic. See James M. Scott, "And Then All Israel Will Be Saved," in *Restoration: Old Testament, Jewish, and Christian Perspectives*, 489–527 (ed. idem; JSJSup 72; Leiden: Brill, 2001), 497–507). All the rest are synchronic: all Israel at a particular point in time.

146. Joseph A. Fitzmyer, *Romans* (AB 33; New York: Doubleday, 1993), 623.

147. For a similar conclusion with a more detailed analysis of the OT evidence, see William L. Osborne, "The Old Testament Background of Paul's 'All Israel' in Romans

Wright placed great emphasis on the presence of "now" in some of the ancient manuscripts in 11:30–31: "Just as you were once disobedient to God but have now received mercy because of their disobedience, so they have now been disobedient in order that, by the mercy shown to you, they too may [*now*] receive mercy." Wright concluded: "The mercy that is shown to Israel according to the flesh is not something for which they will have to wait until some putative final day. . . . It is available 'now'; and Paul's kinsfolk can, he hopes and believes, be provoked into seeking it by being 'jealous' of the way in which Israel's privileges are being enjoyed by Gentiles."[148] Leander Keck commented on this aspect of Wright's reasoning: "The textual uncertainty of the 'now' suggests caution in interpreting this verse."[149] The salvation of "all Israel" is a *future* event that does not detract from the reality of the present situation. Romans 9:1–5 is not a "sham." Romans 10:1 is no "mere formality."[150] With Keck, "Paul does not thereby detract from what he had said in 9:6, because, we may infer, he distinguishes the phenomenon 'Israel' in history (based on election) from the Israel that will be saved on the day of salvation."[151] As Paul puts it in Rom 11:25, a hardening of Israel has taken place "*until* the full number of the gentiles has come in." The temporal limitation of Israel's hardening could not be more clearly expressed. Paul continues: "And *then*/and so all Israel will be saved." Both translations are grammatically possible, and both have merit in this context.[152] Because of these temporal considerations, God can treat the same "hardened" Israel as both "enemies" and "beloved" without fear of contradiction. The disobedience of the

---

11:26a," *AJT* 2 (1988): 284–87: "It is a collective word used for a whole people who may or may not have saving faith" (p. 287). See the discussion of Scott's work below.

148. Wright, "Letter to the Romans," 694.

149. Keck, *Romans*, 285.

150. As Wright, "Letter to the Romans," 689, put it.

151. Keck, *Romans*, 280.

152. For a plausible case for translating καὶ οὕτως as "and then," see Pieter W. van der Horst, "'Only Then Will All Israel Be Saved': A Short Note on the Meaning of καὶ οὕτως in Romans 11:26," *JBL* 119 (2000): 521–5. He demonstrates that the temporal οὕτως (and οὕτω) is amply attested in secular, biblical, and early Christian literature (Thucydides, *Hist.* 3.96.2; Plato, *Prot.* 314c; Plato, *Gorg.* 457d; Xenophon, *Anab.* 7.1.4; Xenophon, *Cyr.* 2.1.1; Aristotle, *Poet.* 17.1455b; *Tabula Cebetis* 19.1; Epictetus, *Diatr.* 2.15.8; *T. Ab.* (rec. A) 7:11; Acts 7:8; 20:11 (note the NRSV's temporal translation); 27:17; 1 Thess 4:16–17). For original texts and translations, see Michael E. Stone, *The Testament of Abraham: The Greek Recensions* (TT 2; Missoula: Society of Biblical Literature, 1972), 18–19; John T. Fitzgerald and L. Michael White, *The Tabula of Cebes* (TT 24; Chico, Calif.: Scholars, 1983), 90–91.

Jews serves a specific, historical role in God's plan. "God's mercy (like God's im-partial justice) treats Gentiles and Jews *in the same way* (all are "imprisoned" in disobedience), but *not at the same time*."[153] A slightly modified version of Keck's chart offers a helpful summary of vv. 30–31.

Past	Agency	Now
As with gentiles who disobeyed,	but by means of Israel's disobedience	have received mercy...
so also with Israel who disobeyed,	but now that gentiles have received mercy	they, also, will receive mercy.

Even as disobedient gentiles have received mercy, so also disobedient, hardened Israelite "enemies" may also receive mercy.[154]

Wright appealed to *m. Sanh.* 10:1 as proof that Paul must be working with a redefined Israel inclusive of the gentiles: "All Israelites have a share in the world to come." Wright concluded that Paul is echoing that tradition. Wright emphasized the exceptions that follow 10:1 enumerating the Israelites that do *not* have a share in the world to come. The exceptions prove to Wright that "all Israelites" does not refer to the majority of ethnic Israel.[155] The rabbis listed as excluded from "all Israel" the Flood generation, the Sodomites, the wilderness generation, the three kings Jeroboam, Ahab, and Manasseh, and the four commoners Balaam, Doeg, Ahitophel, and Gehazi. Also excluded was Korah's group that rebelled against Moses. Apostates were mentioned as excluded. In other words, only the most egregious sinners throughout the history of "Israel" were excluded. They were people who had consciously forsaken the relationship that Israel enjoyed with the God of Abraham, Isaac, and Jacob. The vast majority of ethnic Israel, on the other hand, would enjoy a place in the world to come. Paul's "all Israel," if indeed parallel to the logic regarding "all Israelites" in *m. Sanh.* 10:1, must include the bulk of ethnic Israel.[156]

---

153. Keck, *Romans*, 283.

154. Ibid., 284.

155. Wright, "Letter to the Romans," 689–90.

156. With E. P. Sanders, *Paul and Palestinian Judaism: A Comparison of Patterns of Religion* (Philadelphia: Fortress Press, 1977), 147–50. Wright is certainly correct that Paul has qualified any claim to "Israel" on the basis of faith in Christ, but that does not rule out a future action on behalf of ethnic Israel, as long as such salvation is on the same basis of faith in Christ.

Wright contended that "all Israel" "is best taken as a polemical redefinition, in line with Paul's redefinition of 'Jew' in 2:29, of 'circumcision' in 2:29 and Phil 3:3, and of 'seed of Abraham' in Rom 4, Gal 3, and Rom 9:6–9. It belongs with what seems indubitably the correct reading of 'the Israel of God' in Gal 6:16."[157] No one would dispute Wright's contention that Paul has redefined "circumcision" and the "Jew" in Rom 2:29 or Abraham's descendants in 4:9–12 to include reference to uncircumcised, obedient gentiles. The real question is whether Paul redefines "Israel" in Rom 11:26 to include the gentiles in an analogous fashion, or whether he reserves the term "Israel" in 11:26 to express also his hope for his own people. Wright noted the recent shift in scholarship to favoring "Israel of God" in Gal 6:16 as a reference to the Church.[158] Certainly strong arguments may be marshaled in support of an "Israel of God" inclusive of the gentiles in Gal 6:16. If correctly interpreted, the parallel in Gal 6:16 would render attractive a reading of the Church as Israel in Rom 11:26. Unfortunately, Gal 6:16 is not the clear verse Wright assumed, as the history of scholarship attests. While Paul may be equating "those who will follow this rule" with "the Israel of God," he may also be speaking of two *separate* groups: Paul's gentile readers and a *true* Israel. Paul may be opposing the false "Israel" in the Galatians' midst who were promoting gentile circumcision.[159] The crux is whether "Israel of God" is inclusive of the gentiles in the phrase immediately preceding (an epexegetical καί —renaming the previous group and inclusive of circumcised and uncircumcised) or whether "Israel of God" is exclusive and referring to a *separate* group consisting of Jewish Christians (conjunctive καί).[160] Paul closes the letter in Gal 6:10–16, as he opened it in 1:6–9, on a fiercely polemical note as he contrasts the message of his rivals with the cross of Jesus Christ.[161] In this heated exchange Paul is likely blessing Jewish Christians who are loyal to his gospel message that neither circumcision nor uncircumcision is anything in comparison to the new creation in Christ. He warns against the false brethren in the Galatians' midst (1:8–9; 2:4–5).[162] He distinguishes "Jews by birth" who should recognize

---

157. Wright, "Letter to the Romans," 690.

158. Ibid., 690 n. 458.

159. See the discussion in Das, *Paul and the Jews*, 44–46.

160. For example, Hans Dieter Betz, *Galatians* (Hermeneia; Philadelphia: Fortress Press, 1979), 322–23.

161. Jeffrey A. D. Weima, "Gal. 6:11–18: A Hermeneutical Key to the Galatian Letter," *CTJ* 28 (1993): 90–107.

162. Thus also Gottlob Schrenk, "Der Segenswunsch nach der Kampfepistel," *Judaica* 6 (1950): 177–86. On this point and the OT background to the phrase, see

justification by faith from both gentile "sinners" and "false [Jewish] believers" in Gal 2:4–5, 11–16. While both Jew and Greek are "one" in Christ in 3:29, they do not lose their identities as Jew or Greek.[163] Peter's mission is to the circumcised and Paul's to the uncircumcised in Gal 2:8–9. Paul is therefore denigrating the Jewish Christian Teachers, who demand circumcision as necessary to salvation (contrary to the "rule" of Gal 6:15), by referring to the *true* Israel, the Israel of God. Peter Richardson wrote on the unusual grammar of this verse:

> If it [the second καί] were omitted, the sentence could be interpreted too readily in line with the position of Dahl: namely, "peace and mercy be upon all who walk by this rule, upon the Israel of God" (= RSV), where the last phrase defines the first. But the addition of *kai* should prevent such an interpretation by calling attention to the last four words of the sentence, and by demanding for them special consideration. *Kai* may be construed as ascensive, but only slightly so; the justification for needing any ascensive force at all is that, from the way Paul has argued previously in the letter, one might infer that he was condemning everything about Israel. To forestall this inference he includes this prayer to God for mercy to be shown to Israel.[164]

D. W. B. Robinson, "The Distinction Between Jewish and Gentile Believers in Galatians," *ABR* 13 (1965): 45–48.

163. Analogously, "male" and "female" as such are not abolished even though revalued "in Christ."

164. Peter Richardson, *Israel in the Apostolic Church* (SNTSMS 10; Cambridge: Cambridge Univ. Press, 1969), 82–83. G. K. Beale, "Peace and Mercy upon the Israel of God: The Old Testament Background of Galatians 6, 16b," *Bib* 80 (1999): 204–23, identified an intertextual allusion to Isa 54:10. This may well be the case, but Beale's conclusion that the gentiles will stream into Israel as gentiles does not follow. Isaiah's theology is also fiercely nationalistic. Perhaps Paul's rivals interpreted texts such as Isa 54:10 (and 54:15 LXX) as requiring circumcision of the gentile proselyte. Paul may be appealing to a different trajectory of the interpretation of Isaiah. On the tensions between inclusivism and nationalism in Isaiah, see, for instance, Chris Franke, "Is DI 'PC'? Does Israel Have Most Favored Nation Status? Another Look at 'The Nations' in Deutero-Isaiah," *SBLSP* 38 (Atlanta: Society of Biblical Literature, 1999), 272–91; J. Severino Croatto, "The 'Nations' in the Salvific Oracles of Isaiah," *VT* 55 (2005): 143–62 (who argues that most references to nations streaming into Zion refer to dispersed Jews; the gentiles function entirely negatively); Michael A. Grisanti, "Israel's Mission to the Nations in Isaiah 40–55: An Update," *MSJ* 9 (1998): 39–61; D. W. van Winkle, "The Relationship of the Nations to Yahweh and to Israel in Isaiah XL–LV," *VT* 35 (1985): 446–58; idem, "An Inclusive Authoritative Text in Exclusive Communities," in *Writing and Reading the Scroll of Isaiah: Studies of an Interpretive Tradition* (FIOTL 1; ed. Craig C. Broyles and Craig A. Evans; VTSup 70; Leiden: Brill, 1997) 423–54.

In other words, had Paul wanted to equate "Israel of God" with the Church, he would have omitted the second καί.[165] No early Christian writer applied the phrase "Israel of God" to the Church until Justin Martyr's *Dialogue* in 160 CE.[166] Even assuming that "Israel of God" in Gal 6:16 is a reference to the Church in a fiercely polemical context, Paul is emphasizing a different point in Rom 11:26. The situation at Rome in many ways is the mirror image of the situation at Galatia. Whereas at Galatia, Jewish Christians were promoting circumcision among the gentiles, in Rome some of the gentile Christians did not fully appreciate the Jewish roots of their faith. To the gentile "strong" at Rome and any gentiles less than appreciative of the Jewish origins of the Christian faith, a claim that the Church is Israel to the exclusion of most ethnic Jews would only reinforce a sense of superiority over Israel.

Wright drew attention to Paul's quotation of Isa 59:20–21 without perhaps realizing the challenge this passage poses to his interpretation of Rom 11:26a. Isaiah 59 opens, as Wright explained, with a lament for Israel's continuing sinfulness (vv. 7–8; cited by Paul in Rom 3:15–17 [!]). Yahweh, wearing the breastplate of righteousness and the helmet of salvation, intervenes in Isa 59:17. In 59:20–21 a Deliverer arrives on the scene who banishes ungodliness from Jacob. The Deliverer therefore rectifies the situation of Israel's continuing sinfulness. Israel's unfaithfulness, as lamented by Paul in the words of Isaiah in Rom 11, will give way to a future divinely wrought deliverance.[167] With Rom 11:27 Paul switches from Isa 59 to Isa 27, a passage that speaks of a covenant in which "God will take away Israel's sins" and heal the people of their idolatry and unfaithfulness (cf. 11:23).[168] Wright countered: "[I]t does not make any sense to suppose that in the last minute massive numbers of Jews alive at the time will suddenly arrive at Christian faith."[169] Isaiah, however, envisions a future deliverance from the present unfaithfulness of his people. Paul likewise envisions a future deliverance

---

165. On this point, see also S. Lewis Johnson, Jr., "Paul and the 'Israel of God': An Exegetical and Eschatological Case-Study," *Mishkan* 6–7 (1987): 56–57. Peter Richardson, *Israel in the Apostolic Church*, 74–84, also saw the "Israel of God" as Jewish believers in Christ, but, unlike Betz, he viewed this as a reference to Paul's eschatological hope for Israel, a hope that parallels Rom 11 and is explained there in greater detail.

166. Richardson, *Israel and the Apostolic Church*, 83 n. 2.

167. Contra Wright, see the detailed discussion of Paul's usage of Isa 59:20–21 in J. Ross Wagner, *Heralds of the Good News: Isaiah and Paul in Concert in the Letter to the Romans* (Leiden: Brill, 2002), 280–94.

168. As Wright, "Letter to the Romans," 692, puts it.

169. Ibid.

of his disobedient co-religionists.[170] Wright properly described a suspension of the "hardening" and an "increasing" number of ethnic Jews believing in the Messiah.[171] Certainly gentiles enjoy Israel's privileges as members of God's new people. Gentiles benefit from being grafted onto the olive tree of Israel's gracious heritage. Both believing Israel and the gentiles are together branches on *the same* tree, but instead of Israel losing its identity to the Church, a "third" entity, the gentiles must recognize their dependence upon historic, ethnic Israel's heritage. Although gentiles are benefiting from that heritage, they remain wild branches benefiting *as gentiles.* "All Israel" in Rom 11:26 does not include gentiles.

"All Israel" as the Jewish Remnant throughout History

Ben Merkle recognized that Paul never includes gentiles in "Israel" in Rom 9–11. Merkle offered a thorough, representative case contending that "all Israel" is simply another term for the believing Jewish remnant referred to in Rom 9:1–23 and 11:1–10.[172] "All Israel" in 11:26 refers to believers in Christ throughout time *within* ethnic Israel. This approach takes seriously the categorical statement in Rom 9:6b that "not all Israel is Israel," a distinction Paul maintains in Rom 11:7. Any interpretation of Rom 11, Merkle contended, should be consistent with Rom 9–10, and in those chapters Paul made clear that ethnic Israelites would not be saved on the basis of their ethnic identity (Rom 9:6). Only the elect *within* Israel would be saved (Rom 9:7–10), and they on the basis of faith in Christ (10:12). Merkle concluded that a future conversion of Israel en masse would

---

170. This deliverance will not call into doubt God's impartiality, contra Wright, "Romans," 692, since the basis of that deliverance can be none other than the faith in Christ proclaimed all throughout Romans. Isaiah 27 therefore holds out hope for the people of Israel. As Ross Wagner, *Heralds of the Good News,* 297, put it in his study of Paul's use of Isa 27 in Rom 11: "The branches once pruned from the olive tree due to their unfaithfulness (ἀπιστία, Rom 11:20) have been grafted in again by God, who in removing their sins has *ensured* that they do not remain in ἀπιστία (Rom 11:23)."

171. Wright, "Letter to the Romans," 693.

172. Ben L. Merkle, "Romans 11 and the Future of Ethnic Israel," *JETS* 43 (2000): 709–21; so also François Refoulé, ". . . *Et ainsi tout Israël sera sauvé*": *Romains 11:25–32,* LD 117 (Paris: Cerf, 1984); idem, "Cohérence ou incohérence de Paul in Romains 9–11," *RB* 98 (1991): 51–79; Charles M. Horne, "The Meaning of the Phrase 'And Thus All Israel Will Be Saved,'" *JETS* 21 (1978): 329–34. The remnant approach remains popular in many quarters, e.g., a public lecture by Dr. Greg Beale at Wheaton College in March 2006.

contradict God's express will to save a remnant.[173] The contradiction Merkle perceived between a future mass conversion in 11:26 and the rest of Rom 9–11 is only apparent: God's activity of saving a remnant *in the present* does not rule out the salvation of "all Israel" *in the future*. Paul rhetorically signals that Rom 11 is not repeating the same line of thought as Rom 9–10. In Rom 9:14, 30 Paul asks: "What then are *we* to say?" In Rom 11:1: "*I* say, then, has God rejected his people?" In 11:11: "So *I* ask, have they stumbled so as to fall?"[174] Paul asks the questions as an individual Israelite.

Merkle translated Rom 11:1: "Has God cast off ethnic Israel *altogether?*" In Rom 11:11 Merkle's Paul asks whether the stumbling in Israel have "*completely* forfeited their past privilege." No, Merkle maintained, they have not completely fallen. The presence of a remnant guarantees that God has not cast Israel off completely, in spite of the rejection of the majority.[175] Merkle overlooked the significance of the second half of 11:1, where Paul identifies himself as "an Israelite, a descent of Abraham." As Keck put it so well in his commentary, "Israel *as a people* cannot be rejected if there are Israelites who are not rejected. Paul is not the exception that proves the rule (that Israel is rejected), because *as* a believer he *is* an Israelite (*is* is emphasized in the Greek), a specific instance that demonstrates that God has not rejected the people."[176] Paul then reminds the Romans of Elijah's complaint against Israel and God's revealing the future preservation of seven thousand (1 Kgs 19:18). "For Paul, 'remnant' does not refer simply to what is left over (as in a fabric shop) but to the enduring part that survives disaster and so assures the future."[177] Merkle did not realize that the existence of a "remnant" provides hope for the people *as a whole*.

Gerhard Hasel, in his rather lengthy study of the "remnant" motif throughout the Hebrew Bible and the ancient Near East, explained that the "remnant" motif functions both negatively and positively.[178] Negatively, the existence or complete lack of a remnant attests the destruction of the majority or entirety of a people (Amos 1:6–8; 4:1–3; 5:1–3; 6:9–10; 9:1–4; Isa 10:22–23; 30:15–

---

173. Merkle, "Romans 11," 711–12.

174. Scott Hafemann, "The Salvation of Israel in Romans 11:25–32: A Response to Krister Stendahl," *Ex auditu* 4 (1988): 50.

175. Merkle, "Romans 11," 713.

176. Keck, *Romans*, 264.

177. Ibid., 265.

178. Gerhard F. Hasel, *The Remnant: The History and Theology of the Remnant Idea from Genesis to Isaiah* (Berrien Springs, Mich.: Andrews Univ. Press, 1972). See also, however, Ronald E. Clements, "'A Remnant Chosen by Grace' (Romans 11:5): The Old Testament Background and Origin of the Remnant Concept," in Hagner and Harris, *Pauline Studies*, 106–21.

17). Positively, the existence of a remnant provides hope for the survival and restoration of the people as a whole. *The remnant is never an end in itself.* The remnant, when employed in a positive sense, always provides *the means* for the preservation and restoration of the whole.[179] Noah and those with him function as a "remnant" (וישאר, Gen 7:23b) whose preservation guarantees a future existence for humanity. As in other ancient Near Eastern flood traditions, the remnant bridges humanity's past and its future. Judgment will yield to salvation.[180] Joseph realizes that he had been sent to Egypt to preserve for his family a "remnant" (שארית, Gen 45:7). The family's survival as a whole is dependent upon this "remnant," which would serve as the nucleus for a "great people" in the future. In 1 Kgs 18:22 Elijah recognizes that he is the only one left of the prophets of the Lord at Mt. Carmel.[181] In a darker moment a short while later in 1 Kgs 19:9–18, God reveals to a despondent Elijah at Mount Horeb that he is not the only one left. Seven thousand will survive the impending judgment. They are not an end in themselves but rather the kernel of something larger and greater, a new Israel (similarly Isa 4:2–3, the "holy" "survivors of Israel"; 6:11–13, "the holy seed is its stump"; Isa 10:20–22, "a remnant will return"; Amos 9:11–12 [Edom]; Amos 5:14–15).[182] In Isa 1:8–9, "If the Lord of hosts had not left us a few survivors, we would have been like Sodom and become like Gomorrah." The presence of survivors proffers hope for the continuation of Jerusalem as a city. The Septuagint of Isa 1:9 (cited by Paul in Rom 9:29) describes the survivors as "seed" (σπέρμα) left to Zion. Throughout Isaiah "seed" is the language of promise to the patriarchs (41:8–10) and to Israel itself (43:5; 44:2–3; 45:25; 65:9; 66:22) of a greater, future entity even as God denies a seed to foreign nations in order to remove any possibility of future restoration (14:22, 30; 15:9; 33:2; 48:14).[183] The name of Isaiah's oldest son (Shear-jashub, 7:2–3)

---

179. So also Clements, "Remnant Chosen by Grace." The positive use of the remnant motif functions as a sign of "eschatological hope" "for the restoration of Israel in the future" (p. 112).

180. So also Gen 32 and Jacob's division of his clan so that a remnant would survive should the other group be destroyed.

181. He was the only one left standing publicly on behalf of the Lord. Another hundred were in hiding from Jezebel (1 Kgs 18:4; 19:10, 14).

182. Sir 47:22: a seed of Jacob and the root of David.

183. The "seed of a new generation," "the hope of the world" on the raft guarantees a new generation (Wis 14:6). The seed of Israel will fill the face of the world with their offspring (CD–A II, 11–12). "When Paul appropriates Isaiah's oracle, then, it is with full knowledge of this widely used metaphor of 'seed' as the pledge of a *future* for Israel" (Wagner, *Heralds of the Good News*, 115). Wagner concludes that Rom 11:26 is being anticipated already in the judgment of chap. 9.

means "A-remnant-shall-return," expressing the dual aspects of Isaiah's ministry of announcing *both* judgment *and* hope for the people.[184] Judgment is more imminent, but hope is on the horizon: God-with-*us* (7:14). So even in judgment the prophet draws upon the imagery of the Abrahamic promises: "For though your people were like the sand of the sea, only a remnant of them will return" (Isa 10:20–22; cited in Rom 9:27–28). The prophet contrasts the tiny remnant with the great number promised to Abraham. This is certainly an indicator of the severity of God's judgment, but with Ross Wagner: "At the same time . . . by recalling God's unconditional promise to Abraham, these words remind Israel of God's faithfulness to the covenant he has graciously initiated. The preservation of a remnant of Israel thus holds out hope for a realization of this promise of innumerable descendants on the other side of judgment."[185] In Isa 11:11–12 and 11:16 God gathers from foreign lands the outcasts and dispersed of his people, the remnant (see also Mic 2:12).[186] In Isa 37:30–32, "The surviving remnant of the house of Judah shall again take root downward, and bear fruit upward." The remnant serves as seed for a reconstituted, much larger whole that will spread outward "from Jerusalem" and "from Mount Zion." In Mic 4:7: "The lame I will make the remnant, and those who were cast off, a strong nation." Once again, the remnant is the seed for a "strong nation." In Mic 5:7–8 the prophet looks forward to "the remnant of Jacob" being transformed into something greater and far stronger, "a lion among the animals of the forest." In a somewhat different use of the "remnant" motif in Gen 18:17–33, God announces judgment against

---

184. Clements, "Remnant Chosen by Grace," 108–11, disagreed and interpreted 7:2–3 by means of 10:20–23, where the returning remnant is a sign of judgment rather than hope. The number of those returning in the northern kingdoms will be so few as to be of no consequence. The hopeful remnant passages come from a later period of Isaiah's ministry.

185. Wagner, *Heralds of the Good News*, 102. Isaiah refers to the promise to Abraham of descendants as numerous as the grains of sand in 48:18–19, again in the context of the harsh reality of judgment. God promises that Israel will *not* be eradicated or destroyed. Isaiah 48:20–21 anticipates a new exodus. The prophet refers to the Abrahamic promises again in 51:2–3: God chose to multiply Abraham's descendants and will make Zion prosper. The promise of descendants to Abraham serves as a continual reminder of God's faithfulness and Israel's hope for future blessing. The Septuagintal translation demonstrates that Isa 10:22–23 was perceived also as an oracle of salvation; Wagner, *Heralds of the Good News*, 103–4. Paul in Rom 9:27–29 conflates Isa 10:22–23 with Isa 28:22b to emphasize the shortening of the time of chastisement; Wagner, *Heralds of the Good News*, 104–6.

186. Hasel did not discuss Micah. He limited his overview of the "remnant" motif to Amos and Isaiah. See Dan Johnson, "The Structure and Meaning of Romans 11," *CBQ* 46 (1984): 93–94.

Sodom and the cities of the Plain. Abraham intervenes by questioning whether the majority of evildoers should be destroyed if even ten righteous people dwell in their midst. God concedes that if ten righteous people are present the entire city would be spared. In this instance, hope for the future of a people resides not with the reconstitution of that people from its remnant but with the leavening effect of the few on behalf of the whole: "The minority of a righteous remnant has a preserving function for the wicked majority."[187] To summarize, negatively, the remnant attests to the decisive judgment of a people. Positively, the existence of a remnant in the Hebrew Bible is never an end in itself but always a means to a greater end, whether the reconstitution of the people from that remnant or the remnant's leavening effect on behalf of the whole.

Although most instances of the remnant motif look beyond the remnant to a restored people, the notion of a leavening effect in the Abrahamic narrative may be of significance for the interpretation of Rom 11:16: "If the part of the dough offered as first fruits is holy, then the whole batch is holy; and if the root is holy, then the branches are also holy." Paul refers to the first converts of his ministry in an area as "the first fruits" which foreshadow "the greater, eventual redemptive work of God" (Rom 16:5; 1 Cor 16:5).[188] As Keck commented regarding Rom 11:16:

> The logic of verse 16 is simple and straightforward: What is true of the part is true of the whole. Therefore, Paul implies, when the "fullness" of Israel is actualized, there will be no difference between the present remnant of Israel (= the "first fruits") and the "hardened.". . . Because both the remnant and the hardened are part of the same dough, what is true of the part is ultimately true of the whole as well.[189]

Paul is therefore anticipating v. 26 already in v. 16. The dominant aspect of the remnant motif, however, is the reconstitution of a people from the small remnant left behind. Likewise, in Rom 11 the "remnant" would serve as seed for a reconstituted people in the future. A collected "remnant" from every point in history, as Merkle envisioned, would not change its function as an enduring sign of hope pointing *beyond* itself to the *whole* of Israel at some future point.

Paul draws on the remnant motif in his discussion of Elijah in Rom 11:1–10. Twice in 1 Kgs 9:9–18 Elijah condemns Israel's complete forsaking of God's covenant and says "I alone am left" (vv. 10, 14). The subtext for this story comes

---

187. Hasel, *Remnant*, 389.

188. Johnson, "The Structure and Meaning of Romans 11," 99.

189. Keck, *Romans*, 272–73; so also Hvalvik, "'Sonderweg' for Israel," 90 (following Johnson).

from Exod 32–34. When the Israelites completely forsake the covenant with the Lord at Mt. Sinai in the golden calf incident, God threatens to destroy the apostates and start afresh with Moses (Exod 32:7–10). With Paul's opening focus on himself—"I alone am left"—he appears to be initiating a plea for God to start a new Israel with him. "I myself am an Israelite, a descendant of Abraham, a member of the tribe of Benjamin" (Rom 11:1). The persecuted apostle even expands on this point by saying that Elijah had pleaded "*against* Israel" (11:2). Paul notes, perhaps surprisingly after Rom 11:1, that God *denied* Elijah's suggestion that he act as a substitute for faithless Israel. Elijah (or Paul) as a remnant of one will *not* serve as a replacement for the people of Israel. God will preserve a remnant of seven thousand faithful, which points to an even greater number in the future. Scott Hafemann helpfully summarized the logic:

> The point of the parallel to Elijah is not that Elijah or Paul or the small remnant of the Jews that are currently being saved (cf. 9:27–29) are all alone. The point is the promise to Elijah and to the remnant of Paul's day that their experience points forward to the salvation of a greater number. Rather than judgment on all the rest, the significance of the small, persecuted remnant is that their experience is a symbol of hope for the future of the people.[190]

The remnant is not a replacement for the people as a whole. In Rom 11 the remnant motif has shifted from functioning primarily negatively, as in Rom 9–10, to functioning positively as hope for the future. Those familiar with the remnant motif in the Hebrew Scriptures should not be surprised by this hopeful anticipation.

Merkle explained that the focus in Rom 11 is on the *present:* a present remnant (Rom 11:1, 5), a present hope to render the Jews jealous (11:13–14), and the Jews' present reception of mercy (Rom 11:30–31—assuming with some manuscripts the reading "now" [νῦν]).[191] Merkle noted the argument from Rom 11:23–24 that unbelieving Jews would one day be grafted back onto the olive tree which represents their gracious heritage. As Wayne Meeks articulated it:

---

190. Hafemann, "The Salvation of Israel," 49; Dan Johnson, "Structure and Meaning of Romans 11," 94.

191. If the second νῦν is considered original, it "was probably a way of highlighting the imminence of this second and final phase of 'the now time'" following the first phase of the "now" with mercy to the gentiles and Israel's disobedience; James D. G. Dunn, *Romans 9–16* (WBC 38B; Dallas: Word, 1988), 687. The time of Israel's disobedience is not the same time as Israel's reception of mercy. Moo, *Romans*, 735: "It [the second νῦν] need not mean that the event will infallibly take place within a few years, but it reveals that typical NT perspective which views the new era of fulfillment as already having dawned and all the events belonging to that era as therefore near in time."

"Just as, contrary to all 'natural' expectation, gentiles have been grafted into the people of God, so also, contrary to what now seems evident to gentile Christians, 'all Israel will be saved.'"[192] Merkle responded that Paul is primarily warning against gentile pride. For Merkle, Paul never implied that *all* the branches will be grafted back in. As (some) unbelieving Jews come to faith, they are presently being grafted back in.[193] Merkle is right that Paul refers to present realities in Rom 11, but he also refers to temporal sequences that reach into the future. The remnant is for the *present* time (11:5). The future of Israel will be a time of fullness in contrast to the present (11:12). Paul anticipates Israel's future acceptance (11:15). The hardening of Israel in *the present* is a hardening *until* (ἄχρι οὗ) the fullness of the gentiles comes in, an event which remains in the future. "And then"/"and so" "all Israel will be saved" (11:26).[194] Merkle mistakenly asserted that καὶ οὕτως never has temporal significance.[195] He claimed that the conclusion of the gentile ingathering would be at Christ's return when the hardening

---

192. Wayne A. Meeks, "Judgment and the Brother: Romans 14:1 — 15:13," in *Tradition and Interpretation in the New Testament*, 290–300 (ed. Gerald F. Hawthorne and Otto Betz; Grand Rapids: Eerdmans, 1987), 297.

193. Merkle, "Romans 11," 719.

194. Most commentators translate καὶ οὕτως modally as "and so," and yet maintain a temporal progression with the fullness of the gentiles preceding the salvation of "all Israel." This is for a number of reasons, including the use of ἄχρι in 11:25. Moo wrote: "The 'manner' of Israel's salvation is the process that Paul has outlined in vv. 11–24 and summarized in v. 25b: God imposes a hardening on most of Israel while Gentiles come into the messianic salvation, with the Gentiles' salvation leading in turn to Israel's jealousy and her own salvation. But this means that *houtōs*, while not having a temporal *meaning*, has a temporal *reference*: for the manner in which all Israel is saved involves a process that unfolds in definite stages" (*Romans*, 720).

195. The claim of some scholars that καὶ οὕτως never bears a temporal sense in Greek literature or in the NT is demonstrably wrong (Thucydides, *Hist.* 3.96.2; Plato, *Prot.* 314c; *Gorg.* 457d; Xenophon, *Anab.* 7.1.4; *Cyr.* 2.1.1; Aristotle, *Poet.* 17.1455b; *Tabula Cebetis* 19.1; Epictetus, *Diatr.* 2.15.8; *T. Ab.* [rec. A] 7:11; Acts 7:8; 20:11 [with ἄχρι paralleling Rom 11:25–26]; 27:17; 1 Thess 4:16–17). See van der Horst, "'Only Then Will All Israel Be Saved,'" 521–25, who contends that a temporal sense in Rom 11 is likely because of Paul's use of ἄχρι in the immediate context. James Scott, "And Then All Israel Will Be Saved," 491–92, extended van der Horst's observations: "The Greek Patristic literature in the Thesaurus Lingua Gracae CD-ROM (vol. 3, 1999) shows that καὶ οὕτως in Rom 11:26 was most commonly (73% of 60 citations!) understood in the temporal sense of 'and *then*.' For Greek Patristic texts frequently substitute for καὶ οὕτως some other expression, such as τότε or μετὰ τοῦτο.... Temporal interpretation of Paul's καὶ οὕτως must be [sic] regarded not only as possible on the basis of well-established usage, but also as highly probable in light of the earliest commentaries on our text."

of the Jews would be eschatologically fulfilled but not reversed.[196] The clearly temporal "until," however, is related to *the hardening of Israel's hearts*. The reader therefore anticipates from Paul's "until" *not* the end of the age but rather *a time when Israel's heart will be softened* by the God who has mercy and who hardens (Rom 9:6–29). A removal of hardening suggests a future softening and salvation, which is exactly what Paul claims by the end of v. 26. For Merkle's reading to stand, he must change the referent of "Israel" joltingly within the short span of a single verse from the majority of unbelieving ethnic Israel to a believing minority throughout history.

For Merkle a future conversion of the Jews would contradict Paul's language in 1 Thess 2:14–16 where he claims that God's wrath has come upon the Jews εἰς τέλος, "until the end."[197] Commentators are divided on whether to translate εἰς τέλος as "until the end" (temporal) or "completely" (modal).[198] The eschatological wrath of 1 Thess 2:14–16 is directed, however, against those Jews who persecuted the Judean Christians or those who are deliberately hindering the Christians' missionary work. First Thessalonians 2:14–16 is not a blanket statement of wrath against the Jewish people to the end of time.[199] Abraham Malherbe responded in his commentary to those who connect 1 Thess 2:14–16 and Rom 11:26: "By recognizing that Paul is speaking about his immediate situation in which he was being prevented from preaching to the Gentiles, the need to harmonize the pericope with Romans' history of salvation is removed."[200] Paul employs the apocalyptic language of intra-Jewish polemic with its characteristic

---

196. Merkle, "Romans 11," 715–16.

197. Ibid., 717–18.

198. For a survey of scholars representing both positions, see Jeffrey S. Lamp, "Is Paul Anti-Jewish? *Testament of Levi* 6 in the Interpretation of 1 Thessalonians 2:13–16," *CBQ* 65 (2003): 414.

199. Das, *Paul and the Jews*, 138–39. Frank D. Gilliard, "The Problem of the Antisemitic Comma Between 1 Thessalonians 2.14 and 15," *NTS* 35 [1989]: 481–502), had argued on the basis of syntax that the participial phrase following τῶν ' Ιουδαίων is restrictive and should be set off by a comma. Paul is therefore only pronouncing wrath on these particular Jews. Donald A. Hagner, "Paul's Quarrel with Judaism," in *Anti-Semitism and Early Christianity: Issues of Polemic and Faith* (ed. Craig A. Evans and Donald A. Hagner; Minneapolis: Fortress Press, 1993), 133–34 n. 24, responded that vv. 15–16 broaden the application to all the Jews who are hindering Paul's gospel; so also Lamp, "Is Paul Anti-Jewish?" Paul certainly employs generalizing language, but the "Jews" nevertheless are specified as those who have actively hindered Paul's ministry.

200. Abraham J. Malherbe, *The Letters to the Thessalonians* (AB 32B; New York: Doubleday, 2000), 178–79.

"vituperation and hyperbole" (cf. 2 Cor 10–13; Gal 1:6–8; Phil 3:2, 18–19).[201] To reason directly from 1 Thess 2:14–16 to Rom 11:26 would be an utter misappropriation of the stock hyperbolic rhetoric of intra-Jewish polemic.

Many scholars have difficulty interpreting the "mystery" of Rom 11:25 as anything other than Israel's future conversion. Raymond E. Brown explained that a "mystery" in biblical literature refers either to God's hidden plan, which has not yet been revealed, or to a partial revelation that has not yet been fully understood. God had already revealed the existence of a Jewish remnant in Paul's own day. The fact that a remnant believes in Christ would hardly constitute a "mystery."[202] If by speaking of "all Israel" being saved Paul means nothing more than an elect group of Israelites, then v. 26 would say nothing beyond v. 25. Merkle's interpretation of καὶ οὕτως as "in this manner" leads to the following sequence: the rejection of Israel brings about the acceptance and salvation of the gentiles, which would stir Jewish jealousy of the gentiles' salvation, which would lead to (some) Jewish repentance — a process that would continue until the end of the age. The "mystery" of which Paul speaks, then, would consist of the *interdependence* of Jewish and gentile salvation.[203] Merkle, following Herman Ridderbos, understood the mystery of that interdependence as that "God grants no mercy to Israel without the Gentiles."[204] Paul, however, never says this. He expresses the exact opposite. The gentiles are being grafted onto a tree representing Israel's gracious heritage in 11:17–24. The Messiah is of Israel in 9:5. Certainly Paul hopes to make his own people jealous, but nowhere does Paul say that the present reception of mercy by Israel's remnant is dependent on what God has done for the gentiles. Paul is looking to *the end*. The Jewish people were hardened with positive effects for the gentiles in the present just as the gentiles will one day reach their fullness with positive effects for the Jews.

Merkle interpreted the hardened "part of Israel" in 11:25 as referring to a different sort of "Israel" than the "all Israel" of v. 26. Just as Rom 9:6 distinguishes

---

201. Malherbe, *Letters to the Thessalonians*, 179; Carol J. Schlueter, *Filling up the Measure: Polemical Hyperbole in 1 Thessalonians 2.14–16* (JSNTSup 98; Sheffield: Sheffield Academic, 1994); Hagner, "Paul's Quarrel with Judaism," 133–35. On the apocalyptic elements in 1 Thessalonians, see Das, *Paul and the Jews*, 136–37.

202. Raymond E. Brown, *The Semitic Background of the Term "Mystery" in the New Testament* (FBBS 12; Philadelphia: Fortress Press, 1968).

203. Merkle, "Romans 11," 715, 717, 719–20. Murray Baker, "Paul and the Salvation of Israel: Paul's Ministry, the Motif of Jealousy, and Israel's Yes," *CBQ* 67 (2005): 469–84, has recently argued *against* the interdependence that Merkle hypothesized. If correct, the mystery would more likely refer to Israel's future conversion.

204. Merkle, "Romans 11," 720.

the elect Israel from the ethnic whole and 11:7 distinguishes the elect from the hardened, so Merkle's Paul refers to the hardened "part" in 11:25 as opposed to the elect "all Israel" in 11:26. Merkle's reasoning is flawed, since he ignored both the *temporal contrast* and the *numerical contrast* in this passage. Israel *has been* hardened *in part*, but *all* Israel *will be* saved. The problem that has motivated Paul's concern for Israel in 9:1–5 and throughout his entire discussion in Rom 9–11 is precisely that the vast majority of Israel does not currently believe in Christ. Only a tiny remnant has become Christian. Paul continues to speak of the small number of Jewish Christians in chap. 11. The contrast in language in this chapter is striking: Paul speaks of the "remnant" (λεῖμμα, 11:5–7), "some" (τινές, 11:17), and a "part of Israel" (ἀπὸ μέρους τῷ Ἰσραήλ, 11:25) juxtaposed with "all Israel" (πᾶς Ἰσραήλ, 11:26) or the "full number" (πλήρωμα, 11:12).[205] To put it differently, when v. 25 speaks of "*part* of Israel" being hardened, the verse implies that *another part* of Israel, the remnant, is currently being saved—but "*all* Israel" *will* be saved.[206] Merkle therefore confused the present, partial remnant with the "all" Israel to come. Paul envisions a day when the small numbers of believing Jews will yield to a far greater number.

Since Rom 9:6 Paul has been *bifurcating* Israel into an elect, believing minority, and an unbelieving, hardened majority (11:7). A hardening has therefore come upon *part* of Israel (11:25). Paul consistently distinguishes between two different Israels all through Rom 9–11, but that distinction is precisely why the phrase "all Israel" is so striking. In other words, *in contrast to the division within ethnic Israel* throughout Rom 9–11, Paul envisions a future for "*all Israel*." As Ross Wagner noted regarding Rom 11:8–24,

> Paul's refusal to employ the term "Israel" as a name for either "the elect" or "the rest" in Romans 11:8–24 suggests that "all Israel" in 11:25 includes both groups—"the elect," who have already obtained what "Israel" sought, and "the rest," who have been temporarily rendered insensible but whose future "fullness" and "acceptance" Paul can anticipate with confidence.[207]

Paul is anticipating in 11:8–24 the resolution of Israel's bifurcation in a future oneness (11:26).

---

205. Dunn, *Romans 9–16*, 681.

206. Otfried Hofius, "'All Israel Will Be Saved': Divine Salvation and Israel's Deliverance in Romans 9–11," PSBSup 1 [1990]: 35, wrote: "The clause πᾶς Ἰσραὴλ σωθήσεται, which foretells a future event, is clearly antithetical to the statement in v. 25b that God caused a partial hardening to fall upon Israel at present, so that now only a few receive σωτηρία, namely, the elect 'remnant' of 11:5, 7a."

207. Wagner, *Heralds of the Good News*, 278.

That hardened "Israel" should comprise a significant portion of "all Israel" is rendered more likely by Paul's use of "Israel" in Rom 9–11. "Israelites" are those for whom Paul grieves in Rom 9:4. "Israel" mistakenly pursues the "Law of righteousness" in 9:31. "Israel" in 10:21 is a "disobedient and contrary people." Whenever Paul uses "Israel" apart from a contrast of a part of Israel with the rest, he is typically referring to the disobedient majority. Before distinguishing the elect from the rest in 11:7, Paul begins with "Israel [not "part" of Israel] failed to obtain what it was seeking." Paul hopes to make "Israel" jealous in 11:11. Even after the strong statement in Rom 9:6 about an elect within the ethnic people, Paul nevertheless continues to *include* hardened Israel in his reference to "Israel."[208] "All Israel" in 11:26 must therefore include the hardened.[209]

The apostle is struggling to show that God remains faithful to all Israel even though Israel has to a large extent become hardened and disobedient. A people currently characterized by "rejection" will be characterized by their "acceptance" (v. 15). Paul writes in Rom 11:12: "Now if their stumbling means riches for the world, and their defeat means riches for gentiles, how much more will their full inclusion mean!" (NRSV, mod.). Then in 11:15: "For if their rejection is the reconciliation of the world, what will their acceptance be but life from the dead!" Israel's present "rejection," "defeat," and "stumbling" will yield to their future "full inclusion" and "acceptance." Merkle attempted to counter this reasoning by drawing attention to the "full number" of the gentiles in 11:25 (πλήρωμα, the same word as in 11:12). Since the "full number" of the gentiles refers to the gathering of elect gentiles through history, Merkle reasoned that the "full inclusion" of Israel should refer to the gathering of believing Israelites through history.[210] Merkle added:

> Since verses 12 and 15 are parallel, the "acceptance" of verse 15 also refers to the consummation of all elect Jews. Paul, of course, makes an argument from the lesser to the greater. If the failure of the Jews meant the gospel blessings for the Gentiles, then their acceptance, that is, the coming in of the full number of the elect, will mean nothing less than the resurrection itself ("life from the dead").[211]

---

208. Nils A. Dahl, "Der Name Israel: Zur Auslegung von Gal. 6,16," *Judaica* 6 (1950), 162, therefore distinguished between "Israel" as the preferred term for the unbelieving majority and the believing "remnant" or "elect" (Rom 9:27, 29; 11:5, 7).

209. As Bruce W. Longenecker, "Different Answers to the Different Issues," 97, put it: "When Paul speaks of 'all Israel' in 11.26, what he has in mind is an ethnic group whose members are schismatically divided. In this sense, his point is not so much that all *Israel* will be saved, but that *all* Israel will be saved."

210. Merkle, "Romans 11," 718.

211. Ibid., 718.

Paul is therefore referring to the salvation of the remnant throughout all time, the *full number* of elect Israelites. The flaw in Merkle's reasoning is that he must distinguish as *separate groups* the Israelites who *reject* and the "full number" of Israelites who *accept*. Paul never refers to the "full number *of the remnant.*" Paul does not claim that *some* of those who currently reject, an elect remnant, will come to accept. He claims that *the very Israelites* who reject will come to accept. In other words, the majority of Israel that is hardened and rejecting (*as opposed to* the remnant) will one day accept. Paul's contrast is *not* between two different groups, one that rejects and another that accepts, but rather between *two contrasting receptions* by *the same* people, the majority of ethnic Israel. When Merkle countered on the basis of Rom 9:6 that Paul could be using two different definitions of "Israel" within the same verse, he ignored the fact that Rom 9:6 explicitly clarifies that not all Israel is Israel. Merkle used Rom 11:7 to prove that Paul could shift definitions of "Israel" within the same verse, but the apostle, again, *signals* his distinction of "the elect" from "the rest." The explicit language *signaling* differing conceptions of Israel in Rom 9:6 and 11:7 is absent in Rom 11:12, 15. Nothing in the immediate context of Rom 11:12, 15 suggests a contrast between a hardened majority and an elect minority (even if through time). This is a problem not only for Merkle's interpretation of Rom 11:12 and 11:15 but also for his approach to 11:25–26, where the most natural reading is that Israel's *hardening* will come to an end ("until") at a point of *softening* and salvation, exactly what Paul claims at the end of v. 26. An abrupt change of referent in vv. 25–26 for "Israel" ("part of Israel"; "all Israel") is unnecessary and without contextual warrant.

The phrase "all Israel" poses problems for Merkle. As Wright pointed out, "all Israel" in the Hebrew Bible normally refers to "the great majority of Jews alive at the time."[212] "All Israel" is a corporate expression that does not mean every Israelite who ever lived or even every Israelite at the time when "all Israel" is saved. The phrase *never* emphasizes individuals but rather the fullness of Israel's idealized *twelve-tribal structure*.[213] The phrase does regularly refer to the majority of the people (for example, Exod 18:5; Deut 27:9; Josh 3:17; 8:33; 1 Sam 3:20; 2 Sam

---

212. Wright, "Letter to the Romans," 689 n. 455.

213. The most detailed study in support of this point remains that of James M. Scott, "And Then All Israel Will Be Saved," who offered a full categorization and representative examples. Paul's understanding of the fullness of "all Israel" in 11:26 is defined by the contrast with the presently hardened majority. The future will manifest a restoration of the people as a whole, although not every individual.

8:15; 1 Kgs 4:1, 7; 2 Chr 9:1; 12:1, 38; 17:6; Dan 9:11; *m. Sanh.* 10:1–4).[214] The corporate language of "all Israel" may refer to a representative group, again, in reference to the fullness of Israel's tribal structure (for example, Josh 7:25; 1 Chr 11:1–14; 13:5; 2 Chr 31:1).[215] "All Israel" is *not* a mere collection of believing individuals through time as the remnant reading supposes: "A diachronic view of 'all Israel' puts too much emphasis on Israel being a collection of individuals and not enough on the corporate entity."[216] Or with Scott: "All Israel [in the Hebrew Bible] normally refers to the *contemporary* people of Israel, rather than to the collective manifestation of the people either in the past or in the future" (*more than* 98% of all instances of the phrase are synchronic).[217] The "all Israel" of Rom 11:26, at the end of Paul's discussion of ethnic Israel, parallels the "all Israel" at the beginning of his discussion in Rom 9:6: πάντες οἱ ἐξ᾽ Ἰσραήλ, "all who descend from Israel." "Hence, it is better to understand the πᾶς, 'all,' in a global sense. . . ."[218] With Rom 11:26 Paul has reached full circle (from 9:6) and has finally resolved the pain his people's current rejection poses (9:1–5).

A consistent refrain in the Isaiah passages that Paul employs throughout Rom 11 — indeed throughout Rom 9–11 — is hope for the future salvation of Israel.[219] Paul speaks in 11:8 of Israel's "sluggish spirit," the language of Isa 29:10 LXX. Only a few verses later in the Septuagint: "And in that day the deaf will hear the words of a book, and the darkened and befogged eyes of the blind will see; the poor will rejoice with gladness on account of the Lord, and those without hope will be filled with gladness" (Isa 29:18–19).[220] Wagner commented:

> Just as in Isaiah Israel's blindness will one day give way to sight, its deafness yield to hearing, so in Paul's eschatological vision the spiritual stupor of the 'the rest' of Israel is only temporary. As in Isaiah, so too in Paul's theodicy,

---

214. Hvalvik, "'Sonderweg' for Israel," 100. See also the helpful review of "all Israel" in the Hebrew Bible, especially Chronicles, by William L. Osborne, "The Old Testament Background of Paul's 'All Israel' in Romans 1:26a," *AJT* 2 (1988): 282–93.

215. Moo, *Romans*, 722 n. 55; see the fuller discussion in Scott, "And Then All Israel Will Be Saved," 503–5.

216. Baker, "Paul and the Salvation of Israel," 482 n. 54. Moo, *Romans*, 723: "No occurrence of the phrase 'all Israel' [136 times in the LXX] has a clearly diachronic meaning."

217. Scott, "And Then All Israel Will Be Saved," 507.

218. Romano Penna, *Paul the Apostle: Wisdom and Folly of the Cross* (trans. Thomas P. Wahl; Collegeville, Minn.: Liturgical, 1996), 1:318 n. 86.

219. Argued at length in Wagner's thesis, *Heralds of the Good News*.

220. Wagner's translation, *Heralds of the Good News*, 253.

God will be faithful to redeem and restore those whom he has rendered insensible."[221]

In Rom 11:26–27 Paul quotes a series of texts, beginning with Isa 59:20 and closing with Isa 27:9. These Isaianic texts conform to the larger pattern throughout of Isaiah of Israel's future deliverance from its imminent judgment. Isaiah 59 begins by responding to the people's plight: "The Lord's hand is not too short to save, nor his ear too dull to hear. Rather, your iniquities have been barriers between you and your God, and your sins have hidden his face from you so that he does not hear." After indicting Israel throughout vv. 3–8 (a portion of which Paul draws on in Rom 3:15–17), the prophet narrates Israel's confession (vv. 12–13) and laments God's absence of deliverance (59:9, 11, 14), at which point the Lord sends a deliverer to rescue his people (59:19). God will take away the people's ungodliness (59:20) and will make a covenant with them and grant his Spirit (59:21). With Israel's redemption the nations stream to Zion in Isa 60. "For in my wrath I struck you down, but in my favor I have had mercy on you" (60:10). In an ironic twist, "whereas Isaiah imagined Gentiles carrying the scattered children of Israel home to Zion on their shoulders (Isa 60:3–4, 9), Paul avers that the Gentiles will indeed bring Israel back to God, but only by provoking them to jealousy for their rightful inheritance (Rom 11:13–14)."[222] Paul also cites Isa 27:9 from a context promising the reconciliation of the nations to God (25:6–7), the defeat of death (25:8), and the resurrection of the dead (26:19) even as in Rom 11:15 Israel's rejection has brought about the nations' reconciliation and their future acceptance will result in "life from the dead."[223] Isaiah 27 anticipates Israel's restoration including the eradication of the people's idolatry. As Wagner summarized,

> In claiming that God will be faithful to redeem all Israel, Paul does not lean on the isolated testimony of a few verses from Isaiah. Rather, he taps into a broad and deep stream of thought that is characteristic of Isaiah's vision — a stream of thought, moreover, that is shared by numerous other prophetic texts and that is kept vigorously alive in later Jewish literature.[224]

. . . . . .

> Paul finds in Isaiah's oracles the assurance that God, on account of his abundant mercy and enduring faithfulness to Israel, will do what "the rest"

---

221. Ibid., 254.
222. Ibid., 292.
223. Ibid., 295–96.
224. Ibid.

of Israel cannot do for themselves. God will heal their spiritual blindness and insensibility. God himself will remove their ungodliness and take away their sins, cleansing them of their infidelity and empowering them to keep his covenant.[225]

The God who hardens will in the end soften the hearts of Paul's fellow Israelites.

Paul's expectations have profound implications for a gentile readership. After the first ten chapters of Romans, the gentile audience has learned that they share in Israel's privileges as the elect sons of God. Their status as God's chosen leads Paul to turn to the status of his own kinsfolk. If God acts impartially whether an individual is a Jew or a gentile, is there any advantage for the Jew? Paul begins to answer that question in 3:1 but never really returns to it until Rom 9. In Rom 9:6–29 he qualifies unbelieving Israel's not being God's elect. In Rom 9:30 — 10:21 he faults Israel for its failure to believe. Of course, Paul must again ask in Rom 11:1 if there is any benefit to being a Jew or has God rejected them. For the gentile audience, this question is of supreme relevance: what value is there in this strange, eastern, barbaric heritage? Does faith in Christ render ethnic Israel essentially a relic, a thing of the past? The gentiles dare not think that they have replaced ethnic Israel.[226] "Although Paul was willing to grant Israel's failure, he refused to grant the conclusion that Gentile Christians drew from it, namely, that God had rejected the Jews (11:1)."[227] The image of the olive tree confronts gentile arrogance. Philip Esler provided what has proved to be the most extensive survey of ancient oleiculture to date. He demonstrated that cultivated olive shoots were typically grafted onto wild olive trees in order to render them more fruitful. Paul reverses the imagery to an action that is truly "contrary to nature" (Rom 11:24). In the reversed scheme, wild olive branches would not contribute to a cultivated tree's fruitfulness. In less than flattering imagery, Paul is describing the "barbarianization" of the olive tree by unproductive, parasitic branches.[228] The apostle is removing any possibility of gentile superiority over

---

225. Ibid., 297.

226. Neil Elliott, *The Rhetoric of Romans: Argumentative Constraint and Strategy and Paul's Dialogue with Judaism* (JSNTSup 45; Sheffield: Sheffield Academic, 1990; Fortress Press edition, 2006), wrote: "Far from being overwhelmed by Jewish claims of privilege, they run the risk, in Paul's estimation, of holding God's mercy in contempt by boasting of having 'replaced' Israel (cf. 11:17–24)."

227. Walters, *Ethnic Issues*, 82.

228. Philip F. Esler, "Ancient Oleiculture and Ethnic Differentiation: The Meaning of the Olive-Tree Image in Romans 11," *JSNT* 26 (2003): 121–23. Esler dispelled the use of Columella by A. G. Baxter and J. A. Ziesler, "Paul and Arboriculture: Romans 11.17–24,

the Jews. Gentiles depend on the Jewish tree and its root structure. The gentile branches do not support the Jewish roots, but rather their roots support the gentile branches. The gentiles are benefiting from God's promises to Israel. The Jew remains "first" (Rom 1:16). Gentile engrafting is a matter of unmerited grace (11:20; cf. 9:18; 9:30–32; 10:9; 11:5–6), but the future belongs to Israel.[229] Israel will be grafted back into its own tree (11:23–24), which will result in "riches" beyond measure.[230] As Paul said of the very people for whom he wished himself cut off: "They are Israelites" (9:4).

Israel's fate parallels its Messiah. Israel is currently cut off, just as Christ was cut off, and Paul himself wishes to be cut off for Israel's sake. As Abraham nearly sacrificed Isaac, so God sacrificed his own Son (8:32 and 11:21). In like manner God did not spare his own people and will vindicate them as well through a sort of resurrection — life from the dead in 11:15.[231] In each case, rejection leads to vicarious benefit for others. If the gentiles question Israel's priority, they must question *their own status* in God's plan! "The Gentiles have come to share [Israel's] spiritual blessings" (Rom 15:27).

JSNT 24 (1985): 25–32, since Paul signals an action "contrary to nature" and not an accepted practice. Further, Columella's practice was for unproductive trees, which is not the case in Rom 11. Columella was writing of a recuperative measure for an unproductive tree and not a standard sort of "grafting," which would require differing vocabulary. Finally, Theophrastus does not mention Columella's practice in his description of oleiculture in the Mediterranean east (and considered wild branches unable to contribute to a tree's fruitfulness); Esler, "Ancient Oleiculture," 120–21. On the gentiles as parasitic branches, see also Longenecker, "Different Answers to the Different Issues," 105.

229. Hafemann, "Salvation of Israel," 52.

230. Mark Nanos, *The Mystery of Romans* (Minneapolis: Fortress Press, 1996), 254.

231. Richard B. Hays, *Echoes of Scripture in the Letters of Paul* (New Haven: Yale Univ. Press, 1989), 61; see esp. pp. 60–63. Israel, of course, is currently in ἀπιστία. The shape of their fate may therefore be somewhat ironic.

Conclusion

For years scholars have been working with the assumption that the sixteen-chapter Letter to the Romans was addressed to a mixed audience of both gentiles and Jews. Since the early 1990s, evidence has been mounting that requires a paradigm shift for the encoded audience of the letter.[1] Paul belabors at length the relationship between the Jews as God's historic people and the gentiles. He elaborates on the role of the Mosaic Law and Jewish customs in God's saving plan for the nations. In focusing on these particular issues, the apostle is not merely summarizing his theology as it developed in the East. He knows that these are issues relevant for the Romans' own situation. At various points he betrays knowledge of the Roman congregations (1:8–11, 13; 3:8; 6:17; 13:6–7; 15:14–15, 18–23, 26; 16:27). The instructions to the "strong" in Rom 14:1 — 15:13, for instance, appear tailored to the specific situation as the Romans assembled for worship and common meals. The unique aspects of Paul's instructions deny the conclusion that he was merely repackaging advice originally intended for the church at Corinth. His treatment of food as neither clean nor unclean in itself would have stirred the ire of the Jerusalem Christians had they been the target audience of the letter. Many at Jerusalem would have disagreed with Paul's claim that one's food choices are a matter of indifference. The issues between the weak and the strong in Rom 14:1 — 15:13 as well as the

---

1. A. J. M. Wedderburn, *The Reasons for Romans* (Edinburgh: T&T Clark, 1988), 64, listed three criteria for a viable reconstruction of the concrete situation behind Paul's letter to the Romans: (1) Is the situation presupposed inherently plausible? Does it provide a coherent picture of the life of the Christian community in that place? (2) Is this picture compatible with what we know from other sources concerning the history of the earliest church? Is it similar to anything else we know happened elsewhere in the church of that day? (3) Does it fit in with what Paul's text says? Does it make good sense of that text? Each of these criteria may be affirmatively answered on the assumption of a gentile audience.

instructions in Rom 13:8–10 correspond to the rest of the letter as Paul explains how the Roman congregations are to apply the Mosaic Law in their communal life. What is the precise relationship between gentile Christians and the Jewish origins of their faith? Paul does mention other reasons for writing, even if these reasons are not his central concern. He mentions very briefly his upcoming trip to Jerusalem with the collection and his hope for missionary work in Spain. He does not elaborate on these plans, but the scope of his apostolic itinerary is breathtaking: Jerusalem, Rome, all the way to Spain. The agenda serves a rhetorical purpose in order that the Romans, members of congregations Paul has never visited, will hearken to a stranger's message and advice. All indications suggest a concrete situation at Rome (chap. 1).

Paul clearly identifies his audience as gentiles at various points in the letter (1:5–6, 13; 11:13; 15:15–16). He assumes on the part of the Roman congregations a knowledge of Judaism and the Law that would require interaction with the Jewish synagogues on the part of a significant portion of the audience at some point (chap. 2). The letter also provides evidence that a decisive break from the synagogues has taken place (chap. 3). Serious objections can be raised against the evidence traditionally cited for a significant Jewish minority in the congregations. For instance, the greetings at the end of the letter identify five people who were likely of Jewish ethnicity, two of which were a couple associated with Paul's missionary endeavors to the gentiles (Prisca and Aquila). Similarly, two others who were likely of Jewish ethnicity were also a missionary couple associated with Paul's gentile mission (Andronicus and Junia). These individuals are included in a set of greetings in the third person, which was typical for letters in which the addressees were admonished to greet a third party. In other words, the individuals mentioned in Rom 16 were not themselves members of the Roman congregations at the time Paul wrote. The discussion of the weak and the strong conforms to the widely recognized interest in Jewish food laws and Sabbath observance on the part of gentile God-fearers. Gentiles who had formerly associated with the synagogues were interacting with other gentiles who did not share the same interest in these Jewish practices. As gentiles joined the early Christ-believing movement, many of these newer "converts" would not have experienced synagogue life or at the level of other gentiles. Varying levels of interaction with the synagogues would lead to tension over the role of the Law of Moses in the Christ-believers' communal life (at the conceptual level, though not necessarily at the level of a full-blown conflict between groups or parties). They would have struggled to understand the nature of their relationship as gentile communities of faith to the Jewish people. These issues manifested themselves in the relationship between the weak and the strong in chaps. 14–15. Commentators have frequently noted Paul's obliqueness in not identifying the strong as gentiles and the weak as Jews on the basis of their customs with respect to the Law. Such obliqueness is understandable if the letter is addressed entirely to gentiles. James C. Miller faulted several major approaches to the Romans debate for not integrating the evidence of both the letter-frame and the letter-body.[2] Paul's identification of a gentile audience in the letter's frame as well as the neglected evidence for a gentile encoded readership in the letter's body (for example, 6:19) need to be taken seriously.

The extant external evidence confirms the reconstruction of gentile Christian communities based on the internal evidence (chap. 4). The edict of Claudius was a response to disputes over the significance of Christ in the Jewish synagogues. Since only Luke and Suetonius recorded the expulsion, only those actually involved in the dispute were the ones likely affected. The Romans would have been dependent on the Jewish community in administering the expulsion. The Jewish community would have singled out those who posed the greatest threat to their social cohesiveness, namely, Jewish and proselyte advocates of Christ. Gentile God-fearers, on the other hand, were not as integrated into the Jewish community and, in the face of pressure from the imperium, would have been able to reintegrate with gentile social groupings. With the expulsion of the Jewish Christians and possibly the most vocal God-fearers during the conflict, the remaining gentiles would have been forced to worship Christ apart from the synagogues. These new worshiping communities would have included both gentiles with a knowledge of Judaism and its customs from their prior, close interaction with the synagogues as well as gentiles without the same appreciation for Judaism, particularly among newer members. In other words, the best reconstruction of the external evidence agrees with what may be concluded from the letter itself.

Reviewers complained that Stanley Stowers and Neil Elliott spent an inordinate proportion of their defense of a gentile audience on Rom 1–4. A strong case for a gentile audience, as Stowers himself demonstrated, may be made in connection with the identity of the "I" in Rom 7:7–25, a section that develops the various motifs from Paul's address of his audience in the surrounding frame of 7:5–6 and 8:2 (chap. 5). Recent commentaries on Romans have yet to interact with Stowers's case for a gentile "I" in 7:7–25.[3] Romans 9–11, especially Rom

---

2. James C. Miller, *The Obedience of Faith, the Eschatological People of God, and the Purpose of Romans* (SBLDS 177; Atlanta: Society of Biblical Literature, 2000), 16–17. In Miller's own case, he did not account for the evidence of the letter-frame for a gentile audience and opted for a Jewish minority, which would correspond, in his scheme, to the Jewish issues in the body of the letter.

3. For example, Ben Witherington (with Darlene Hyatt), *Paul's Letter to the Romans: A Socio-Rhetorical Commentary* (Grand Rapids: Eerdmans, 2004), 193–206; Charles H. Talbert, *Romans* (SHBC; Macon, Ga.: Smyth & Helwys, 2002), 185–212.

11:26, confronts gentile arrogance against the Jewish people. Paul reminds his gentile audience that they have been grafted onto the olive tree of Israel and its heritage. As Robert Gagnon put it, Paul has "trapped" his audience.[4] Paul censures the "Jew" in 2:17 — 3:9. He affirms the impartiality of God toward both Jew and gentile in matters of judgment and salvation. In Rom 8 he applies to the gentiles the designations of an elect people of Israel. When he turns to his own Jewish people in Rom 9:1 — 10:21, the apostle seems to continue a train of thought that denies any advantage for ethnic Israel. Readers might conclude, then, that God offers no advantage for the Jewish people at all. With Rom 11:1 Paul changes course and reaches a climax in 11:26 with the surprising expectation that "all Israel" will be saved (chap. 5). The time of the gentiles will be fulfilled, and the moment for ethnic Israel's affirmation of the Jewish Messiah will arrive!

All the pieces of the puzzle for Paul's letter to the Romans fit. The apostle is writing to a gentile audience. Approaching Romans as written to an all-gentile audience would take seriously both the explicit identification of the audience in the letter as well as the full range of evidence for the edict of Claudius and its scope. Evidence from the letter-frame corresponds neatly to the content of the body of the letter. Since the situation presupposed is inherently plausible, the time has come for a paradigm shift in the interpretation of the Roman situation. Future readings of Romans must take seriously the rhetorical impact of Paul's writing to an encoded gentile audience.

---

4. Robert A. J. Gagnon, "Why the 'Weak' at Rome Cannot Be Non-Christian Jews," *CBQ* 62 (2000), 74.

Abbreviations

AASF	Annales Academiae scientarum fennicae
AB	Anchor Bible
ABR	*Australian Biblical Review*
AcadB	Academia Biblica
AIPHOS	*Annuaire de l'Institut de philologie et d'histoire orientales et slaves*
AJA	*American Journal of Archaeology*
AJT	*Asia Journal of Theology*
ANTC	Abingdon New Testament Commentaries
ARS	*Annual Review of Sociology*
BAR	*Biblical Archaelogy Review*
BDAG	Bauer, W., F. W. Danker, W. F. Arndt, and F. W. Gingrich, *Greek-English Lexicon of the New Testament and Other Early Christian Literature*
BECNT	Baker Exegetical Commentary on the New Testament
BETL	Bibliotheca ephemeridum theologicarum lovaniensium
BevT	Beiträge zur evangelischen Theologie
BHR	Bibliotheca Helvetica Romana
Bib	*Biblica*
BibS(F)	Biblische Studien (Freiburg 1895–)
BJRL	*Bulletin of the John Rylands Library*
BJS	Brown Judaic Studies
BNTC	Black's New Testament Commentaries
BR	*Biblical Research*
BSac	*Bibliotheca Sacra*
BTB	*Biblical Theology Bulletin*
CA	*Classical Antiquity*
CBET	Contributions to Biblical Exegesis and Theology
CBQ	*Catholic Biblical Quarterly*

CCWJCW	Cambridge Commentaries on Writings of the Jewish and Christian World 200 BC to AD 200
CIJ	*Corpus inscriptionum judaicarum*
CIL	*Corpus inscriptionum latinarum*
CIRB	*Corpus Inscriptionum Regni Bosporani*
CJ	*Concordia Journal*
CMG	Corpus Medicorum Graecorum
ConBNT	Coniectanea biblica: New Testament Series
CPJ	*Corpus papyrorum judaicarum*
CPSSup	Cambridge Philological Society Supplements
CRBR	*Critical Review of Books in Religion*
CSEL	Corpus scriptorum ecclesiasticorum latinorum
CTJ	*Calvin Theological Journal*
CTQ	*Concordia Theological Quarterly*
CurBS	*Currents in Research: Biblical Studies*
CurTM	*Currents in Theology and Mission*
EKKNT	Evangelisch-katholischer Kommentar zum Neuen Testament
ExpTim	*The Expository Times*
FAS	Forschungen zur Antiken Sklaverei
FB	Forschung zur Bibel
FIOTL	Formation and Interpretation of Old Testament Literature
FRLANT	Forschungen zur Religion und Literatur des Alten und Neuen Testaments
HABES	Heidelberger althistorische Beiträge und epigraphische Studien
HHS	Harvard Historical Studies
HKNT	Hand-Kommentar zum Neuen Testament
HNT	Handbuch zum Neuen Testament
HTKNT	Herders theologischer Kommentar zum Neuen Testament
HTR	*Harvard Theological Review*
HTS	Harvard Theological Studies
HUCA	*Hebrew Union College Annual*
IB	*Interpreter's Bible*
IBS	*Irish Biblical Studies*
ICC	International Critical Commentary
Int	*Interpretation*
ITQ	*Irish Theological Quarterly*
JAC	Jahrbuch für Antike und Christentum
JBL	*Journal of Biblical Literature*
JETS	*Journal of the Evangelical Theological Society*
JQR	*Jewish Quarterly Review*

JRS	*Journal of Roman Studies*
JSJ	*Journal for the Study of Judaism in the Persian, Hellenistic, and Roman Periods*
JSJSup	Journal for the Study of Judaism Supplements
JSNT	*Journal for the Study of the New Testament*
JSNTSup	Journal for the Study of the New Testament: Supplement Series
JSP	*Journal for the Study of the Pseudepigrapha*
JSS	*Jewish Social Studies*
JTS	*Journal of Theological Studies*
Jud	*Judaica*
Judaica	*Judaica: Beiträge zum Verständnis des jüdischen Schicksals in Vergangenheit und Gegenwart*
KNT	Kommentar zum Neuen Testament
LCL	Loeb Classical Library. Cambridge: Harvard University Press
LD	Lectio divina
LSJ	Liddell, H. G., R. Scott, H. S. Jones, *A Greek-English Lexicon*. 9th ed.
LTP	*Laval théologique et philosophique*
NIB	*The New Interpreter's Bible*
NICNT	New International Commentary on the New Testament
NovT	*Novum Testamentum*
NovTSup	Novum Testamentum Supplements
NPNF	*Nicene and Post-Nicene Fathers*
NTAbh	Neutestamentliche Abhandlungen
Numen	*Numen: International Review for the History of Religions*
PEHS	Papers of the Ecclesiastical History Society
PG	Patrologia graeca. Edited by J.-P. Migne.
PHC	*A People's History of Christianity* (Fortress Press)
PL	Patrologia latina. Edited by J.-P. Migne.
PSB	*Princeton Seminary Bulletin*
PSBSup	Princeton Seminary Bulletin Supplements
PTS	Patristische Texte und Studien
RB	*Revue Biblique*
ResQ	*Restoration Quarterly*
RH	*Revue Historique*
RSR	*Religious Studies Review*
RTR	*Reformed Theological Review*
RUB	*Revue de l'université de Bruxelles*
SBL	Society of Biblical Literature
SBLDS	Society of Biblical Literature Dissertation Series

SBLSP	*Society of Biblical Literature Seminar Papers*
SBLSymS	Society of Biblical Literature Symposium Series
SBLWAW	Society of Biblical Literature Writings from the Ancient World
SBM	Stuttgarter biblische Monographien
SCJ	Studies in Christianity and Judaism
SD	Studies and Documents
SDODB	Sintesi Dell'oriente e Della Bibbia
SE	*Studia evangelica*
SFSHJ	South Florida Studies in the History of Judaism
SHBC	Smyth & Helwys Bible Commentary
SIHC	Studies in the Intercultural History of Christianity
SJLA	Studies in Judaism in Late Antiquity
SJT	*Scottish Journal of Theology*
SKKNT	Stuttgarter kleiner Kommentar, Neues Testament
SNT	Studien zum Neuen Testament
SNTIW	Studies of the New Testament and Its World
SNTSMS	Society for New Testament Studies Monograph Series
SNTSU	Studien zum Neuen Testament und seiner Umwelt
SP	Sacra Pagina
SPSH	Scholars Press Studies in the Humanities
ST	*Studia Theologica*
TB	Theologische Bücherei
TDNT	*Theological Dictionary of the New Testament*
TF	*Theologische Forschung*
TJT	*Toronto Journal of Theology*
TT	Texts and Translations
TU	Texte und Untersuchungen
TUGAL	Texte und Untersuchungen zur Geschichte der altchristlichen Literatur
TZ	*Theologische Zeitschrift*
VT	*Vetus Testamentum*
VTSup	Vetus Testamentum Supplements
WBC	Word Biblical Commentary
WGRW	Writings from the Greco-Roman World
WUNT	Wissenschaftliche Untersuchungen zum Neuen Testament
WW	*Word and World*
ZNW	*Zeitschrift für die neutestamentliche Wissenschaft*
ZPE	*Zeitschrift für Paypyrologie und Epigraphik*
ZTK	*Zeitschrift für Theologie und Kirche*

Bibliography

Aasgaard, Reidar. *'My Beloved Brothers and Sisters!' Christian Siblingship in Paul.* Journal for the Study of the New Testament: Supplement Series 265. London: T & T Clark, 2004.

Achtemeier, Paul J. *Romans.* Interpretation. Atlanta: John Knox, 1985.

———. "Romans 3:1–8: Structure and Argument." Pages 77–87 in *Christ and His Communities: Essays in Honor of Reginald H. Fuller.* Edited by Arland J. Hultgren and Barbara Hall. Cincinnati, Ohio: Forward Movement Publications, 1990.

———. "'Some Things in Them Hard to Understand': Reflections on an Approach to Paul." *Interpretation* 38 (1984): 254–67.

———. "Unsearchable Judgments and Inscrutable Ways: Reflections on the Discussion of Romans." Pages 521–34 in *1995 SBL Seminar Papers.* Edited by Eugene H. Lovering, Jr. Atlanta, Ga.: Scholars Press, 1995. Repr. (with corrections) pages 3–21 in *Looking Back, Pressing On.* Vol. 4 of *Pauline Theology.* Edited by E. Elizabeth Johnson and David M. Hay. SBL Symposium Series 4. Atlanta: Scholars, 1997.

Adams, Edward. "Paul's Story of God and Creation: The Story of How God Fulfils His Purposes in Creation." Pages 19–43 in *Narrative Dynamics in Paul: A Critical Assessment.* Edited by Bruce W. Longenecker. Louisville: Westminster John Knox, 2002.

Aland, Kurt. "Der Schluss und die Ursprüngliche Gestalt des Römerbriefes." Pages 284–301 in *Neutestamentliche Entwürfe.* Theologische Bücherei 63. München: Chr. Kaiser, 1979.

Augustine. *The City of God.* In vol. 2 of *The Nicene and Post-Nicene Fathers,* Series 1. Edited by Philip Schaff. 1886–1889. 14 vols. Repr. Peabody, Mass.: Hendrickson, 1994.

———. *The City of God.* Translated by George E. McCracken and William M. Green. 7 vols. Loeb Classical Library. Cambridge: Harvard University Press, 1957–1972.

Baker, Murray. "Paul and the Salvation of Israel: Paul's Ministry, the Motif of Jealousy, and Israel's Yes." *Catholic Biblical Quarterly* 67 (2005): 469–84.

Banks, Robert. *Paul's Idea of Community.* Rev. ed. Peabody, Mass.: Hendrickson, 1994.

Barclay, John M. G. "'Do We Undermine the Law?' A Study of Romans 14.1—15.6." Pages 287–308 in *Paul and the Mosaic Law.* Edited by James D. G. Dunn. Tübingen: J. C. B. Mohr (Paul Siebeck), 1996.

———. *Jews in the Mediterranean Diaspora: From Alexander to Trajan (323 BCE–117 CE)*. Edinburgh: T & T Clark, 1996.

———. "Paul among Diaspora Jews: Anomaly or Apostate?" *Journal for the Study of the New Testament* 60 (1995): 89–120.

———. "Πνευματικός in the Social Dialect of Pauline Christianity." Pages 157–67 in *The Holy Spirit and Christian Origins: Essays in Honor of James D. G. Dunn*. Edited by Graham N. Stanton, Bruce W. Longenecker, and Stephen C. Barton. Grand Rapids: Eerdmans, 2004.

———. Review of Stanley K. Stowers, *A Rereading of Romans*. *Journal of Theological Studies* 46 (1995): 646–51.

———. "Thessalonica and Corinth: Social Contrasts in Pauline Christianity." *Journal for the Study of the New Testament* 47 (1992): 49–74.

Barnes, T. D. "Legislation against the Christians." *Journal of Roman Studies* 58 (1968): 32–50.

Barnett, Paul W. "Jewish mission in the era of the New Testament and the apostle Paul. Pages 263–83 in *The Gospel to the Nations: Perspectives on Paul's Mission in Honour of Peter T. O'Brien*. Edited by Peter Holt and Mark Thompson. Downers Grove, Ill.: InterVarsity, 2000.

Barrett, C. K. *A Commentary on the Epistle to the Romans*. 2d ed. Black's New Testament Commentaries. Peabody, Mass.: Hendrickson, 1991.

Bartchy, S. Scott. "Community of Goods in Acts: Idealization or Social Reality?" Pages 309–18 in *The Future of Early Christianity: Essays in Honor of Helmut Koester*. Edited by Birger A. Pearson. Minneapolis: Fortress Press, 1991.

Bartsch, H. W. "Die historische Situation des Römerbriefes." Pages 281–91 in part 1 of vol. 4 of *Studia Evangelica*. Texte und Untersuchungen zur Geschichte der altechristlichen Literatur 102. Berlin: Akademie, 1968.

Bassler, Jouette M. Review of Stanley K. Stowers, *A Rereading of Romans: Justice, Jews, and Gentiles*. *Journal of Biblical Literature* 115 (1996): 365–68.

Bauckham, Richard. *Gospel Women: Studies in the Named Women in the Gospels*. Grand Rapids: Eerdmans, 2002.

Baumgarten, Albert. "Graeco-Roman Voluntary Associations and Ancient Jewish Sects." Pages 93–111 in *Jews in a Graeco-Roman World*. Edited by Martin Goodman. Oxford: Oxford University Press, 1998.

Baur, Ferdinand Christian. *Paul, the Apostle of Jesus Christ: His Life and Works, His Epistles and Teachings; A Contribution to a Critical History of Primitive Christianity*. 2 vols. London: Williams & Norgate, 1873–1875. Repr. Peabody, Mass.: Hendrickson, 2003.

———. "Über Zweck und Veranlassung des Römerbriefs und die damit zusammenhängenden Verhältnisse der römischen Gemeinde. *Tübinger Zeitschrift für Theologie* 3 (1836): 59–178. Repr., pages 147–266 in *Historishe Untersuchungen zum Neuen Testament*. Vol. 1 of *Ausgewählte Werke in Einzelausgaben*. Stuttgart/Bad Cannstatt: Friedrich Frommann, 1963.

Baxter, A. G., and J. A. Ziesler. "Paul and Arboriculture: Romans 11.17–24." *Journal for the Study of the New Testament* 24 (1985): 25–32.

Beale, G. K. "Peace and Mercy upon the Israel of God: The Old Testament Background of Galatians 6, 16b." *Biblica* 80 (1999): 204–23.

Beker, J. Christiaan. *Paul the Apostle: The Triumph of God in Life and Thought.* Philadelphia: Fortress Press, 1990.

Bell, Richard H. *Provoked to Jealousy: The Origin and Purpose of the Jealousy Motif in Romans 9–11.* Wissenschaftliche Untersuchungen zum Neuen Testament, 2 Reihe 63. Tübingen: J. C. B. Mohr (Paul Siebeck), 1994.

Bellen, Heinz. "Die Assuage einer bosporanishen Freilassungsinschrift (CIRB 71) zum Problem der 'Gottfürchtigen." Jahrbuch für Antike und Christentum 8 (1965): 171–76.

Belleville, Linda. "᾽Ιουνιαν: A Re-examination of Romans 16.7 in Light of Primary Source Materials." *New Testament Studies* 51 (2005): 231–49.

Bendemann, Reinhard von. "Die kritische Diastase von Wissen, Wollen und Handeln: Traditionsgeschichtliche Spurensuche eines hellenistischen Topos in Römer 7." *Zeitschrift für die neutestamentliche Wissenschaft und die Kunde der älteren Kirche* 95 (2004): 35–63.

Benko, Stephen. "The Edict of Claudius of A.D. 49 and the Instigator Chrestus." *Theologische Zeitschrift* 25 (1969): 406–18.

———. *Pagan Rome and the Early Christians.* Bloomington, Ind.: Indiana University Press, 1984.

Betz, Hans Dieter. *Galatians.* Hermeneia. Philadelphia: Fortress Press, 1979.

———. *Lukian von Samosata und das Neue Testament: Religionsgeschichtliche und Paränetische Parallelen.* Texte und Untersuchungen zur Geschichte der altchristlichen Literatur 76. Berlin: Akademie, 1961.

Binder, Donald D. *Into the Temple Courts: The Place of Synagogues in the Second Temple Period.* Society of Biblical Literature Dissertation Series 169. Atlanta: Society of Biblical Literature, 1999.

Blass, F., A. Debrunner, and R. W. Funk. *A Greek Grammar of the New Testament and Other Early Christian Literature.* Chicago: University of Chicago Press, 1961.

Bömer, Franz. *Untersuchungen über die Religion der Sklaven in Griechenland und Rom.* 2 vols. 2d ed. Forschungen zur Antiken Sklaverei 14. Weisbaden: Franz Steiner, 1981.

Borg, Marcus J. "A New Context for Romans xiii." *New Testament Studies* 19 (1972–73): 205–18.

Borgen, Peder. "The Contrite Wrongdoer—Condemned or Set Free by the Spirit? Romans 7:7–8:4." Pages 181–92 in *The Holy Spirit and Christian Origins: Essays in Honor of James D. G. Dunn.* Edited by Graham N. Stanton, Bruce W. Longenecker, and Stephen C. Barton. Grand Rapids: Eerdmans, 2004.

Bornkamm, Günther. "The Letter to the Romans as Paul's Last Will and Testament." Pages 16–28 in *The Romans Debate.* Rev. and enl. ed. Edited by Karl P. Donfried. Peabody, Mass.: Hendrickson, 1991. Repr. from *Australian Biblical Review* 11 (1963): 2–14.

Bornkamm, Günther. "Sin, Law and Death: An Exegetical Study of Romans 7." Pages 87–104 in *Early Christian Experience.* New York: Harper and Row, 1969.

Borse, Udo. "Schlußwort des Römerbriefes: Segensgruß (16,24) statt Doxologie (VV.25–27)." Studien zum Neuen Testament und seiner Umwelt. Serie A 19 (1994): 173–92.

Botermann, Helga. *Das Judenedikt des Kaisers Claudius: Römischer Staat und Christiani im 1. Jahrhundert.* Hermes-Einzelschriften 71. Stuttgart: Franz Steiner, 1996.

Boyarin, Daniel. *A Radical Jew: Paul and the Politics of Identity.* Berkeley: University of California Press, 1994.

Brändle, Rudolf, and Ekkehard W. Stegemann. "The Formation of the First 'Christian Congregations' in Rome in the Context of Jewish Congregations." Pages 117–27 in *Judaism and Christianity in First-Century Rome.* Edited by Karl P. Donfried and Peter Richardson. Grand Rapids: Eerdmans, 1998.

Branham, R. Bracht, and Daniel Kinney, eds. and trans. *Petronius.* Berkeley: University of California Press, 1996.

Brindle, Wayne A. "'To the Jew First': Rhetoric, Strategy, History, or Theology?" *Bibliotheca Sacra* 159 (2002): 221–33.

Brown, Raymond E. *The Semitic Background of the Term "Mystery" in the New Testament.* Facet Books, Biblical Series 12. Philadelphia: Fortress Press, 1968.

Brown, Raymond E., and John P. Meier. *Antioch & Rome: New Testament Cradles of Catholic Christianity.* New York: Paulist, 1983.

Bruce, F. F. "Christianity under Claudius." *Bulletin of the John Rylands Library* 44 (1961): 309–26.

———. "The Romans Debate — Continued." *Bulletin of the John Rylands Library* 64 (1981–82): 334–59. Repr. pp. 175–94 in *The Romans Debate.* Rev. and enl. ed. Edited by Karl P. Donfried. Peabody, Mass.: Hendrickson, 1991.

Bryan, Christopher. *A Preface to Romans: Notes on the Epistle in Its Literary and Cultural Setting.* Oxford: Oxford University Press, 2000.

Burer, Michael H. and Daniel B. Wallace. "Was Junia Really an Apostle? A Re-examination of Rom 16.7." *New Testament Studies* 47 (2001): 76–91.

Burke, Trevor J. *Family Matters: A Socio-Historical Study of Kinship Metaphors in 1 Thessalonians.* Journal for the Study of the New Testament: Supplement Series 247. London: T & T Clark, 2003.

Butts, James R. "The Progymnasmata of Theon: A New Text with Translation and Commentary." Ph.D. diss., Claremont Graduate School, 1986.

Byrne, Brendan. *Romans.* Sacra Pagina 6. Collegeville, Minn.: Liturgical, 1996.

Campbell, Douglas A. "Determining the Gospel through Rhetorical Analysis in Paul's Letter to the Roman Christians." Pages 315–36 in *Gospel in Paul: Studies on Corinthians, Galatians and Romans for Richard N. Longenecker.* Edited by L. Ann Jervis and Peter Richardson. Journal for the Study of the New Testament: Supplement Series 108. Sheffield: Sheffield Academic, 1994.

———. *The Rhetoric of Righteousness in Romans 3.21–26.* Journal for the Study of the New Testament: Supplement Series 65. Sheffield: Sheffield Academic, 1992.

Campbell, William S. "Did Paul Advocate Separation from the Synagogue? A Reaction to Francis Watson: Paul, Judaism and the Gentiles: A Sociological Approach." *Scottish Journal of Theology* 42 (1989): 457–67.

————. *Paul's Gospel in an Intercultural Context: Jew and Gentile in the Letter to the Romans.* Studies in the Intercultural History of Christianity 69. Frankfurt am Main: Peter Lang, 1991.

————. "Why Did Paul Write Romans." *Expository Times* 85 (1973–74): 264–69.

Caragounis, Chrys C. "From Obscurity to Prominence: The Development of the Roman Church between Romans and *1 Clement.*" Pages 245–79 in *Judaism and Christianity in First-Century Rome.* Edited by Karl P. Donfried and Peter Richardson. Grand Rapids: Eerdmans, 1998.

Carson, D. A. "An Introduction to the Porter/Fanning Debate." Pages 18–25 in *Biblical Greek Language and Linguistics: Open Questions in Current Research.* Edited by Stanley E. Porter and D. A. Carson. Journal for the Study of the New Testament: Supplement Series 80. Sheffield: Sheffield Academic, 1993.

Carter, Warren. "Rome (and Jerusalem): The Contingency of Romans 3:21–26." *Irish Biblical Studies* 11 (1989): 54–68.

Cary, Phillip. *Augustine's Invention of the Inner Self: The Legacy of a Christian Platonist.* Oxford: Oxford University Press, 2000.

Champlin, Edward. *Nero.* Cambridge: Harvard University Press, 2003.

Chestnut, Glenn F. "Eusebius, Augustine, Orosius, and the Later Patristic and Medieval Christian Historians." Pages 687–713 in *Eusebius, Christianity, and Judaism.* Edited by Harold W. Attridge and Gohei Hata. Detroit: Wayne State University Press, 1992.

Cicero. Translated by C. MacDonald, J. E. King et al. 29 vols. Loeb Classical Library. Cambridge: Harvard University Press, 1954–1999.

Clarke, Andrew D. "Jew and Greek, Slave and Free, Male and Female: Paul's Theology of Ethnic, Social and Gender Inclusiveness in Romans 16." Pages 103–25 in *Rome in the Bible and the Early Church.* Edited by Peter Oakes. Grand Rapids: Baker, 2002.

————. *Serve the Community of the Church: Christians as Leaders and Ministers.* First Century Christians in the Graeco-Roman World. Grand Rapids: Eerdmans, 2000.

Clements, Ronald E. "'A Remnant Chosen by Grace' (Romans 11:5): The Old Testament Background and Origin of the Remnant Concept." Pages 106–21 in *Pauline Studies.* Edited by Donald A. Hagner and Murray J. Harris. Grand Rapids: Eerdmans, 1980.

Cohen, Shaye J. D. *The Beginnings of Jewishness: Boundaries, Varieties, Uncertainties.* Berkeley: University of California Press, 1999.

————. "Crossing the Boundary and Becoming a Jew." *Harvard Theological Review* 82 (1989): 13–33. Repr. and rev. pages 140–74 in *The Beginnings of Jewishness: Boundaries, Varieties, Uncertainties.* Berkeley: University of California Press, 1999.

————. "Religion, Ethnicity, and 'Hellenism' in the Emergence of Jewish Identity in Maccabean Palestine." Pages 204–23 in *Religion and Religious Practice in the Seleucid Kingdom.* Edited by Per Bilde, Troels Engberg-Pedersen, Lise Hannestad, and Jan Zahle. Studies in Hellenistic Civilization 1. Aarhus, Denmark: Aarhus University Press, 1990.

————. "'Those Who Say They Are Jews and Are Not': How Do You Know a Jew in Antiquity When You See One?" Pages 1–45 in *Diasporas in Antiquity.* Edited by Shaye J. D. Cohen and Ernest S. Frerichs. Brown Judaic Studies 288. Atlanta:

Scholars, 1993. Repr. and rev. pages 25–68 in *The Beginnings of Jewishness: Boundaries, Varieties, Uncertainties*. Berkeley: University of California Press, 1999.

Collins, John J. "A Symbol of Otherness: Circumcision and Salvation in the First Century." Pages 163–86 in *"To See Ourselves as Others See Us": Christians, Jews, "Others" in Late Antiquity*. Edited by Jacob Neusner and Ernest S. Frerichs. Scholars Press Studies in the Humanities. Chico, Calif.: Scholars, 1985.

Collins, Raymond, F. "The Case of a Wandering Doxology: Rom 16,25–27." Pages 293–303 in *New Testament Textual Criticism and Exegesis: Festschrift J. Delobel*. Edited by A. Denaux. Bibliotheca ephemeridum theologicarum lovaniensium 161. Leuven: Leuven University Press, 2002.

Crafton, Jeffrey A. "Paul's Rhetorical Vision and the Purpose of Romans: Toward a New Understanding." *Novum Testamentum* 32 (1990): 317–39.

Cranfield, C. E. B. "Changes of Person and Number in Paul's Epistles." Pages 280–89 in *Paul and Paulinism: Essays in honour of C. K. Barrett*. Edited by Morna D. Hooker and Stephen G. Wilson. London: SPCK, 1982.

———. *A Critical and Exegetical Commentary on the Epistle to the Romans*. 2 vols. Edinburgh: T & T Clark, 1975, 1979.

Cranford, Michael. "Election and Ethnicity: Paul's View of Israel in Romans 9.1–13." *Journal for the Study of the New Testament* 50 (1993): 27–41.

Croatto, J. Severino. "The 'Nations' in the Salvific Oracles of Isaiah." *Vetus Testamentum* 55 (2005): 143–62.

Cullmann, Oscar. *Peter: Disciple, Apostle, Martyr*. Translated by Floyd V. Filson. Philadelphia: Westminster, 1958.

Cumont, F. "Un rescrit imperial sur la violation de sepulture." *Revue Historique* 163 (1930): 241–66.

Curtis, Heath R. "A Female Apostle?: A Note Re-examining the Work of Burer and Wallace Concerning ἐπίσημος with ἐν and the Dative." *Concordia Journal* 28 (2002): 437–40.

Dabourne, Wendy. Review of Neil Elliott, *The Rhetoric of Romans: Argumentative Constraint and Strategy and Paul's Dialogue with Judaism*. *Journal of Theological Studies* 43 ns (1992): 607–9.

———. "Euodia and Syntyche and Paul's Letter to the Philippians." Pages 3–15 in *The Social World of the First Christians: Essays in Honor of Wayne A. Meeks*. Edited by L. Michael White and O. Larry Yarbrough. Minneapolis: Fortress Press, 1995.

Dahl, Nils A. "Der Name Israel: Zur Auslegung von Gal. 6,16." *Judaica* 6 (1950): 161–70.

Dalbert, Peter. *Die Theologie der hellenistisch-jüdischen Missionsliteratur unter Ausschluss von Philo und Josephus*. Theologische Forschung 4. Hamburg-Volksdorf: Herbert Reich, 1954.

Das, A. Andrew. "1 Corinthians 11:17–34 Revisited." *Concordia Theological Quarterly* 62 (1998): 187–208.

——— "Another Look at ἐὰν μή in Galatians 2:16." *Journal of Biblical Literature* 119 (2000): 529–39.

———. *Paul, the Law, and the Covenant*. Peabody, Mass.: Hendrickson, 2001.

———— *Paul and the Jews*. Library of Pauline Studies. Peabody, Mass.: Hendrickson, 2003.

Daube, David. "Rabbinic Methods of Interpretation and Hellenistic Rhetoric." *Hebrew Union College Annual* 22 (1949): 239–62.

DeGraff, David. "Some Doubts about Doubt: The New Testament Use of ΔΙΑΚΡΙΝΩ." *Journal of the Evangelical Theological Society* 48 (2005): 733–55.

Deissmann, Adolf. *Light From the Ancient East*. Translated by Lionel R. M. Strachan. New York: George H. Doran, 1927.

Dewey, Arthur J. "ΕΙΣ ΤΗΝ ΣΠΑΝΙΑΝ: The Future and Paul." Pages 321–49 in *Religious Propaganda & Missionary Competition in the New Testament World: Essays Honoring Dieter Georgi*. Edited by Lukas Bormann, Kelly Del Tredici, and Angela Standhartinger. Novum Testamentum Supplements 74. Leiden: Brill, 1994.

Dill, Samuel. *Roman Society from Nero to Marcus Aurelius*. London: Macmillan, 1911.

Dio Cassius. *Roman History*. Translated by Earnest Cary. 9 vols. Loeb Classical Library. Cambridge: Harvard University Press, 1914–1927.

Diodorus Siculus. Translated by C. H. Oldfather et al. 12 vols. Loeb Classical Library. Cambridge: Harvard University Press, 1933–1967.

Dodd, Brian. *Paul's Paradigmatic "I": Personal Example as Literary Strategy*. Journal for the Study of the New Testament: Supplement Series 177. Sheffield: Sheffield Academic, 1999.

Donaldson, Terence L. *Paul and the Gentiles: Remapping the Apostle's Convictional World*. Minneapolis: Fortress Press, 1997.

————. "Proselytes or 'Righteous Gentiles'? The Status of Gentiles in Eschatological Pilgrimage Patterns of Thought." *Journal for the Study of the Pseudepigrapha* 7 (1990): 3–27.

Donfried, Karl Paul. "False Presuppositions in the Study of Romans." *Catholic Biblical Quarterly* 36 (1974): 332–58. Repr. pp. 102–25 in *The Romans Debate*. Rev. and enl. ed. Edited by Karl P. Donfried. Peabody, Mass.: Hendrickson, 1991.

————. "A Short Note on Romans 16." Pages 44–52 in *The Romans Debate*. Rev. and enl. ed. Edited by Karl P. Donfried. Peabody, Mass.: Hendrickson, 1991. Repr. from *Journal of Biblical Literature* 89 (1970): 441–49.

Dülmen, Andrea van. *Die Theologie des Gesetzes bei Paulus*. Stuttgarter biblische Monographien 5. Stuttgart: Katholisches Bibelwerk, 1968.

Dunn, James D. G. *The Acts of the Apostles*. Valley Forge, Pa.: Trinity Press International, 1996.

————. Review of Mark D. Nanos, *The Mystery of Romans*. *Journal of Theological Studies* 48 (1997): 599–602.

————. "Rom. 7,14–25 in the Theology of Paul." *Theologische Zeitschrift* 31 (1975): 257–73.

————. *Romans 1 — 8*. Word Biblical Commentary 38A. Dallas: Word, 1988.

————. *Romans 9 — 16*. Word Biblical Commentary 38B. Dallas: Word, 1988.

Du Toit, Andreas B. "Persuasion in Romans 1:1–17," *Biblische Zeitschrift* ns 33 (1989): 192–209.

Elliott, Neil. "Asceticism among the 'Weak' and 'Strong' in Romans 14–15." Pages 231–51 in *Asceticism and the New Testament*. Edited by Leif E. Vaage and Vincent L. Wimbush. New York: Routledge, 1999.

———. "Disciplining the Hope of the Poor in Ancient Rome." Pages 177–97 in *Christian Origins*. Vol. 1 of *A People's History of Christianity*. Edited by Richard A. Horsley. Minneapolis: Fortress Press, 2005.

———. *Liberating Paul: The Justice of God and the Politics of the Apostle*. Sheffield: Sheffield Academic, 1995.

———. "'*Paulus Contra Gentiles*': Comments on Mark Nanos, *The Mystery of Romans*." *Critical Review of Books in Religion* 11 (1998): 149–52.

———. *The Rhetoric of Romans: Argumentative Constraint and Strategy and Paul's Dialogue with Judaism*. Journal for the Study of the New Testament: Supplement Series 45. Sheffield: Sheffield Academic, 1990.

Ellis, E. Earle. "Paul and His Co-Workers." Pages 183–89 in *Dictionary of Paul and His Letters*. Edited by Gerald F. Hawthorne, Ralph P. Martin, and Daniel G. Reid. Downers Grove, Ill.: InterVarsity, 1993.

Epictetus. *The Discourses as Reported by Arrian*. Translated by W. A. Oldfather. 2 vols. Cambridge: Harvard University Press, 1925–1928.

Epp, Eldon Jay. *Junia: The First Woman Apostle*. Minneapolis: Fortress Press, 2005.

Esler, Philip F. "Ancient Oleiculture and Ethnic Differentiation: The Meaning of the Olive-Tree Image in Romans 11." *Journal for the Study of the New Testament* 26 (2003): 103–24.

———. *Conflict and Identity in Romans: The Social Setting of Paul's Letter*. Minneapolis: Fortress Press, 2003.

———. *Galatians*. New Testament Readings. London: Routledge, 1998.

Euripides. Edited and translated by David Kovacs. 6 vols. Cambridge: Harvard University Press, 1994–2002.

Fahy, T. "St. Paul's Romans were Jewish Converts." *Irish Theological Quarterly* 26 (1959): 182–91.

Fanning, Buist M. "Approaches to Verbal Aspect in New Testament Greek: Issues in Definition and Method." Pages 46–62 in *Biblical Greek Language and Linguistics: Open Questions in Current Research*. Edited by Stanley E. Porter and D. A. Carson. Journal for the Study of the New Testament: Supplement Series 80. Sheffield: Sheffield Academic, 1993.

Fee, Gordon D. *The First Epistle to the Corinthians*. New International Commentary on the New Testament. Grand Rapids: Eerdmans, 1987.

Feldman, Louis H. *Jew & Gentile in the Ancient World: Attitudes and Interactions from Alexander to Justinian*. Princeton, N.J.: Princeton University Press, 1993.

———. "Jewish Proselytism." Pages 372–408 in *Eusebius, Christianity, and Judaism*. Edited by Harold W. Attridge and Gohei Hata. Detroit: Wayne State University Press, 1992.

———. "The Omnipresence of the God-Fearers," *Biblical Archaelogy Review* 12/5 (1986): 58–69.

———. "Reflections on Rutger's 'Attitudes to Judaism in the Greco-Roman Period.'" *Jewish Quarterly Review* 86 (1995): 153–70.

―――. Review of Leonard Victor Rutgers, *The Jews in Late Ancient Rome: Evidence of Cultural Interactions in the Roman Diaspora. Jewish Quarterly Review* 86 (1995): 439–43.

Finger, Reta Haltmann. "Open Homes and Fictive Kin Groups: Jesus Invents the Family." *Daughters of Sarah* 20.1 (1994): 18–22.

Finlan, Stephen. *The Background and Content of Paul's Cultic Atonement Metaphors.* Academia Biblica 19. Atlanta: Society of Biblical Literature, 2004.

Finn, Thomas M. "The God-fearers Reconsidered." *Catholic Biblical Quarterly* 47 (1985): 75–84.

Fiorenza, Elisabeth Schüssler. "Missionaries, Apostles, Coworkers: Romans 16 and the Reconstruction of Women's Early Christian History." *Word & World* 6 (1986): 420–33.

Fitzgerald, John T., and L. Michael White. *The Tabula of Cebes.* Texts and Translations 24. Chico, Calif.: Scholars, 1983.

Fitzmyer, Joseph A. *Romans.* Anchor Bible 33. New York: Doubleday, 1993

Franke, Chris. "Is DI 'PC'? Does Israel Have Most Favored Nation Status? Another Look at 'The Nations' in Deutero-Isaiah." Pages 272–91 in *SBL Seminar Papers, 1999.* Society of Biblical Literature Seminar Papers 38. Atlanta: Society of Biblical Literature, 1999.

Fredriksen, Paula. *From Jesus to Christ: The Origins of the New Testament Images of Jesus.* New Haven: Yale University Press, 1988.

―――. "Paul and Augustine: Conversion, Narratives, Orthodox Traditions, and the Retrospective Self." *Journal of Theological Studies* 37 (1986): 3–34.

Frend, W. H. C. *Martyrdom and Persecution in the Early Church.* Oxford: Basil Blackwell, 1965.

Frey, Jean-Baptiste. *Corpus Inscriptionum Judaicarum: Jewish Inscriptions from the Third Century B.C. to the Seventh Century A.D.* Vol. 1: *Europe.* The Library of Biblical Studies. New York: Ktav, 1975.

Freyne, Sean. "Behind the Names: Samaritans, *Ioudaioi,* and Galileans." Pages 389–401 in *Text and Artifact in the Religions of Antiquity: Essays in Honour of Peter Richardson.* Edited by Stephen G. Wilson and Michel Desjardins. Studies in Christianity and Judaism 9. Waterloo, Ontario: Wilfrid Laurior University Press, 2000.

Friedrich, Johannes, Wolfgang Pohlmann, and Peter Stuhlmacher. "Zur historischen Situation und Intention von Rom 13, 1–7." *Zeitschrift für Theologie und Kirche* 73 (1976): 131–66.

Fuchs, Ernst. *Hermeneutik.* 2d ed. Bad Cannstatt: R. Müllerschön, 1958.

Gabba, Emilio. *Iscrizioni greche e latine per lo studio della Bibbia.* Sintesi Dell'oriente e Della Bibbia 3. Torino, Italy: Marietti, 1958.

Gager, John G. "Jews, Gentiles, and Synagogues in the Book of Acts." *Harvard Theological Review* 79 (1986): 91–99.

―――. *The Origins of Anti-Semitism.* Oxford: Oxford University Press, 1983.

―――. *Reinventing Paul.* Oxford: Oxford University Press, 2000

Gagnon, Robert A. J. "The Meaning of ῾ΥΜΩΝ ΤΟ ῾ΑΓΑΘΟΝ in Romans 14:16." *Journal of Biblical Literature* 117 (1998): 675–89.

―――. "Why the 'Weak' at Rome Cannot Be Non-Christian Jews." *Catholic Biblical Quarterly* 62 (2000): 64–82.

Galen: On the Doctrines of Hippocrates and Plato. Edited and translated by Phillip De Lacy. Corpus Medicorum Graecorum 5.4.1. Berlin: Akademie, 1984.

Gamble, Harry Jr. *The Textual History of the Letter to the Romans.* Studies and Documents 42. Grand Rapids: Eerdmans, 1977.

Garland, David E. "Composition and Unity of Philippians." *Novum Testamentum* 27 (1985): 141–73.

Garnsey, Peter. "Religious Toleration in Classical Antiquity." Pages 1–27 in *Persecution and Toleration.* Edited by W. J. Sheils. Papers of the Ecclesiastical History Society. Oxford: Blackwell, 1984.

Gaston, Lloyd. *Paul and the Torah.* Vancouver: University of British Columbia, 1987.

———. "Reading the Text and Digging the Past: The First Audience of Romans." Pages 35–44 in *Text and Artifact in the Religions of Mediterranean Antiquity: Essays in Honour of Peter Richardson.* Edited by Stephen G. Wilson and Michel Desjardins. Studies in Christianity and Judaism 9. Waterloo, Ontario: Wilfrid Laurier University Press, 2000.

Gathercole, Simon J. "A Law unto Themselves: The Gentiles in Romans 2.14–15 Revisited." *Journal for the Study of the New Testament* 85 (2002): 27–49.

Gaventa, Beverly Roberts. *Acts.* Abingdon New Testament Commentaries. Nashville: Abingdon, 2003.

Gignac, Alain. "Déconstruire notre lecture de *Romains* pour reconstruire notre théologie? Á propos de l'ouvrage de S.K. Stowers: *A Rereading of Romans.*" *Laval Théologique et Philosophique* 54 (1995): 181–93.

Gilliard, Frank D. "The Problem of the Antisemitic Comma Between 1 Thessalonians 2.14 and 15." *New Testament Studies* 35 (1989): 481–502.

Glad, Clarence E. *Paul and Philodemus: Adaptability in Epicurean and Early Christian Psychagogy.* Novum Testament Supplements 81. Leiden: Brill, 1995.

Godet, F. *Commentary on St. Paul's Epistle to the Romans.* Translated by A. Cusin. New York: Funk & Wagnalls, 1883.

Goldenberg, Robert. Review of John G. Gager, *The Origins of Anti-Semitism: Attitudes Toward Judaism in Pagan and Christian Antiquity. Religious Studies Review* 11 (1985): 335–37.

Goodman, Martin. *Mission and Conversion: Proselytizing in the Religious History of the Roman Empire.* Oxford: Oxford University Press, 1994.

Grieb, A. Katherine. *The Story of Romans: A Narrative Defense of God's Righteousness.* Louisville: Westminster John Knox, 2002.

Grisanti, Michael A. "Israel's Mission to the Nations in Isaiah 40–55: An Update." *The Master's Seminary Journal* 9 (1998): 39–61.

Gruen, Erich S. *Diaspora: Jews amidst Greeks and Romans.* Cambridge, Mass.: Harvard University Press, 2002.

Guerra, Anthony J. *Romans and the apologetic tradition: The purpose, genre and audience of Paul's letter.* Society for New Testament Studies Monograph Series 81. Cambridge: Cambridge University Press, 1995.

———. "Romans: Paul's Purpose and Audience with Special Attention to Romans 9–11." *Revue Biblique* 97 (1990): 219–37.

Gundry, Robert H. "The Moral Frustration of Paul Before His Conversion: Sexual Lust in Romans 7:7–25." Pages 228–45 in *Pauline Studies: Essays Presented to Professor F. F. Bruce on his 70th Birthday*. Edited by Donald A. Hagner and Murray J. Harris. Grand Rapids: Eerdmans, 1980.

———. *Soma in Biblical Theology with Emphasis on Pauline Anthropology*. Society for New Testament Studies Monograph Series 29. Cambridge: Cambridge University Press, 1976.

Hafemann, Scott. "The Salvation of Israel in Romans 11:25–32: A Response to Krister Stendahl." *Ex auditu* 4 (1988): 38–58.

Hagner, Donald A. "Paul's Quarrel with Judaism." Pages 128–50 in *Anti-Semitism and Early Christianity: Issues of Polemic and Faith*. Edited by Craig A. Evans and Donald A. Hagner. Minneapolis: Fortress Press, 1993.

Harland, Philip A. *Associations, Synagogues, and Congregations: Claiming a Place in Ancient Mediterranean Society*. Minneapolis: Fortress Press, 2003.

———. "Familial Dimensions of Group Identity: 'Brothers' ('Αδελφοί) in Associations of the Greek East." *Journal of Biblical Literature* 124 (2005): 491–513.

Harrill, J. Albert. *Slaves in the New Testament: Literary, Social, and Moral Dimensions*. Minneapolis: Fortress Press, 2006.

Harrisville, Roy A., III. *The Figure of Abraham in the Epistles of St. Paul: In the Footsteps of Abraham*. San Francisco: Mellen Research University Press, 1992.

Hasel, Gerhard F. *The Remnant: The History and Theology of the Remnant Idea from Genesis to Isaiah*. Berrien Springs, Mich.: Andrews University Press, 1972.

Hays, Richard B. "Adam, Israel, Christ: The Question of Covenant in the Theology of Romans: A Response to Leander E. Keck and N. T. Wright." Pages 68–86 in *Romans*. Edited by David M. Hay and E. Elizabeth Johnson. Vol. 3 of *Pauline Theology*. Minneapolis: Fortress Press, 1995.

———. *Echoes of Scripture in the Letters of Paul*. New Haven: Yale University Press, 1989.

———. "'The Gospel Is the Power of God for Salvation to Gentiles Only'? A Critique of Stanley Stowers' *A Rereading of Romans*." *Critical Review of Books in Religion* 9 (1996): 27–44.

———. "'Have We Found Abraham to be Our Forefather According to the Flesh?' A Reconsideration of Rom 4:1." *Novum Testamentum* 27 (1985): 76–98.

———. "Three Dramatic Roles: The Law in Romans 3 — 4." Pages 151–64 in *Paul and the Mosaic Law*, ed. James D. G. Dunn. Wissenschaftliche Untersuchungen zum Neuen Testament 89. Tübingen: J. C. B. Mohr (Paul Siebeck), 1996.

Hedner-Zetterholm, Karin. "The Jewish Communities of Ancient Rome." Pages 131–40 in *The Synagogue of Ancient Ostia and the Jews of Rome: Interdisciplinary Studies*. Edited by Birger Olsson, Dieter Mitternacht, and Olof Brandt. Stockholm: Svenska Institutet i Rom, 2001.

Heil, John Paul. "From Remnant to Seed of Hope for Israel: Romans 9:27–29." *Catholic Biblical Quarterly* 64 (2002): 703–20.

Hemer, Colin J. *The Book of Acts in the Setting of Hellenistic History*. Wissenschaftliche Untersuchungen zum Neuen Testament 49. Tübingen: J. C. B. Mohr (Paul Siebeck), 1989. Repr., Winona Lake, Ind.; Eisenbrauns, 1990.

Hengel, Martin, and Anna Maria Schwemer. *Paul between Damascus and Antioch.* Louisville: Westminster John Knox, 1997.

Hidal, Sten. "The Jews as the Roman Authors Saw Them." Pages 141–44 in *The Synagogue of Ancient Ostia and the Jews of Rome: Interdisciplinary Studies.* Edited by Birger Olsson, Dieter Mitternacht, and Olof Brandt. Stockholm: Svenska Institutet I Rom, 2001.

Hoehner, Harold W. *Ephesians: An Exegetical Commentary.* Grand Rapids: Baker, 2002.

Hoerber, Robert G. "The Decree of Claudius in Acts 18:2." *Concordia Theological Monthly* 31 (1960): 690–94.

Hofius, Otfried. "'All Israel Will Be Saved': Divine Salvation and Israel's Deliverance in Romans 9–11." *Princeton Seminary Bulletin.* Suppl. 1 (1990): 19–39.

Holland, Glenn S. "The Self against the Self in Romans 7.7–25." Pages 260–71 in *The Rhetorical Interpretation of Scripture: Essays from the 1996 Malibu Conference.* Edited by Stanley E. Porter and Dennis L. Stamps. Journal for the Study of the New Testament: Supplement Series 180. Sheffield: Sheffield Academic, 1999.

Horace. *Satires, Epistles and Ars Poetica.* Rev. ed. Translated by H. Rushton Fairclough. Cambridge: Harvard University Press, 1929.

Horne, Charles M. "The Meaning of the Phrase 'And Thus All Israel Will Be Saved.'" *Journal of the Evangelical Theological Society* 21 (1978): 329–34.

Horsley, Richard A. "Synagogues in Galilee and the Gospels." Pages 46–69 in *Evolution of the Synagogue: Problems and Progress.* Edited by Howard Clark Kee and Lynn H. Cohick. Harrisburg, Pa.: Trinity Press International, 1999.

Horst, Pieter W. van der. *Ancient Jewish Epitaphs: An Introductory Survey of a Millennium of Jewish Funerary Epigraphy (300 BCE–700 CE).* Contributions to Biblical Exegesis and Theology 2. Kampen: Kok Pharos, 1991.

———. "'Only Then Will All Israel Be Saved': A Short Note on the Meaning of καὶ οὕτως in Romans 11:26." *Journal of Biblical Literature* 119 (2000): 521–25.

Howard, George. "The Beginnings of Christianity in Rome: A Note on Suetonius, Life of Claudius XXV.4." *Restoration Quarterly* 24 (1981): 175–77.

Hurtado, Larry W. "The Doxology at the End of Romans." Pages 185–99 in *New Testament Textual Criticism: Its Significance for Exegesis: Essays in Honour of Bruce M. Metzger.* Edited by Eldon Jay Epp and Gordon D. Fee. Oxford: Oxford University Press, 1981.

Hvalvik, Reidar. "A 'Sonderweg' for Israel: A Critical Examination of a Current Interpretation of Romans 11.25–27." *Journal for the Study of the New Testament* 38 (1990): 87–107.

Janne, Henri. "Impulsore Chresto." *Annuaire de l'Institut de philologie et d'histoire orientales et slaves* 2 (1934): 531–53.

Jervell, Jacob. "The Letter to Jerusalem." *Studia Theologica* 25 (1971): 61–73. Repr. pp. 53–64 in *The Romans Debate.* Rev. and enl. ed. Edited by Karl P. Donfried. Peabody, Mass.: Hendrickson, 1991.

Jervis, L. Ann. "'The Commandment Which Is for Life' (Romans 7.10): Sin's Use of the Obedience of Faith." *Journal for the Study of the New Testament* 27 (2004): 193–216.

————. *The Purpose of Romans: A Comparative Letter Structure Investigation.* Journal for the Study of the New Testament: Supplement Series 55. Sheffield: Sheffield Academic, 1991.

Jewett, Robert. *A Chronology of Paul's Life.* Philadelphia: Fortress Press, 1979.

————. "Ecumenical Theology for the Sake of Mission: Romans 1:1–17 + 15:14–16:24." Pages 89–108 in *Romans.* Edited by David M. Hay and E. Elizabeth Johnson. Vol. 3 of *Pauline Theology.* Minneapolis: Fortress Press, 1995.

————. "Paul, Phoebe, and the Spanish Mission." Pages 142–61 in *The Social World of Formative Christianity and Judaism: Essays in Tribute to Howard Clark Kee.* Edited by Jacob Neusner, Peder Borgen, Ernest S. Frerichs, and Richard Horsley. Philadelphia: Fortress Press, 1988.

————. "The Question of the 'Apportioned Spirit' in Paul's Letters: Romans as a Case Study." Pages 193–206 in *The Holy Spirit and Christian Origins: Essays in Honor of James D. G. Dunn.* Edited by Graham N. Stanton, Bruce W. Longenecker, and Stephen C. Barton. Grand Rapids: Eerdmans, 2004.

————. "Romans as an Ambassadorial Letter." *Interpretation* 36 (1982): 5–20.

————. "Tenement Churches and Communal Meals in the Early Church: The Implications of a Form-Critical Analysis of 2 Thessalonians 3:10." *Biblical Research* 38 (1993): 23–43.

Johnson, Dan. "The Structure and Meaning of Romans 11." *Catholic Biblical Quarterly* 46 (1984): 91–103.

Johnson, E. Elizabeth. "A Critical Assessment of Mark Nanos, *The Mystery of Romans.*" *Critical Review of Books in Religion* 11 (1998): 153–62.

————. *The Function of Apocalyptic and Wisdom Traditions in Romans 9–11.* Society of Biblical Literature Dissertation Series 109. Atlanta: Scholars, 1989.

Johnson, Luke Timothy. *Reading Romans: A Literary and Theological Commentary.* Reading the New Testament. New York: Crossroad, 1997.

Johnson, S. Lewis, Jr. "Paul and the 'Israel of God': An Exegetical and Eschatological Case-Study." *Mishkan* 6–7 (1987): 49–65.

Josephus. Translated by H. St. J. Thackeray et al. 10 vols. Loeb Classical Library. Cambridge: Harvard University Press, 1926–1965.

Juel, Donald. *Messianic Exegesis: Christological Interpretation of the Old Testament in Early Christianity.* Philadelphia: Fortress Press, 1988.

Judge, E. A. and G. S. R. Thomas. "The Origin of the Church at Rome: A New Solution?" *Reformed Theological Review* 25 (1966): 81–94.

Karlberg, Mark W. "Israel's History Personified: Romans 7:7–13 in Relation to Paul's Teaching on the 'Old Man.'" *Trinity Journal* 7 (1986): 65–74.

Karris, Robert J. "Romans 14:1–15:13 and the Occasion of Romans." *Catholic Biblical Quarterly* 25 (1973): 155–78. Repr. pp. 65–84 in *The Romans Debate.* Rev. and enl. ed. Edited by Karl P. Donfried. Peabody, Mass.: Hendrickson, 1991.

Käsemann, Ernst. *Commentary on Romans.* Grand Rapids: Eerdmans, 1980.

Keck, Leander E. *Romans.* Abingdon New Testament Commentaries. Nashville: Abingdon, 2005.

———. "What Makes Romans Tick?" Pages 3–29 in *Romans*. Edited by David M. Hay and E. Elizabeth Johnson. Vol. 3 of *Pauline Theology*. Minneapolis: Fortress Press, 1995.

Kee, Howard Clark. "Defining the First-Century C.E. Synagogue: Problems and Progress." Pages 7–26 in *Evolution of the Synagogue: Problems and Progress*. Edited by Howard Clark Kee and Lynn H. Cohick. Harrisburg, Pa.: Trinity Press International, 1999.

Kennedy, George A. *Progymnasmata: Greek Textbooks of Prose Composition and Rhetoric*. Writings from the Greco-Roman World 10. Atlanta: Society of Biblical Literature, 2003.

Kettunen, Markku. *Der Abfassungszweck des Römerbriefes*. Annales Academiae Scientarum Fennicae: Dissertations Humanarum Litterarum 18. Helsinki: Suomalainen Tiedeakatemia, 1979.

Kinoshita, Junji. "Romans — Two Writings Combined." *Novum Testamentum* 7 (1964): 258–77.

Kittel, G., and G. Friedrich, eds. *Theological Dictionary of the New Testament*. Translated by G. W. Bromiley. 10 vols. Grand Rapids: Eerdmans, 1964–1976.

Klein, G. *Der älteste christliche Katechismus und die jüdische Propaganda-Literatur*. Berlin: Georg Reimer, 1909.

Klein, Günter. "Paul's Purpose in Writing the Epistle to the Romans." Pages 29–43 in *The Romans Debate*. Rev. and enl. ed. Edited by Karl P. Donfried. Peabody, Mass.: Hendrickson, 1991. [Translation of "Der Abfassungszweck des Römerbriefes." Pages 129–44 in *Rekonstruktion und Interpretation: Gesammelte Aufsätze zum Neuen Testament*. Beiträge zur evangelischen Theologie 50. Münich: Chr. Kaiser, 1969.]

Klijn, A. F. J. *An Introduction to the New Testament*. Leiden: Brill, 1967.

Kloppenborg, John S. "Collegia and *Thiasoi*: Issues in Function, taxonomy and membership." Pages 16–30 in *Voluntary Associations in the Graeco-Roman World*. Edited by John S. Kloppenborg and Stephen G. Wilson. London: Routledge, 1996.

Kloppenborg, John S. "Edwin Hatch, Churches and *Collegia*." Pages 212–38 in *Origins and Method: Towards a New Understanding of Judaism and Christianity: Essays in Honour of John C. Hurd*. Edited by Bradley H. McLean. Journal for the Study of the New Testament: Supplement Series 86. Sheffield: Sheffield Academic, 1993.

Knox, John. "The Epistle to the Romans: Introduction." Pages 355–72 of vol. 9 of *The Interpreter's Bible*. Edited by George Arthur Buttrick et al. 12 vols. Nashville: Abingdon, 1951–1957.

Kraabel, A. Thomas. "The Disappearance of the God-Fearers." *Numen: International Review for the History of Religions* 18 (1981): 113–26. Repr. pages 120–30 in *Diaspora Jews and Judaism: Essays in Honor of, and in Dialogue with, A. Thomas Kraabel*. Edited by J. Andrew Overman and Robert S. MacLennan. South Florida Studies in the History of Judaism 41. Atlanta: Scholars, 1992.

———. "Immigrants, Exites, Expatriates, and Missionaries." Pages 71–88 in *Religious Propaganda & Missionary Competition in the New Testament World: Essays Honoring Dieter Georgi*. Edited by Lukas Bormann, Kelly Del Tredici, and Angela Standhartinger. Novum Testamentum Supplements 74. Leiden: Brill, 1994.

————. "Synagoga Caeca: Systematic Distortion in Gentile Interpretations of Evidence for Judaism in the Early Christian Period." Pages 219–46 in *"To See Ourselves as Others See Us": Christians, Jews, "Others" in Late Antiquity*. Edited by Jacob Neusner and Ernest S. Frerichs. Scholars Press Studies in the Humanities. Chico, Calif.: Scholars, 1985. Repr. pages 35–62 in *Diaspora Jews and Judaism: Essays in Honor of, and in Dialogue with, A. Thomas Kraabel*. Edited by J. Andrew Overman and Robert S. MacLennan. South Florida Studies in the History of Judaism 41; Atlanta: Scholars, 1992.

Krodel, Gerhard. "Persecution and Toleration of Christianity Until Hadrian." Pages 255–67 in *Early Church History: The Roman Empire as the Setting of Primitive Christianity*. Edited by Stephen Benko and John J. O'Rourke. London: Oliphants, 1971.

Kümmel, Werner Georg. *Introduction to the New Testament*. Rev. and enl. ed. Translated by Howard Clark Kee. Nashville: Abingdon, 1975.

————. *Römer 7 und das Bild des Menschen im Neuen Testament*. Theologische Bücherei 53. Munich: Chr. Kaiser, 1974.

La Piana, George. "Foreign Groups in Rome During the First Centuries of the Empire." *Harvard Theological Review* 20 (1927): 183–403.

Laato, Timo. *Paul and Judaism: An Anthropological Approach*. Translated by T. McElwain. South Florida Studies in the History of Judaism 115. Atlanta: Scholars Press, 1995.

Lake, Kirsopp. *The Earlier Epistles of St. Paul: Their Motive and Origin*. 2d ed. London: Rivingtons, 1919.

————. "Proselytes and God-Fearers." Pages 74–96 in vol. 5 of *The Acts of the Apostles*. Part 1 of *The Beginnings of Christianity*. Edited by F. J. Foakes Jackson and Kirsopp Lake. London: Macmillan, 1933. Repr. Grand Rapids: Baker, 1979.

Lambrecht, Jan. "Paul's Lack of Logic in Romans 9,1–13: A Response to M. Cranford's 'Election and Ethnicity.'" Pages 55–60 in *Pauline Studies*. Leuven: Leuven University Press, 1994.

Lamp, Jeffrey S. "Is Paul Anti-Jewish? *Testament of Levi* 6 in the Interpretation of 1 Thessalonians 2:13–16." *Catholic Biblical Quarterly* 65 (2003): 408–27.

Lampe, Peter. *From Paul to Valentinus: Christians at Rome in the First Two Centuries*. Translated by Michael Steinhauser. Minneapolis: Fortress Press, 2003.

————. "The Roman Christians of Romans 16." Pages 216–30 in *The Romans Debate*. Rev. and enl. ed. Edited by Karl P. Donfried. Peabody, Mass.: Hendrickson, 1991.

————. "Zur Textgeschichte des Römerbriefes." *Novum Testamentum* 27 (1985): 273–77.

Lane, William L. "Social Perspectives on Roman Christianity during the Formative Years from Nero to Nerva: Romans, Hebrews, 1 Clement." Pages 196–244 in *Judaism and Christianity in First-Century Rome*. Edited by Karl P. Donfried and Peter Richardson. Grand Rapids: Eerdmans, 1998.

Leenhardt, Franz J. *The Epistle to the Romans: A Commentary*. London: Lutterworth, 1961.

Leon, Harry J. *The Jews of Ancient Rome*. Updated ed. Peabody, Mass.: Hendrickson, 1960.

Levinskaya, Irina. *The Book of Acts in Its Diaspora Setting*. Vol. 5 of *The Book of Acts in Its First-Century Setting*. Edited by Bruce W. Winter. Grand Rapids: Eerdmans, 1996.

Lietzmann, Hans. *Einführung in die Textgeschichte der Paulusbriefe an die Römer.* 5th ed. Handbuch zum Neuen Testament 8. Tübingen: J. C. B. Mohr (Paul Siebeck), 1933. Repr., 1971.

Lieu, Judith M. "Do God-Fearers Make Good Christians?" Pages 329–45 in *Crossing the Boundaries: Essays in Biblical Interpretation in Honour of Michael D. Goulder.* Edited by Stanley E. Porter, Paul Joyce, and David E. Orton. Biblical Interpretation Series 8. Leiden: Brill, 1994.

———. *Neither Jew Nor Greek? Constructing Early Christianity.* Studies of the New Testament and Its World. London: T & T Clark, 2002.

Lifshitz, Baruch. "Notes d'épigraphie grecque." *Revue Biblique* 76 (1969): 92–98.

Lightfoot, J. B. *Biblical Essays.* New York: Macmillan, 1893. Repr., Grand Rapids: Baker, 1979.

———. *The Epistle of St. Paul to the Galatians.* 3d ed. Grand Rapids: Zondervan, 1962.

Linderski, Jerzy. *Roman Questions: Selected Papers.* Heidelberger althistorische Beiträge und epigraphische Studien 20. Stuttgart: Steiner, 1995.

Lipsius, Richard Adelbert. *Briefe an die Galater, Römer, Philipper.* Vol. 2 of *Hand-Commentar zum Neuen Testament.* 2d ed. Freiburg: J. C. B. Mohr (Paul Siebeck), 1892.

———. *Chronologie der römischen Bischöfe bis zur Mitte der vierten Jahrhunderts.* Kiel: Schwers'sche, 1869), 40–76.

Longenecker, Bruce W. "Different Answers to the Different Issues: Israel, the Gentiles and Salvation History in Romans 9–11." *Journal for the Study of the New Testament* 36 (1989): 95–123.

Longinus. *On the Sublime.* Translated by W. H. Fyfe. Loeb Classical Library. Cambridge: Harvard University Press, 1995.

Lüdemann, Gerd. *Early Christianity according to the Traditions in Acts: A Commentary.* Translated by John Bowden. Minneapolis: Fortress Press, 1989.

———. *Paul, Apostle to the Gentiles: Studies in Chronology.* Translated by F. Stanley Jones. Philadelphia: Fortress Press, 1984.

Lutjens, Ronald. "'You Do Not Do What You Want' What Does Galatians 5:17 Really Mean?" *Presbyterion* 16/2 (1990): 103–17.

Lyonnet, S. "L'historie du salut selon le chapitre VII de l'épitre aux Romains." *Biblica* 43 (1962): 117–51.

MacLennan, Robert S. and A. Thomas Kraabel. "The God-Fearers — A Literary and Theological Invention." *Biblical Archaeology Review* 12/5 (1986): 46–53, 64. Repr. pages 131–43 in *Diaspora Jews and Judaism: Essays in Honor of, and in Dialogue with, A. Thomas Kraabel.* Edited by J. Andrew Overman and Robert S. MacLennan. South Florida Studies in the History of Judaism 41. Atlanta: Scholars, 1992.

MacMullen, Ramsey. *Enemies of the Roman Order: Treason, Unrest, and Alienation in the Empire.* Cambridge: Harvard University Press, 1966.

Maier, Harry O. *The Social Setting of the Ministry as Reflected in the Writings of Hermas, Clement, and Ignatius.* Ontario: Wifrid Laurier Univ. Press, 1991.

Malherbe, Abraham J. *The Letters to the Thessalonians.* Anchor Bible 32B. New York: Doubleday, 2000.

Malherbe, Abraham J. "*Me Genoito* in the Diatribe and Paul." Pages 25–33 in *Paul and the Popular Philosophers*. Minneapolis: Fortress Press, 1989. Repr. from *Harvard Theological Review* 73 (1980): 231–40.. "*Me Genoito* in the Diatribe and Paul." Pages 25–33 in *Paul and the Popular Philosophers*. Minneapolis: Fortress Press, 1989. Repr. from *Harvard Theological Review* 73 (1980): 231–40.

———. *Social Aspects of Early Christianity*. 2d ed. Philadelphia: Fortress Press, 1983.

Malina, Bruce J. "'Religion' in the World of Paul." *Biblical Theology Bulletin* 16 (1986): 92–101.

———., and Jerome H. Neyrey. "Honor and Shame in Luke-Acts: Pivotal Values of the Mediterranean World." Pages 25–65 in *The Social World of Luke-Acts: Models for Interpretation*. Edited by Jerome H. Neyrey. Peabody, Mass.: Hendrickson, 1991.

Manson, T. W. "St. Paul's Letter to the Romans — and Others." Pages 225–41 in *Studies in the Gospels and Epistles*. Edited by M. Black. Manchester: Manchester University Press, 1962. Repr. pages 3–15 in *The Romans Debate*. Rev. and enl. ed. Edited by Karl P. Donfried. Peabody, Mass.: Hendrickson, 1991.

Manson, William. *The Epistle to the Hebrews: An Historical and Theological Reconsideration*. London: Hodder and Stoughton, 1951.

Marcovich, Miroslav, ed. *Iustini Matyris Apologiae Pro Christianis*. Patristische Texte und Studien 38. Berlin: Walter de Gruyter, 1994.

Marcus, Ralph. "The Sebomenoi in Josephus." *Jewish Social Studies* 14 (1952): 247–50.

Marshall, I. Howard. "Romans 16:25–27 — An Apt Conclusion." Pages 170–84 in *Romans and the People of God: Essays in Honor of Gordon D. Fee on the Occasion of His 65th Birthday*. Edited by Sven K. Soderlund and N. T. Wright. Grand Rapids: Eerdmans, 1999.

Marxsen, Willi. *Introduction to the New Testament: An Approach to its Problems*. Translated by G. Buswell. Philadelphia: Fortress Press, 1968.

Mason, Steve, "'For I Am Not Ashamed of the Gospel' (Rom. 1.16): The Gospel and the First Readers of Romans." Pages 254–87 in *Gospel in Paul: Studies on Corinthians, Galatians and Romans for Richard N. Longenecker*. Edited by L. Ann Jervis and Peter Richardson. Journal for the Study of the New Testament: Supplement Series 108. Sheffield: Sheffield Academic Press, 1994.

———. "Paul, Classical Anti-Jewish Polemic, and the Letter to the Romans." Pages 181–223 in *Self-Definition and Self-Discovery in Early Christianity*. Edited by David J. Hawkin and Tom Robinson. Lewiston, N.Y.: Edwin Mellen, 1990.

McCready, Wayne O. "*Ekklesia* and Voluntary Associations." Pages 59–73 in *Voluntary Associations in the Graeco-Roman World*. Edited by John S. Kloppenborg and Stephen G. Wilson. London: Routledge, 1996.

McDonald, J. I. H. "Was Romans XVI a Separate Letter?" *New Testament Studies* 16 (1969–70): 369–72.

McEleney, Neil J. "Conversion, Circumcision and the Law." *New Testament Studies* 20 (1974): 319–41.

McKay, K. L. "Time and Aspect in New Testament Greek." *Novum Testamentum* 34 (1992): 209–28.

McKnight, Scot. *A Light among the Gentiles: Jewish Missionary Activity in the Second Temple Period.* Minneapolis: Fortress Press, 1991.

McLean, Bradley H. "The Agrippinilla Inscription: Religious Associations and Early Church Formation." Pages 239–70 in *Origins and Method: Towards a New Understanding of Judaism and Christianity: Essays in Honour of John C. Hurd.* Edited by Bradley H. McLean. Journal for the Study of the New Testament: Supplement Series 86. Sheffield: Sheffield Academic, 1993.

Meagher, John C. "As the Twig Was Bent: Antisemitism in Greco-Roman and Earliest Christian Times." Pages 1–26 in *Anti-Semitism and the Foundations of Christianity.* Edited by Alan T. Davies. New York: Paulist, 1979.

Meeks, Wayne A. "Breaking Away: Three New Testament Pictures of Christianity's Separation from the Jewish Communities." Pages 93–115 in *To See Ourselves as Others See Us: Christians, Jews, "Others" in Late Antiquity.* Edited by Jacob Neusner and Ernest S. Frerichs. Scholars Press Studies in the Humanities. Chico, Calif.: Scholars, 1985.

Meeks, Wayne A. *First Urban Christians.* New Haven: Yale University Press, 1983.

———. "Judgment and the Brother: Romans 14:1 — 15:13." Pages 290–300 in *Tradition and Interpretation in the New Testament.* Edited by Gerald F. Hawthorne and Otto Betz. Grand Rapids: Eerdmans, 1987.

Merkle, Ben L. "Romans 11 and the Future of Ethnic Israel." *Journal of the Evangelical Theological Society* 43 (2000): 709–21.

Metzger, Bruce M. "The Nazareth Inscription Once Again." Pages 221–38 in *Jesus und Paulus: Festschrift für Werner Georg Kümmel zum 70. Geburtstag.* Edited by E. Earle Ellis and Erich Gräßer. Göttingen: Vandenhoeck & Ruprecht, 1975.

———. *A Textual Commentary on the Greek New Testament.* Stuttgart: United Bible Societies, 1971.

Meyer, Paul W. "The Worm at the Core of the Apple: Exegetical Reflections on Romans 7." Pages 62–84 in *The Conversation Continues: Studies in Paul and John in Honor of J. Louis Martyn.* Edited by Robert T. Fortna and Beverly R. Gaventa. Nashville: Abingdon, 1990.

Middendorf, Michael Paul. *The "I" in the Storm: A Study of Romans 7.* St. Louis: Concordia Academic Press, 1997.

Miller, James C. *The Obedience of Faith, the Eschatological People of God, and the Purpose of Romans.* Society of Biblical Literature Dissertation Series 177. Atlanta: Society of Biblical Literature, 2000.

———. "The Romans Debate: 1991–2001." *Currents in Research: Biblical Studies* 9 (2001): 306–49.

Milne, D. J. W. "Romans 7:7–12, Paul's Pre-conversion Experience." *Reformed Theological Review* 43 (1984): 9–17.

The Mishnah. Translated by Herbert Danby. Oxford: Oxford University Press, 1933.

Mitchell, Margaret M. *Paul and the Rhetoric of Reconciliation: An Exegetical Investigation of the Language and Composition of 1 Corinthians.* Louisville: Westminster John Knox, 1991.

Mitchell, Stephen. "The Cult of Theos Hypsistos between Pagans, Jews, and Christians." Pages 81–148 in *Pagan Monotheism in Late Antiquity*. Edited by Polymnia Athanassiadi and Michael Frede. Oxford: Clarendon, 1999.

Momigliano, Arnaldo. *Claudius: The Emperor and His Achievement*. Rev. ed. Cambridge: W. Heffer & Sons, 1961.

Moo, Douglas J. *The Epistle to the Romans*. New International Commentary on the New Testament. Grand Rapids: Eerdmans, 1996.

———. "Israel and the Paul in Romans 7.7–12." *New Testament Studies* 32 (1986): 122–35.

Morgan, Robert. "Romans Re-visioned." Review of Neil Elliott, *The Rhetoric of Romans*. *Expository Times* 102 (1991): 279–80.

Morris, Leon. *The Epistle to the Romans*. Grand Rapids: Eerdmans, 1988.

Mullins, Terence Y. "Greeting as a New Testament Form." *Journal of Biblical Literature* 87 (1968): 418–26.

Munck, Johannes. *Paul and the Salvation of Mankind*. Atlanta: John Knox, 1959.

Murphy-O'Connor, Jerome. "Lots of God-Fearers? *Theosebeis* in the Aphrodisias Inscription." *Revue Biblique* 99 (1992): 418–24.

———. *Paul: A Critical Life*. Oxford: Oxford University Press, 1996.

———. "Paul and Gallio." *Journal of Biblical Literature* 112 (1993): 315–17.

Nanos, Mark D. *The Irony of Galatians*. Minneapolis: Fortress Press, 2002.

———. "The Jewish Context of the Gentile Audience Addressed in Paul's Letter to the Romans." *Catholic Biblical Quarterly* 61 (1999): 283–304.

———. *The Mystery of Romans: The Jewish Context of Paul's Letter*. Minneapolis: Fortress Press, 1996.

———. "A Rejoinder to Robert A. J. Gagnon's 'Why the "Weak" at Rome Cannot Be Non-Christian Jews.'" 37 pages. Created 14 July 2000. Updated 20 June 2003. Cited 1 August 2005. Online: http://mywebpages.comcast.net/nanosmd/Gagnon-rejoinder-6–20–03.pdf.

———. "Response." *Critical Review of Books in Religion* 11 (1998): 167–78.

Noack, Bent. "Current and Backwater in the Epistle to the Romans." *Studia Theologica* 19 (1965): 155–66.

Nock, A. D. "Religious Developments from the Close of the Republic to the Death of Nero." Pages 465–511 in vol. 10 of *The Cambridge Ancient History*. Edited by S. A. Cook, F. E. Adcock, and M. P. Charlesworth. Cambridge: Cambridge University Press, 1934.

Nolland, John. "Uncircumcised Proseyltes?" *Journal for the Study of Judaism in the Persian, Hellenistic, and Roman Periods* 12 (1981): 173–94.

Nygren, Anders. *Commentary on Romans*. Philadelphia: Fortress Press, 1949.

O'Neill, J. C. O. *Paul's Letter to the Romans*. Baltimore, Md.: Penguin Books, 1975.

Ollrog, Wolf-Henning. "Die Abfassungsverhältnisse von Röm 16." Pages 221–44 in *Kirche: Festschrift für Günther Bornkamm zum 75. Geburtstag*. Edited by Dieter Lührmann und Georg Strecker. Tübingen: J. C. B. Mohr (Paul Siebeck), 1980.

Omerzu, Heike. Review of Angelika Reichert, *Der Römerbrief als Gratwanderung: Eine Untersuchung zur Abfassungsproblematik*. *Journal of Biblical Literature* 123 (2004): 767–71.

Orosii, Pauli. *Historiarum Adversum Paganos. Libri VIIL Accedit Eiusdem Liber Apolo-geticus.* Corpus Scriptorum Ecclesiasticorum Latinorum 5. Vindobonae: Apud C. Geroldi Filium Bibliopolam Academiae, 1882.

Osborne, William L. "The Old Testament Background of Paul's 'All Israel' in Romans 1:26a." *Asia Journal of Theology* 2 (1988): 282–93.

Overman, J. Andrew. "The God-Fearers: Some Neglected Features." *Journal for the Study of the New Testament* 32 (1988): 17–26. Repr. pages 145–52 in *Diaspora Jews and Judaism: Essays in Honor of, and in Dialogue with, A. Thomas Kraabel.* Edited by J. Andrew Overman and Robert S. MacLennan. South Florida Studies in the History of Judaism 41; Atlanta: Scholars, 1992.

Ovid. *Metamorphoses.* Rev ed. Translated by Frank Justus Miller. 2 vols. Loeb Classical Library. Cambridge: Harvard University Press, 1977–1984.

Packer, J. I. "The 'Wretched Man' in Romans 7." Pages 621–27 in *Studia Evangelica,* vol. 2: *Papers Presented to the Second International Congress on New Tesatment Studies Held at Christ Church, Oxford, 1961,* part 1: *The New Testament Scriptures.* Edited by F. L. Cross. Texte und Untersuchungen 87. Berlin: Akademie, 1964.

Patrologia graeca. Edited by J.-P. Migne. 162 vols. Paris, 1857–1886.

Patrologia latina. Edited by J.-P. Migne. 217 vols. Paris, 1844–1864.

Pedersen, Sigfred. "Theologische Überlegungen zur Isagogik des Römerbriefes." *Zeitschrift für die neutestamentliche Wissenschaft und die Kunde der älteren Kirche* 76 (1985): 47–67.

Penna, Romano. *Paul the Apostle: Wisdom and Folly of the Cross.* 2 vols. Translated by Thomas P. Wahl. Collegeville, Minn.: Liturgical, 1996.

Peterlin, Davorin. *Paul's Letter to the Philippians in the Light of Disunity in the Church.* Supplements to Novum Testamentum 79. Leiden: Brill, 1995.

Peterson, Jeffrey. Review of Stanley K. Stowers, *A Rereading of Romans. Restoration Quarterly* 39 (1997): 50–53.

Petronius. *Satyricon.* Translated by Michael Heseltine. Loeb Classical Library. Cambridge: Harvard University Pres, 1969.

Philo. Translated by F. H. Colson et al. 10 vols. and 2 suppl. vols. Loeb Classical Library. Cambridge: Harvard University Press, 1929–1962.

Philostratus. *Life of Apollonius of Tyana.* Edited and translated by Christopher P. Jones. 2 vols. Cambridge: Harvard University Press, 2005.

Picirilli, Robert E. "The Meaning of the Tenses in New Testament Greek: Where Are We?" *Journal for the Study of the New Testament* 48 (2005): 533–55.

Plutarch. *Lives.* Translated by Bernadotte Perrin. 11 vols. Loeb Classical Library. Cambridge: Harvard University Press, 1914–1926.

Ponsot, Hervé. "Et ainsi tout Israel sauvé; Rom., XI, 26a." *Revue Biblique* 89 (1982): 406–17.

Porter, Stanley E. *Idioms of the Greek New Testament.* 2d ed. Biblical Languages: Greek 2. Sheffield: Sheffield Academic, 1994.

———. "In Defense of Verbal Aspect." Pages 26–45 in *Biblical Greek Language and Linguistics: Open Questions in Current Research.* Edited by Stanley E. Porter and

D. A. Carson. Journal for the Study of the New Testament: Supplement Series 80. Sheffield: Sheffield Academic, 1993.

———. *Verbal Aspect in the Greek of the New Testament, with Reference to Tense and Mood.* Studies in Biblical Greek 1. New York: Peter Lang, 1989.

Poythress, Vern S. "Is Romans 1:3–4 a *Pauline* Confession After All?" *Expository Times* 87 (1975–76): 180–83.

Quintilian. Translated by H. E. Butler. 4 vols. Cambridge: Harvard University Press, 1920–1922.

Rajak, Tessa, and David Noy. "*Archisynagogoi:* Office, Title and Social Status in the Greco-Jewish Synagogue." *Journal of Roman Studies* 83 (1993): 75–93.

Rauer, Max. *Die "Schwachen" in Korinth und Rom nach den Paulusbriefen.* Biblische Studien 21. Freiburg: Herder, 1923.

Reasoner, Mark. "Rome and Roman Christianity." Pages 850–55 in *Dictionary of Paul and His Letters.* Edited by Gerald F. Hawthorne, Ralph P. Martin, and Daniel G. Reid. Downers Grove, Ill.: InterVarsity, 1993.

———. *The Strong and the Weak: Romans 14:1–15:13 in Context.* Society of New Testament Studies Monograph Series 103. Cambridge: Cambridge University Press, 1999.

Reichert, Angelika. *Der Römerbrief als Gratwanderung: Eine Untersuchung zur Abfassungsproblematik.* Forschungen zur Religion und Literatur des Alten und Neuen Testaments 194. Göttingen: Vandenhoeck & Ruprecht, 2001.

Refoulé, François. "Cohérence ou incohérence de Paul in Romains 9–11." *Revue Biblique* 98 (1991): 51–79.

———. "*... Et ainsi tout Israël sera sauvé*": *Romains 11:25–32.* Lectio Divina 117. Paris: Cerf, 1984.

Reynolds, Joyce M., and Robert F. Tannenbaum. *Jews and God-fearers at Aphrodisias: Greek Inscriptions with Commentary: Texts from the Excavations at Aphrodisias Conducted by Kenan T. Erim.* Supplementary volume 12. Cambridge: Cambridge Philological Society, 1987.

Rhoads, David. "Children of Abraham, Children of God: Metaphorical Kinship in Paul's Letter to the Galatians." *Currents in Theology and Mission* 31 (2004): 282–97.

Riccobono, Salvator, G. Baviera, C. Rerrini, G. Furlani, and V. Aragnio-Ruiz, eds. *Iuris Romani Antejustiniani.* Editio altera aucta et emendata. Florentiae: Apud S. A. G. Barbèra, 1940–1943.

Richardson, Peter. "Augustan-Era Synagogues in Rome." Pages 17–29 in *Judaism and Christianity in First-Century Rome.* Edited by Karl P. Donfried and Peter Richardson. Grand Rapids: Eerdmans, 1998.

———. *Building Jewish in the Roman East.* Waco, Tex.: Baylor University Press, 2004.

———. "Early Synagogues as Collegia in the Diaspora and Palestine." Pages 90–109 in *Voluntary Associations in the Graeco-Roman World.* Edited by John S. Kloppenborg and Stephen G. Wilson. London: Routledge, 1996.

———. *Israel in the Apostolic Church.* Society of New Testament Studies Monograph Series 10. Cambridge: Cambridge University, 1969.

Ridderbos, Herman. *Paul: An Outline of His Theology.* Translated by John Richard De Witt. Grand Rapids: Eerdmans, 1975.

Riesner, Rainer. *Paul's Early Period: Chronology, Mission Strategy, Theology.* Grand Rapids: Eerdmans, 1998.

Robinson, D. W. B. "The Distinction Between Jewish and Gentile Believers in Galatians." *Australian Biblical Review* 13 (1965): 29–48.

Runesson, Anders. "A Monumental Synagogue from the First Century: The Case of Ostia." *Journal for the Study of Judaism in the Persian, Hellenistic, and Roman Periods.* 33 (2002): 171–220.

———. *The Origins of the Synagogue: A Socio-Historical Study.* Coniectanea biblica: New Testament Series 37. Stockholm: Almqvist & Wiksell, 2001.

———. "The Synagogue at Ancient Ostia: The Building and Its History from the First to the Fifth Century." Pages 29–99 in *The Synagogue of Ancient Ostia and the Jews of Rome: Interdisciplinary Studies.* Edited by Birger Olsson, Dieter Mitternacht, and Olof Brandt. Stockholm: Svenska Institutet i Rom, 2001.

Russell, Walt. "Insights from Postmodernism's Emphasis on Interpretive Communities in the Interpretation of Romans 7." *Journal of the Evangelical Theological Society* 37 (1994): 511–27.

Russell, Walter B., III. "An Alternative Suggestion for the Purpose of Romans." *Bibliotheca Sacra* 145 (1988): 174–84.

Rutgers, Leonard Victor. "Archaeological Evidence for the Interaction of Jews and Non-Jews in Late Antiquity." *American Journal of Archaeology* 96 (1992): 101–18.

———. "Attitudes to Judaism in the Greco-Roman Period: Reflections on Feldman's *Jew and Gentile in the Ancient World,*" *Jewish Quarterly Review* 85 (1995): 361–95.

———. "Roman Policy toward the Jews: Expulsions from the City of Rome during the First Century C.E. *Classical Antiquity* 13 (1994): 56–74. Repr. pages 93–116 in *Judaism and Christianity in First-Century Rome.* Edited by Karl P. Donfried and Peter Richardson. Grand Rapids: Eerdmans, 1998.

Sampley, J. Paul. "Romans in a Different Light: A Response to Robert Jewett." Pages 109–29 in *Romans.* Edited by David M. Hay and E. Elizabeth Johnson. Vol. 3 of *Pauline Theology.* Minneapolis: Fortress Press, 1995.

Sanday, William, and Arthur C. Headlam. *A Critical and Exegetical Commentary on the Epistle to the Romans.* 5th ed. International Critical Commentary. Edinburgh: T & T Clark, 1902.

Sanders, E. P. *Jesus and Judaism.* Philadelphia: Fortress Press, 1985.

———. "Jewish Association with Gentiles and Galatians 2.11–14." Pages 170–88 in *The Conversation Continues: Studies in Paul and John in Honor of J. Louis Martyn.* Edited by R. T. Fortna and B. R. Gaventa. Nashville: Abingdon, 1990.

———. *Judaism: Practice and Belief, 63 BCE–66 CE.* Philadelphia: Trinity Press International, 1992.

———. *Paul and Palestinian Judaism: A Comparison of Patterns of Religion.* Philadelphia: Fortress Press, 1977.

Sandnes, Karl Olav. *Belly and Body in the Pauline Epistles.* Society for New Testament Studies Monograph Series 120. Cambridge: Cambridge University Press, 2002.

Sandnes, Karl Olav. *A New Family: Conversion and Ecclesiology in the Early Church with Cross-Cultural Comparisons.* Studies in the Intercultural History of Christianity 91. Bern: Peter Lang, 1994.

Schlatter, Adolf. *Romans: The Righteousness of God.* Translated by Siegfried S. Schatzmann. Peabody, Mass.: Hendrickson, 1995. Orig. *Gottes Gerechtigkeit: Ein Kommentar zum Römerbrief.* Stuttgart: Calwer, 1935.

Schlier, Heinrich. *Der Römerbrief.* HTKNT 6. Freiburg: Herder, 1977.

Schlueter, Carol J. *Filling up the Measure: Polemical Hyperbole in 1 Thessalonians 2.14–16.* Journal for the Study of the New Testament: Supplement Series 98. Sheffield: Sheffield Academic, 1994.

Schmeller, Thomas. *Paulus und die "Diatribe": Eine vergleichende Stilinterpretation.* Neu testamentliche Abhandlungen n.s. 19. Münster: Aschendorff, 1987.

Schmidt, Daryl D. "Verbal Aspect in Greek: Two Approaches." Pages 63–73 in *Biblical Greek Language and Linguistics: Open Questions in Current Research.* Edited by Stanley E. Porter and D. A. Carson. Journal for the Study of the New Testament: Supplement Series 80. Sheffield: Sheffield Academic, 1993.

Schmithals, Walter. *Der Römerbrief als historisches Problem.* Studien zum Neuen Testament 9. Gütersloh: Gütersloher Verlagshaus Gerd Mohn, 1975.

———. *Der Römerbrief: Ein Kommentar.* Gütersloh: Gerd Mohn, 1988.

Schnackenburg, Rudolf. "Apostles Before and During Paul's Time." Pages 287–303 in *Apostolic History and the Gospel: Biblical and Historical Essays presented to F. F. Bruce on his 60th Birthday.* Edited by W. Ward Gasque and Ralph P. Martin. Grand Rapids: Eerdmans, 1970.

Schneider, André, ed. *Le Premier Livre* Ad Nationes *de Tertullien: Introduction, Texte, Traduction et Commentaire.* Bibliotheca Helvetica Romana 9. Rome: Institut Suisse de Rome, 1968.

Schneider, Nelio. *Die 'Schwachen' in der christlichen Gemeinde Roms.* Theologie 5. Münster: Lit, 1996.

Schreiner, Thomas R. *Romans.* Baker Exegetical Commentary on the New Testament 6. Grand Rapids: Baker, 1998.

Schrenk, Gottlob. "Der Segenswunsch nach der Kampfepistel." *Judaica: Beiträge zum Verständnis des jüdischen Schicksals in Vergangenheit und Gegenwart* 6 (1950): 170–90.

———. "Was bedeutet 'Israel Gottes'?" *Judaica: Beiträge zum Verständnis des jüdischen Schicksals in Vergangenheit und Gegenwart* 5 (1949): 81–94.

Scott, James M. *Adoption as Sons: An Exegetical Investigation into the Background of* ΥΙΟΘΕΣΙΑ *in the Pauline Corpus.* Wissenschaftliche Untersuchungen zum Neuen Testament 2/48. Tübingen: J. C. B. Mohr (Paul Siebeck), 1992.

———. "And Then All Israel Will Be Saved." Pages 489–527 in *Restoration: Old Testament, Jewish, and Christian Perspectives.* Edited by James M. Scott. Journal for the Study of Judaism: Supplement Series 72. Leiden: Brill, 2001.

Scott, S. P., trans. *The Civil Law Including The Twelve Tables, The Institutes of Gaius, The Rules of Ulpian, The Opinions of Paulus, The Enactments of Justinian, and The Constitutions of Leo.* 17 vols. Cincinnati: Central Trust, 1932.

Scramuzza, Vincent M. *The Emperor Claudius*. Harvard Historical Studies 44. Cambridge: Harvard University Press, 1940.

———. "The Policy of the Early Roman Emperors towards Judaism." Pages 277–97 in vol. 5 of *The Acts of the Apostles*, part 1 of *The Beginnings of Christianity*. Edited by F. J. Foakes Jackson and Kirsopp Lake. London: Macmillan, 1933. Repr. Grand Rapids: Baker, 1979.

Segal, Alan F. *Paul the Convert: The Apostolate and Apostasy of Saul the Pharisee*. New Haven, Conn.: Yale University Press, 1990.

Seifrid, Mark A. *Justification by Faith: The Origin and Development of a Central Pauline Theme*. Novum Testamentum Supplements 68. Leiden: Brill, 1992.

Seneca. *Hercules, Trojan Women, Phoenician Women, Medea, Phaedra*. Translated by John G. Fitch. Loeb Classical Library. Cambridge: Harvard University Press, 2002.

Shogren, Gary Steven. "'Is the Kingdom of God About Eating and Drinking or Isn't It?' (Romans 14:17)." *Novum Testamentum* 42 (2000): 238–56.

Silva, Moisés. *Biblical Words and Their Meaning: An Introduction to Lexical Semantics*. Rev. ed. Grand Rapids: Zondervan, 1994.

———. "A Response to Fanning and Porter on Verbal Aspect." Pages 74–82 in *Biblical Greek Language and Linguistics: Open Questions in Current Research*. Edited by Stanley E. Porter and D. A. Carson. Journal for the Study of the New Testament: Supplement Series 80. Sheffield: Sheffield Academic, 1993.

Slingerland, H. Dixon. "Chrestus: Christus?" Pages 133–44 in *The Literature of Early Rabbinic Judaism: Issues in Talmudic Redaction and Interpretation*. Vol. 4 of *New Perspectives on Ancient Judaism*. Edited by Alan J. Avery-Peck. Lanham: University Press of America, 1989. Repr. and rev. pp. 203–17 in *Claudian Policymaking and the Early Imperial Repression of Judaism at Rome*. South Florida Studies in the History of Judaism 160. Atlanta: Scholars, 1997.

———. *Claudian Policymaking and the Early Imperial Repression of Judaism at Rome*. South Florida Studies in the History of Judaism 160. Atlanta: Scholars, 1997.

———. "Suetonius *Claudius* 25.4, Acts 18, and Paulus Orosius' *Historiarum Adversum Paganos Libri VII*: Dating the Claudian Expulsion(s) of Roman Jews." *Jewish Quarterly Review* 83 (1992): 127–44. Repr. and rev. pp. 111–29 in *Claudian Policymaking and the Early Imperial Repression of Judaism at Rome*. South Florida Studies in the History of Judaism 160. Atlanta: Scholars Press, 1997.

———. "Suetonius *Claudius* 25.4 and the Account in Cassius Dio." *Jewish Quarterly Review* 79 (1989): 305–22. Repr. and rev. pp. 89–110 in *Claudian Policymaking and the Early Imperial Repression of Judaism at Rome*. South Florida Studies in the History of Judaism 160. Atlanta: Scholars Press, 1997.

Smallwood, E. Mary. "The Alleged Jewish Tendencies of Poppaea Sabina." *Journal of Theological Studies* 10 (1959): 329–35.

———. *Documents Illustrating the Principates of Gaius, Claudius, and Nero*. London: Cambridge University Press, 1967.

———. *The Jews under Roman Rule: From Pompey to Diocletian*. Studies in Judaism in Late Antiquity 20. Leiden: Brill, 1976.

Smiga, George. "Romans 12:1–2 and 15:30–32 and the Occasion of the Letter to the Romans." *Catholic Biblical Quarterly* 53 (1991): 257–73.

Snow, David A., and Richard Machalek. "The Convert as a Social Type." Pages 259–89 in *Sociological Theory 1983*. Edited by Randall Collins. The Jossey-Bass Social and Behavioral Science Series. San Francisco: Jossey-Bass, 1983.

———. "The Sociology of Conversion." *Annual Review of Sociology* 10 (1984): 167–90.

Song, Changwon. "Reading Romans through the Macrostructure of the Diatribe." Pages 260–77 in *SBL Seminar Papers, 2001*. Society of Biblical Literature Seminar Papers 40. Atlanta: Society of Biblical Literature, 2001.

Stanley, Christopher D. *Arguing with Scripture: The Rhetoric of Quotations in the Letters of Paul*. New York: T & T Clark, 2004.

———. "'Neither Jew Nor Greek': Ethnic Conflict in Graeco-Roman Society." *Journal for the Study of the New Testament* 64 (1996): 101–24.

Stegemann, Ekkehard W., and Wolfgang Stegemann. *The Jesus Movement: A Social History of Its First Century*. Translated by O. C. Dean, Jr. Minneapolis: Fortress Press, 1999.

Stendahl, Krister. "The Apostle Paul and the Introspective Conscience of the West." *Harvard Theological Review* 56 (1963): 199–215. Repr. pages 78–96 in *Paul Among Jews and Gentiles and Other Essays*. Philadelphia: Fortress Press, 1976.

———. "Paul among Jews and Gentiles." Pages 1–77 in *Paul among Jews and Gentiles*. Philadelphia: Fortress Press, 1976.

Stern, Menahem, ed. and trans. *Greek and Latin Authors on the Jews and Judaism*. 3 vols. Jerusalem: The Israel Academy of Sciences and Humanities, 1974.

Stirewalt, Martin Luther, Jr. "The Form and Function of the Greek Letter-Essay." Pages 147–71 in *The Romans Debate*. Rev. and enl. ed. Edited by Karl P. Donfried. Peabody, Mass.: Hendrickson, 1991.

Stone, Michael E. *The Testament of Abraham: The Greek Recensions*. Texts and Translations 2. Missoula, Mont.: Society of Biblical Literature, 1972.

Stowers, Stanley K. "Apostrophe, Προσωποποιία and Paul's Rhetorical Education." Pages 351–69 in *Early Christianity and Classical Culture: Comparative Studies in Honor of Abraham J. Malherbe*. Edited by John T. Fitzgerald, Thomas H. Olbricht, and L. Michael White. Supplements to Novum Testamentum 110. Leiden: Brill, 2003.

———. "An Assessment of Mark Nanos's *Mystery of Romans*." *Critical Review of Books in Religion* 11 (1998): 163–66.

———. *The Diatribe and Paul's Letter to the Romans*. Society of Biblical Literature Dissertation Series 57. Chico, Calif.: Scholars, 1981.

———. "Misreadings of a Rereading: A Response to Richard Hays." Unpublished paper.

———. "Paul's Dialogue with a Fellow Jew in Rom. 3.1–9." *Catholic Biblical Quarterly* 46 (1984): 707–22.

———. *A Rereading of Romans: Justice, Jews, and Gentiles*. New Haven: Yale University Press, 1994.

———. Review of Runar M. Thorsteinsson, *Paul's Interlocutor in Romans 2*. *Journal of Theological Studies* 56 (2005): 561–65.

———. "Romans 7.7–25 as a Speech-in-Character (προσωποποιία)." Pages 180–202 in *Paul in His Hellenistic Context*. Edited by Troels Engberg-Pedersen. Minneapolis: Fortress Press, 1995.

———. "Social Stature, Public Speaking and Private Teaching: The Circumstances of Paul's Preaching Activity." *Novum Testamentum* 26 (1984): 59–82.

Strange, James F. Pages 27–45 in "Ancient Texts, Archaeology as Text, and the Problem of the First-Century Synagogue," in *Evolution of the Synagogue: Problems and Progress*. Edited by Howard Clark Kee and Lynn H. Cohick. Harrisburg, Pa.: Trinity Press International, 1999.

Struve, V. V., ed. *Corpus Inscriptionum Regni Bosporani (CIRB)*. Leningrad: Nauka, 1965.

Stuhlmacher, Peter. *Paul's Letter to the Romans: A Commentary*. Translated by Scott J. Hafemann. Louisville: Westminster John Knox, 1994.

———. "The Purpose of Romans." Pages 231–42 in *The Romans Debate*. Rev. and enl. ed. Edited by Karl P. Donfried. Translated by Reginald and Ilse Fuller. Peabody, Mass.: Hendrickson, 1991. Translation of "Der Abfassungszweck des Römerbriefes." *Zeitschrift für die neutestamentliche Wissenschaft* 77 (1986): 180–93.

Suetonius. Translated by J. C. Rolfe. 2 vols. Loeb Classical Library. Cambridge: Harvard University Press, 1997–1998.

Suggs, M. Jack. "'The Word is Near You': Romans 10:6–10 Within the Purpose of the Letter." Pages 289–312 in *Christian History and Interpretation*. Edited by W. R. Farmer, C. F. D. Moule, and R. R. Niebuhr. Cambridge: Cambridge University Press, 1967.

Tacitus. The Histories and The Annals. Translated by C. H. Moore and J. Jackson. 4 vols. Loeb Classical Library. Cambridge: Harvard University Press, 1937.

Talbert, Charles H. *Romans*. Smyth & Helwys Bible Commentary. Macon, Ga.: Smyth & Helwys, 2002.

Tannenbaum, Robert F. "Jews and God-Fearers in the Holy City of Aphrodite." *Biblical Archaeology Review* 12 (September/October 1986): 54–57.

Taylor, John W. "From Faith to Faith: Romans 1.17 in the Light of Greek Idiom." *New Testament Studies* 50 (2004): 337–48.

Tcherikover, Victor A. *Corpus papyrorum judaicarum*. 3 vols. Cambridge: Harvard University Press, 1957–1964.

———. "Jewish Apologetic Literature Reconsidered." *Eos* 48 (1956): 169–93.

Theissen, Gerd. *Psychological Aspects of Pauline Theology*. Edited by John P. Galvin. Philadelphia: Fortress Press, 1987.

Theobald, Michael. *Kapitel 1–11*. Vol. 1 of *Römerbrief*. 3rd ed. Stuttgarter Kleiner Kommentar 6. Stuttgart: Verlag Katholisches Bibelwerk, 2002.

Theobald, Michael. *Kapitel 12–16*. Vol. 2 of *Römerbrief*. 2nd ed. Stuttgarter Kleiner Kommentar 6. Stuttgart: Verlag Katholisches Bibelwerk, 2001.

Thompson, Michael. *Clothed with Christ: The Example and Teaching of Jesus in Romans 12.1–15.13*. Journal for the Study of the New Testament: Supplement Series 59. Sheffield: Sheffield Academic, 1991.

Thorsteinsson, Runar M. "Paul's Missionary Duty towards Gentiles in Rome: A Note on the Punctuation and Syntax of Rom 1.13–15." *New Testament Studies* 48 (2002): 531–47.

———. *Paul's Interlocutor in Romans 2: Function and Identity in the Context of Ancient Epistolography.* Coniectanea Biblica New Testament Series 40. Stockholm: Almqvist & Wiksell, 2003.

Tobin, Thomas H. *Paul's Rhetoric in Its Contexts: The Argument of Romans.* Peabody, Mass.: Hendrickson, 2004.

Tomson, Peter J. Review of Mark D. Nanos, *The Mystery of Romans. Journal for the Study of Judaism* 28 (1997): 345–47.

———. "What Did Paul Mean by 'Those Who Know the Law'? (Rom 7.1)." *New Testament Studies* 49 (2003): 573–81.

Trebilco, Paul R. *Jewish Communities in Asia Minor.* Society for New Testament Studies Monograph Series 69. Cambridge: Cambridge University Press, 1991.

Vielhauer, Philipp. *Geschichte der urchristlichen Literatur: Einleitung in das Neue Testament, die Apokryphen und die Apostolichen Väter.* Berlin: Walter de Gruyter, 1975.

Wagner, J. Ross. *Heralds of the Good News: Isaiah and Paul in Concert in the Letter to the Romans.* Leiden: Brill, 2002.

Wallace, Daniel B. *Greek Grammar Beyond the Basics: An Exegetical Syntax of the New Testament.* Grand Rapids: Zondervan, 1996.

Walters, James C. *Ethnic Issues in Paul's Letter to the Romans: Changing Self-Definitions in Earliest Roman Christianity.* Valley Forge, Pa.: Trinity Press International, 1993.

———. "Romans, Jews, and Christians: The Impact of the Romans on Jewish/Christian Relations in First Century Rome." Pages 175–95 in *Judaism and Christianity in First-Century Rome.* Edited by Karl P. Donfried and Peter Richardson. Grand Rapids: Eerdmans, 1998.

Waltzing, Jean-Pierre. *Étude historique sur les corporations professionnelles chez les Romains depuis les origins jusqu'à la chute de l'empire d'Occident.* 4 vols. Bologna: Mémoires couronnés et autres mémoires publiée par l'Académie Royale des Sciences, des Lettres et des Beaux-Arts de Belgique 50, 1895–1900.

Wang, Lisa. "Jesus as Messiah in Galatians and Romans: A Response to John Gager's *Reinventing Paul.*" *Toronto Journal of Theology* 19 (2003): 173–82.

Watson, Francis. *Paul, Judaism, and the Gentiles: A Sociological Approach.* Society for New Testament Studies Monograph Series 56. Cambridge: Cambridge University Press, 1986.

———. "The Two Roman Congregations: Romans 14:1–15:13." Pages 94–105 in *Paul, Judaism, and the Gentiles: A Sociological Approach.* Society for New Testament Studies Monograph Series 56. Cambridge: Cambridge University Press, 1986. Repr. pp. 203–15 in *The Romans Debate.* Rev. and enl. ed. Edited by Karl P. Donfried. Peabody, Mass.: Hendrickson, 1991.

Watson, N. M. "The Interpretation of Romans VII." *Australian Biblical Review* 21 (1973): 27–39.

Watts, Rikki E. "'For I Am Not Ashamed of the Gospel': Romans 1:16–17 and Habakkuk 2:4." Pages 3–25 in *Romans and the People of God: Essays in Honor of Gordon*

D. *Fee on the Occasion of His 65th Birthday.* Edited by Sven Soderlund and N. T. Wright. Grand Rapids: Eerdmans, 1999.

Wedderburn, A. J. M. "Adam in Paul's Letter to the Romans." Pages 413–30 in *Studia Biblical 1978: III.* Edited by E. A. Livingstone. Sheffield: JSOT Press, 1980.

———. "The Purpose and Occasion of Romans Again." *Expository Times* 90 (1979): 137–41. Repr. pp. 195–202 in *The Romans Debate.* Rev. and enl. ed. Edited by Karl P. Donfried. Peabody, Mass.: Hendrickson, 1991.

———. *The Reasons for Romans.* Studies of the New Testament and Its World. Edinburgh: T & T Clark, 1988.

Weima, Jeffrey A. D. "Gal. 6:11–18: A Hermeneutical Key to the Galatian Letter." *CTJ* 28 (1993): 90–107.

———. "Preaching the Gospel in Rome: A Study of the Epistolary Framework of Romans." Pages 337–66 in *Gospel in Paul: Studies on Corinthians, Galatians and Romans for Richard N. Longenecker.* Edited by L. Ann Jervis and Peter Richardson. Journal for the Study of the New Testament: Supplement Series 108. Sheffield: Sheffield Academic, 1994.

Weiss, Bernhard. *A Commentary on the New Testament.* 4 vols. Translated by George H. Schodde and Epiphanius Wilson. New York: Funk & Wagnalls, 1906.

Wenham, David. "The Christian Life: A Life of Tension? A Consideration of the Nature of Christian Experience in Paul." Pages 80–94 in *Pauline Studies: Essays Presented to Professor F. F. Bruce on his 70th Birthday.* Edited by Donald A. Hagner and Murray J. Harris. Grand Rapids: Eerdmans, 1980.

Wenham, John. *Redating Matthew, Mark & Luke: A Fresh Assault on the Synoptic Problem.* Downers Grove, Ill.: InterVarsity, 1992.

White, John L. *Light from Ancient Letters.* Philadelphia: Fortress Press, 1986.

White, L. Michael. *The Social Origins of Christian Architecture.* 2 vols. Harvard Theological Studies 42. Valley Forge, Pa.: Trinity Press International, 1997.

———. "Synagogue and Society in Imperial Ostia: Archaeological and Epigraphic Evidence." Pages 30–68 in *Judaism and Christianity in First-Century Rome.* Edited by Karl P. Donfried and Peter Richardson. Grand Rapids: Eerdmans, 1998.

Whitsett, Christopher G. "Son of God, Seed of David: Paul's Messianic Exegesis in Romans 2 [sic]:3–4." *Journal of Biblical Literature* 119 (2000): 661–81.

Whittaker, Molly. *Jews & Christians: Graeco-Roman Views.* Cambridge Commentaries on Writings of the Jewish & Christian World 200 BC to AD 200. Vol. 6. Cambridge: Cambridge University Press, 1984.

Wiefel, Wolfgang. "The Jewish Community in Ancient Rome and the Origins of Roman Christianity." Pages 85–101 in *The Romans Debate.* Rev. and enl. ed. Edited by Karl P. Donfried. Peabody, Mass.: Hendrickson, 1991. Repr. from "Die jüdische Gemeinschaft im antiken Rom und die Angfänge des römischen Christentums." *Judaica* 26 (1970): 65–88.

Wieseler, Karl. *Chronologie des apostolischen Zeitalters bis zum Tode der Apostel Paulus und Petrus.* Göttingen: Vandenhoeck und Ruprecht, 1848.

Wilcox, Max. "The 'God-Fearers' in Acts — A Reconsideration." *Journal for the Study of the New Testament* 13 (1981): 102–22.

Wilckens, Ulrich. *Der Brief an die Römer.* 3 vols. Evangelisch-katholischer Kommentar zum Neuen Testament 6. Neukirchen-Vluyn: Neukirchener, 1978–1982.

Wilken, Robert L. "Collegia, Philosophical Schools, and Theology." Pages 268–91 in *Early Church History: The Roman Empire as the Setting of Primitive Christianity.* Edited by Stephen Benko and John H. O'Rourke. London: Oliphants, 1971.

Williams, Margaret H. "The Meaning and Function of *Ioudaios* in Graeco-Roman Inscriptions." *Zeitschrift für Paypyrologie und Epigraphik* 116 (1997): 249–62.

———. "The Structure of the Jewish Community in Rome." Pages 215–28 in *Jews in a Graeco-Roman World.* Edited by Martin Goodman. Oxford: Oxford University Press, 1998.

———. "'θεοσεβὴς γὰρ ἦν'—The Jewish Tendencies of Poppaea Sabina." *Journal of Theological Studies* 39 (1988): 97–111.

Wilson, Stephen G. "ΟΙ ΠΟΤΕ ΙΟΥΔΑΙΟΙ: Epigraphic Evidence for Jewish Defectors." Pages 354–71 in *Text and Artifact in the Religions of Antiquity: Essays in Honour of Peter Richardson.* Edited by Stephen G. Wilson and Michel Desjardins. Studies in Christianity and Judaism 9. Waterloo, Ontario: Wilfrid Laurior University Press, 2000.

———. *Related Strangers: Jews and Christians 70–170 C.E.* Minneapolis: Fortress Press, 1995.

Winkle, D. W. van. "An Inclusive Authoritative Text in Exclusive Communities." Pages 423–54 in *Writing and Reading the Scroll of Isaiah: Studies of an Interpretive Tradition.* Vol. 1 of *Formation and Interpretation of Old Testament Literature.* Edited by Craig C. Broyles and Craig A. Evans. Vetus Testamentum Supplements 70. Leiden: Brill, 1997.

———. "The Relationship of the Nations to Yahweh and to Israel in Isaiah XL–LV." *Vetus Testamentum* 35 (1985): 446–58.

Winston, David. *The Wisdom of Solomon.* Anchor Bible 43. New York: Doubleday, 1979.

Winter, Bruce. "Roman Law and Society in Romans 12–15." Pages 67–102 in *Rome in the Bible and the Early Church.* Edited by Peter Oakes. Grand Rapids: Baker, 2002.

Witherington, Ben, III. *The Acts of the Apostles: A Socio-Rhetorical Commentary.* Grand Rapids: Eerdmans, 1998.

Witherington, Ben, III (with Darlene Hyatt). *Paul's Letter to the Romans: A Socio-Rhetorical Commentary.* Grand Rapids: Eerdmans, 2004.

———. *Women in the Earliest Churches.* Society for New Testament Studies Monograph Series 59. Cambridge: Cambridge University Press, 1988.

Wolfson, Harry Austryn. *Philo: Foundations of Religious Philosophy in Judaism, Christianity, and Islam.* 2 vols. Cambridge: Harvard University Press, 1948.

Wright, N. T. *Climax of the Covenant: Christ and the Law in Pauline Theology.* Minneapolis: Fortress Press, 1991.

———. "The Letter to the Romans: Introduction, Commentary, and Reflections." Pages 393–770 in vol. 10 of *The New Interpreter's Bible.* Nashville: Abingdon, 2002.

————. "Romans and the Theology of Paul." Pages 30–67 in *Romans*. Edited by David M. Hay and E. Elizabeth Johnson. Vol. 3 of *Pauline Theology*. Minneapolis: Fortress Press, 1995.

Xenophon. Translated by E. C. Marchant et al. 7 vols. Loeb Classical Library. Cambridge: Harvard University Press, 1968.

Yavetz, Zwi. *Julius Caesar and his Public Image*. Ithaca, N.Y.: Cornell University Press, 1983.

Zahn, Theodor. *Der Brief des Paulus an die Römer*. Kommentar zum Neuen Testament 6. 2 Aufl. Leipzig: A. Deichert (Georg Böhme), 1910.

————. Vol. 1 of *Introduction to the New Testament*. Grand Rapids: Kregel, 1953.

Zeller, Dieter. *Juden und Heiden in der Mission des Paulus: Studien zum Römerbrief*. Forschung zur bibel 1. Stuttgart: Katholisches Bibelwerk, 1973.

Zetterholm, Magnus. *The Formation of Christianity in Antioch: A Social-Scientific Approach to the Separation between Judaism and Christianity*. London: Routledge, 2003.

Zielinksi, Thaddée. "L'empereur Claude et l'idée de la domination mondiale des Juifs." *Revue de l'Université de Bruxelles* 32 (1926–27): 128–48.

Ziesler, J. A. "The Role of the Tenth Commandment in Romans 7." *Journal for the Study of the New Testament* 33 (1988): 41–56.

Zuntz, G. *The Text of the Epistles: A Disquisition Upon the* Corpus Paulinum. London: British Academy, 1953.

Index of Authors

Index of Subjects

Index of Primary Sources

NEW TESTAMENT